The Tennessee Brigade
A History of the Volunteers of the
Army of Northern Virginia

by
Randy Bishop

ROOFTOP
publishing

Rooftop Publishing™
1663 Liberty Drive, Suite 200
Bloomington, IN 47403
Phone: 1-800-839-8640

First published by Rooftop Publishing 11/01/07

Publisher: Kevin King
Acquisitions Editor: Nick Obradovich
Senior Editor: Lesley Bolton
Cover Design: April Mostek
Book Design: Jessica Sheese
Production Manager: Aaron Schultz
Senior Publicist: Shannon White

ISBN: 978-1-60008-066-1 (sc)
ISBN: 978-1-60008-078-4 (dj)

Library of Congress Control Number: 2007936645

Printed in the United States of America
Bloomington, Indiana

This book is printed on acid-free paper.

Dedication

To my parents, Wayne and Margaret, for their personal nurturing and instilling a love of history in their youngest child, and to Sharon, Jay, and Ben, whose love, encouragement, and support truly make life worth living.

Preface

A lack of knowledge of the history of one's state and its significance in
American history seems commonplace in today's society. As a veteran
history teacher and longtime student of the Civil War, I discovered this
on a personal basis when I made my first visit to the hallowed battlefield at
Gettysburg, Pennsylvania. Here I realized I was ignorant of the contributions
of an overlooked and understudied group of Tennessee Civil War soldiers.

Initially using the Battle of Gettysburg and this group of Tennesseans
commonly referred to as Archer's Tennessee Brigade, I embarked on the task
of researching and writing my first book. Further research brought about a
wealth of information related to this group of men and their participation
in an overwhelming number of the battles in which the Army of Northern
Virginia participated.

Leaving their homes and families in Middle Tennessee, the soldiers of
the Tennessee Brigade achieved fame, served their country, and suffered
tremendous casualties in states hundreds of miles from their homes. One
member of the brigade proposed that in these battles he and his comrades
had seen many "Yankee backs" and could therefore attest to their running
qualities as well as any other two brigades from Tennessee. Whether or not
this proclamation is exaggerated is to be debated, yet the significance of the
contributions of the men of the Tennessee Brigade is certain.

It is not my intention in writing this book to provide a history of any
of the battles in which the Tennessee Brigade fought; that has been done in
a large number of books and in a much more efficient manner than I could
perform. It is also not the intent to imply that the Tennessee Brigade acted
alone in any of the engagements discussed, yet the book is written to highlight

the actions of the brigade and its part in serving the Army of Northern Virginia and the Confederate States of America.

Containing one regiment that was formed prior to Tennessee's secession, the Tennessee Brigade fought at Fredericksburg, Chancellorsville, Antietam, and Gettysburg, as well as a host of other struggles before surrendering at Appomattox with a fraction of the men from its original ranks. In each of these battles, a significant contribution was made using the efforts and blood of the men of the Tennessee Brigade.

Randy Bishop

James Jay Archer, prominent commander of the Tennessee Brigade.
Drawing by Kim Moore.

Acknowledgments

It would be completely erroneous to delete the name of Cliff Detwieler from the list of those who deserve a special thank you in relation to the completion of this book. Without his literal guidance around the Gettysburg battlefield, his mention of the significance of the Tennessee Brigade at that historic Civil War site, and the additional comment that a suitable brigade history was absent, this work would have remained un-started. However good this work is remains to be seen, yet the credit for the inspiration to write it goes to Mr. Cliff, the certified battlefield guide on my family's trip to Gettysburg.

H. Boyer Butler deserves special recognition as well for unselfish and unhesitating willingness to share three diaries of his ancestor, Archibald Debow Norris, for use in writing the history of the Tennessee Brigade. Norris's comments and entries make an unequaled impact upon the composition of the text. To Mr. Butler, a deep thank you is certainly an understatement. Mrs. Elizabeth Mitchell provided a photograph of Mr. Norris, her grandfather, and for this act I am also greatly indebted.

Don Griffin of Pelham, Alabama provided a host of photographs related to the Fifth Alabama Battalion, a unit to which his grandfather, Elihu Griffin, belonged. Mr. Griffin's contributions to this work are also highly appreciated, as are his phone calls, gifts, and desire to share with the readers of this text the contributions of individuals such as his ancestor.

County historians across parts of Tennessee shared knowledge, compiled works, and supplied valuable leads for the book. These included Mr. Thomas G. Webb of DeKalb County, Yolanda Reid of Robertson, and Eleanor Williams of Montgomery County. Mrs. Floydaline Limbough of the Franklin County Historical Society likewise provided valuable information and assistance in relation to Turney's First Tennessee Regiment, as did Mrs. J. R. Brock, the longtime chairman of the Franklin County Tennessee Historical Society. No work containing information on the Seventh Tennessee Regiment could be complete without the valuable assistance and contributions of Jack and Ruth Cato. The assistance of Judy Philps likewise proved unequaled. To each of these individuals my level of gratitude is unending.

Tom Clemens of Hagerstown Community College, Jerry Blevins of Huntsville, Alabama, and Dr. C. Wallace Cross of Austin Peay readily shared information and their own published materials for use in the book, each proving to be a total professional and extremely knowledgeable. Paul Gibson openly shared photographs from his collection for use in the book and allowed the free use of information contained in his book as well.

Historians at numerous national battlefields gave of their time and knowledge without reservation, a fact impressive to a novice such as myself. These individuals included: James Burgess of Manassas, John Heiser and Troy Harmon of Gettysburg, Robert E.L. Krick of Richmond, Donald Phanz and Frank O'Reilly at Fredericksburg, and Colleen Clark at Antietam. Patrick A. Schroeder at Appomattox supplied an unbelievable amount of documents, photographs, and leads that proved invaluable to the completion of this book. Greg Coco of Gettysburg also contributed worthwhile information and photos and is deserving of praise as well. Jimmy Jobe of Ft. Donelson allowed me to photograph a company flag in the park's museum, a task that required the elimination of lighting from the room to obtain a clear photo; I appreciate his cooperation.

Cara Griggs, library assistant at the Museum of the Confederacy, was a joy to work with and provided the highest level of guidance during this project. A special thank you is due to Darla Brock, Kassie Hassler, and Anita Coursey from the Tennessee State Library and Archives. Tim Pulley of the Reference and Genealogy Department at the Clarksville-Montgomery County Public Library spent several hours assisting this first-time author, all with patience and understanding. Local librarians such as Norma Humphries and Karan Taylor of the Jack McConnico Memorial Library in Selmer, Tennessee provided access to the official records in a setting close to home and totally stress-free. Lee Evans of the Maryland State Archives and Andy Phrydas, military records archivist at the Georgia Department of Archives and History, each supplied helpful resources and assistance. From the State of Alabama Department of Archives and History, Dr. Norwood A. Kerr, Ms. Rickie Brummer, and Jerome Wiley provided access and procurement of a vast amount of information on the Alabama units that served in the Tennessee Brigade. Larry Alford of the University of North Carolina Library allowed me to use the Renfroe document that relates so passionately the love a brother feels for his lost sibling.

Arthur W. Bergeron Jr., PhD, historian at Pamplin Historical Park, Barbara Franklin, manager of the Ashland, Virginia Visitor's Center, along with Martha L. Bennett of the Fort Delaware Society and Christy Carter, park naturalist at Point Lookout State Park, each provided unique information and/or photos for use in the text. The ability to use photographs from the collections of Mikel Urigen and Steve Tokarcik is deeply appreciated. Ray Miller, Lt. Commander of the Savage-Goodner SCV Camp, also supplied a hard-to-come-by picture of John Goodner for use in these pages. In addition, descendents of several of the brigade members included photographs of their ancestors for use in the book and these are noted, where applicable, with the respective photo.

Dave Roth of *Blue and Gray* as well as Jim Vogler of *Confederate Veteran*, each unequaled professionals and editors, agreed without reservation to assist me, a virtual unknown, to any degree by which I could compose a more complete work on the Tennessee Brigade. The references, photographs, and poems from each of these works are without a doubt essential to this work. Mr. Roth, in turn, designed the maps that add an infinite amount of understanding to the text. To these two men I am eternally grateful.

Numerous fellow Civil War relic collectors and dealers agreed for me to use their documents within these pages. Again, the document and the respective owner are duly noted. Friends and family who allowed access to their Civil War libraries and encouragement along the way are also to be thanked at this point. Though I attempted to keep an active list of the professionals and others who made some level of contribution to this work, I undoubtedly missed someone in this section. To him, her, or them, I am truly sorry and, in turn, grateful for your contribution.

Mrs. Sue Shelly, my all-time favorite teacher and a true inspiration and motivation to complete this text, volunteered a great deal of time to proofreading. Constructive comments and a lot of suggestions came from her and are greatly appreciated.

I would be ashamed if I failed to mention these individuals. My students, friends, fellow church members, and others know the high value I place upon my family. For my parents, Wayne and Margaret Bishop, I am thankful daily. Their support, encouragement, willingness to proofread this document, and so many other feats are, to say the least, appreciated.

In conclusion, Sharon, Jay, and Ben—my wife and sons—deserve special recognition as well. I would be misleading if I were to say that the completion of this book took little time away from being the husband and daddy I should have been. While attempts were made to work on this project only at times when it took away little from them, I inevitably found myself wrapped up in the text. For the trips to battlefields, sifting through books at state archives, listening to my tales of frustration, and smiling through it all, I say thank you and I love you to the three people that keep me going. God has truly blessed me.

Randy Bishop
Middleton, Tennessee
December 2004

"More intelligent or braver soldiers the sun has never shone upon."
Gen. William McComb

Table of Contents

CHAPTER ONE

War Seeds Are Planted

Conditions in the state of Tennessee in 1860 mirrored those present in the United States in the decades prior to the Civil War. Just as sectionalism abounded in the United States for years, it also flourished within the Tennessee borders. As the economic bases varied nationwide, a similar diversification existed between Memphis in southwest Tennessee and the mountains of east Tennessee. Most significantly, varying political loyalties were present statewide as well as across the nation, leading to literal divisions in each that exist to this day.

The presidential election of 1860 would prove to be one of the most pivotal in the history of the United States. Likewise, the citizens of Tennessee turned out to exercise their political responsibility and voice individual opinions related to national leadership. Republican candidate Abraham Lincoln was the only presidential office seeker lacking organized support in Tennessee. The Republicans opposed the growth of slavery in any form and therefore elected to not supervise a political crusade in the state.[1]

Stephen Douglas had a small West Tennessee following, yet within the state the election eventually showcased John Bell and John C. Breckinridge. Bell's Constitutional Union Party used barbeques, meetings, and parades to garner support. Breckinridge and the Democrats promoted their love of the South to appeal to Tennessee voters. This was aided through statements that accused Bell of disloyalty to the South and, in turn, to slavery.[2]

Although Bell carried Tennessee over Breckinridge by approximately 4,650 votes, Lincoln won the nationwide election with his ability to obtain

1

large numbers of Northern electoral votes while gathering less than 40 percent of the popular votes. Lincoln's Northern stronghold overwhelmed the electoral division of Southern states among Bell, Breckinridge, and Douglas. When totaled, the electoral votes stood as: Lincoln-180, Douglas-12, Bell-39, and Breckinridge-72.[3]

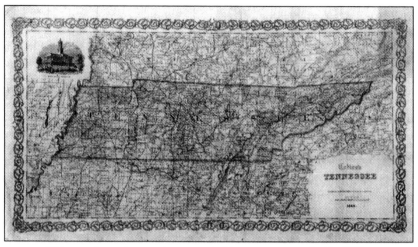

This map shows the counties present in Tennessee prior to the Civil War. Courtesy of the Tennessee State Library and Archives.

On December 20, 1860, South Carolina seceded, largely in protest to Lincoln's election. In February of 1861, six other states—Georgia, Alabama, Florida, Louisiana, Texas, and Mississippi—established a provisional government in Montgomery, Alabama. These Southern states objected to Lincoln's election for numerous reasons, yet the objections were primarily based upon the premise that the election had been accomplished "by one section and by a minority vote."[4] As secessionist fever grew throughout the South, Tennessee began to feel the infection as well.

Soon one Memphis newspaper called for Union loyalty while John Bell called for the support of Lincoln, who Bell stated had been constitutionally elected. Tennessee Governor Isham G. Harris asserted though that a sectional party totally committed against slavery in the South had acquired the White House. Meanwhile, political figures from Harris to Andrew Johnson offered a variety of compromises related to the slavery issue as a means of avoiding war.[5]

At the request of Harris, the people of Tennessee would decide the secession issue on the legislatively appointed date of February 9, 1861. On this day Tennesseans voted for or against a convention of secession, and delegates were to be selected in order to eliminate the need for a second poll, should the convention's authorization take place. The outcome was vaguely pro-Union, with 69,675 voting against the convention and 57,798 approving it. East Tennesseans supported the convention, while an equal split occurred in the middle section of the state,[6] epitomizing the sectionalism within the state and reflecting the opposing attitude present in the nation. The rejection of the convention failed to heal the divisions or resolve the secession issue within the state. The resolution actually seemed to divide the state more deeply. The people had spoken, as in elections of the past, yet the minority secessionists strongly desired recognition.

For example, Franklin County, located in south-central Tennessee, bordered Alabama, one of the founding members of the new nation of the Confederate States of America. In the February election related to the secession convention, Franklin County residents had voted 1240 to 206, a six-to-one ratio, as pro-secessionist. Fifteen days after voting, Franklin County residents gathered in the county seat of Winchester, strongly objecting to the decision of their fellow Tennesseans. Franklin County secessionist Peter Turney led the development of a petition that asked that Franklin County be annexed to Alabama, as the county's residents felt forced by fellow statesmen to remain in the Union against their wills and desires, for their hearts, sympathies, and feelings lay with the Confederate States of America.[7]

Turney was a large man, carrying approximately 240 pounds on his six-foot, three-inch frame. His presence certainly worked in his favor, as he called for a secession-slanted town square meeting in Winchester. On February 24, 1861, some two weeks after Tennesseans had voted to defeat the convention referendum, the thirty-four-year-old Turney and his fellow Franklin County secessionists placed their thoughts and beliefs into action.[8]

Turney held the belief that "secession is a constitutional and inalienable right" and that it was the duty of the Southern states to secede. The crowd that gathered for Turney's meeting was as robust and unruly as Turney himself yet was quickly brought to order when Col. Thomas Finch, a Mexican War veteran, was asked to chair the meeting. Finch was a gray-haired aristocrat and served as a justice of the peace and chairman of the county court. Two men were elected to serve as secretaries of the meeting; one was Nathan Frizzell, a circuit court clerk whose neatly handwritten records are presently still in Franklin County's courthouse. Cotton planter J.F. Syler, a wealthy county resident, served as the second secretary.[9]

The record of the secession meeting reveals a secession resolution was drafted. The resolutions, reprinted with permission of the Franklin County Historical Society, read as follows:

Resolutions

1. Resolved, That the action of the State of Tennessee, on the 9th inst, is to us a source of unfeigned mortification, and regret, as we hoped that her course would have been so different, as to have, by the 4th day of March next, divorced Tennessee forever from her present bonds of political union, and have united her fate-for weal or woe, with her seven proud and gallant sisters of the South, which have so divorced themselves.

2. Resolved, That while against our wills and earnest desire, we as Tennesseans are forced to remain citizens of the Federal Union, our hearts, sympathies and feelings are with the Confederate States of America, and we still hope that the day will review and reverse her action, and give birth to another State upon the National Flag of the Southern Republic.

3. Resolved, That we hope that the Northern fanatics have read the speeches of the Presidents-Davis and Lincoln, (made enroute for the respective seats of government) and seen the difference, and from it learned a lesson of common sense, which will cause them to hush their insane croaking about the ignorance of the Southern people, since, they must see that while the Confederate States have for their representative a gentleman, a scholar and a statesman, the Federal Union has a wag, a mental dwarf.

4. Resolved, That the speeches of President Lincoln, intimating coercion, deserve, and will receive, the supreme contempt of every true Southern heart; and when the Federal Government, under the administration of Mr. Lincoln, shall call for troops to invade or coerce the seceding States, old Franklin will respond as becomes freemen who know their rights, and dare maintain them-not to aid the Federal Government, but to resist, even unto death, the Federal policy. If war must come, our fate is, and shall be, with our sisters of the South; their cause shall be our cause—with them we will stand, or with them fall.

5. Resolved, That we earnestly petition the Legislatures of Alabama and Tennessee through them, and by ourselves, and all other authorities that can give us any aid in the matter, to change the line between the States, so as to transfer the count of Franklin to the State of Alabama, unless, before this can be done, Tennessee secede from the Union, thereby giving to us a government having our consent. And that copies of this and

the next resolution be sent to the Governors of Alabama and Tennessee as early as can be.

6. Resolved, That upon the conditions of the 5th resolution, we declare ourselves out of the Union, subject to be ratified by the States of Alabama and Tennessee, as provided in said resolution, which we again earnestly request may be early attended to.

Then I.T. Carr, Esq., being called on, after making a few appropriate remarks, submitted the following resolutions which were unanimously adopted:

1. Resolved, That we have ever stood by the Constitution, its impacts and compromises, but they have been ruthlessly set aside by the Republican party and the Chicago platform adopted instead thereof, and we are now duty bound to the framers of the Constitution, the Revolutionary sires, our ancestors, to posterity, our homes, and our sacred honor, to adhere to it now as reaffirmed by the Confederate States of America.

2. Resolved, That in as much as the movements now made in the Congress of the United States of North America, and the incoming administration thereof, threaten to blockade our ports, force revenues, suspend postal arrangements, destroy commerce, ruin trade, depreciate currency, invade sovereign States, burn cities, butcher armies, gibbet patriots, hang veterans, oppress freemen, blot our liberty, beggar homes, widow mothers, orphan children, and desolate the peace and happiness of the nation with fire and sword, --these things to do, and not to disappoint the expectation of those who have given him (Mr. Lincoln) their votes. Now, against these things we, in the name of right, the Constitution, and a just God, solemnly enter our protest; and further, when that which is manifested shall have come upon the country, we say to Tennessee: let slip the dogs of war and cry havoc !

3. Resolved, That we commend in the highest the true and loyal chivalry of the sons of the South who have resigned their offices under the late Federal government of the United States, in the army, navy, and otherwise.

Then F.T. Estill, Esq., Dr. Childs and others addressed the crowd. Afterwards Mr. A. Jourdan sang a Southern Marseilles, which was highly appreciated by all, and for which all joined in hurrahs and loud and protracted applause for Mr. Jourdan.

THOS. FINCH, Ch'N,
J.F. Syler,
N. Frizzell,
Secretaries
(Winchester, Tennessee)
(February 25, 1861)[10]

It must be noted that it is assumed copies of the resolution were sent to the Alabama and Tennessee legislatures. No records of the receipt or resulting action or lack thereof are known to exist.[11]

Today it seems unlikely that Tennesseans and/or their governor would fail to take just action against Turney and Franklin County. The best explanation lies in the fact Governor Harris was a native Franklin County resident. A true Southerner in many senses of the word, Harris had received his education in Winchester and was personally acquainted with a vast majority of the county's influential citizens. Turney's father, Hopkins L. Turney, had been a close friend of Harris.[12] The number of circumstances tilted Harris toward the new nation of the South.

This sign notes the location of Peter Turney's attempt at leading Franklin County's secession from Tennessee. Photo by author.

6

By the end of March 1861, Turney had recruited 1,165 men to fight for the Confederacy. The Confederate War Department in Montgomery sent Turney a letter, received April 9, ordering the troops to be ready for a call to fight. Orders to report to action were not received for some time, as the Montgomery-based government avoided the possibility of offending Tennessee, a potential ally state. Turney and his regiment would wait until April 25, the day after Virginia's secession, to assemble.[13]

While Turney and other Franklin County residents organized for a possible struggle, the state capital of Nashville became the site of a battle of words. The Nashville-based *Union and American*, a Democratically biased periodical, referred to Lincoln's inauguration as "a declaration of war against the seceded states" and stated that within a month war would result. The *Banner*, a more Republican-slanted newspaper, felt the inaugural address had been "mild and conservative" and declared it would be no fault of Lincoln's if a state of war should arise.[14]

As the internal pressures increased in Tennessee, the stress between the United States and the newly formed Confederate States passed the proverbial boiling point. At Ft. Sumter, South Carolina Confederate forces under P.G.T. Beauregard gained the surrender of Robert Anderson's command following a bombardment of the installation. Ironically this confrontation yielded no major casualties, a stark contrast to the war the event would effectively create. On April 15, President Lincoln, as a means of ending what he felt was only an insurrection, called for 75,000 volunteers.

Upon receiving Lincoln's request for volunteers, Tennessee Governor Harris called for an April 25 extra General Assembly session. Calling Lincoln's request an "unholy crusade" in which "no gallant son of Tennessee will ever draw his sword," Harris exclaimed that not a single soldier would be given to benefit the United States. If need be, Harris added, 50,000 men could be called to defend the rights of the fellow men of the South.[15]

Peter Turney, leader of the Franklin County secession movement and the founder of the First Tennessee Infantry Regiment. Courtesy of Confederate Veteran.

In Winchester the field officers from Peter Turney's Franklin County recruits were elected on April 27 and Turney was elected colonel. The regiment massed at Turney's home, Wolf's Craig, parading back and forth under a tall tree that carried a Confederate flag, supposedly the first to fly in Franklin County and one of the earliest, if not the earliest, to fly in Tennessee. The next three days were filled with songs, dancing, and parties, as the troops marched daily around the courthouse.[16]

A tragedy of lost history is noted on this sign showing the location of the remains of Turney's home of Wolf's Craig. Photo by author.

Three hundred and fifty girls from Mary Sharpe College gathered to bid farewell to Turney's recruits, gathered on the college grounds. Turney had served as president of the college's board of trustees for several years, and his entry onto the campus while atop a magnificent horse assured the young ladies of a Southern victory. The college president, Dr. Graves, gave a stirring speech followed by cheers from the soldiers. Turney dismounted his horse and with a trembling voice noted the words of Graves and the faces of the young ladies would inspire his men and him in the days and events to come. Turney then mounted his horse to leave as many of the girls began crying.[17]

On May 1, Turney's regiment prepared to march to Decherd, two miles east of Winchester. Here they would board a train on the North Carolina and St. Louis Railroad to be transported to Virginia. As the men lined up in the town square, the citizens of the area began cheering wildly. The soldiers responded with what was afterward labeled the "rebel yell." It is sometimes stated then that the rebel yell originated in Turney's regiment.[18]

As the troops prepared to leave, a fatigued runner made his way to Col. Turney and forced a note into his hand. After reading the note, Turney threw back his head and laughed. The note had come from "Aunt" Annie Finch, a beloved elderly lady and one of the strongest secessionists in the county. She was inviting Turney and his men to her home, located one mile northwest of town on the Tullahoma Road, where she would "sing them a song." Turney's men, a crowd of spectators, and a collection of animals proceeded to Finch's home, where they discovered the old lady. Finch, with assistance from Turney, perched herself precariously in a chair placed upon a stack of boxes on her porch.[19]

Aunt Annie sang the first two lines of "Hail Columbia" and then explained that those were all she knew. Turney raised the lady from her chair as the soldiers responded with unbridled cheers. The elderly lady kissed Turney and half a dozen soldiers as tears ran down her cheeks. The regiment returned to town, singing Finch's song as they marched. As loved ones followed, many of the soldiers in Turney's regiment saw their homes for the last time. The town of Winchester, Tennessee now seemed abnormally quiet, as the army of Franklin County went to war.[20]

An article in the May 3, 1861 *Daily Gazette* from Nashville announced the departure of Turney's regiment from Franklin. The group of 1,200 men, leaving for Lynchburg, Virginia, marched from the area over a path "literally strewn with flowers from the hands of ladies and children, who … pronounced … a hearty 'God Bless you.'"[21]

The Tennessee General Assembly passed a May 6 ordinance that ended the Federal connection that had existed since 1796 between the United States and Tennessee. Acting upon Harris's proposal to cease this relationship if decided upon by popular vote, the assembly's declaration was voted on by Tennesseans on June 8, 1861. In addition to this suggestion, Harris felt the "people's voices" should be heard on the issue of Tennessee's admission to the Confederacy. Both time and cost would be minimized using this course of action rather than pursuing a convention.[22]

An interesting aspect of the chain of events that transpired in Tennessee between the February and June votes was the increase in secessionist mindsets over those of the pro-Union faction. The attitudes of Franklin County residents, seen as revolutionary following the February election, became the majority opinion by June. Middle Tennessee, in turn, became the catalyst for the state's call for secession.

The fall of Ft. Sumter and Lincoln's petition for recruits are often cited as the major causes for a change in attitude among the people of Middle Tennessee.

Spring Hill resident Major Campbell Brown explained this changing sentiment following Sumter's capture. Brown noted an extremely pro-Union attitude in Nashville only a few weeks prior to the attack on the South Carolina fort. Instantaneously following Sumter's fall, Brown marveled at the fact that pro-secession parades and Confederate flags abounded and that he found "secession ... at every corner."[23]

The change of heart among Middle Tennesseans in conjunction with the increase in the number of secession-minded individuals in West Tennessee created obvious results for the June vote. The seeds of secession had matured. Now the seeds of war were ready for growth, perhaps to be supplied the needed nutrients through the blood of Tennesseans.

Only five West Tennessee counties voted against secession, and just three Middle Tennessee counties followed the pro-Union faction. The latter is somewhat difficult to comprehend, as this outcome required some twenty thousand Middle Tennesseans to change their minds in four short months. Over 80 percent of the voters in twenty-two Middle Tennessee counties had favored secession in the February vote, while no pro-Union votes were supposedly cast in three counties of the area. Accusations of intimidation, unlawful voting, and subduing of Union-minded speakers in the west and middle sections of the state led many citizens to believe the election was dishonest.[24]

In East Tennessee only six counties favored secession. Even in this Union stronghold, though, pro-secessionist feeling had increased 11 percent since February. However, approximately 33,000 of the 47,238 pro-Union votes cast in Tennessee came from East Tennessee. Unlike the farmlands of West Tennessee, where the need for field hands was great, East Tennessee was mountainous, and slaves were used primarily in homes, functioning as household servants. Slaves were, in turn, treated as family members in many cases throughout the eastern section.[25]

This area of the state again mirrored the division over secession prevalent across the nation and Tennessee. Knoxville voted for secession by a vote of 786 to 377, yet in Knox County, secession lost 3,196 to 1,226. Separation also prevailed in Chattanooga 421 to 51, yet its parent county of Hamilton went into the pro-Union column by a vote of 1,260 to 854.[26]

Montgomery, Alabama, the Confederate capital, paid great attention to the episodes in Tennessee. The officials of the Confederacy were well aware of Tennessee's waterways and the fact that the state would provide a cushion for the deeper South states such as Alabama.[27] It appears these two characteristics were far too tempting for the secession leaders to ignore and led to the subsequent courting of the state to call for secession.

Alabama citizen Henry W. Hilliard, serving as a type of Confederate ambassador to Tennessee, had paid a visit to Nashville prior to the June vote, making it known that he would gladly consent to a request to speak in front of the General Assembly concerning the formation of a partnership between the Confederate states and Tennessee. With the extension of the invitation to speak and the subsequent acceptance of the same, Hilliard spoke to the assembly on April 20. Having been well received and reported by the newspapers as having given a splendid speech, Hilliard returned to the Confederate capital proclaiming that he had achieved the purpose of his mission.[28]

Another act of the period prior to the June vote called for fifty-five thousand volunteers to serve in a provisional army. Of this number twenty-five thousand would be placed into active service; the remainder in reserve. Authorization was given for the circulation of 5 million dollars in state bonds to muster capital to back the troops.[29] This pact with the Confederacy, the call for volunteers, and the issuance of bonds added to the popular majority's call to secede only fanned the flame in relation to the anti-secessionists of East Tennessee. This stronghold of Unionists had no plans to follow their fellow statesmen in an act of obedience to popular sovereignty.

While the overwhelming majority of Southern senators gave up their seats as their respective states seceded, East Tennessean Andrew Johnson refused to follow suit. Johnson left Tennessee in July 1861 with Confederate troops neglecting to impede his escape. This failure to apprehend Johnson would prove critical for the Confederacy. Johnson would be appointed by Lincoln to be Tennessee's military governor in 1862, following his pledge to keep the plight of East Tennesseans in the minds of the Northern people. The Confederates envisioned, as Lincoln encouraged, that East Tennessee would receive military aid.[30] Johnson clearly had numerous reasons to flee the state.

Prior to Johnson's departure, his Greeneville home was the site of the June 17 East Tennessee Convention. The meeting would last through the twentieth, with all East Tennessee counties but Rhea providing delegates. One proposal of this delegation was to proclaim that the document written to declare Tennessee independent as well as other acts of the state's government relating to secession were void due to their unconstitutionality.[31]

Eventually these individuals desired to secede from Tennessee, yet their proposal failed in the democratically controlled legislature. The assembly simply adjourned, taking no action on this issue. This idea bore great similarity to that of the people of Western Virginia, who formed West Virginia at the midpoint of the Civil War. Many East Tennesseans would remain loyal to the Union, despite the failure of their attempt to disconnect from their mother state.[32] The Confederate forces would prove capable of ending most attempts of East Tennesseans to "take matters into their own hands" until the fall of 1863.

On June 24, 1861, with the notification of Governor Harris, Tennessee officially became a "free and independent" government. This condition would exist until July 22, when Tennessee became a legitimate member of the Confederate States of America, becoming the last state to do so.

Isham G. Harris served as Tennessee's governor at the outbreak of the Civil War. Courtesy of Confederate Veteran.

In August of 1861, Tennesseans diverted attention from the secession issue and the arrival of preparation for war. Governor Isham Green Harris was then seeking his third term in office. The major opposition to the incumbent's quest was William Polk.

Polk was the brother of former president James K. Polk and began charging Harris with possessing plans to become a military dictator and for being at fault for Tennessee's secession. Harris seemed to proclaim that his goal was the fulfillment of his job's requirements and that he was simply defending the state he'd been elected to govern. It was written in the Memphis *Appeal* that anyone who voted against Harris would be guilty of treason. Harris was eventually reelected, gathering 75,300 votes in comparison to 43,495 for Polk. As with almost every other matter placed before the state, East Tennesseans went against the majority's decision. Polk had carried a majority of East Tennessee votes by approximately 12,000 votes.[33]

In October 1861, the new Tennessee legislature met and elected Gustavus Adolphus Henry and Landon Carter Haynes to the Confederate Senate. On November 6, Tennesseans chose eleven Confederate representatives created by the recently empowered legislature. East Tennesseans again provided a problem for the matter at hand. In the first, second, and third congressional districts, Confederate candidates had been defeated. This allowed Andrew Johnson to keep the US Senate seat he secured before Tennessee's secession. As a result, East Tennessee, from 1861 to 1863, would be represented at Montgomery and Washington, D.C.[34]

Only twenty days before Governor Harris had overseen the admission of his state to the new Southern government, he offered to Confederate President Davis twenty-two infantry regiments that were equipped and ready for combat. In addition, two cavalry regiments and ten artillery regiments were presented in the hope that the Confederates would protect Tennessee from a Union invasion.[35]

The circumstances of the secession of Tennessee as well as the division among its sections and their residents led to a virtual civil war within the state. Tennesseans readily voted to express thoughts and convictions, yet they also proved their willingness to express opinions and beliefs in a more forceful manner, responding to a call to arms by both sides. This call often seemed to come from neighbors or friends, notably in East Tennessee.

The eastern section was the site of military actions such as raiding enemy communications, attacking enemy troops, and aiding kindly soldiers. In addition, political undertakings included harassing, intimidating, and sometimes murdering advocates of the opposition government. Theft and assault were common criminal aspects of guerilla campaigns present in the area.[36]

Within a year of secession, Tennessee had responded well to the need of troops for the Confederacy and their training. More than twenty Confederate camps and forts existed throughout the state in 1862. In addition, Tennessee would provide more than 120,000 men to fight for the Confederacy. This number was from the approximate Southern total of 750,000 and more than the number that came from any other state. Thirty-six Confederate generals would come from Tennessee; twenty-seven would serve as brigadier generals.[37]

Proving the division so prevalent in the state, Tennessee would also have a large number of its native sons fighting for the Union. East Tennessee again provides the example of the minority thought pattern and action found within the state during this period. The United States had approximately 2 million men fighting for its preservation. Of this total, approximately thirty-eight thousand came from Tennessee, more US military personnel than was supplied by any other Confederate state and more than came from five northern states. A majority of these individuals left their homes in East Tennessee to fight for the Union. Among these Union Tennesseans were Knox County's David Farragut, the nation's first full admiral, and Samuel Carter of Carter County, the only man in history to hold the ranks of brigadier general and rear admiral.[38] These numbers clearly exemplify the strong commitment of Tennesseans to a cause in which they strongly believed.

It is a widely accepted fact that Tennessee ranks second to Virginia in the number of Civil War battles fought within its boundaries. Shiloh, Ft. Henry, Ft. Donelson, and Murfreesboro were the sites of high levels of bloodshed in the first half of the war. In addition to the destruction of property and loss of life in the areas of these battlegrounds, Union forces captured the city of Memphis in mid-1862. Nashville was also taken over by Union troops, becoming the first Confederate state capital to hold that distinction.

With the initial entry of Union soldiers into the nearby Mississippi cotton region in early 1862, many Tennessee planters, unable to ship their cotton, simply burned it. While this appears to have been a means of boldly displaying patriotism, many cotton growers were aware of the fact that Confederate officers would destroy the cotton of those planters unwilling to do so themselves. This was seen as a means of eliminating the chance for the valuable crop to fall into Union hands.[39] The more infamous cases of destruction of Southern property are usually associated with federal troops.

Mark Cockrill of Davidson County lost 20,000 bushels of corn, 26 horses, 60 head of cattle, 220 sheep, 200 tons of hay, 2,000 bushels of oats, and 2,000 pounds of cured bacon to pillaging Union soldiers. Murfreesboro resident Bettie Ridley Blackmore recorded that her house was burned and her father's property destroyed by Northern soldiers.[40]

By March of 1862, Tennessee and six other Southern state legislatures had passed various relief acts directed toward the families of Confederate soldiers. The funds were limited to the families of volunteers and were to be collected through state, county, or local taxes for distribution by the county authorities. This "county unit system" met limited success, as many counties suffered droughts that led to failed crops. Many sections were heavily laden with poverty, while others saw the successful collection of taxes. The number of needy individuals heavily overburdened the available reserves.[41]

These facts were undoubtedly known throughout the ranks of Tennessee military personnel of the North and South. While Tennesseans loyal to the North saw the fall of Nashville as a loss of the protective buffer that existed for the deep-South states, it also signified to them that possession of the complete South was also possible. The Tennessee Confederates, who championed the cause of secession and saw the destruction and capture of their state, were well aware of the need to take the war northward.

CHAPTER TWO

Formation of the Tennessee Brigade Regiments

Multi-volume works have been dedicated to the establishment of the numerous regiments, Union and Confederate, organized in Tennessee between 1861 and 1865. A large number of counties within the state produced more than one regiment, often with families being split over the national flag under which they would fight.

A total of fifty-three federal regiments were organized in Tennessee for use in the Civil War. In addition, one battalion and a single detached company from the state fought on the Union's behalf. The number of militia and other type units is almost impossible to ascertain. While these numbers are impressive, those contributed to the Confederacy are astonishing. By the war's end, Tennessee had provided 110 regiments to the Confederate States of America; 33 battalions, along with 54 separate batteries or companies were added to the Southern cause.[1]

These numbers communicate little to individuals totally lacking or possessing minimal comprehension of the military organization of the period.

Consisting of 101 officers and enlisted men, the Confederate infantry *company* served as the basic unit. Platoons, as known today, were nonexistent in the Civil War. The *battalion* was the next level of organization, consisting of at least four companies. Unlike today, this unit was often a separate or even independent unit, not a part of the regiment, with a major or lieutenant colonel directing. Ten companies were ordinarily assigned to a *regiment*, using letter designations from A to K. The letter J, through some conventional rationale, was omitted. Usually consisting of five regiments was the *brigade*. The Confederate army brigades were identified by the names of their commanders, unlike the Union's use of numerical designations. The latter practice was used among various Confederate units before the battle of Shiloh. Afterward the use of names being attached to the brigade units became commonplace.[2]

In most cases three brigades were organized into a *division*. Two or more divisions comprised a *corps*. Confederate *armies* consisted of two or more corps, named after the department or state of origin or the area of its major campaigns. While infantry units were arranged into brigades, divisions, and corps, the assignment of a regiment into an elevated unit was not eternal. The brigade assignment did tend to involve a longer time frame for a regiment than did its assignment to a division or corps.[3] As will be noted in this text, assignments to a specific brigade were far from permanent.

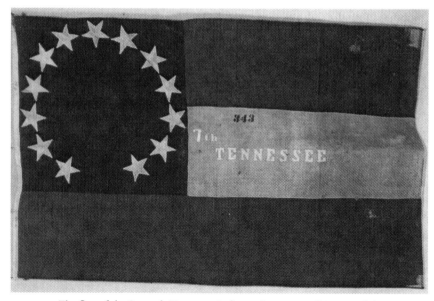

The flag of the Seventh Tennessee Infantry Regiment. Courtesy of the Tennessee State Museum Collection.

The Seventh Tennessee Infantry (7th TN) was organized at Camp Trousdale near Gallatin, Tennessee in Sumner County in late May 1861. In July of the same year, after weeks of "perfecting itself in discipline and drill," the regiment was mustered into Confederate service and transferred to Virginia. Brig. Gen. Samuel R. Anderson commanded the Seventh Tennessee at this time as it, along with the Fourteenth Tennessee Infantry (14th TN),

formed the original Tennessee Brigade. Ten companies combined to form the
Seventh, consisting of men who hailed primarily from four counties in the
north-central portion of the state.[4]

Six of the companies in the Seventh Tennessee—D, F, G, H, I, and
K—were from Wilson County. Sumner County provided Companies C and
E. Company A called DeKalb County home. Capt. John Fite led Company
B from Smith County. "The Harris Rifles" associated with Company D;
Company F, "The Statesville Tigers"; Company G and "The Hurricane
Rifles" were akin, as were Company I and "The Silver Spring Guards."
Ironically Company H was "The Grays" and Company K, "The Blues."
Sumner County's Company E had been formed under the name "Fite's
Guards" in honor of the individual who uniformed it, Mr. S. B. Fite. The
company had left home for Nashville, camping on the south side of town
at the old fairgrounds until meeting with the rest of the brigade at Camp
Trousdale, which the troops reached by rail.[5]

The Fourteenth Tennessee Infantry Regiment was formed following
Governor Isham G. Harris's first call for troops. While the date of organization
varies from April to June 6, 1861, accounts are nearly unanimous as to
the site of the regiment's organization: Camp Duncan, in the vicinity
of Clarksville, Montgomery County, Tennessee. Montgomery County, in
addition to its east and west neighboring counties of Robertson and Stewart
respectively, provided the bulk of individuals who filled the ranks of this
group of fighting men.[6]

Originally, the Fourteenth Tennessee contained eleven companies, with
approximately one thousand men on roster. Companies A, B, G, H, K, and
L were composed of men from Montgomery County. Stewart County was
home to the men of Companies D, E, and F; the latter of which would
be disbanded in May 1863 and its thirty-two remaining men transferred
to Company E. The remaining companies, I and C, consisted largely of
Robertson County natives. The men of Company C were also known as
the "Pepper Guards."[7]

Camp Duncan was near Dunbar Cave and served as the headquarters
of the Fourteenth for approximately two weeks. At that time the regiment
was moved roughly ten miles to a better water supply. From the regiment's
new base of Camp Quarles, the Fourteenth was called to Virginia. Quarles
was accessible by rail and the Russellville Pike and lay across the Red
River. The guns the men of the Fourteenth used while training at Camp
Quarles had been converted from flint to percussion locks. Few complaints
were made concerning these outdated muskets, for they were the only type
available at the time. In turn, they were used as the soldiers' perfected
military drills.[8]

The Fourteenth Tennessee Infantry Regiment battle flag, St. Andrew's Cross pattern. Courtesy of the Tennessee State Museum Collection.

The men of the Fourteenth from Clarksville, Tennessee became well known for quickly responding to the governor's call for troops. Many left college to enter the service of the Confederacy. Led by Capt. William A. Forbes, the boys of Company A marched in front of the Bank of Tennessee, entertaining one of the first meetings of its type. A large crowd attended and heard speeches filled with patriotism. Ben Haskins of Clarksville was one of the almost one hundred young men from Stewart College who followed Forbes, a mathematics professor at the college, in response to Governor Harris's call for volunteers. Forbes, a Virginian and a graduate of Virginia Military Institute, helped transform the campus of Stewart College into a military camp, which it served as until Company A moved to Camp Quarles.[9]

Clarksville Judge C.W. Tyler proposed that the efforts of men from Clarksville and Montgomery County were seldom if ever equaled in one aspect by any other Southern county or state. Boys and men, married and single, volunteered their services to the military at such a rate that eventually more than two thousand men from the Tennessee county filled the ranks of various companies. This number, according to Tyler, "exceeded the entire white population subject to military duty."[10]

Dr. Ben Haskins in post-war photo. Haskins served as a first lieutenant in the Fourteenth Tennessee until he was captured at Gettysburg on July 1. Exchanged in time to meet his regiment at Petersburg, Haskins served until the war's end. A bursting shell had wounded him at Chancellorsville, and he wore this "cross of honor" until his February 11, 1912 death at the age of seventy. Never married, the veteran was buried beside his parents in Clarksville, Tennessee. Photo courtesy of Confederate Veteran.

J.O. Shackelford, in a speech, urged his son Robert, a private in Company A, to be willing to die for his country, should the situation arise. Private Robert Shackelford heeded his father's advice while dying at Gettysburg. The battlefield served as his final resting place.[11]

While circumstances like Shackelford's were commonplace, many of the men who joined regiments throughout the South did so with mixed emotions. It is a well-established fact that one of the Confederacy's greatest generals, Robert E. Lee, was torn between his allegiance to the United States and his home state of Virginia. This emotional turmoil was not relegated to the upper echelon of military ranks. An example of the emotional struggles is recorded in the diary of Archibald Debow Norris of Rome in Smith County, Tennessee. The twenty-two-year-old private, known to his friends as Archie, was the son of a prominent farmer, John Blakemore Norris, and his wife, Margaret. Archibald was the June 1860 Valedictorian at Allegheny College in Meadville, Pennsylvania. Upon his graduation, he served as headmaster at White Sulphur Springs College in his hometown. True to his upbringing, Norris also farmed.

On January 28, 1861, Norris's diary entry stated his compassion to preserve the Union. He wrote, "Went to hear … Esquire McClain speak on the Union … The Union ball is in motion, may it continue to roll and increase."[12]

Norris had noted earlier in his diary his studies of pro-Union writings, sermons, and speeches. His January 22, 1861 entry was recorded as:

> Finished reading Andrew Johnson's speech. He takes the following positions That a state has no right to secede. That the government has no right to coerce a state, but has the right to coerce the individuals thereof. He thinks that a dissolution of the Union would hasten the very evils which are assigned as the cause. He is for maintaining our rights in the Union, not out of it.

The next day, a Wednesday, Norris noted his further study upon the issue of secession:

> Read Mr. Toombs speech in the USS in which he presents as the ultimatum to the North, five demands … That the Northern states repeal their personal liberty bills. That the government promptly execute the fugitive slave law of 1860. That the south have free access to the territories with their slaves. An amendment to the effect that slavery can never be abolished but by the people of the states where it exists. I have forgotten the last.[13]

On the twenty-sixth of January, Norris revealed his dedication to unity within the church and his nation as a whole as he wrote, "Went to hear Mr.

Baldwin preach … Think he will be able to harmonize the hitherto discordant elements of the church … He is for the Union now and forever."[14]

In the entries of February 3 through 5, Norris recorded his growing compassion for the Union to prevail. The subject consisted of a significant majority of each entry for these dates. He explained:

> Went over to Uncle Lamb's and thence to Dr. Sinks. Had strong Union conversations. Think Tennessee will remain in the Union. Hope So … Every day seems to develop more clearly the policy to be pursued by Tennessee. She should maintain an "armed neutrality" and assume the office of mediation between the conflicting sections of the country. The evils which our once happy but now distracted country is suffering, have all been the work of demagogues, of politicians who have made their efforts subservient to partisan aims and have wielded the government as an instrument for the upbuilding and upholding of political parties.[15]

On the seventh, Norris's convictions grew louder as he expressed himself openly in a larger group. He stated, "Went to Rome last night to hear speaking. They however called on me first. I talked a little, disconnectedly and scatteringly avowing my adherence to the Union."[16]

As did many individuals across the state of Tennessee, Norris voted no on the issue of the convention on February 9. He proudly noted this fact in his journal entry for the day and the information that his local precinct held an opinion similar to his by voting down the convention proposal by a vote of 82 to 20. Within a week, Norris wrote of his belief that the preservation of the Union could not be accomplished without bloodshed. Over the next month, he recorded the burning of twenty-two homes in and around Rome.[17]

For some reason the pages from April 1 through May 10 were torn from Norris's journal. These could have provided some insight into how the events of the period had altered his mindset. Regardless of what they were, their effect was evident, as the variation became clear in his May 10, 1861 entry that said, "Went to Lebanon today. Times are becoming very serious. The necessity of arming the State is becoming more apparent. Saw the three military companies parade today. They presented a very fine appearance. Great many people there."[18]

Norris felt obliged to protect his state's honor, yet did so with sadness over his father's reaction:

> Returned to Lebanon, joined the company of Robt. Hatton, did it reluctantly, regretted the necessity and yet hope there will

be no necessity for my services. I went into this measure with the conviction that it was my imperative duty. I owe allegiance to my State and though I may regret the steps which my State may take, yet it is my imperative duty to support it in such appalling crisis as this and to it will my support be given … Pa is very grieved at my having joined the volunteers, and had I not joined I would not now merely for his sake. It is grievious [sic] to see him so sorrowful.[19]

Capt. A.D. Norris, Seventh Tennessee. Norris's recollections of the early phases of the war provide unlimited insight and information for this text. Photo courtesy of Elizabeth L. Mitchell, granddaughter of Capt. Norris.

As would his fellow infantrymen, Norris soon experienced his indoctrination into the military lifestyle. As thousands experienced before and since, Norris felt the deep painful emotions of serving a state and a cause that took him from his home. On May 20, 1861, Private Archibald D. Norris remarked:

Left home this morning for the camp as a volunteer in Capt. Hatton's Company. Sad was the parting, saddest of all the partings I ever had. Sad too was the thought that I might be placed in conflict with some of my once best friends, but my duty to my State constrains me. I do not approve altogether of the course of the people of the State, yet I am a Tennessean. May Heaven avert the effusion of fraternal blood and restore peace to our land.[20]

More patriotic correspondence arose from Col. John F. Goodner in a letter to Miss Lizzie Floyd on June 18, 1861. Writing from Camp Trousdale, Goodner praised the ladies of the area for producing a stand of colors for the regiment and asked them to deliver it personally. Goodner's attraction to the ladies was reciprocated, at least in his own opinion, as he wrote ten days later that they were regularly sending him fresh vegetables and sweetmeats while complimenting him as being the finest-looking officer in the field.[21]

John F. Goodner replaced Robert Hatton as colonel of Co. A, 7th TN. Goodner served in this capacity almost a year before resigning. Courtesy of Ray Miller, Savage-Goodner SCV Camp #1513.

The military lifestyle was known to have an adverse effect on many Southern soldiers who were used to far different sets of rules and "home cooking." Life in camp added to the intake of foodstuffs basically foreign to a body, and a longing for home made the events once taken for granted gain a new level of appreciation. Little more than six weeks after leaving home, Norris made this entry on July 5, 1861: "Staid [sic] at the Commercial last night, saw Grandma. Had a pleasant time. First time I ate at a civilized table in a long time, seemed new and somewhat unnatural."[22]

The pressures of military camp life, even prior to the entry into battle, obviously caused some individuals to question their decision of enlistment. These often led to thoughts of desertion, yet the sight of a fellow soldier being punished for such an act undoubtedly deterred many from following suit. Norris noted such an event in his July 11, 1861 entry:

> Witnessed the infliction of the first sentence of a Court Martial on a deserter named McHenry. He was divested of his uniform, clad in calico breeches and shirt, pants rolled above the knees, head half shaved, uncovered, barefooted, shoes in his hand and two huge horns projecting from his forehead. In this condition he was led along the line of regiments drawn up for his reception. He looked despicable indeed. After being drummed along the line he was turned loose and told to "Slope," which he did in short order.[23]

After a few weeks at Camp Trousdale, where regimental members drilled for six hours a day, the men of the Seventh made their way toward Nashville, accompanied by the Fourteenth, whose members had spent the same period at Camp Quarles. On July 16, 1861, the new recruits began their journey toward their new assignment. The event was recorded in Norris's entry of that day:

> Before day we took up the line of march to Richland station where we arrived at five. Left on the cars at nine, arrived at Nashville at about twelve, ate part of a dinner that Grandma sent me. Were marched to the academy grounds where we rested and were treated to drinks of cold water by the beautiful Acd'y girls, left about 6 p.m. for Chattanooga. Some of our boys got "Gloriously drunk," had sleepless ride over and through the Cumberland Mountains.[24]

Leaving from Nashville in response to the need for all available units, the Seventh and Fourteenth regiments traveled by train to Chattanooga, changing trains several times. In open cars and encountering an unpleasantly cool evening, the troops reached Knoxville, ready to join the action and reinforce Beauregard and Johnston, waiting at Manassas. From Knoxville the regiments journeyed to Haynesville, Tennessee through a heavy rainstorm. This portion of the journey was completed with far fewer men than had begun the trip eastward. Approximately thirty men from the Fourteenth alone had been left in Knoxville, suffering from fever, dysentery, and measles.[25]

The trip to Knoxville had been comprised of a showing of might on the part of the Confederate inductees. Pvt. Norris posted the following: "Very hard drill, lasting five hours, some spectators out from Knoxville ... marched through Knoxville in the evening. Made quite a display. Were complimented by the Col."[26]

The Fourteenth Tennessee, under Col. William Forbes, had arrived in Knoxville with approximately one thousand men. The strength of the regiment was reported by a Knoxville resident to one Col. Carter, an individual who was organizing a Federal regiment that was bivouacked only six miles from the Tennessean's camp. Carter ordered his men home in an effort to avoid a conflict for which they were ill prepared and to wait until a more opportune time to make a stand.[27]

After moving to Haynesville, the Seventh and Fourteenth Tennessee regiments were joined by Col. George Maney's First Tennessee Regiment. Tents were pitched and the waiting began as the units were informed of the news that the first battle at Manassas had been fought. This Confederate victory brought about a change in orders, placing the Tennessee regiments in the Department of Northwestern Virginia, under the command of Robert E. Lee. Brigadier Samuel R. Anderson's Brigade, containing the First, Seventh, and Fourteenth Tennessee infantry regiments, was formed at this time.[28]

Anderson was from Nashville and had served in the Mexican War. It is noteworthy at this point to mention that Maney's First Tennessee Regiment, not Turney's First Tennessee Regiment, was an original member of the brigade. A.D. Norris recorded the arrival of Maney's First Tennessee on Monday July 29, 1861 and noted that the event immediately preceded the brigade's departure for "Millborough."[29]

The Tennessee regiments now formed to create Anderson's Brigade. The group proceeded eastward, reaching Millboro in August 1861. This town was a Virginia Central Railroad way station and the nearest railroad station to the brigade's destination. The brigade indulged in a "long and tedious march," reaching Big Springs by mid-August. Private Robert E. McCulloch, Co. H., 14th TN, expressed his elation about arriving in Big Springs, as it offered rest for the "weary and footsore" soldiers.[30]

Anderson's Brigade joined Donelson's Tennesseans, Gilham's Virginia Infantry Brigade, W.H.F. Lee's Virginia Cavalry, and Capt. Alexander's Tennessee cavalry company in forming Gen. Loring's division. J.H. Moore, 7th TN, stated that his inexperienced cohorts had not yet "entered upon the realities of war" and that they spent a great deal of their time at Big Springs and "indulged in hunting and fishing the game ... abundant in the mountains of west Virginia."[31]

Gen. Samuel R. Anderson, early commander of the Tennessee Brigade. Courtesy of the Urigen Collection.

The Tennesseans received a welcomed visitor at this point of their existence. A paymaster, sent by Tennessee Governor Harris, arrived and paid the men with money from their home state. This was the first payment the soldiers had received since enlisting. Many individuals lacked the knowledge that the state of Tennessee, as William McComb stated, "took care of the boys for several months after we enlisted."[32]

In addition to the money he was given, Archibald Norris shared Moore's relishing of the area's natural beauty. His entry of August 14, 1861 emphasized how the unspoiled beauty and resources impressed the young teacher/farmer/soldier. As he fought for the nation his home state had recently joined, he forecast the impending entry of civilization into the region by writing,

"During my stay at Mr. Lamb's as Picket guard I had a good opportunity to study the character and resources of Western Va. This country is much wilder and less cultivated than a Tennessean would think any portion of the Old dominion to be. The mountains are studded with undergrowth. In some places the Laurel has superceded [sic] every other kind of growth. deer, bear, wild Turkeys etc. still abound in this locality. In a short fishing excursion on Elk river, a deer going up the stream passed within six paces of where I was lying concealed. The cleared land readily produces grass which is indigenous and consequently luxuriant. The great forte of this country is raising cattle. There they find sustenance summer and winter. Capitalists discerning this have monopolized the land and are instrumental in keeping this land out of cultivation. An ordinary farmer here owns from two to 5 thousand acres of land. Another great resource is the water power, But it will require ages to enable this feature to be amply developed."[33]

Greed had an impact on some men in areas such as these, where needs were fully met. Norris saw this event to be as tragic as the war itself. He wrote, "Each new day adds new evidences of the destructiveness not to say the horrors of war even before we have reached its acme—a battle. The march of an army through a friendly country is attended with much loss of food and property to the citizens along the line of march. How much more destructive then must be the march of a hostile army who regard ever species of property as their legitimate booty." [34]

Pvt. Norris exhibited his desire to right the wrongs of his companions by visiting a household to offer compensation for a portion of the stolen goods.

"Touched with sympathy and suspecting her loss due to some of our soldiers I offered her a V which was all I had and only half of that was mine. She hesitated to accept but finally kept saying she would return it in a day or two. A few moments reflection convinced me I had acted imprudently in offering money to one who did not need it half so much as myself and moreover had brought suspicion on myself for taking of goods by being too impulsive."[35]

While some members of the Tennessee regiments resorted to stealing as a means of quenching their desires, others in the Seventh Tennessee longed for simple possessions. Pvt. John S. Close of Company A wrote to his friend Wingate Robinson in their home county of DeKalb, Tennessee. He stated:

> I would have writ sooner if I could have got paper but this is the first paper I have got hold of … We had a fine time while we was on the cars. We run on the cars to Milburow Va. and then we had to walk 40 miles, that went very hard with us … we have plenty of beef and bread and coffee but other pervision [sic] ain't quite so plentyful

[sic] as they was at camp trousdal. Wingate, we have lots of fun and
some hard times, hits [sic] rained every day since we have bin hear
[sic] and the guards has to ly [sic] on the wet ground only when they
are sanding at thare [sic] post. Our picket guard is from 5 to 7 miles
from camps and has to stay out 48 hours at a time.[36]

Sgt. Robert T. Mockbee, 14th TN, shared the assertion of his comrade J.H.
Moore that the realities of war had failed to be fully grasped among his fellow
infantrymen. He noted guard duty and daily drilling had intervals that were
usually filled with innocent games, sport, or other forms of recreation. There
were those who played cards for money, and nighttime was often made more
festive with the playing of a fiddle in many companies. Stag dances sometimes
arose, with a handkerchief tied around the right arm of men designated as
female partners. True to their Southern upbringing, the men were graceful
to their so-called lady partners who responded with curtsies and polished
motions. Mockbee explained that many of the members of the Fourteenth
Tennessee had been taught dance by males from the various Middle Tennessee
counties in which the regiment had recruited members.[37] Perhaps this activity
relieved some levels of homesickness among its participants.

Junius "June" Kimble, Co. A, 14th TN, of Clarksville, Tennessee,
recalled his fondness for the Fourteenth Tennessee Glee Club, which so
often entertained the soldiers. This faction of the regiment was begun at the
time of the regiment's organization and remained intact throughout the war.
Kimble played violin for the group; there was also flautist, a song leader, and
three singers. In addition to delighting the infantrymen, the glee club was
often asked to entertain at the homes of families, "native and cultured alike,"
near the brigade camp or along the paths of marches. Usually visiting without
additional followers, these talented musicians found that "the simple, frank,
modest maid of the mountains was as cordial and courteous in her way as the
more cultured, refined daughter of the proud planters of the Virginia plains
in their way." The entertainers were always well received and valued by those
they visited. Kimble noted that these times were "a Godsend in the humdrum
of ... soldier life" and, as such, a true source of contentment.[38]

Leaving their camp at Big Springs after almost four weeks of rest,
Anderson's brigade members placed five days of rations into their haversacks
and followed orders directing them to Cheat Mountain.[39] A.D. Norris recorded
the circumstances:

Soon after dinner we received orders to cook five days rations.
Left camp at eight o'clock ... morning. Anderson and Donnelson
[sic] brigade both marched out. We went along the base of Cheat

Mountain crossing several very high knobs, becoming very weary. About night fall we started after a short bivouac and marched about two miles. Some of the regiments getting away from the main body.[40]

On September 11, 1861, Norris wrote, "Resumed our march over mountain paths and frequently with no paths, through the roughest country I ever saw. It was rocky, steep and wet … Expect to fight tomorrow."[41]

Located in the Parkersburg Turnpike in Western Virginia, the objective of Cheat Mountain was a fortified mountain pass. The left wing of the federal army, under the command of Gen. Rosecrans, held the position. If the Confederate forces could ensnare the cut, the communication lines between the two wings of Rosecrans's army would be obstructed, requiring his withdrawal from most of Western Virginia.[42]

The Tennesseans were to gain and hold positions on the Parkersburg Road and the rear of the pass, preventing the retreat or reinforcements of the federal stronghold. The garrison would receive a frontal and right-side attack from troops under Col. Rust and Gen. Henry Jackson. In order to reach its assigned position, Anderson's Brigade traveled approximately forty miles over mountains without the benefit of passable roads. The relentless rains added to the use of Appalachian trails that necessitated single-file marching. This ended the brigade's hopes of a quick and eventful campaign. Upon approaching the turnpike, the brigade's previously peaceful march was fired upon by a lone enemy soldier who escaped through the thick underbrush. The result of the enemy's shot was the wounding of a soldier surnamed Crunk, the first Anderson Brigade member wounded in the war.[43]

Reaching their objective, the brigade was positioned around Parkersburg Road. Immediately the brigade received and returned fire, resulting in a Federal retreat. The brigade suffered few casualties yet recorded the successful capture of five Federal soldiers, including a lieutenant.[44]

Unaware or unimpressed at the capture of members of the enemy, Norris nonetheless was highly cognizant of the other events of the day: "This morning, proceeded a short distance when one … was wounded very severely by a rifle shot from an unseen foe. After a miles rugged march we came to the Huttonsville and Staunton road. Had two Skirmishes with the enemy in which two of our men were killed and several wounded."[45]

Jackson and Rust ordered the withdrawal of their commands, feeling a frontal assault would be impractical. Anderson's Brigade was also ordered to pull back, ending its first campaign. Following a three-day march, retracing its steps of a few days prior, the brigade returned to Big Springs.[46]

The incidents of the Cheat Mountain campaign and the subsequent march had a demoralizing effect upon several members of the brigade. Norris stated:

> Resumed our march early toward our old camping ground … Travelled [sic] very slowly over a very muddy road, reached camp about twelve o'clock, almost exhausted. Thus ended the most difficult fatiguing and profitless weeks march perhaps that was ever attempted or executed on the American Continent … Rested a short time only from our fatigue. About ten o'clock an order was issued to move over to dry Branch about half way between our camp on Mingo Flats and the old one near Big Spring. We had to carry every thing on our shoulders, including tents and cooking vessels and that too over the worst of roads, through mud sometimes knee deep. A general backward move of the army seems to be the program … On going back we found it was a ruse to get us back and that the real object of our return was to bring over the sick, which we did on litters.[47]

Norris relished the food he and others in his brigade found in abundance in the area. One day he explained, "Had a hearty feast of black berries" while two days later noting that while camping on "a nice little hill, had peaches, [and] apples." The prolific supply of food failed to harbor Norris's proclamation of the first campaign he and his fellow Tennesseans had recently experienced. He wrote, "The 'valley mountain' expedition seems to have been a failure. Two months, a million of money, and many fine soldiers worn out and nothing done. It was not the enemy but nature that thwarted us with high mountains and muddy roads."[48]

William McComb, 14th TN, said, "The expedition was a complete failure," though he also felt it was well planned. With the initiation of firing by troops on the east side of Cheat Mountain, those on the west side were to charge from the rear. Those on the east side never fired a shot, and as McComb wrote, "I never heard why the attack was not made on the east side of the mountain. We never heard any more of the general in command; so we all returned to Valley Mountain." Agreeing with Norris's assertion of the abundance of food, McComb also noted that the days following the campaign were ones in which "the boys had a fine living on venison."[49]

Robert Mockbee regarded the long march "through tangled undergrowth over mountains without roads" as well as what was labeled "mountain fever" as the major hardships of the campaign. With warm days, cold nights, and rains for some twenty days prior to the march that began the struggle for Cheat Mountain, several members of Mockbee's regiment had developed an extremely high fever that often advanced into a strain of typhoid fever. Few ambulances were present to transfer the sick, whose numbers, Mockbee described, increased hourly. Supply wagons were converted to carry the individuals, yet the nearly nonexistent roads traveled by the makeshift vessels only increased their misery. When the soldiers finally reached "Camp Edna" and were ordered into camp, many of the individuals were beyond medical assistance. More than thirty members of the Fourteenth Tennessee were buried near Camp Edna. Many others who prevailed long enough to reach Warm Springs and Hot Springs, where hotels were transformed into hospitals, "gave their lives for their country" as honestly as did those on the battlefields to come.[50]

Capt. John Amenas Fite, Co. B, 7th TN, recalled in his memoirs that one of his company, Frank Rieves, was stricken with typhoid fever and looked as though he had only hours to live. Fite requested Hatton's permission to stay with Rieves and bury him upon his death, yet with Hatton's subsequent unsuccessful plea to Gen. Loring, Fite's petition was denied. Rieves was placed into one of a series of wagons, each carrying four to six sick soldiers bound for Warm Springs. Rieves fortunately survived the ordeal and the war.[51]

Mockbee felt that the ineptness of the medical department ranked high on his list of improvements needed within his regiment, the Fourteenth Tennessee, before embarking on future military actions. A primary example he provided was that the medical department "made worse the conditions by which we were surrounded." One regimental surgeon had an uncontrollable desire for strong drink and actually expended a great deal of the supply of alcohol allotted for the sick. His over-consumption led to a state of drunken stupor and an inability to perform his duties. He did soon resign and was replaced by an individual whose abilities were equal to the tasks at hand.[52] Nonetheless, help had come too late for many.

At least one physician contributed his part to dismissing Mockbee's perception of the ineptness of the army's medical personnel. Dr. Walter Drane left his profitable Clarksville, Tennessee practice for a visit to the Fourteenth Tennessee presently located near Cheat Mountain. Two of Dr. Drane's sons, James and Hugh, had enlisted the previous May and were currently serving in the Tennessee Brigade.

Volunteering his surgical services, Dr. Drane wrote other family members frequently, detailing the poor health condition of the brigade, noting large numbers of soldiers were suffering from dysentery and typhoid fever. In a mid-September 1861 letter to his son Walt, Dr. Drane noted the preparations for battle present all around. The facts of the existence of strong enemy fortifications occupied by a superior force, combined with the reduction of

Confederate troops due to illness, left little doubt in the doctor's mind of a Union victory.[53]

Dr. Drane's interest in the brigade's health soon took a personal stance as both sons lay ill. In the same letter to Walt, Dr. Drane explained that Hugh was suffering from night sweats and James had survived a difficult night, yet both boys had improved from their previous states. The doctor's optimism appeared high as he explained that he would take the boys home on furlough as soon as they were able to be moved. This trip was necessitated by the young men being "so thoroughly broken up in constitution that they will be unfit for duty anymore, during the present campaign."[54]

Three days later Dr. Drane wrote to his wife from Randolph County, Virginia, expressing his hope to be home within three weeks. This was proclaimed despite the certainty that their sons were in no condition to be moved. Obviously keenly aware of the severity of both sons' conditions, Dr. Drane prompted his wife to believe no information other than his in regard to their offsprings' health.[55]

The following day, September 19, 1861, Dr. Drane wrote of his having to move his sons a short distance out of necessity to maintain a position near the moving army and avoid Union scouting parties. James was currently in a highly endangered state yet had handled the movement far better than Dr. Drane had expected. Hugh, though far from well, was improving. Drane's analysis of the brigade was filled with skepticism as he stated that the hardships and exposure had left "our army … in a ruined condition."[56]

On September 26, Dr. Drane sent a message from Charlottesville via the South Western Telegraph Company; its contents: "James is dead—I have his remains—Hugh is with me in a feeble state, returning home."[57] Unfortunately the Dranes had experienced the loss of a son in a manner that thousands of other families would come to endure.

June Kimble, Co. A, 14th TN, recalled that the arrival in camp following the Cheat Mountain campaign was met with strict orders forbidding theft of property from civilians and promising severe reprimands to any soldier who disobeyed. One member of Maney's First Tennessee was known for a lack of respect for rules and military discipline and left camp late one night with the knowledge or permission of no one. His return was not as well concealed, as early in the morning, a lone sheep appeared on a hill overlooking the Confederate camp. Soon the departed soldier became visible and the lamb darted toward camp, chased closely by the soldier. Cheers and yells erupted from the three thousand or so Confederates as the lamb darted to and fro in an attempt to flee his intent captor.[58]

Gen. Anderson emerged from his tent at that time, threatening to arrest the soldier who had disobeyed his order. As the sheep made its way to

34

within seventy-five yards of Anderson's tent, the general's demeanor suddenly changed as he cursed and shouted for someone to catch the sheep and not let it get away. The next morning, a hindquarter of hot, freshly cooked lamb greeted Gen. Anderson at his table; no disciplinary action was taken toward the soldier.[59]

The Cheat Mountain campaign, though not successful from a Confederate standpoint, is noteworthy, as it was Robert E. Lee's first Civil War campaign. One Tennessean's first impression of Gen. Lee was less than spectacular, as A.D. Norris explained: "Saw General Lee before a house in which the principal officers of the house were quartered. He wore a slouched hat and looked more like a teamster than a general."[60]

Robert T. Mockbee of the Fourteenth Tennessee was more complimentary of Lee in his first sighting of the great Confederate leader. He recalled the event as the time he and many others "looked upon the face and form" of the individual who would soon "take his place among the greatest military leaders the world ever produced."[61]

CHAPTER THREE

Winter of Indecision, 1861-1862

In early October of 1861, Archibald Norris began feeling the effects of illness that had run rampant among his comrades in the Tennessee Brigade. For a week he suffered from the mumps and created the corresponding entries:

> Felt a soreness in my right jaw yesterday which last night became manifestly "the mumps" … no more inopportune time could have been selected but "Not my will but Thine be done" … Read several chapters in the Testament. Talked and whiled the time away drearily. Wrote a letter home … Jaws considerably swollen and a little painful. The day is gloomy. I heard today from what … would seem good authority that we were to leave this place, and five other places were mentioned most positively as our destination.[1]

Norris felt well enough a week later to search for food with a fellow soldier. On Sunday, October 13, 1861, he wrote, "David Phillips and I went chestnut hunting this morning … rambled some two miles from camp … I almost forgot that I have had the mumps."[2]

The following day, Norris kept his journal entries on the course of obtaining nourishment. He described camp routine as well as his quest for food in writing the following:

The daily routine of camp life in the mountains seem so indelibly fixed on the memory as to need no place here, yet I will transcribe them per chance they may serve to refresh the memory here after. To begin then with the time when we draw rations ... beef comes first, a pretty full allowance as cattle are abundant here. The only requisite is that they be fat ... they come free, from the aged cow or veteran bull to the tender yearling. Next come flour and salt just enough to no more than will cleverly sustain a soldier. Sometimes coffee and sugar are allowed. For supper we have (when we can get it) coffee and biscuit with now and then a little stake [sic]. For breakfast we have beef soup and biscuit. For dinner, a mess of "cush" is prepared consisting of biscuit cut up very fine and boiled beef hashed, boiled up together.[3]

Norris's health improved, along with that of men in the Tennessee regiments serving under Gen. Anderson. The receipt of clothing, blankets, medicine, and other items from family and friends at home seemed to be major factors in this improvement. In addition, regiments within the brigade began building log cabins near Huntersville. Complete with stick and mud chimneys, these structures had pine boards placed on the roofs and in the cracks of the walls.[4]

On October 20, 1861, Norris received a letter from his father stating that he had sent clothing for him. On November 4, Norris made this entry: "Our clothes were brought here to be distributed. A great deal of confusion ... many did not receive their parcels. Mine came safely to hand and good time for I was needing them."[5]

In early December 1861, the brigade was moved to Winchester, Virginia to serve under Gen. Thomas J. "Stonewall" Jackson, who had intentions of driving the enemy from Northern Virginia. Jackson had taken command in the Shenandoah Valley in November.[6]

The move to Winchester was accomplished using familiar methods for the Tennesseans: marches and railroad transportation. William McComb, Fourteenth Tennessee, remembered passing through Warm Springs, New Market, and Strausburg. Archibald Norris recorded this as well in his diary when writing, "A few miles march then brought us to Warm Springs through which we passed before on August 1." On December 19, Norris entered this passage: "Left camp quite early this morning, myself and two or three others from our company going ahead by permission. Reached New Market about ten o'clock ... came this side of Mt. Jackson Depot and camped, making 12 miles."[7]

Norris's quest for food and his ability to procure it had a devastating effect on his person in this march of the brigade.

> Made arrangements to ride on a wagon today, but it was so cold as to be uncomfortable, so I walked on the railroad. Was quite sick in consequence of eating too many persimmons. Reached Strasburg about 11 o'clock having marched 74 miles in six days over the finest pike through the finest valley I ever saw.[8]

Norris had also entered earlier notations regarding a now-traditional act of the Tennesseans in explaining that half of one regiment had begun the trip on train cars with the other half to follow the next day. Two days later the other half left, epitomizing the military's ability to drag its feet.[9]

The log cabins had given many of the brigade members a literal home away from home from which they were summoned and which aided many of the Seventh Tennessee members in overcoming the threat of illness, adverse weather, and obvious homesickness. Norris noted that between November 25 and 29:

> Turned cold yesterday evening. Snow fell to the depth of two inches ... It is now definitely fixed that we stay in the houses in this vicinity. The increasing sickness admonishes us to occupy them soon. Most of our company today occupied the rooms assigned to them either in the church or dwelling house ... I think we would enjoy better health in the tents than in the heated impure air of the church ... a number of us went out ... to see if we could not get a room for ourselves. We succeeded ... The greatest difficulty is its distance from the company ... at our abode at "Owls Nest" as we termed our new intended abode ... rented some furniture that was in the room, went up took possession and entered upon a course of bachelor housekeeping One of our party engaged some milk and butter for tomorrow, in short we are going to have a glorious time ... finished moving today. We ate our first meal of our own, cooked our first dinner at a fireplace, and entered on our career for the winter at "Owls Nest" gloriously. Everything wore an air of coziness and comfort, hard to describe but easy to imagine by those who have entered a home of their own after a long absence.[10]

The next day brought panic and disappointment to Norris and his fellow housekeepers. He explained:

> Two of our party went out soon this morning ... they got ... a fine buck, saw a wild turkey. On going to town, we found our

company packed up ready to leave. Orders came last night for our reg't to go ... about to leave us. We hurried back, packed up, and were off, having everything to carry with us.

This sudden migration was to prove indicative of what lay ahead. Having been in Strasburg for nearly a week, several of the Tennesseans, according to a member of the Fourteenth Tennessee, "had made some preparations for celebrating Christmas."

A.D. Norris noted the events of the week, beginning with his December twenty-second entry: "Many of the ladies of Strasburg visited the camp. The boys are as noisy as ever. Col. Goodner had dress parade ... I suppose for the gratification of the ladies for whom he has a strong liking." The following day, Norris expressed disgust at the lack of supplies when writing, "Today we drew a few tents and ... cooking vessels ... owing to the inefficiency of the quartermaster or the scarcity of such articles, we did not draw more than half camp. The day was very blustery. Many tents were blown down."[11]

Norris also explained that on the twenty-third of December, the First and Fourteenth Tennessee regiments joined the Seventh Tennessee at Strasburg, to become "more united under Gen. Anderson." The joy of the Christmas season was darkened with the accidental killing of a member of the Seventh Tennessee. Norris stated:

> The most melancholy accident of the season was the shooting of Clack Harrison of the grays last night in town. It was purely accidental and the result of carelessness and drunkenness on the part of numbers of the 14th. He was a clever soldier. How many of our brave boys will thus be stricken down before they sustain the country's honor on the battlefield! This is the 2nd of our reg't thus killed.[13]

Norris's Christmas celebration was ended with the order to move to Winchester. The timing could not have been worse, as Norris revealed in his Christmas Day, 1861 entry:

> A merry Christmas over an eggnog breakfast and a turkey for dinner. Such was the anticipation of our boys this morning. They got the former in large doses and most of them were gloriously merry when just as they were through drinking and preparing to eat, an order came to strike tents and prepare to march towards Winchester immediately. It was promptly, though reluctantly obeyed. We came 7 miles down the Shenandoah.[14]

Norris detailed the brigade's December 27 arrival in Winchester, the town that he documented as marking "another hundred to the 300 miles we have marched since being in the service." The next two days were spent in camp, performing a more routine military lifestyle. Norris provided this record:

> Attended the Episcopal Church at Winchester today. Heard Dr. Quinlard of the 1ˢᵗ reg't. He preached a good sermon. Today I am 23 years old. Of all the years of my life the last has been the most eventful. How different my situation from the same a year ago! Then I was at home surrounded by friends and kindred, now in a military camp a few miles from the enemy … General inspection came off today and was the closest inspection of the kind we have passed through. Knapsacks, cartridge boxes, etc. were inspected. In the forenoon I helped to make out the pay rolls for our company for the two months ending tomorrow. I have the worst cold I have had since being in the service.[15]

On New Year's Eve, the brigade was again ordered to move with little warning. Norris recalled the command to depart Winchester: "Dress parade came off this evening at which orders were issued for the regiments to have five days rations on hand and one days rations ahead cooked, and to be ready to march early tomorrow morning. The Colonels were also ordered to draw cartridges. Where we are going is … secret."[16]

Sgt. Robert T. Mockbee, 14ᵗʰ TN, felt the march of January 1, 1862 was one that inspired the men. The pleasant weather and hopes of an encounter with enemy provided the stimulus. William McComb also recalled the roads traveled on the first were "pretty good." Norris added his analysis of the situation: "The new year opens propitiously. The weather mild, health good … early this morning we struck tents, packed up and prepared to leave our camp at Winchester to go we knew not whither. About 9 a.m. the troops began to move. The road was full of wagons men and artillery for several miles. We started towards Romney … took a right … to Pughtown … camped."[17]

Mockbee described resting that night in a well-forested valley where the bright stars provided the tired men, resting on beds made from piles of leaves, with a "sweet sleep." The next morning, the group awakened to the order to prepare to move, only to be covered with snow atop their blankets. Norris substantiated Mockbee's recollection with his January 2 entry:

> The wind got on a frolic last night and blew nearly all our tents down. Ours was a new one and stretched for the first time, we cared not to expose it to the danger of falling for the second time, so did not repitch it. Thus we slept in the open air confronting the stars of

Heaven … This morning it was very cold. We set out before day, but
were kept back so much by the wagons that we made little progress.
We were going all day and till late at night and finally camp without
tent, food or blankets.[18]

Gen. Loring had ordered the men to establish camp and cook rations,
then informed Gen. Jackson of his decision, one that was much to Jackson's
dismay. The latter's plans to move to Ungoe's Store had been delayed by
this bivouac order that must be cancelled, exclaimed Jackson. McComb
continued:

That made General Loring furiously mad, and he dashed
through the camp, ordering everything back in the wagons at
once. Part of the bread was half cooked and the rest in the dough.
Consequently the boys got no supper, and the teams ate very little.
But we obeyed orders and prized and shoved wagons from that
time until after day the next morning and did not advance three
hundred yards. Then, after Gen. Jackson took in the situation the
next morning, he ordered us in bivouac and to cook two days'
rations. This was our first acquaintance with General Jackson …
we were not very favorably impressed.[20]

On the third the weather remained cold and the road conditions
unsatisfactory. Norris reflected:

Went back 2 miles to our wagons to get breakfast, which I ate
with relish consequent on my last nights exposure. We started on the
march about ten o'clock. Traveled ahead of the wagons going over
an ordinary public road through a union settlement. About dusk we
halted, loaded our guns then forwarded at double quick about two
miles, when we came up with the advance brigade of the army who
had had a skirmish with a strong Yankee picket, killing thrice and
driving them in. Loss on our side 4 wounded. Here within 2 miles
of Bath we bivouacked, the Col. telling us to make fires of rails or
anything else. Soon after nightfall snow fell. Our wagons came up
2 hours before day.[21]

The Tennesseans arrived in Bath the next day with the objective to destroy
a nearby railroad bridge. As the Confederate forces approached, the enemy
retreated across the Potomac to Hancock, Maryland, and the Tennesseans
witnessed Jackson's artillery bombardment of Hancock on the following
day.[22]

William McComb was serving as adjutant of the Fourteenth Tennessee at this point and recalled the night of the Union retreat as being extremely cold. The temperature and snow on the ground resulted in the men gathering in circles and moving their feet to keep them from freezing. McComb and others in Anderson's Brigade had been ordered to halt upon gaining sight of Hancock. Within the hour, generals Loring and Jackson arrived with Jackson, asking to what extent the skirmish line extended frontward.[23]

As the Fourteenth was in the front of the brigade, Col. Forbes, in command of the Fourteenth, ordered McComb to "ride down and find out" the location of the skirmish line. McComb located it at the riverbank, where the soldiers explained that only the cavalry had crossed the Potomac, leaving no one behind. McComb returned to the generals and reported the statements of those on the skirmish line, at which point Jackson turned to Loring and instructed him to move his command forward. This was done immediately.[24]

As the regiments completed approximately half of the three-quarter-mile march to the river, an order was given to halt. Following another thirty minutes of the men moving about in circles to lessen the chance of freezing, another order was given; this one to countermarch. Following the completion of the latter, camp was established. Loring and Anderson had loudly protested the possibilities of the brigade having to cross the Potomac under such extreme conditions, an event that caused irreparable damage to the command.[25]

A.D. Norris recorded the specific events of January 4 and 5 as the brigade positioned itself and noted the bombardment:

> After a sleepless night in the snow, we got an early start towards Bath. We would go about three hundred yards then halt, build rail fires and just as they began to burn would forward. We halted within ¾ of a mile to town, a plan of attack made. 3 companies of our reg't were detached to guard 2 pieces of artillery designed to batter down a stone house which served as a fort for the enemy, ours was one of the number. In the meantime, the enemy was thundering away with artillery doing little injury to anyone. Here for the 1st time I heard the roar of cannon. After we had made all arrangements about 4 p.m. we were ready to advance when news came that the enemy had beat a hasty retreat. Our cavalry had charged on them and driven them off. We marched to town immediately and on in quick pursuit. 6 miles brought us to the "Upper Potomac." Our men occasionally fired a ball or bomb into Hancock, just on the other shore in Maryland. Now and then a reply was heard. We were kept standing on the pike about two hours in the cold. Then the firing ceased and we returned

building rail fires. We slept about 2 hours ... wagons failed to come up, so we passed the night tentless and supperless ... The sun rose bright this morning (Jan. 5th). The sky was perfectly clear and the air very cold and piercing especially to those who like us have been foodless one day and sleepless 4 nights. About 8 o'clock a flag of truce was sent over to Hancock requesting the enemy to remove the women and children from the place within a given time. The artillery was stationed on a hill in our front, unlimbered and loaded, about 1 o'clock the cannonading commenced and was kept up briskly on both sides during half and hour, it then slackened and finally ceased entirely, no damage done. About three we were ordered to fall back half a mile to our wagons which we did very cheerfully, we hastily cooked our supper, breakfast and dinner and as greedily ate all three together. We then pitched our tent dug away the frozen earth and snow, and prepared to spend the night as comfortably as possible. Before nightfall I went to the top of the hill on which we were encamped and looked across Maryland to the bleak hills of Pennsylvania only 5 miles distant. We expect the attack to be made tomorrow. Some of the boys are shivering at the prospect of wading the Potomac.[26]

The shelling of the town coincided with the construction of a pontoon bridge under the direction of Col. William A. Forbes of the Fourteenth Tennessee. Gen. Jackson had ordered Gen. Anderson to supply as many men as possible with axes to cut logs from a cliff west of Hancock. These logs were to be rolled into the river in order to form the bridge. The inexperience of the men in using axes in the harshly cold environment soon resulted in sore hands that became almost incapable of grasping the handles. Fresh details were frequently sent in as the cold weather only added to the soldiers' frustration as woodsmen. The bridge, intended to serve as a troop passage, was never used, as the Federal retreat occurred prior to its completion.[27]

A.D. Norris recalled a day spent waiting for possible action against the enemy:

Broad day light came before we awoke. Soon after sunup the "long roll" was beat and we fell in hastily with guns, cartridge boxes ... regiment was formed, we stacked arms and returned to our fires; in 15 minutes we were again ordered to "fall in," and again in 5 minutes dismissed. We returned to our tents, knocked off the snow which during the night had fallen to the depth of 2 or 3 inches. About 10 o'clock the enemy commenced firing bombs into our camp. They wounded one man in the 14 Tennessee and caused a general falling back of officers and men out of the reach of danger.[28]

The next day the brigade returned to Bath. A member wrote:

> Before daylight this morning we were roused up and having cooked a hasty breakfast packed up the wagon and prepared to leave. The wagons began moving slowly back toward Bath. Their progress was slow, we remained till about 12 … began to move but halted every hundred yards to wait for the wagons. We reached Bath a short time after dark. There we remained standing in the cold during an hour, we then came on very slowly indeed; the night was intense by cold. Some of the boys got frost bitten. About 9 o'clock, we came up with the wagons. We stretched our tent, cooked supper and went to bed by 12.[29]

William McComb added that the purpose of the trip to Bath was to have the horses' shoes made rough in an attempt to enable them to walk without slipping on the slick road surfaces. This would allow the troops to make a faster journey to their next destination, a point unknown to most of the individuals. The objective was then sarcastically dubbed "Camp Suspense" among members of the brigade.[30]

Norris recalled the ineffectiveness of the purpose behind the trip to Bath in his January 8, 1862 entry. He wrote:

> Slept very soundly last night … except when interrupted by fits of coughing. The night was the coldest of the winter. At 4 we were roused up and cooked breakfast. Soon after daylight the wagons started. Their progress was slow and tedious. The road was slick as glass. The horses slipped and fell often, crippling several. It was dangerous walking for a man. Several got hard falls. The reg't started about 10 o'clock, halted often and long. We crossed several creeks on ice which was several inches thick. We marched about 10 miles.[31]

Extreme winter weather in the area riddled the Tennessee soldiers. Rain, sleet, snow, high winds, and fierce cold battered the men of Jackson's command. Only the confidence of his men in Jackson's past victories saved his career at this point, as many men suffered from exposure and snow-covered blankets. On one occasion, several individuals cursed Jackson, blaming him for their situation, unaware that he lay nearby, under a tree, also suffering in the weather. After he listened quietly for some time, Jackson shook the snow from his blanket and acknowledged his own discontent with the situation.

As news of the event circulated in camp, Jackson's popularity was largely restored.[32]

The brigade's geographical goal of Romney eventually became known among those in the brigade. Romney lay approximately forty miles away[33] and the process of reaching this point required more days of frustrating marches, stops, and negotiations with the weather.

Norris's January 14 entry exemplified the frustration he felt. "At an early hour we began the 'halting process' … camped half a mile beyond on the Romney road making 8 miles. News came this evening that the enemy had fled … contrary to our expectations journeying hither." The following day he wrote:

> Snow and sleet fell during most of the night last night. We slept comfortable in our tent having raked the snow off and digged [sic] up the earth. The start this morning was anything but promising. Rain and snow mingled together continued to fall till late in the evening. The roads were sloppy. We crossed Capon River on a temporary bridge. One of our wagons got the tongue broke in the middle of the river and had to be unloaded by carrying its contents out on horseback. 4 of my mess got supper in the evening—a good meal. First time I have ate at a table this year! Marched … to within 15 miles of Romney.[34]

Continuing the process, the brigade moved slowly but steadily the next day, reaching a point "within 4 miles of Romney," where Norris saw that "most of the houses have been burned." Reflecting upon the damage brought to the community, Norris counted eleven houses, one mill, and a tannery burned to the ground. He continued, "There they stand like ghosts to haunt the imaginations of their ruthless destroyers. Truly the invading army is a terrible scourge. Nothing is sacred to them. They spare not churches, dwellings or farms."[35]

The following day Norris continued to express disgust, though not toward the enemy. He entered:

> Military genius is undoubtedly a rare quality and displays itself in rare ways. We had a fine exhibition of it this morning. After a moderately early breakfast, orders were issued to strike tents and prepare for a march. We obeyed. The wagons, started, we passed them almost at 'double quick.' Went to within sight of Romney, got our blood warmed up, perspiration started, halted at the Yankee fortifications. Remained standing in the cold 2 hours. Then, here is the genius part, turned around and came back to our last night's camping place, to stay we don't know how long![36]

On January 18 the brigade received supplies enhanced with the distribution of whiskey and butter. These were welcome sights to the regular coffee, sugar, bacon, flour, and salt the members usually obtained. Winter clothing was slow in coming though as the brigade members waited for their arrival from Winchester.[37]

With a majority of the members of the Seventh Tennessee having only four months left in their term of service, frustration grew throughout the ranks. Men spent days in their tents, avoiding the heavy rains and snows of the period. Norris noted this as "the most unpleasant time of the soldier's life" and that he spent one day venturing to a mill some three miles from camp. After purchasing fifty pounds of flour and fourteen pounds of pork and lard, Norris and a friend named Justiss spent the night in the home of the miller, exclaiming, "We fared well, had a good supper and a first rate breakfast. We slept on a feather bed for the first time this year." Norris's adventures away from camp must have been commonplace in the brigade, as he never noted any repercussions for his frequent forays.

The flour used to bake bread was proof of the phrase that necessity is the mother of invention. Even in heavy winds the brigade often faced, with the coals and ashes being blown from the fire, baking prevailed. The dough would be placed in an oven lid and propped up against the fire.[38] In this manner, the men of the brigade found a means of survival.

On January 23, 1862, the Tennessee Brigade witnessed the passing of the Stonewall Brigade on its way to Winchester. The men of Anderson's command became angry, feeling that Jackson was showing off during the departure. That same night the Tennesseans received orders to prepare early the next morning to move again in the direction of Romney.[39]

Upon their arrival at the outskirts of Romney, the Tennesseans discovered the town had not only been quickly vacated but also that supplies had been left behind in the nearby Union camp.[40]

Norris explained:

> Romney ... is a desolate place indeed. The yards to the finest houses are covered with the entrails of beefes [sic]. The fences burned, everything polluted. A portion of our troops were quartering in the town. It was once a beautiful place. After leaving Romney our route was down the South fork of the Potomac. We passed through what had been the enemy's camp. The remnant of kettles, pots, pans, stoves, plank etc were strown [sic] all around all rendered useless by the former owners.[41]

Jackson's departure left only Gen. Loring's men to control the area around Romney. Jackson's conduct brought about accusations of favoritism, in that he had returned his former brigade to the more amiable accommodations in Winchester while Loring's division was left to suffer the hardships of weather and the continual threat of the nearby enemy.[42]

The hardships of traveling through the countryside were far from over. Despite the merriment surrounding a new snowfall, the arrival of supplies brought about difficulties for the brigade. Two wagons per company had a distance of one and a half miles to cover in the four inches of snow that had fallen the night before. One of the wagons turned over as soon as the trip started, emptying its contents into a stream. Attempts to upend the overturned wagon delayed the entire train. Using two chains, A.D. Norris and a detachment of his company "fastened them to the end of the tongue, hitched ourselves horse fashion to them and pulled the wagon to company camping ground." After such a grueling exercise, the men of the Seventh grew more disenchanted with military life when they found that their winter clothing was not among the contents of any of the wagons in the train.[43]

The gradual arrival of supplies tended to give a brief respite from the threat of attack from the ever-present Union troops. Norris spent the next three days walking to a nearby cobbler and paying $1.25 to have his shoes half-soled and taps placed on the heels, buying twenty-cent-per-pound ham and reading a collection of letters from family and friends. On January 28, Norris joined a group of his company in constructing a structure to serve as a buffer from the weather. He explained, "rain, hail and snow began to fall this morning about daybreak ... We went to work on 'Pine Fort' as we have christened our ground hut. We digged [sic] down about three feet, cut out a fireplace, run up a rude chimney making a far more comfortable abode than we have had before."[44]

The brigade's long-awaited winter clothing finally arrived on January 29. Norris noted also that "most of us rec'd our pacoges [sic], overeating abounded." The celebration over the packages and their contents was brought to an end at eleven o'clock that night when the men quickly put on their cartridge boxes and prepared for action. Norris recalled the confusion of the night:

> As soon as we got ready the drums tapped the signal for forming the companies. Some confusion attended the forming of the reg't on account of the darkness. Some of the men got lost from their companies. Companies couldn't find their places in the reg't. As last amid brush, stumps and mud holes the line was formed. The column began to move toward the bridge as intelligence had been received that the enemy expected to attack us there during the night, drive our pickets in, take our forces by surprise and force us to retire.

Our route to the bridge was through lanes rendered soft and oozy by the melting of the snow, a film of which still remained on the ground and across fields sown in what, which we sank half a foot in the wet earth at every step. In about an hour from the time of starting we gained our position on the bank of the river above the bridge, our line of battle running parallel with stream. There we remained five hours with wet feet and no fire. Our feet got very cold, we had to keep "marking time" to keep them from being frostbitten. About 5 o'clock we were relieved by the 14th with two cannon, we retired behind the bank of the stream built rail fires and staid [sic] with them till about 9 o'clock. Snow was falling thick and fast ... It was ascertained that the enemy had abandoned their design. We returned to camp, feeing drowsy and dull from the night's exposure.[45]

Norris's desire was to get a good night's rest following the events of the twenty-ninth and thirtieth, yet the Seventh Tennessee was ordered to prepare for attack at four in the afternoon on the thirty-first. Norris wrote:

The 'long roll' was beaten, we snatched our guns ... double quicked to the river; remained there an hour or two. Finally it was ascertained that nothing was the matter, about dark we returned to camp no much wiser and no better than when we started from camp. The following evening another alarm was given and once again, after a brief time spent at the bridge, the decision was made that nothing serious was at hand.[46]

Something serious of a different nature was taking place while the false alarms of late January were transpiring. Gen. Loring had written the Confederate Secretary of War, detailing the circumstances, situations, and complaints against Gen. Jackson. Gen. Stevenson, Loring's adjutant, carried the message to Richmond. In turn, Gen. Loring and his command, including the three Tennessee regiments, were ordered to return to Winchester. As neither the latter decree nor Loring's tell-all letter went through Jackson's possession, Jackson tendered his resignation to the secretary of war. Influential citizens such as Virginia governor Letcher intervened, seeing Jackson's potential, and were able to convince officials not to accept the resignation.[47]

The Tennesseans joined Loring's command in the return to Winchester, an event that began on February 2, 1862. The march and its events were recorded in the ever-efficient diary of Archibald Norris:

An order came to cook up two days rations and be ready to load the wagons in one hour. We hurriedly cooked a few biscuits.

Struck tents and within the time prescribed the wagon was loaded. We started, reached the foot of the hill on which we camped, there they "hung up." Everything governmental and a great deal of private property was thrown out and the next morning burned tents, cooking vessels, water buckets, meat, flour … The Reg't remained on the camping ground till the morning of Monday, Feb. 3rd. … Burned everything combustible and destroyed everything that might be converted to use by the enemy. Amid a heavy fall of snow we left our "winter quarters" … We started toward Winchester passed by the charred remains of many wagons that had been stalled. Our wagons which traveled all night last night reached "Hanging Rock" 15 miles from Romney. We went 9 miles…when the troops got very much scattered, camping where best suited them … slept comfortably from 12 till day on had laid on plank, the latter lying on the snow which is about 6 inches deep.[48]

Rounding up scattered troops constituted the majority of the day on February 4 while the brigade moved to "Capon Bridge" on the fifth. The brigade neared its former campground on the sixth, yet an ill A.D. Norris joined a few men in going into Winchester. There Norris and his comrades purchased supper at a restaurant yet, unable to find a boarding house in which to spend the night, slept a second consecutive night on the snow-covered ground.[49]

Sgt. Robert Mockbee of the Fourteenth Tennessee remembered the arrival in Winchester and being placed "into camp again" as welcome relief from the difficulties encountered during the previous month. Many members of the Fourteenth Tennessee were sent to hospitals where treatment was given for exposure. Numerous others had sore or frostbitten feet that also required attention.[50]

CHAPTER FOUR

Realignment

The first seven months of existence for Anderson's Tennessee Brigade had been filled largely with minor action and occasional recruitment of personnel. Promotions, disease, and casualties had inflicted a mere fraction of the results that were to come. The climactic effects of the Civil War would soon be felt in the Tennessee Brigade regiments, as they had and would be nationwide.

The conditions encountered at the Winchester camp were received with elation among most of the Tennesseans. The simplicities of everyday life took precedence in A.D. Norris's diary as he wrote of trips to town for shopping and visiting the local barber. News from home began to replace the humdrum existence of the brigade members, and recently confronted hardships rekindled loyalty to the Confederacy in the minds of many of the brigade members. Norris wrote what many in the brigade were discussing when he noted, "News ... today of the capture of Fort Henry by the Yanks on the 5th ... They thus have command of the Tennessee River."[1]

Almost immediately the ramifications of the fall of the Tennessee fort took effect. On February 10, the day after Norris noted the receipt of the news concerning the fall of Ft. Henry, Norris recorded, "Winchester was full of soldiers today, a large number from Jackson's Brigade are taking the 60 day furlough and reenlisting for the war. Some of our boys seem disposed to take it also." As rheumatism affected Norris's health, his journal entries continued the reflection of the brigade's mindset as he proclaimed, "It never rains but it pours is an old proverb and just now applies to the condition of public affairs in the Confederacy."[2]

Valentine's Day 1862 brought A.D. Norris a welcomed package and a rumor that would soon create a significant transformation for the brigade. Norris wrote, "J.B. Hale arrived from home today bringing news and a pair of gloves … A rumor prevailed today that a portion of Loring's command are ordered to Knoxville, Tenn. The Tennessee boys are much rejoiced at the prospect of treading on Tennessee soil from which we have so long been banished."[3]

Several members of the Fourteenth Tennessee had been mustered into Confederate service at Ft. Donelson, Tennessee. On February 16 and 17, news from that area was far from encouraging. Norris's details of the events were, "The newspapers this morning gave accounts of the attack on Fort Donelson on the Cumberland River on Thursday last. The cannonade commenced on the evening of the 12th and continued till the afternoon of the 13th. Up to that time our forces had repulsed the enemy and kept them back. May God grant them success in defending our own homes and firesides."[4]

News arrived in camp on February 18 that Maney's First Tennessee Regiment was being ordered to Knoxville. Maney's return to the west was requested in order that the regiment may join Confederate forces gathering at Corinth, Mississippi in an attempt to halt Gen. U.S. Grant's advance into the area. For the remainder of the war, Maney's, later Field's, Regiment would serve in the Army of Tennessee. As part of this military unit, Maney's First Tennessee Regiment would see action at Shiloh, Murfreesboro, Chickamauga, Franklin, and Nashville. After being consolidated into part of Palmer's Brigade in Cheatham's division, the regiment was surrendered at Durham, North Carolina by Gen. Joseph E. Johnston on April 26, 1865. Only 125 of the 1,200 officers and men whose names appeared on the rolls of the regiment were present at the surrender.[5]

The removal of Maney's First Tennessee from the Tennessee Brigade drew little written notice in Norris's diary. The continuation of news from home comprised the bulk of his entries, which well recorded the emotions of his comrades. On February 18, the day Maney's regiment was reassigned, Norris placed the news in a secondary position to that from the events in Tennessee. He wrote, "Indescribable gloom was … on the faces of our men today by the news that Fort Donelson had fallen and Nashville was in the hands of the enemy. We hope it is not true, in the meantime we are very anxious to go to Tennessee. The 1st Reg't is ordered to Knoxville; ours and the 14th to Fredericksburg. Great efforts are being made to get our destiny changed."[6]

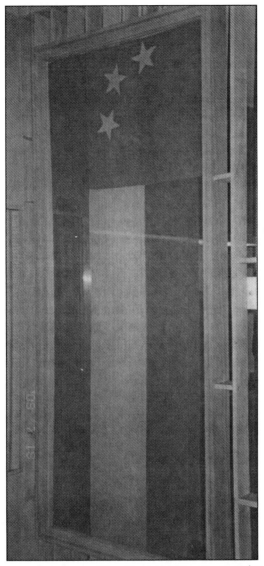

This flag was the property of Pvt. Daniel McCoy, Co. D, 14ᵗʰ TN. It is generally regarded that McCoy was among a group of men who returned home for recruiting purposes, only to be captured upon the fall of Ft. Donelson. The battle-scarred flag, with seven stars opposite the three shown on this side, now rests in the museum at Ft. Donelson NMP. Courtesy of Jimmy Jobe, historian, Ft. Donelson. Photo by author.

The next day found the two remaining Tennessee regiments, the Seventh and Fourteenth, remaining stationary in a rainstorm. The men of the regiments received some positive news from home in among the bad, as Norris explained, "The news of the fall of Fort Donelson is confirmed though the capture of Nashville is denied. Few particulars are given, though the fight is represented as a most desperate one ... Our men are almost crazy to go to Tennessee."[7]

The desperation to obtain news from home added to the cold and windy conditions the Tennesseans faced in Virginia. "Every eye is turned toward Tennessee. Every new arrival from town is questioned with intense eagerness as to the 'latest news' from Tennessee ... Many propositions are made to go to Tennessee with or without the order of the war department."[8] The wait for the members who would survive the fighting that lay ahead would last three more years.

As the incidents in Tennessee prevailed in importance among the Tennesseans serving the Confederacy in Virginia, significant personnel developments were evolving within eyesight. Gen. Loring, the individual whose pleas had sheltered the Tennesseans from numerous hardships, left the brigade's command in response to orders that placed him in the army's Mississippi Department.[9]

Replacing Maney's First Tennessee Regiment at Winchester was Col. Peter Turney's First Tennessee, also known as the First Tennessee Volunteer Infantry Regiment, Provisional Army, Confederate States of America. Turney's First Tennessee, along with Col. Robert Hatton's Seventh Infantry Regiment and Col. William A. Forbes's Fourteenth Tennessee Infantry Regiment, joined to form a brigade known for the remainder of the war as the Tennessee Brigade. While minor changes would occur in relation to additional regiments as brigade members, the First, Seventh, and Fourteenth Tennessee Regiments would remain the core components of the group until Appomattox.[10]

With the addition of Turney's First Tennessee, the brigade was truly destined for glory and greatness, yet few members of the brigade could have imagined the years of bloodletting that lay ahead. Known to few of the members was the fact that Turney and his regiment had created for themselves several noteworthy accomplishments prior to becoming part of the Tennessee Brigade. These facts are noteworthy in relation to the regiment's contributions to Civil War trivia.

On May 8, 1861, Turney's regiment was mustered into Confederate service at Lynchburg, Virginia. From here the regiment went to Richmond aboard trains to receive instruction from a Virginia Military Institute cadet group. Ten companies comprised the regiment at the time of its alignment with the Confederacy, a venture that would last until Appomattox. The regiment consisted primarily of men from the south-central Tennessee counties of Grundy, Coffee, Franklin, Bedford, and Lincoln. Several companies of the First Tennessee entered the war with colorful names.

Company C, for example, contained men largely from Col. Turney's home of Franklin County and was known as "The Mountain Boys." Company E was the "Lynchburg Rangers," Company G the "Fayetteville Guards"; and Company H used the name "The Shelton Creek Volunteers." Companies I and K were known as the "Tullahoma Guards" and "Boon's Creek Minute Men" respectively.[11]

This regiment spent a brief time under the command of Thomas J. Jackson at Harper's Ferry. Assigned to the later commands of Barnard Bee and William Whiting, Turney's First Tennessee was placed under the leadership of Maj. Gen. Theopolus H. Holmes on February 9, 1862. At this point the regiment had left Virginia and its assignment in the Army of Northern Virginia to return to Tennessee. There it would remain until the formation of the Tennessee Brigade on March 8, 1862.[12]

The St. Andrew's cross pattern battle flag of Turney's First Tennessee Infantry Regiment. Photo courtesy of the Tennessee State Museum collection.

When Turney's men had left Franklin County, the train ride was the first or most probably the longest train trip for many of the enlisted men. The track on which they rode was less than ten years old, and many of these men still held a great deal of distrust for the railroads. The train passed through Chattanooga, Knoxville, Greenville, Bristol, moving onward to central Virginia. In Knoxville, the group of secession-minded Tennessee soldiers experienced their first ridicule. While their train was sidetracked to allow another to pass, the soldiers noticed the passing train was filled with Union sympathizers en route to Nashville to protest to Governor Isham Harris the second secession referendum that would later lead to Tennessee's secession.[13]

Accounts vary as to the point at which Turney's regiment joined the two remaining Tennessee regiments in the brigade. The Seventh and Fourteenth had been ordered in late February to move toward Manassas. Norris failed to recognize the arrival of Turney's regiment within the pages of his otherwise highly accurate and efficient journal. Norris did record the events of the brigade's march toward, arrival in, and subsequent tour of the Manassas battlefield.

On February 22, Norris wrote:

> Today we celebrated the anniversary of Washington's birthday by leaving our comfortable camp near Winchester and marching 15 miles over a good turnpike toward Manassas. The march was devoid of incidents save a few touching and eloquent remarks by Col. Hatton counseling good order and cheerful obedience to higher authorities even though we did not get to go and defend our own dear homes and firesides.[14]

As the march progressed, rains turned the roads into slick mud. The spirits of the men seemed high as their route took them through beautiful country. The men crossed the Shenandoah River in boats "built for that purpose, two companies crossing at a time." The soldiers enjoyed a wonderful view of the Shenandoah Valley before camping nine miles from the river following an eighteen-mile march for the day.[15]

After marching to the town of Aldie on the twenty-fourth, the brigade encountered frozen roads on the twenty-fifth. The wagons moved slowly as the men waited anxiously for them. Individuals grew tired of the lack of progress and "went away from the regiment having a mind to look at the country and see the inhabitants." One brigade member obtained a free supper at the home of a man named Foley and shared a visit with Foley's sisters. The ladies were proclaimed to be interesting and intelligent ladies who left quite an impression on the young soldier. The man rejoined the regiment before night, camping near a railroad.[16]

The following day, Wednesday, February 26, Norris joined his comrades of the Seventh Tennessee in marching to the site of the battle of First Manassas. He wrote:

> Col. Hatton took the regiment over a portion of the battlefield of the 21st of July. It is a desolate dreary looking place. Old fields worn out, here and there interspersed with clusters of green pine present the only varieties in the appearance of the country. The bushes about the scene of conflict were cut and pierced with balls from cannon and small arms. I saw a tree six inches in diameter that had been cut off

by a cannon ball. On the eminence where the Sherman Battery was planted and afterwards captured, the bones of several horses were lying where they were shot down by our artillery. A short distance below was a long ditch in which the dead were buried, bodies … were found lying on the ground, bones were found scattered around. The plains of Manassas … are yet the source of sorrow and anguish to many a Mother's heart. Many a widow breathes a sigh as the scene of a husband's death is mentioned. Many a sister laments a brother slain … We camped within 1½ miles of the Junction.[17]

The next week was largely uneventful, yet the record reveals the boy-like wonderment soldiers are capable of displaying. On February 27, the Fourteenth Tennessee joined the Seventh in receiving afternoon orders to prepare to board trains at eight o'clock that night. The group proceeded to Taylorsville Junction, where a few members were accidentally left behind. The Tennesseans crossed Acquia Creek and came to a point along the march where the troops were enabled to glimpse "a view of the 'broad Potomac … 1 7/8 miles wide … a grand sight though seen on a cloudy day." After viewing Yankee gunboats and batteries, the men settled down for the night, yet many "got quite merry" over their cups of whiskey.[18]

Using pine brush for a roof, Norris was soaked by the rains of March 3. He and his mess gained tents that once belonged to the Fourteenth Alabama and drew full rations that night, though they had received no breakfast. As the days passed, occasional firing from Federal gunboats passed overhead, failing to harm any of the Tennesseans. On March 5, Norris wrote:

About an hour before day … the boom of cannon was heard in the direction of the river … till 78 discharges were heard. The long roll was heard … near by …and our own drummers rattled it off at 'double quick.' We got hastened through … darkness about halfway to the river when we were ordered back … The cannonading was kept up most of the day.[19]

On March 8, 1862, the official announcement was made concerning the organization of the Tennessee Brigade. Brigadier Samuel R. Anderson retained command of the brigade that had previously bore his surname as its designation.[20] The remaining days of March were primarily spent in drills, fighting sickness, and waiting for the arrival of warmer weather. On March 9, after spending the night in dense woods, the Seventh Tennessee formed under orders from Col. Hatton.

A member recalled, "Drilled us some time in the manual. Gave the officers a lecture about staying with their companies and then ordered us forward. The reg't kept close up to our wagons, consequently our progress was slow ... We camped in a beautiful wood about 2 ½ miles from Fredericksburg. Every convenience ... was there."[21]

Sabers were given to the brigade on March 10, creating what one brigade member called a "formidable appearance" to the troops. The following day the regiment was ordered to strike their tents and headed toward Fredericksburg. Three cheers were given to Gen. Anderson as the brigade passed him en route to a forest of oak, hickory, and pine, where they camped only a mile from the previous day's camp.[22]

News from home again filled the conversations of brigade members as letters received "represent everything as in a deplorable condition at home. They advise recipients not to reenlist." The demeanor of the brigade officers began to change in perspective of the enlisted men. One member wrote, "Our officers are becoming exceedingly military." Spirits were lifted on March 27 as the Tennesseans drew two months' wages. The weather began warming as well, leading a member to proclaim, "Spring is upon us almost."[23]

April began as March had gone. However, in addition to drills, news on the national scale caused quite a stir among Anderson's Tennessee Brigade. A.D. Norris noted, "The message of Pres. Davis recommending the filling of the army by conscription and the forcible draft of all men over 18 and under 35 is the theme of conversation now. Nearly everyone deplores it as the surest means of introducing anarchy and mutiny in our army. A few contemplate desertion if the bill passes." Norris saw the possible passage of the conscription bill in a negative way himself, stating, "I greatly fear the consequence of its passage will be the disaffection of most of the volunteers whose term of service is nearly out."[24]

On April 4, Gen. Joseph E. Johnston paid the brigade a visit and reviewed the troops. While making quite an impression on Norris, Johnston was positively compared to Gen. Lee, who had somehow gained stature in Norris's eyes since his first glimpse of the man he originally viewed as a teamster. Norris penned, "At 3 p.m. we were on the field, our brigade extending about ¼ of a mile in length ... Johnston is a fine specimen of a general, next in point of appearance to Gen. Lee. Wears a heavy moustache, was dressed in a suit of gray ... horsemanship is splendid ... dignified without having any of the military strut." [25]

Events in Tennessee again gained the attention of the brigade members. The news not only took place in their home state but also involved Maney's First Tennessee and their former brigade members. Norris recorded the events surrounding the brigade's notification of the battle of Shiloh:

The long roll was beaten, every man seized his gun expecting to be hurried into a battle. A great many caps were burst to dry the tubes. The reg't was formed in the road and then closed in mass ... Gen'l Anderson mounted on a fine spirited steed ... appeared before us ... he said 'Officers and men of the Seventh regiment of Tennessee, I have the pleasure of announcing to you a glorious triumph of our arms in Tennessee ... our forces attacked the enemy near Pittsburg Landing ... completely routed the enemy ... loss heavy on both sides including that of A.S. Johnston' ... General Anderson proposed three cheers for the brave boys in Tennessee. We responded heartily.[26]

On the morning of April 8, in a pelting rain, the order had been given to move toward Richmond. The men moved ten miles, going to sleep without supper due to the delay of the wagons. The next day five miles were made through the rain; three the next, over bad roads. On the eleventh, the brigade marched nineteen miles, arriving at a telegraph road near Ashland Station. A break from marching was given to the fatigued soldiers on the thirteenth. Rations were ordered to be quickly cooked on the fourteenth in preparation of more marching, and on April 15 the brigade moved within one mile of Hanover Court House.[27]

The sixteenth allowed the brigade members to view wealthy farms and discuss the passage of the heavily debated conscription bill. Norris recalled, "Got an early start this morning, traveled through an old rich and long settled country. Fields of 500 acres ... people seem ... to be aristocrats ... We camped ... after a march of 18 and 20 miles. Our boys today received the first authentic news of the passage of the ... Conscription bill. Many of its most determined opponents have become its warmest advocates."[28]

On the seventeenth, the brigade moved approximately sixteen miles, crossing the Richmond and York River Railroad. Warm, dusty roads greeted the troops and they became worn out in covering twenty-two miles on the eighteenth. On the nineteenth, the brigade marched nine miles toward Yorktown and camped near the church of Lebanon, thus completing a week's march of nearly 150 miles, much of it in the rain.[29]

The Tennessee Brigade was given the task of maintaining a position approximately halfway between the York and James rivers. Gen. George McClellan, the commander of the Army of the Potomac, had begun to move toward the Confederate capital using this peninsula, an action that had gained the increased attention of Confederate commanders. At Yorktown the presence and threat from the enemy were constant. One soldier wrote, "About noon today we were ordered to cook a hasty snack having to go to a portion of our entrenchments as pickets. We got to the ditches about 3 p.m.

… pickets of four from each company were placed in front of the ditch being relieved every hour. In front of the ditch was a stream of water, dammed up so as to be about 200 yards wide, a most formidable barrier."[30]

One brigade member noted the term in Yorktown as being stressful. June Kimble, 14th TN, remembered that the Tennessee Brigade, with Smith's entire division, held an extremely dangerous piece of ground. Being stationed in the rear and in close proximity to the Confederate works, the Tennesseans were well within range of the gunboats McClellan had positioned on the York and James rivers. In addition, the brigade was in harm's way from the Federal siege guns. Noise and demonstrations of any type were prohibited, and for several days and nights, the order was strictly adhered to.[31]

The arrival of a Virginia brigade and its attempt to establish camp flushed a rabbit from its hiding place, resulting in a free-for-all attempt from both the Virginians and the Tennesseans to kill the animal. Hundreds of men apparently joined the festivities, creating a high level of noise that resulted in the appearance of "Old Sam" Anderson, clad only in his shirt and shoes. Cursing, threats of arrests, and warnings to catch the cottontail resounded throughout the camp until the worn-out animal ventured too closely to "a great burly brute with a club in his hand." Thus ended the life of the rabbit. The event was recalled in Kimble's notes years later, as he had no answer to why the enemy guns failed to fire on the Tennessee Brigade's position that was made so apparent by the noise.[32]

While in Yorktown, the Seventh and Fourteenth Tennessee regiments approached the end of their first year of service to the Confederate States of America. The political wheels turned within each company and names that would prove to become well known internally and externally of their respective regiments were elected as officers. Norris's April 25 entry revealed a small amount of the process: "It was announced this morning that the regiment was to be reorganized tomorrow. A host of candidates was the result. After much wavering it was determined that I should be run against the present incumbent. Great electioneering and some betting."[33] The following day, Norris's fellow company members revealed their admiration of him by electing him captain of his company.

Robert L. Hatton, captain of Company K, Fourteenth Tennessee, at the time of the regiment's organization, was elected colonel. John F. Goodner, once Company A's captain, became lieutenant colonel. The original captains of each company in the Seventh Tennessee had been: A, R.N. Wright; B, John A. Fite; C, James Baber; D, J.M. Anderson; E, D.C. Douglass; F, Nathan Oakley; G, S.G. Sheperd; H, W.H. Williamson; I, J.A. Anthony; and K, T.H. Bostick.[34]

In Company F of the Seventh Tennessee, known as the Statesville Tigers, Nathan Oakley chose not to run for reelection as his company's commander; the position was quickly filled by Asoph Hill. In the May 1861 election for the same position, Hill had lost to Oakley by two votes, a result largely accredited to Hill's young age. At Camp Trousdale, during the organization of the Seventh Tennessee, Hill received a promotion from private to sergeant major at Col. Hatton's request. Hatton would later give honorable mention to Hill for the faithfulness with which he performed his duties. The acknowledgement Hatton gave Hill obviously removed any doubts as to the latter's ability to lead; Hill's fellow Statesville Tigers responded in due fashion.[35]

Members of the First Tennessee also received promotions during the time spent at Yorktown. Felix G. Buchanan had begun his Confederate service in Turney's First Tennessee as second lieutenant of Company G, the Fayetteville Guards, only one year earlier. At Yorktown, Buchanan was advanced to captain of the same group.[36]

These individuals served in varying capacities during the duration of their companies. On the twenty-seventh and twenty-eighth of April, Archibald Norris explained his activities as captain of Company K, which was comprised largely of men from Wilson County, Tennessee:

> Rec'd our certification of election from General Anderson. The newly elected officers enter on the discharge of their duties tomorrow. ... Took charge of the Wilson Blues today. Felt somewhat embarrassed in my new position. Drilled the company one hour and a half in the morning, one hour in the evening. In the interval at the time for officers drill, Col. Hatton gave us a lecture in which was embodied some good advice.[37]

Voters in the Fourteenth Tennessee saw the election or reelection of William Forbes as colonel; George A. Harrell, lieutenant colonel; and William McComb, major. The captains at this point were: Company A, William W. Thompson; B, William J. Jennings; C, A.C. Dale; D, Charles L. Martin; E, Clay Robertson; F, Bruce L. Phillips; G, Issac Brunson; H, William S. Moore; K, James W. Lockert; and L, John W. Mallory. One soldier recalled that the promotion of men to captain from lower ranks and the removal of those who had held commissioned offices resulted in most leaving the Fourteenth for armies in the west.[38]

CHAPTER FIVE

Yorktown

The First, Seventh, and Fourteenth Tennessee regiments were now set for what would become their first true test together. Following the aforementioned elections, promotions, and reenlistments, twice-a-day drills became the routine for a short period of time. The complacency of this lifestyle was soon replaced with the warning of impending danger. On May 1, 1862, the brigade was issued orders to cook four days' rations and, in accordance with a late-night order, have the wagons packed by daylight.[1]

The next day involved the brigade forming at daylight, yet the march failed to begin until sundown. The men of the brigade traveled through a swampy forest and found themselves involved in another rain-hampered march, this time resulting in a broad scattering of the troops. At two o'clock in the morning of May 3, the bulk of the brigade passed through Williamsburg, reaching their destination an hour and a half later.

A.D. Norris stated that his new command was as scattered as others in the brigade and that he arrived in the new camp with only five men of his company. Little else was done on the third, yet on May 4 the brigade followed orders to form hastily and began marching. Passing through Williamsburg again, the Tennesseans sensed battle was near.[2]

Norris recalled, "We went about 2 miles from the town, loaded our guns and prepared for a fight. After halting a while near a mill pond, we faced about and returned to camp. Immediately on our return we were ordered to cook two days rations which occupied the boys till about midnight. We rested till one when we were called up to be ready to march. We started before daylight in the rain. Marched through the rain most of the day camping near nightfall … Our wagon train was threatened during the day by the enemy but the presence of a few brigades checked them. Our company lost many of our cooking utensils and blankets."[3]

This movement had been necessitated by what William McComb recalled as an action wherein "General McClellan had sent several gunboats and transports up [the] York River." The Tennessee Brigade, which at the time contained Braxton's Fredericksburg artillery in addition to the three Tennessee regiments, was given the task of keeping the road to Richmond open to allow Gen. Johnston's artillery to retreat from the reach of what appeared to be an overwhelming Union force.[4] The success of this effort would protect Richmond from McClellan's army arriving by land or water.

In conjunction with Hood's Texas Brigade, Anderson's Tennesseans were ordered to Yorktown. They soon encountered a large Federal force of some twenty thousand men, aided by gunboats near West Point. The Union detachment appeared to be attempting to divide the columns of the retreating armies. While the losses of the Seventh Regiment were minimal, both the First and Fourteenth Tennessee regiments "suffered considerably in the loss of both officers and men." J.H. Moore of Centerville, Tennessee and a member of the Seventh Tennessee noted that, despite the heavy fighting and significant losses, the Texans and Tennesseans bravely exchanged fire with the Federals as they "met and repulsed them, and forced them to seek the shelter of their gunboats."[5]

As the line of battle had been drawn, 2nd Lt. James T. Crusman, 14th TN, was positioned near the front, alongside Gen. Anderson and his staff. The opening volleys from the Union forces shattered Anderson's field glasses, leaving them dangling at his side. In addition, Crusman was seriously wounded as gunshots caused a compound fracture of the thigh. The latter wound would lead to his eventual resignation.[6]

In response, the Fourteenth Tennessee was thrown into a state of confusion that took the officers' full efforts to transform. A new line of battle was formed, utilizing the other regiments. Sgt. Robert Mockbee explained this tactical movement was above Anderson's ability, as he had gained no open-country fighting experience in the Mexican War; instead he had fought only in towns with narrow streets.[7]

June Kimble, Co. A, 14th TN, recalled that the Federal line had no intention of retreating and no indication of panic as volleys of shot rattled the Confederate ranks and knocked Anderson from his horse. A profanity-laced command to charge was given and carried out. Hood's Brigade now fronted the assault as the enemy boarded their transports. This position was maintained until the next afternoon, at which time the Confederate artillery and wagons had passed.[8] A.D. Norris recalled the series of events:

Cannon and small arms were being fired continually. We saw several bombs burst high in the air. At length we reached our brigade and formed, then rested in our places having stationed two pickets in front of each company. Here we learned that the 14th had a sharp skirmish in the morning in which General Anderson ran a narrow risk of losing his life. Here too we were entertained by the almost unearthly shrieking of bombs and occasionally of balls. The enemy fell back to their gunboats.[9]

The Tennessee Brigade then served as the rear guard until it reached the Chickahominy River, a few miles from Richmond. Norris noted the sequence of events: "We crossed the Chickahominy after nightfall, came about a mile farther camping about nine o'clock. Drew rations and cooked supper, went to bed, slept soundly, waked [sic] up on the morning of the 16th much refreshed."[10]

Norris continued, "Were ordered to go back beyond the bridge to act as the rear guard of the army. The wagons went forward. Our brigade formed a line of battle beyond the bridge, remained till about noon, then crossed to the Richmond side, there remained till near sundown having had nothing to eat except a little corn since breakfast. We then fell back to a beautiful pine wood a mile and a half from the bridge where we bivouacked for the night. Early on the morning of the seventeenth, we got up ate a snack consisting of a quarter of a pone of bread and two slices of meat—our days rations. The morning was glorious … our repose was broken by the rattling of small arms and the rapid discharge of several cannon."[11]

June Kimble remembered the experience of his company's introduction to the Federal gunboats and weapons when writing, "We had learned to regard as formidable, most destructive as engines of war, and to be dreaded." Kimble added that he recalled, "…upon that day the profound bow or rather squat made with military precision by the 14th Tenn. Regt., when the first shell passed over our heads, true it was two or three hundred feet high and aimed at troops on the high hills, a mile to our rear, nevertheless it commanded our respect … it sounded much like a barrel full of combustibles about to explode, and shower upon us all sort of slugs, scrap iron and what not, such was … our imagination … later on, it lost its power of frightening the veterans of Lee's army."[12]

Kimble, recently promoted to sergeant, also transcribed a little-known incident from the Confederate retreat from Yorktown. Kimble recalled after McClellan's advance had been successfully hampered, Gen. Anderson moved forward, leaving Maj. William McComb and the Fourteenth Tennessee to bring up the rear. Evidently growing bored, McComb seized an opportunity near Richmond to strike the Federal cavalry and selected a corner of a small field along the road to Richmond as the site of his attack.[13]

Using a pine thicket in the northwest corner of the field as cover, McComb established a five-hundred-yard skirmish line to attract the enemy. Across the road from that field lay a much larger field. McComb felt the enemy would soon emerge from this point, as ineffective artillery fire was already being sent in McComb's direction, falling distantly overhead. The Union cavalry arrived as predicted, "in columns of four, with sabers drawn." Focusing on the skirmishers, the Federal cavalry passed within sixty yards of McComb's main force, unaware of its presence. The cavalry entered a full gallop, creating a charge that Kimble stated "was indeed awe-inspiring, if not dreadful."[14]

Only upon hearing McComb's command to fire did the Fourteenth open upon the advancing column, already parallel to the right of McComb's regiment. One thousand guns, in near unison, fired from the pine thicket in a volley that sent men and horses, killed or wounded, to the ground. Riderless horses led the retreat to their starting point, and shots continued until few cavalrymen remained.[15]

Without taking time to count what was estimated to be a large Federal loss, McComb's men returned to the brigade. The pine thicket, emptied by the Tennesseans, was bombarded as the Union batteries "soon converted it into a howling wilderness." Kimble explained the futility of the enemy fire, in that even the birds had long since left the thicket.[16]

Another documented account of several witnesses during the retreat from Yorktown took place near Williamsburg. Second Lt. W. E. Donaldson in Company F of Turney's First Tennessee corroborated the story of C. C. Cummings, a member of the Seventeenth Mississippi. A young blond-haired lady rushed onto the porch of her large house, demanding that the soldiers passing her home turn back and defend "this old town, the cradle of American freedom." With two pistols around her waist, she offered her services as a captain, should the duly-appointed captains refuse to return to the sound of the guns. At almost the same instant, orders were received from elsewhere, sending the Mississippians back toward the direction of the small arms fire. This fully convinced the young lady that her appeal was the motivating factor. The Mississippians missed the action the young lady felt she had recruited them for, and the Tennesseans were destined to move elsewhere. The young lady, explained Donaldson, was "entitled to credit for the inspiration she imparted in encouraging the troops."[17]

The events the brigade encountered around West Point and Richmond were largely successful. The marches, halting, and countermarches continued, though, as one soldier remembered: "Left camp this morning. Started towards Richmond, traveled about two miles, halted. Remained on the Roadside till evening, then faced about, retraced our steps and camped 8 miles from Richmond."[18]

On May 24, the brigade's presence reached a more active level. The action was recorded as follows: "About 7 o'clock on the morning of Saturday May 24, we started towards the enemy. We took position in a wood on both sides of the road. Col. Forbes on the left of the road, Col. Turner [sic] on the R.R. The right wing of our reg't behind the battery on the right of the road in the edge of the woods, the left wing on the extreme left about half a mile from the road at the point where left it. About 10 a.m. a fire from the skirmishers on both sides commenced and was kept up briskly, soon afterward Capt. Braxton's artillery opened on the enemy who after an interval replied. Brisk cannonading was kept up for two hours, when our battery was removed. We retained our positions about half an hour after the batter left. Were then ordered to fall back as the enemy appeared in superior numbers. We fell back in good order till a piece of the enemy's cannon preceded by cavalry came up and opened on us with grape shot. This threw the line into confusion, some of the boys threw away knapsacks and blankets, only two from the reg't were missing. Altogether the retreat of our forces in the presence of the enemy was almost miraculous. We formed in an open field while the grape was still whistling over our heads."[19]

Union soldiers were not the only enemy the Confederate soldiers faced at Yorktown and in battles to come. William Clendening, Co. E, 7th TN, stated that it was humorous to see a member of his regiment hiding behind a tree looking for "graybacks." The number of men who encountered lice in a personal respect is one of numerous statistics left to speculation. Clendening was ashamed of his infestation "until the secret became a common one." As the Army of Northern Virginia moved farther into the peninsula, it became more and more common for Confederate soldiers to pass others sitting on the roadside, bootless, and removing "graybacks" from their bodies.[20]

The action the brigade encountered was manifested with the abrupt resignation of Gen. Anderson during this course of events. Robert Hatton had been promoted, replacing the first brigadier of the Tennessee Brigade. Opinions vary as to the basis of Anderson's withdrawal from military service. Some indications are that failing health was the foremost cause; others point to the rigorous lifestyle military leadership necessitates. Criticism of his ability to lead his men effectively is a distinct possibility in regard to Anderson's departure. Regardless of the reasons for his decision, the fifty-eight-year-old Mexican War veteran left the brigade with no intention to return. In November of 1864, Anderson was reappointed brigadier general in charge of conscription for Tennessee.[21]

CHAPTER SIX

Hatton and Seven Pines

General Anderson's resignation necessitated the appointment of a new and vibrant leader for the Tennessee Brigade. In May of 1862, Robert Hopkins Hatton was promoted to the rank of brigadier general and given command of the Tennesseans. Hatton had previously served as a colonel with the Seventh Tennessee Regiment, having formed Company K, the Lebanon Blues. Hatton's promotion took place amid an atmosphere of mutual admiration and respect for those he was to lead.[1] This esteemed military rank, unlike the personal affection from and toward his subordinates, would unfortunately be short-lived.

Hatton's pre–Civil War career was as impressive as his Civil War record. Born on November 2, 1826 in Youngstown, Ohio, Hatton was the fifth of six children. After moving to Tennessee, he attended Lebanon's Cumberland University, graduating in 1847. He opened a law practice after passing the bar in 1850 and married two years later. From 1855 to 1857, Hatton served in the state house of representatives and made an unsuccessful run for the governorship of Tennessee in 1857. This setback proved minor for the ambitious young man who, as a Know Nothing candidate, served in the US Congress from 1859 to 1861.

As did numerous Tennesseans, Hatton had felt the Union should prevail though secession talk abounded. Reflecting the mental transition of many in his state, Hatton eventually changed his mind and chose to defend Tennessee and the South.[2] These feelings and action led him to the position he now held, leading others to halt the attack on Richmond.

Robert Hatton. The beloved Christian general met his fate at Seven Pines. Courtesy of the Urigen Collection.

As a prominent member of Tennessee, Hatton pleaded with leaders of the North and South alike to attempt to diffuse the impending war. One such late 1860 petition received a foreboding reply from former president Millard Fillmore. It stated:

> To Hon. Robert Hatton: Sir: I have your letter of the 13th, and have reflected seriously on your suggestion that I should address a letter to my Southern friends against secession and in favor of the Union, and have come to the conclusion that it could do no good. If arguments could avail, they have been presented in a much more forcible manner than I could hope to present them ... In 1850 I

approved and executed the fugitive slave law, because I thought the constitution required it and it was necessary to restore peace to the country. I am happy to say it had that effect. The consequence, however, was that I was sacrificed at the North and not sustained by the South. I have no regrets ... I did my duty and at the close of my administration left the country in peace and prosperity.

In 1856 I saw the gathering storm, and did what I could to allay it ... I stood between the contending factions ... and received the poisoned shafts of both ... it was an evidence of my devotion to the Union more decided and convincing than anything I could now say.

I must say that I look with horror upon the approaching conflict. It will be terrible for us at the North, but more terrible for you in the South. Ours will be a civil war, but the horrors of a servile war will probably be added to our brethren in the South, and the last hope of human freedom will perish with our institutions. May God avert this terrible calamity!

Truly yours Millard Fillmore[3]

Under Hatton the Tennessee Brigade soon established a camp within view of Richmond. From this point, a waiting game began between the forces of Johnston in defense of the Confederate capital and those of McClellan. If McClellan attacked, he would leave his supply base undefended and vulnerable to attack. If the Union army were to divide, a virtual swamp would separate the parts of the Federal forces. Johnston was far from being without a personal dilemma, for attacking either half of McClellan's army would leave Richmond more defenseless and prone to capture.[4]

By May 26, 1862, the Federal army had moved within eight miles of Richmond and reached Seven Pines. On the Richmond side of the Chickahominy River, two corps under Heintzleman and Key led the Federal advance. The feeling seemed highly evident: Richmond should now be either evacuated or fully supported.[5]

New to the position of brigadier and facing a major decision regarding battle assignments, Gen. Hatton was "the peer of any man in the Confederacy." Hatton was the son of a Methodist preacher and was well known for his consistent church attendance, critiquing of sermons, and regular Bible reading. A Nashville preacher expressed that Hatton stood purposefully for "what he believed to be right, cost what it might."[6]

As the time of battle approached, Gen. Hatton wrote to his wife, mother, and father the following expressions of "tenderness, heroism, and manly fortitude":

Camp of Tennessee Brigade

Near Richmond, VA., May 28, 1862.

My Dear Wife: My Brigade will move in an hour from its encampment ... on the Chickahominy ... We go to attack the enemy on tomorrow beyond the river. A general engagement between our forces and the enemy's all along our entire line is expected to ensue. May the God of right and justice smile upon us in the hour of conflict! The struggle will no doubt be bloody. That we shall triumph, and that gloriously, I am confident. Would that I might bind to my heart before the battle my wife and children! That pleasure may never again be granted me. If so, farewell; and may the God of all mercy be to you and ours a Guardian and Friend!

Affectionately your husband, R. Hatton

A word to my dear mother: I go early to-morrow, mother, en route for the field of battle. A terrible and bloody fight is promised us. In the midst of the confusion of getting ready I sit down to say to you, dear mother, God bless you! You have been to me all a mother ever was to a man—loving, kind, unremitting in your efforts for my comfort and happiness. If I should not return, be a mother to my wife and children. God bless you, my own dear old mother!

Affectionately, R. Hatton.

A word to my dear old father: God bless you, my dear father! A tenderer, more loving father never lived. To me you have been the best of fathers. If I never return, let all your affection lavished in the past upon me be transferred to Sophie and her children. Let her never be left alone, but be comforted and cheered by the company of my parents.

Affectionately, R. Hatton[7]

The Chickahominy River lay approximately four miles northeast of Richmond in mid-1862. Flowing southeast, the river was crossed by a multitude of bridges. Meadow Bridge was located six miles north of the opening point of Richmond's Williamsburg Road; Bottom Bridge was positioned approximately eleven miles from Richmond and was also part of the Williamsburg Road. These points formed a triangle that constituted an area that would serve as the strategic field during the battle of Seven Pines.[8]

A heavy rain hit the Richmond area, creating rumors that it was of the extent to raise the Chickahominy to a level capable of washing away area bridges and prohibiting building replacements for days. With the main Federal army on the south side of the river, Key and Heintzleman, each with eighteen thousand men, would be isolated. The Confederate officers agreed that the two corps of Heintzleman and Key should be annihilated before being given the opportunity to retreat or receive reinforcements. The Tennessee Brigade was ordered to move. The march to Seven Pines began after sundown with Turney's First Tennessee leading.[9]

Along the Williamsburg Road stood seven loblolly pines from which the Confederates would acquire the name of the battle they faced. In contrast, the Fair Oaks railroad station was located nearby, giving the Union army its name for the same battle. Nestled at the intersection of the Williamsburg and Nine Mile roads, Seven Pines was approximately seven miles east of Richmond, with the small railway station known as Fair Oaks one mile farther.[10]

The Tennessee Brigade, recently assigned to Gen. Gustavas Smith's division, joined Smith's troops on Nine Mile Road for the purpose of eliminating a Federal retreat or troop reinforcement. The ill Smith had been taken to a farmhouse located on the Williamsburg Road two days earlier. Gen. Huger was to begin an attack on the Union left on the Charles City Road while D.H. Hill and Longstreet struck the center at Seven Pines. Huger was also to provide the signal guns used to mark the moment of attack on the part of the Confederates. Longstreet and Hill delayed the beginning of the attack while impatiently awaiting Huger's signal. By one o'clock, unable to wait any longer, Hill and Longstreet began the battle in Huger's absence.[11]

The Confederates quickly gained the advantage in the battle, as Key's Federal corps abandoned each of its assigned positions. Heintzleman managed to reinforce Key, momentarily slowing the Confederate advance. Soon the Federals were again driven from every point, nearing the river and eventual annihilation. Union troops under Sumner had now successfully crossed the river, finally halting the Confederate advance. Sumner's arrival had saved the Union forces of Key and Heintzleman, yet not before the latter had retreated an estimated mile and a half. As these events unfolded, the Tennesseans spent their time listening to the sounds of the battle. Plank Road had served as a resting place for their rifles, yet the yells of fellow Confederates following each successful charge had created a difficulty among the Tennessean's commanders in restraining the troops from joining the action.[12]

Two Tennessee leaders, Gen. Hatton and Col. Turney, visited, seated atop a fence. The men had different political party backgrounds, yet they indulged in conversation in which they seemed to agree on a united country. In the midst of the conversation, the gentlemen were interrupted with the arrival of a courier seeking Gen. Hatton. Hatton was informed of his being ordered into battle and responded by ordering his men to take arms.[13]

Gustavus W. Smith, with Joseph E. Johnston, served as Confederate Commander at Seven Pines. Courtesy of Confederate Veteran.

The Federal army had gained the advantage in the battle, managing to bring in thousands of fresh troops despite the muddy roads and strong Confederate positions designed to hamper such an event.[14] The late-afternoon request for intervention from the Tennesseans led to a host of memorable events in the life of the brigade.

The order to reinforce Longstreet and Hill had arrived at approximately six o'clock in the evening. Adhering to the courier's message from Johnston to hasten to the front, Hatton, with a single bound, was in his saddle. Hampton's Legion was given the same order as the Tennesseans, and upon learning of this, Hatton remarked, "I'll beat Hampton!" and then commanded the brigade to move forward double quick. Mist had fallen most of the day, and the afternoon had become especially humid. The order to move in a fast pace over a distance of four miles under such conditions was desperate but was carried out successfully in less than one hour.[15]

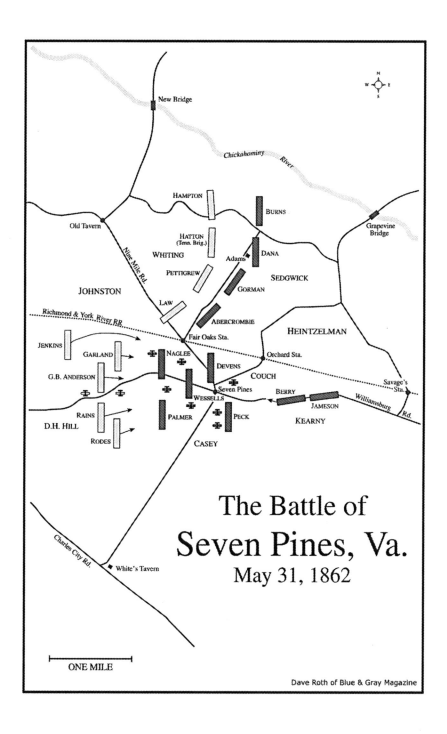

The Battle of
Seven Pines, Va.
May 31, 1862

ONE MILE

Dave Roth of Blue & Gray Magazine

Gen. Hatton formed the brigade on the road leading to Seven Pines. As he sat on his horse, he spoke to his brigade and, in the words of brigade member H.T. Childs, exclaimed, "Boys, before the dawn of another day we will be engaged in deadly conflict with the enemy. We are the only representatives of the gallant little commonwealth of Tennessee upon the soil of Virginia. I appeal to you as Tennesseans. Show yourselves worthy sons of noble ancestry. Just in our rear is the capital city of the Confederacy. Around our capital city has been gathered a vandal horde of Yankees. Their object, their aim, their purpose is to plunder and pillage our capital. Shall it be sacked?" Childs reported, "Just then, the stentorian voice of Colonel Turney rang out upon the night air: 'No, never!' and every boy snatched off his hat, caught up the refrain, and made the welkin ring with the shout of 'No, never!'"[16]

On the rushed approach to the front, the Tennessee Brigade passed Confederate president Jefferson Davis along with his staff and escorts, present to witness the battle. T.H. Benton recalled that Davis looked toward Hatton and said, "General Hatton, I want you Tennesseans to charge those people." Gen. Hatton then replied, "All right, Mr. President, if you say so." The Tennesseans saluted their leader with the rebel yell and proceeded forward.[17]

The brigade reached an old schoolhouse located on the side of the road. Upon a mound was positioned Gen. Johnston, wearing his glasses and sitting upon his horse to obtain a better view. Johnston inquired, "What command is this?" Hatton's reaction was, "Tennessee Brigade!" Johnston then said, "Put them right in."[18]

Gen. Hatton turned to the Tennesseans and ordered them to load their weapons. Company officers repeated the command and steel rattled as it was carried out. One of Johnston's staff sat near him, moving his head from side to side as if dodging the bullets and shells that filled the air. Johnston smiled and told the colonel there was no need to dodge the bullets, as their passing preceded the noise they made.[19]

At that instant a projectile landed near Johnston, throwing him from his horse, wounding the general's knee and knocking him unconscious. Drury L. Armistead, Johnston's courier, carried Johnston back approximately one-quarter of a mile, safe from the danger of enemy fire. Johnston's wound necessitated his removal from the field and closed his tenure as commander of the Confederate forces in Virginia. This position would soon be delegated to Robert E. Lee.[20]

Riding in front of the Tennesseans, Gen. Hatton emphasized the magnitude of the battle. He explained that now that they had met the enemy, they should conduct themselves in the tradition of their home state.

Robert E. Lee, Commander of the Army of Northern Virginia.
Courtesy of Confederate Veteran.

A petition was offered to the soldiers to act as heroes, for their conduct would determine Hatton's character. Cowards, he explained, could never behold the bright eyes of their sons.[21]

The command to "Fix bayonets!" resounded from Hatton's lips. With "Forward, guide center" ringing in their ears, the Tennesseans followed Hatton toward the Union position. The objective was one-fourth of a mile across sloping land and a swampy area with three inches of water and, as Thomas Herndon, Co. L, 14th TN, estimated, "one hundred yards full of fallen tree trunks in a partly decayed state."[22]

The three Tennessee regiments proceeded forward with the stars and bars flying overhead. A member of the First Tennessee called to mind the perfect line that never faltered, despite grapeshot and the canister shot exploding above and around the soldiers while the earth exploded in front of and behind them. The brigade had covered one hundred yards when Col. Peter Turney of the First Tennessee yelled for his regiment to "charge front, forward on first company." The First Tennessee now headed north, passing through the previous night's Union campsite. With dusk approaching, the First Tennessee halted and lay in a small stand of timber as treetops fell around them. Across a small field, in another line of trees, the Union army was forming to charge. Company officers called out, "Up boys!" and the regiment's members stood, guns loaded, and began firing. Darkness and smoke soon covered the area, and each side fired at the flash of the enemy's guns. The First Tennessee received ninety-six casualties, including fourteen dead. Among the wounded were James Massey, Felix Boyle, George Garnett, Arthur Cunningham, and C.A. Morres. James Bland of Company K was one of the members of Turney's regiment to be killed in the first stages of the battle.[23]

Capt. Will J. Muse, Co. B., 1st TN, recorded the casualties of his regiment as eighty-five killed and wounded in a span of fifteen minutes. Muse also recalled the roar of muskets as being so loud that the ability to hear any commands was made impossible. One of the minié balls fired from the Federal lines entered Muse's right thigh, requiring his transportation to a nearby railroad junction. He lay there throughout the night on cold, wet grass awaiting evacuation. Muse proposed that the situation gave him a cold that settled in his wound and created a large amount of trouble during his stay at the Third Alabama Hospital in Richmond.[24]

Turney's First Tennessee moved northward while the Seventh and Fourteenth Tennessee regiments followed Hatton westward. Gen. Hatton rode his horse and encouraged his men, shouting, "Forward, my brave boys, forward!" D.C. Kelley remembered the charge, as Hatton's image led his command "in the uncertain light of that closing day and smoking field his gray gabardine and gleaming sword marked the way for the line which followed him..."[25]

The Union army held a strong position, and its superior numbers caused panic in Hampton's lines as they entered the ranks of the Seventh and Fourteenth Tennessee regiments. Gen. Smith arrived and replaced the wounded Gen. Johnston. Smith made a futile attempt, with Hampton and Hatton, to reform the lines. Hampton himself was wounded.[26]

Near a swampy lagoon, Gen. Hatton fell from his horse, mortally wounded. Capt. Asoph Hill, Co. F, 7th TN, in his first battle as commander of his company, was near Hatton when the general fell. Hill, fellow company member "Esquire" Davis, and T.J. Holloway, Co. H, 7th TN, carried Hatton from the field.[27]

Capt. John Fite, Co. B, 7th TN, recalled that his company had proceeded two hundred yards or less before encountering the enemy fire that killed Gen. Hatton. He also estimated the opposing lines to have been only 150 to 200 yards apart, as fire was exchanged beyond the arrival of darkness. When the firing ended, the Seventh Tennessee moved back another two hundred yards, remaining there until morning. They then determined the Union forces in that area had pulled back during the night. The Seventh and Fourteenth were forced to retire, having spent approximately thirty minutes in battle.[28]

Gen. Robert Hatton's grave in Cedar Grove Cemetery, Lebanon, Tennessee. The monument states, "General Robert Hatton Born Nov. 2, 1826, fell May 31, 1862 while leading his Tenn. Brigade in the battle of Seven Pines, VA. Elected to the General Assembly of Tenn in 1855 ... House of Representatives of the U.S. Congress in 1859 ... Colonel of the 7th TN Reg. May 27, 1861 ... appointed Brig. Gen. May 23, 1862 ... In youth he embraced Christianity as the true science of manhood." Photo courtesy of Jack Cato.

The loss of Hatton was "severely felt and universally regretted." A brigade member wrote that Gen. Hatton's death was "the greatest loss of all." D.C. Kelley proclaimed that Hatton "fell while heroically discharging his duty in his first great battle." Full of affection for and from his command, Gen.

Robert Hatton was known for his stern discipline that never caused hard feelings among his staff. His widow continued to mourn her late husband's loss until her own dying day.[29]

Hatton's body was returned to Tennessee, yet Federal occupation of Middle Tennessee at the time led to his temporary burial in Knoxville. After the war, on March 23, 1866, Robert Hopkins Hatton was reburied in Cedar Grove Cemetery in Lebanon, Tennessee.[30]

The morning after Hatton's death, Col. Pryor of the US Army returned and walked the area of the battlefield where Gen. Hatton had fallen. Noticing a pistol in the mud, Pryor picked it up and discovered it had belonged to Hatton. Pryor sent the pistol to his home in New York, where it remained for thirty years. At that point, Pryor related the story of the pistol to a former Confederate soldier. Feeling a desire to return the pistol to Hatton's family, the former Union soldier secured the appropriate address and restored the ownership of the relic to the Hatton family, explaining the events in a courteous letter.[31]

Thomas E. Buford, Co. H, 7th TN, was killed at the battle of Seven Pines on May 31, 1862. Photo Courtesy of Confederate Veteran.

In addition to Hatton and the aforementioned casualties in Turney's First Tennessee, the Seventh Tennessee also suffered losses. At least five members of Company A of the Seventh lay dead on the Seven Pines battlefield, including G.W. Driver, J.B. Garrison, P.J. Mason, James Vanatta, and T.W. Sewell. One of the wounded of the Seventh was Capt. William N. Tate of Company H. Tate had earlier been detailed to care for the sick of his company, rejoining his comrades a day prior to the march to Cheat Mountain. Another member of the Seventh recalled additional fatalities included J.A. Womack, W.P. Rice, Tom Rice, Dick Baird, Watson Sewell, John Garrett, Martin Roberts, and Sam Ragland.[32]

J.M. Jones, Co. C, 14th TN, became a prisoner of war. Jones had advanced into thick woods with members of his regiment when he and others in his company realized they were a great distance ahead of and separated from their regiment. The soldiers began a hasty retreat toward what they felt was a safe direction, only to be met with a volley of musket shots. Eventually the firing stopped and Jones heard the rapid firing of two or three cannon in quick succession. As "a deathlike stillness prevailed," Jones realized the battle was over. Restarting his quest for safety, Pvt. Jones encountered a line of soldiers in the shadows at wood's edge. "Halt!" echoed throughout the area, and Jones realized those he stood near were Yankees. He was taken to their major, who offered Jones a toast of brandy that was accepted to counter his hunger and chill. Jones was led to a farmhouse nearby, where he spent the night with other Confederate prisoners of the battle.[33]

Robert Hatton in his prewar days. Courtesy of Dave Simpson.

The next morning, Jones was part of a detail to cover the battlefield, now within Federal lines, to search for the wounded. He found a groaning individual, sheltered by a pine bush from the midday June sun. The wounded Confederate touched his fingers to his lips, requesting water. Jones found a fellow prisoner to help bear the wounded soldier to the hospital, and Jones felt the wounded man held a stronger resemblance to "a corpse than a living being." Jones delivered the man to a hospital and was moved with others to Ft. Delaware. Accompanying Jones were J.J. Martin, Fayette Hutchins, James Weaver, William Jones, W.C. Griffin, J.M. Jones, E.M. Spurgeon, Ben Slavely, Richard Rout, James Bevest, and Charles Donoho.[34]

Two months later a prisoner exchange was made, and Jones made his way to Richmond in an attempt to rejoin the Fourteenth. On the way to a train station, Jones passed a hospital where he was greeted with a request from a young Confederate soldier. Asking Jones to stop, the young man asked, "Do you not remember the wounded boy who was carried from the battlefield of Seven Pines to a Yankee hospital?" Jones stated that he did, and the young Confederate exclaimed, "I am the boy." Jones was given "the most profound gratitude … expressed in voice and countenance." The young man also explained that in spite of his severe wounds, he was clear-minded during the events of Seven Pines and knew he owed his life to Jones.[35]

Jones, Hatton, and others contributed to the total losses of the Tennessee Brigade at Seven Pines. The final numbers for Hatton's command were 44 killed, 187 wounded, and 13 captured or missing, creating a total casualty figure of 244 for the brigade at Seven Pines.[36]

CHAPTER SEVEN

Archer Assumes Control

The death of Gen. Robert Hopkins Hatton was a tremendous loss for the Tennessee Brigade. His proven record as a leader of outstanding character and his unlimited potential are points to reflect upon and ponder as to the impact he may have made on the entire scope of the war. Another man who possessed a distinguished record and high potential was chosen as Hatton's successor: James Jay Archer. Archer's life and military record prior to the Civil War were filled with adventure and distinction.

Archer had been born in Stafford, Harford County, Maryland, on December 19, 1817 to Dr. John Archer and his wife Ann. The eighth of eleven children, James attended Princeton, Bacon College, and the University of Maryland, where he studied civil engineering and law, briefly practicing the latter. He served in the Mexican War and returned to civilian life, only to rejoin the army in 1855, serving as a captain in the Pacific Coast service. There he spent the next six years of his life.[1]

A Presbyterian by faith, Archer would remain a bachelor his entire life. Perhaps he felt Oregon was no place for a wife. His duties included serving many of his years as a captain in the U.S. Army after then Secretary of War Jefferson Davis commissioned him. Rumors would circulate regarding Archer's bachelorhood and his mannerisms that were often regarded as feminine in nature. While at Princeton, Archer was known by his nickname of "Sally," which he received because of his good looks. Mary Chesnut, in her August 27, 1861 diary entry, explained that Archer's good looks still remained, yet the ruggedness of his time in the military had permanently "destroyed all softness and girlishness."[2]

James J. Archer. In this photo the girlish appearance that earned the future Tennessee Brigade leader the nickname "Sally" is clearly evident. Courtesy of the Urigen Collection.

Archer irregularly received mail at his post, lessening his ability to properly gain knowledge of the increasing tension between the Northern and Southern sections of the nation. Writing from Ft. Colville on March 1, 1861, Archer chastised his friends and family in a letter to his mother for their failure to mention what he called "the one all absorbing topic of interest and anxiety, the 'impending crisis.'" C.A. Porter Hopkins proposed that Archer held a great level of concern for his family, friends, and the direction his home state of Maryland would take regarding secession, creating a high degree of personal turmoil. Archer's isolation, Hopkins states, clearly provided him the opportunity to decide his own path relative to the oncoming war.[3]

On March 17, 1861, Archer again wrote his mother, apparently disgusted with his sister, Nannie. He was amazed that she could possibly "ignore the great events that are transpiring." While Nannie's opinions of the secession movement and impending struggle had begun to matter less to him, Archer deeply desired "to know what part all our friends and relatives are taking." He explained that he saw an obvious course for Maryland and that it should be achieved with a unanimous vote in response to "a revolution with the devil and black Republicanism," exhibiting a show of force. Archer further expressed how he felt both the Constitution and Union had been destroyed and that a solution only lay in "something that will give security to the minority against the ... majority for all time to come."[4]

Archer, in his own words, eventually grew thoroughly disgusted with the direction in which Maryland appeared to be headed. He had expressed to his brothers in a January 1861 letter that should Maryland secede: "I desire her to consider my services at her disposal—I will ... immediately come." In a series of letters from May through August 1861, Archer detailed his intention to file an application for a leave of absence and his decision to tender his resignation. The latter action was taken although family members pleaded with him to forgo such an absolute action. In the last sentence of his July 16, 1861 letter to his mother, Archer nonchalantly mentioned that he had received a sixty-day leave of absence due to his May 10 resignation and then noted, "so I am no longer a U.S. officer." Archer's decision was undoubtedly stressful and perplexing. He felt his position would have allowed him to remain on the Pacific Coast with no outside disturbances for the war's duration, yet he expressed a need to assist his fellow Marylanders, many of whom he wrote would be the early victims of the struggle.[5]

On August 16, 1861, Archer left his post at Ft. Yamhill to move toward his new assignment. Fearing arrest, Archer progressed eastward using steamboats, stagecoaches, and trains as modes of transportation. Traveling through Portland, San Francisco, and Salt Lake City evidently presented few problems for Archer. From St. Joseph, Missouri through Indianapolis and into Louisville, Archer explained that he passed through Northern camps and actually shared the same cars as battalion-sized groups of Union soldiers. Archer arrived in Nashville on August 23, soon passed through Lynchburg, and reached Richmond on August 26, 1861.[6]

Once in Richmond, Archer began the political tactics of attempting to gain a transfer for his brother, Robert, then assigned to Gaither's company of Maryland cavalry. Archer offered advice to Robert, whom he referred to as "My dear Bob" to avoid talking about others to officers, as it appeared "mutinous" and could hamper the transfer process. In September Archer wrote Robert of the improving prospect of the latter being commissioned a major, quite an improvement from a private. Archer warned his younger brother of the possibility of failing at gaining promotion and that such an event should not cause disheartenment. On September 27, 1861, Archer again wrote Robert on the course of the attempt to gain the young man's promotion. Archer's actions often tended to accentuate the performance and well-being of others ahead of his own, oftentimes resulting in a lack of due credit being given to him. However, the pursuit of his brother's promotion took such an important portion of Archer's mindset that on September 27 he informed Robert that he had resigned his commission in the Confederate army, creating a vacancy as a lieutenant colonel, a spot that he had arranged to give to Robert. The day after filing his resignation, though, Archer was given command of sixteen Texan companies and appointed to the rank of colonel in the Provisional army.[7]

In late January, 1862, Col. James J. Archer again wrote Robert, informing him of the latest facet of their military association. Robert was told that he would make a perfect selection as his older brother's aide-de-camp, should James be appointed brigadier. The possibility but not probability existed for such advancement, wrote the elder Archer brother.[8]

Two months later James sent yet another letter to Robert concerning promotions. James lamented the role over the determination of military matters that politics played. Noting the absence of Maryland representation in the Confederate Congress, Archer proclaimed that he could see "no likelihood of my being promoted" yet quickly added to Robert, "I think I desire your success and happiness more than my own."[9] References to the hope of a promotion appeared in a number of Archer's subsequent letters to his brother.

In direct opposition to the amount of attention and longing given to the likeliness of advancement, James Archer seemed largely serene upon his notification of his receiving a brigade command. Offering neither sympathy toward anyone for Hatton's death nor apprehension toward his subordinates, Archer's message to Bob, dated June 3, 1862, was straightforward and imperative. The contents were simply that Archer had been appointed brigadier in command of the Tennessee Brigade. "Come over and be my aid de camp," was Archer's plea.[10] Thus originated an extremely successful yet under-studied command: Archer's Tennessee Brigade.

Archer's tenure with the Tennesseans began with a rather lukewarm reception. One can only speculate the effects that his West Coast isolation had upon him in a variety of ways. The lack of home-front communication and stress of anticipation of a possible promotion undoubtedly had a bearing on Archer's interpersonal skills at the time of his assignment to command the Tennessee Brigade.

Fergus S. Harris, Co. H, 7th TN, was initially unimpressed with the man whom he termed as puzzling. His dislike for Archer was shared among others of the brigade. He explained, "His exterior was rough and unattractive, small of stature and angular of feature, his temper was irascible and so cold was his manner that we thought him at first a Martinet. Very noncommunicative, and the bearing and extreme reserve of the old army officer made him, for a time, one of the most intensely hated of men."[11]

Gen. James J. Archer. Courtesy of Blue and Gray.

J.H. Moore of the Seventh Tennessee recalled that a majority of the remainder of June entailed "the ordinary routine of camp and picket duty."[12] It was during this period that John Fite, one of Moore's fellow regiment members, first encountered Archer in what he recollected as being an unpleasant experience.

Fite was serving on a picket line when Archer was introduced to him and inquired as to whom the command fell for that particular detachment. Fite informed Archer of his uncertainty on the matter but that he believed a captain or lieutenant held the distinction. Archer ordered Fite to take command, a request that Fite explained was not in keeping with past tradition, as it required a field officer being in charge of the sentry. Archer quickly and forcefully enlightened Fite and others around him that past practices were of no concern to the current leadership of the brigade. Within minutes Archer had increased Fite's picket command to a force of over three hundred men. Fite held this position for forty-eight consecutive hours in spite of the relief and substitution of others in the guard.[13]

Cursing Archer from a safe distance, a fellow brigade member came to Fite during the time and informed him that he had approached Archer concerning Fite's lengthy uninterrupted duration as picket commander. The individual apparently had become irate over the fact that Archer had told him that he would request the services of individuals when he needed them. At this revelation, Fite proceeded toward camp, where he confronted Gen. Archer with his frustrations. Fite stated that he had been at the difficult post for more than his fair share of time and that the stress and danger of the intermittent firing from the enemy necessitated his being relieved. Archer said any man not anticipating danger should stay out of the army. Fite then dejectedly returned for another day of picket duty.[14]

Events such as these made Archer's early days as brigadier of the Tennessee Brigade unpleasant for those whom he commanded. The events of late June 1862 would forever change this perception of James J. Archer in the hearts and minds of the men of the Tennessee Brigade.

CHAPTER EIGHT

Seven Days

During the period prior to the significant episodes of the Seven Days' Battles, the Tennessee Brigade was given a new assignment. Selected to serve in Maj. Gen. Ambrose Powell Hill's Light Division, Archer's Tennessee Brigade would make its greatest contributions to the Southern cause and gain its highest level of praise and recognition. The First, Seventh, and Fourteenth Tennessee regiments therefore joined the Fifth Alabama Infantry Battalion and Nineteenth Georgia in the Army of Northern Virginia.

The Fifth Alabama Infantry Battalion consisted of four companies at the time of its assignment to the Tennessee Brigade. Though Company D, the Daniel Boone Rifles from Mobile County, would be disbanded at the midpoint of the war. Its members would be divided among the remaining three companies, creating a level of trust within the ranks of Lee's army. At approximately the same time of the consolidation of the Fifth into three companies, the battalion would also be given the duty of provost guard for the remainder of the war. This assignment, though, in no way would signal the end of the contributions in battle from this group of fine soldiers. Their course of action will be noted throughout the remainder of this text.

Company A of the Fifth Alabama was organized at Gainesville in Sumter County, Alabama on May 26, 1861. In honor of their county, the members of the company fought under the designation of the North Sumter Rifles. Leaving Gainesville on June 17 in direct response to an order to move to Richmond, the company was mustered into the service of the Confederate States of America at Lynchburg, Virginia on June 23, 1861. A countermand was issued regarding the order to report to Richmond; in response to another order, the company arrived at Manassas on July 5, remaining there for several months. A December 2, 1861 special order resulted in the company's relocation to Dumfries, Virginia, where it became an integral part of the Fifth Alabama Battalion. Following assignments to picket duty at Cockpit Point, Virginia and Fredericksburg as a detachment of Whiting's Brigade, the company was briefly assigned to Field's Brigade. On June 14, 1862, the company was transferred to Archer's Tennessee Brigade.[1]

*Fifth Alabama Infantry Battalion battle flag. Courtesy of the Alabama
Department of Archives and History.*

Company B, the Calhoun Sharpshooters, had been organized at Jacksonville, Alabama on August 10, 1861. Thomas Bush had contributed greatly to the company's organization and would serve as its first captain. In October the company began service as a temporary battalion at Yorktown, where it assisted in the defense of the city. The temporary battalion was disbanded and reported to Dumfries, Virginia. There it joined members of Company A of the Fifth Alabama.[2]

Company C, the White Plains Rangers, was raised in White Plains, Alabama and left its hometown on May 3, 1861. In addition to Company B, this group hailed from Calhoun County, Alabama and their points of service from that time forward duplicate those of the two previously discussed companies of the battalion.[3]

The Nineteenth Georgia Regiment had an approximately six-month-long assignment to the Tennessee Brigade, during which time the Seven Days' battles occurred. Over nine hundred officers and enlisted men joined the Confederacy with this unit in the summer of 1861. The men of Company C, the Palmetto Guards, and those in G Company, the Henry Guards, had reported for duty at Camp Pickens, Virginia and had served in Hampton's Brigade prior to aligning with Archer's Tennesseans.[4] Though its time in the Tennessee Brigade would be short-lived, the Nineteenth would make large contributions to the brigade's successes of the period before being assigned to Colquitt's Brigade.

The regiments of the Tennessee Brigade joined others in Maj. Gen. A.P. Hill's Light Division, including Brig. Gen. Charles Field's Brigade of the Fortieth, Forty-Seventh, Fifty-Fifth, and Sixtieth Virginia regiments; Brig. Gen. Maxcy Gregg's First, Twelfth, Thirteenth, and Fourteenth South Carolina regiments; Brig. Gen. Joseph A. Anderson's Fourteenth, Thirty-Fifth, Forty-Fifth, and Forty-Ninth Georgia regiments and the Third Louisiana Battalion. Also incorporated into the Light Division were Brig. Gen. Branch's Seventh, Eighteenth, Twenty-Eighth, Thirty-Third, and Thirty-Seventh North Carolina regiments; as well as William D. Pender's Second Arkansas Battalion, Twenty-Second Virginia Battalion, and the Sixteenth, Twenty-Second, and Thirty-Fourth North Carolina regiments. Approximately eleven Confederate infantry divisions, in addition to artillery and cavalry units, combined to create an estimated 80,000 to 90,000 effectives in the series of struggles known as the Seven Days. Struggling against 105,445 Union troops[5], the Southern attack had to be made at the enemy's weakest point or erupt as a complete surprise.

J. H. Moore, 7th TN, expressed an opinion that Robert E. Lee sought some method of reducing the enemy's pressure upon the Confederate capital. Gen. J.E.B. Stuart had determined the right side of the Union lines to be the weakest point with the rear also poorly protected. These factors combined in late June of 1862 and led Lee to order an attack. The plan of the attack, Moore explained, was for Gen. Thomas J. "Stonewall" Jackson to attack the enemy from the rear, while generals Magruder and Huger fronted Richmond. A.P. Hill's division, including Archer's Brigade, was to attack the same position as Jackson, differing only in that the Tennesseans and the rest of the Light Division would make a frontal assault intended to force the enemy's right wing into a retreat. Hill's planned success would open a bridge spanning the Chickahominy and provide a crossing for generals D.H. Hill and Longstreet.[6]

Union general George McClellan had determined that moving his base south of the Chickahominy would allow his army to be more able to receive Naval support. He placed seventy thousand men under the command of Maj. Gen. Fitz John Porter, on the Southern banks of the river. Another thirty thousand men were located north of the Chickahominy and were ordered to proceed past Fredericksburg and join McClellan.[7]

On the night of June 25, 1862, Archer's Brigade was ordered to cook rations. In advance of the lighting of fires to cook their rations, the brigade members were ordered to fall in, fully knowledgeable of the fact that a battle was at hand. Blankets and knapsacks were thrown into wagons as the Tennesseans, Alabamians, and Georgians of Archer's Brigade readied themselves for what lay ahead.[8]

The Union army was within ten miles of Richmond when Company C of the Fifth Alabama Battalion began the march toward the point of attack but stopped suddenly. Company officers within the Fifth made the men aware that the following day they would be engaged in battle and told them to be brave while standing firm. The company commanders talked with their respective groups, and the men of Company C were shown their flag and informed that there was no regular color-bearer and told that a volunteer to do so should step forward. M.T. Ledbetter stepped out and took the company's flag and was quickly joined by five men volunteering as the flag's guards. At that point, the march continued for the Fifth Alabama.[9]

That night W.F. Fulton and William Frost were detailed from Company A of the Fifth Alabama to guard one end of a covered bridge spanning the Chickahominy. They were warned of the enemy's close proximity, yet they were to fire a shot only if it was considered to be absolutely necessary. Situating themselves on the bridge's large abutment, the two Alabama farm boys, relatively new to the ways of a soldier's life, began watching for any signs of the hidden enemy. Adding to the men's nervousness at such a demanding and new experience was what Fulton referred to as "one of those inky dark nights." In addition, the patience of Fulton and Frost was tried to the fullest extent by a large number of frogs, creating "the most dismal noise it was ever my misfortune to listen to." Fulton recalled the sounds appeared as if each successive frog was attempting to surpass the previous one during the Chickahominy swamp "frog celebration."[10]

In the minutes preceding sunrise on the twenty-sixth, a Yankee picket on the opposite bank struck a match to light his pipe. Fulton jumped at the sight, falling from the bridge in obvious panic, subconsciously attempting to dodge a bullet that had yet to be fired. Fulton's fall caused Frost to double up in laughter at Fulton's vain impulse to preserve his life. The laughter would soon cease for the duo and others of the Tennessee Brigade.

At noon large numbers of the brigade lay beside the road and took a well-deserved and much-needed rest. Ledbetter, the recently self-appointed flag-bearer of the Fifth Alabama, wrote that due to his advanced fatigue, he lay by his flag and speedily fell asleep.[11]

Gen. A.P. Hill arrived at the designated position at the agreed-upon time, but Jackson was not in position. Jackson's guide had taken a wrong road and was therefore out of position. Hill waited until two o'clock in the afternoon and then, without Jackson's support, began the attack cannon and small-arms fire, which awakened M.T. Ledbetter as those around him pounded his side and enlightened him of the situation. Becoming aware of the magnitude of the fight, Ledbetter arose and moved with his brigade into the thick of the battle.[12]

Robert T. Mockbee noted that Hill's troops were the first to cross the Chickahominy and open Meadow Bridge for Longstreet. Archer's Brigade continued moving forward through large felled trees whose tops were entangled with vines and saplings. The undergrowth and heavy enemy fire led to high numbers of casualties in each regiment of the brigade. Ledbetter was forced to wrap his flag tightly around the staff as he made his way through the thick underbrush. He later recalled that some ten bullet holes were discovered in his flag following this incident and that a section of wood was shot from the flag staff less than a foot above his head. Two of his friends, Murphy and Lambert, fell dead by his side, yet Ledbetter remained unharmed.[13]

Capt. W.F. Fulton, 5th AL, recalled the Federal shells "would pass over our heads with a peculiar whizzing sound" and men, positioned in long lines, crouched with each discharge. The latter action became entertaining to those viewing the barrage, as the shells were actually exploding one hundred yards behind the soldiers who were rhythmically ducking their heads.[14]

Capt. Pegram's Maryland artillery passed to the left of the Tennessee Brigade whose members cheered and sang "Maryland, My Maryland." As the artillery duel unfolded between Pegram's Confederates and the enemy's battery, Fulton and his fellow Fifth Alabama members moved toward the woods that lay ahead. As Fulton carried the flag into action, he felt his demeanor altered. He recalled, "My heart beat quick, my lips became dry, my legs appeared weak, and a prayer rose to my lips as we entered those woods. The artillery redoubled its firing, the muskets began to roar like a storm … the fear had passed away and I forgot the danger amid the excitement."[15]

The amusement of Fulton and those around him was not felt among all members of Archer's Brigade. John Fite, 7th TN, spent the early stages of the artillery duel stooped beside a small pine until a cannonball struck the ground near him, bounced, and struck him, knocking him senseless. Fite regained his composure and was sent with Mitchel Anderson, under orders from Goodner, toward the rear. A nearby pond provided Fite with a refreshing drink, and he spent the remainder of the night leaned against a pine tree, unable to lie down, as this caused him to lose his breath. At sunrise Fite began throwing up blood. He made his way to the field hospital, where Dr. McGuire informed Fite that his breastbone was broken and several ribs were damaged. Fite's wound was wrapped and he was sent to Richmond, where, for over a month, he denied himself deep breaths for fear of injuring himself again. The wound resulted in a deep ridge across his breastbone, and for the remainder of his life, especially in wet weather, it caused the soldier a great deal of pain.[16]

Gen. Porter was able to leave Mechanicsville during the night of the twenty-sixth; the Tennessee Brigade also fell back a short distance, gathering in nearby woods. William McComb proposed that Porter's ability to exit the area around Mechanicsville would have been made more unlikely had Gen. Jackson arrived as scheduled.[17]

Gen. Lee saw an opportunity to attack the enemy on the following day, June 27, 1862. Gen. Porter was then positioned at Gaines Mill, where the Confederates pursued him in an attempt to dislodge the Federal troops from their fortified defenses. J.H. Moore, 7th TN, noted that the Federal defenses at Gaines Mill were impossible to capture using a frontal assault. The Union troops stood atop a steep ridge fronted by Powhite Creek. Infantry located on the bluff could fire down upon the enemy, the rear line being in no way encumbered by the front.[18]

Capt. John Keely of the Nineteenth Georgia added that the creek, which fed a mill, had been dammed. Union soldiers had placed stakes breast high and leaning in the direction of the would-be attackers. Trees were cut with their tops toward the Confederates, adding to the protection of the Federal hilltop position and making the ascent a near impossibility.[19]

J.H. Moore asserted that some fifty artillery pieces backed the Union infantry. Keely proposed that one man, with great difficulty, could have possibly made his way through the maze, yet a gun and forty rounds of ammunition lessened his chances of success. The above factors, not in any means attempting to cause one to forget the two lines of Federal firepower, gave Porter's Union command a far superior position.[20]

M.T. Ledbetter recalled the bittersweet approach to Gaines Mill. Federal cannonading had furiously hit the woods where he and others of the Fifth Alabama rested following the previous day's action. The hour-long bombardment had been used for protection of Porter's men as they retreated to Gaines Mill. Pursuing the Union army at nine o'clock on the morning of the twenty-seventh, Ledbetter saw dead Confederates stuck in the knee-deep mud near Meadow Ridge. The heavy earthworks and headlogs posed a situation that Ledbetter felt "looked like foolishness to undertake to move them, but they had to be moved."[21]

M.T. Ledbetter, color-bearer of the Fifth Alabama Infantry Battalion. Wounded twice during the war, Ledbetter regularly attended reunions of his comrades until his death in 1908 at the age of sixty-seven. Courtesy of Confederate Veteran.

William McComb explained that the Tennessee Brigade formed in an open field near Gaines Mill with Hill's division positioned to their left. The order to advance came at approximately four o'clock in the afternoon, and the Tennessee Brigade advanced forward one hundred yards. The soldiers began moving double quick when the Federal position came into clear view. The Confederate cannon of Capt. Braxton began firing toward the Federal position in front of the Tennesseans as the brigade pressed on.[22]

Capt. John Keely became somewhat philosophical when reflecting upon the early stages of the attack. Keely recalled how knee-high corn grew in the open field through which Archer's Brigade advanced. Virtually cut down under the charging soldiers' feet, the corn would soon afterward be periodically covered under corpses of its destroyers. The dead bodies sometimes remained on the field following the battle, only to fertilize the earth and enhance the next year's crop in an attempt to compensate for the earlier destruction.[23]

W.F. Fulton, 5th AL, added that the men in his portion of the charging Confederate line were told to pass along the message to not hurry and keep in line. Fulton felt the distance to be covered while crossing the field was so great that the warning to slow down was a request to save energy for the task that lay ahead. Lt. Crittenden, a young man on Gen. Archer's staff, led Company A of the Fifth Alabama across the field. Crittenden's words rang clearly: "My brave Alabamians, I know I may depend on you." Fulton stated that though he heard these words and fully understood them, he was too focused on the hill positioned in front of him. The hill "all in a flash … was ablaze from top to bottom."[24]

The Tennessee Brigade proceeded toward the enemy and soon passed Field's Brigade, positioned in woods to the left of the Tennesseans and failing to join the Confederate charge. The Tennessee Brigade continued a distance of another hundred yards when the Federal guns opened with a concentration on Archer's Tennessee Brigade. Archer had moved forward with no support from other troops. A.P. Hill later stated that his division fought two hours before being reinforced.[25]

This first charge upon the Union position had showcased the bravery of twenty-six-year-old Lt. Col. John C. Shackelford of Turney's First Tennessee. Shackelford had joined Turney's regiment prior to Tennessee's secession and had fought at Seven Pines and Mechanicsville. Those assigned to his command noted he possessed nerves of steel and respected the young man for his coolness in battle. Shackelford stood waving his sword above his head, urging his men forward, as he was shot. The heavy barrage of fire during the failed first assault had created a situation necessitating a retreat, yet Shackleford refused the offered assistance from another soldier to remove him from the field. The young officer's reply was, "No it is no use. Take care of yourself."[26]

The Seventh Tennessee suffered seventy-two total casualties at Mechanicsville and Gaines Mill and also lost Lt. Col. John K. Howard in the first charge. Howard was a popular officer among the men, and his courage under fire was well known throughout the regiment. Howard's mortal wound in the early stages of the battle would have prophetic ramifications as every field officer of the Seventh Tennessee would be killed or wounded at battle's end. W.C. Boze and B.B. Thackston of Co. B, 7th TN, were two of the individuals responsible for carrying Howard to the field hospital. Thackston, Boze, and six others survived the battle to become the only eight men of Company B without wounds or unable from exhaustion to answer at roll call.[27]

Col. W.A. Forbes, 14th TN, suffered a severe wound in the initial charge, making it necessary for the command of the regiment to pass to William McComb. At the time of Forbes' wounding, Gen. Archer, who now had a clear view of the battle, ordered a retreat.[28]

M.T. Ledbetter, still carrying the flag of the Fifth Alabama Battalion, recalled halting at the face of a knoll graced with an apple orchard. He and his comrades evidently mistook the call to retreat as an order to lie down and buried themselves among the obstacles. W.F. Fulton felt the odds were too great for the Tennessee Brigade and remembered the apple orchard provided sources of protection for Archer's men. Fulton reached an apple tree in the orchard and was determined to hide behind it, but he found a series of men—one hugging the tree, another hugging him, and so on—making the tree virtually unable to provide any degree of safety.[29]

Fulton hid behind a fellow battalion member nicknamed Bee Gum who was known for frequently wearing a tall black beaver hat. Fulton noticed canister and grapeshot that kicked up dust all around him, and he began to make his way to another tree. He found William Frost lying on the ground and moaning deeply. After asking Frost what was causing his pain, Fulton heard his friend explain that he'd been shot clear through as a projectile had entered his chest and exited under his shoulder blade. Examining the wound, Fulton found Frost had actually received a blister on his back, possibly caused by a shell fragment, and that the rest of his injuries were only imagined. Frost sat up, breathed deeply, and said, "Well, I thought I was gone."[30]

William Tolley calculated that the first attack, before stalling in a retreat, came within twenty steps of the enemy works, well protected in the woods. The small number of men, less than one thousand in Tolley's estimation, were unable to hold the relatively victorious position, as it later took seven brigades to reach the same point.[31]

A courier eventually approached Gen. Archer. The estimations of the elapsed time between the call to retreat and the arrival of the courier at Archer's position vary considerably. William McComb remembered the duration as being some thirty minutes; Ledbetter, "an hour or so."[32]

The message of the courier caused Archer to walk among his command and order the brigade forward. Ledbetter described how the Federal fire poured into the Tennesseans following the receipt of the order for a Confederate charge. A man from Company C of the Fifth Alabama stood to the side of Ledbetter and was shot through his arm.[33]

Ledbetter recorded that "the fire from the enemy's … lines was furious and the boys began to waver." At this point of the attack, General Archer waved his sword above his head and called to his men, "Follow me!" Archer's order was no sooner proclaimed than M.T. Ledbetter was shot. Ledbetter turned to ascertain the location of his color guard when he was shot through the right hip. He determined that death awaited him whether he stood or lay down, yet the better option rested in attempting to flee. Making a futile attempt to stand, Ledbetter decided he would successfully escape only by dragging his wounded leg. He caught a glimpse of four members of his color guard on the ground, yet Ledbetter was unable to detect a sign of life in any one of them. A minié ball then hit his left wrist, shattering it and detaching his thumb. Reaching the safety of a gully, Ledbetter was motivated to retreat farther to the rear in order to avoid being captured. Sgt. George Williams aided Ledbetter in this stage of his flight to the rear. The dead and wounded littered Ledbetter's route as canister rounds filled the air.[34]

Despite the killing and wounding of scores of others within the brigade, the Tennesseans and the balance of Hill's division trudged forward. Gen. Hood's Texans joined the charge, resulting in the sounding of the rebel yell. McComb wrote that Archer and Hood were not only friends but also "both as brave as the bravest." The determination and leadership of these two men left little doubt of the decision to raise the rebel yell. Capt. William P. Tolley explained that Hood was the only mounted officer in the battle of Gaines Mill and led his army into action that day in line. Hood's line joined that of Archer's and pushed forward into the Federal works.[35]

William McComb proposed that the breeching of the Union fortifications was made largely possible with the fear the rebel yell inflicted. A Union commander had explained their position could be held against attack; but his men, attending six of the finest steel-rifled cannon on the field, trembled in their boots at the sound of the yell. In response, their decision to leave and the implementation of that recourse were virtually simultaneous.[36]

The confidence of the Federal artillerymen was also recorded by Dick Pike. The soldier had been wounded during the first charge and captured immediately afterward. McClellan supposedly informed Pike of his doubt of the rebels ever driving the Federals from their position.[37]

Portions of Archer's Brigade and Hood's Fourth Texas and Eighteenth Georgia regiments were recorded in Tolley's words as the first units to break the Union lines. The fire from the Federals allowed the Confederates to move forward only a few paces, drop to their knees and fire, and listen for Archer's call to get "up and at them!" Reaching the enemy lines, the Confederates saw close up the "strong lines of breastworks, each heavily manned ... while the plateau behind them was a solid park of artillery."[38]

William McComb recalled an approximately eighteen-year-old boy named Sam Taylor, 14th TN, as being the first man to enter the Federal breastworks at the Tennessee Brigade's point of attack. Taylor had taken over the duties, as his predecessor had been wounded in the first charge. Taylor was offered but declined a sword for his achievement of crossing the breastworks and planting his flag on a cannon.[39]

The brigades of Archer and Hood captured the cannon of the Federals and presented six of them to Capt. Braxton's Fredericksburg battery. The men of both brigades mingled around the captured guns in the area where "some of the best blood of Tennessee was poured out." Capt. Braxton gave names to two of the guns. One he called "Forbes" for the wounded colonel of the Fourteenth Tennessee; the other he named "Taylor" after the young color-bearer who breeched the Union barricade.[40]

Braxton's battery was not the only Confederate unit to improve its firepower following Gaines Mill, as Springfield and Enfield rifles replaced the smooth bore muskets of the Fourteenth Tennessee. Thousands of small arms and stores of supplies were confiscated as the Confederates retrieved the goods located among the dead and wounded Union soldiers. A large number of Union prisoners also fell into Confederate hands. In a period of less than thirty minutes from Archer's call for a second charge, the entire Federal position was in Confederate hands as the right wing of McClellan's army hastened toward the sanctuary of the Chickahominy. M.T. Ledbetter, the Fifth Alabama's flag-bearer, survived his wounds at Gaines Mill, sheltered behind a large oak tree. Four litter-bearers fashioned a US blanket and used it to move Ledbetter to a field hospital. The bearers lost their way in the darkness, and Ledbetter was carried to a North Carolina battlefield hospital, where he received substandard care. After two days at the North Carolina location, Ledbetter was sent to Richmond for recovery and his future return to the Tennessee Brigade.[41]

Gen. Longstreet had marched fourteen miles on June 29, stopping three miles southwest of Frayser's Farm. Intending to cut off a Federal retreat,

Longstreet placed his batteries in strategic locations, keeping A.P. Hill's troops, including the Tennessee Brigade, in reserve.[42]

Longstreet felt it a certainty that generals Jackson and Huger would be in position to attack; Jackson from the north toward the Federal position at Charles City Crossroads and Huger from the west. Longstreet was to wait for a signal from these generals to begin his attack. Mid-afternoon arrived and with it Longstreet's entire division stood in position as Longstreet conversed with Gen. Lee and Confederate president Jefferson Davis in a small field concealed by trees and undergrowth.[43]

Artillery fire opened near the point Huger was to attack, yet the Union batteries' response proved near fatal for the Confederacy. A shell exploded near the party of the Confederate leaders, killing two horses and wounding their riders. Longstreet ordered an officer forward to silence the Federal battery, but this effort, intended to safeguard a delegation of Confederate officials and commanders, created an all-out engagement between the two armies. Gen. McCall's Federal troops had employed the use of fallen timbers and breastworks that had proven effective during the recent clashes with the Confederates. McCall's soldiers were pushed back in heavy hand-to-hand fighting, though the task was accomplished without the presence of Huger and Jackson.[44]

The Tennessee Brigade stood in reserve, intended to be used in pursuit of the Union army following its retreat. Archer's Tennesseans and the rest of Hill's ten thousand reserves were ordered forward to assist Longstreet's men, now exhausted from their vicious struggle. One unbroken portion of the Federal lines remained as the Tennessee Brigade reached the scene of the attack. Joining Gen. Anderson's South Carolina troops, Archer's men succeeded in driving the Federals from the field and capturing several artillery pieces.[45]

Heavy fighting took place the next day, July 1, at Malvern Hill, where the Tennessee Brigade was again held in reserve. Heavy Federal artillery and gunboat fire pelted the brigade's position, causing a small number of casualties. The large shells coming from the riverboats were called nail kegs among the brigade's members. The experience at Malvern Hill, explained Sgt. Mockbee of the Fourteenth Tennessee, was "more trying" than had been the fighting on the front in the previous days. McClellan found safety in his gunboats along the James River. Gen. Lee evidently ended his desire to pursue and capture his enemy at that point and ordered his armies to Richmond.[46]

In the Seven Days campaign, the Tennessee Brigade suffered a heavy casualty rate. Of the 2,500 effectives, 92 members of the brigade lay dead on the fields of the weeklong struggle for the area around Richmond. A total of 443 wounded, and missing brigade members brought the total casualty figure to 535.[47]

Of the ninety-nine casualties Turney's First Tennessee reported, Capt. J. B. Turney remembered that among those killed were J.T. Turney, Henry Dyer, J.F. Downing, and S.W. Gill. The wounded of Company K included W.G. Massey, John Massey, and James Alsup. Privates David Neville and George Nowlin were two members of Company A of the First Tennessee killed at Gaines Mill. Hugh Northcutt was one of several members of Company A of the First Tennessee to be wounded during the action around Richmond. Northcutt was given a furlough and returned home to recover from his wounds. He was captured and sent to prison, where he remained for the rest of the war. The Seventh Tennessee lost heavily at Mechanicsville with seventy-two casualties suffered. Every field officer of the regiment was killed or wounded. The Fifth Alabama had nineteen killed and seventy-nine wounded out of the approximately two hundred effectives seeing action.[48]

The July 22, 1862 issue of the *Clarksville Chronicle* listed the casualties the Fourteenth Tennessee suffered during the battle of Seven Pines and in the Seven Days Battles. These included Company A: R.D. Duke and J.M. Hatton were killed and nine were wounded. Company B: W.J. Martin was killed and eighteen were wounded. Company C: J. Gambill, J.M. Jones, B.F. Anderson, James and Titus Powell were killed and thirteen were wounded. Of the wounded, Richard Pike and William Erwin died by the date of publication. Company D: Capt. C.L. Martin, J. Cherry, and W.E. Largin killed and nine wounded. Company E: four wounded. Company F: R.T. Brooks killed and fourteen wounded. Company G: Dallas Booth killed and of the twelve wounded, T.H. Collins and William Hamilton soon died. Company H: C.C. Tilley and W.H. Reagan killed and thirteen wounded; T.M. Broaddus of the list died. Of the severely wounded was Capt. J.J. Crusman. Company I: W.T. Baber and Richard Chandler killed (the former on picket) and seven wounded. Company K: J.W. Gunn killed and fourteen wounded. G.A. Tompkins, who was among the wounded, died soon afterward. Adjutant R.C. Bell was mortally wounded in this series of battles.[49]

These numbers, while great, were a fraction of the devastation the brigade would soon encounter.

CHAPTER NINE

With Stonewall

Following the Seven Days Battles of late June 1862, the Tennessee Brigade received a well-deserved rest. The members were involved in no military actions during the entire month of July, yet changes and action were taking place in regard to military assignments.

On the first of August, Gen. A.P. Hill's Light Division was ordered to join Gen. Thomas J. "Stonewall" Jackson, who was positioned to the north in the Culpepper and Orange counties of Virginia. Jackson's objective was to hinder the movement of Maj. Gen. John Pope's Army of Virginia. Spearheading Pope's Federal movement was Maj. Gen. Nathaniel Banks's Second Corps.[1]

The Tennessee Brigade left its camp south of Richmond and moved to Gordonsville, Virginia aboard trains. The troop trains bested the supply wagons' journey by twenty-four hours, leaving the brigade without food for more than a day. The Tennessee Brigade joined the remainder of Hill's Light Division and spent the next few days at Gordonsville. On the night of August 8, 1862, they camped across the Rapidan from the Union army.[2]

One of the best insights into the mindset of an Archer's Tennessee Brigade member appeared in the *Rome Courier*. Writing from his camp near Gordonsville, a member of the Nineteenth Georgia Regiment, identifying himself as "B," provided interested parties "back home" a first-hand account of camp life and the anticipation of looming battle.

B explained that during his lonely nights in camp he had been given regular relief when reading news from the pages of the *Courier*, and he felt it his duty to return the favor. B stressed the beauty of the area, with its invigorating mountain air, was a welcome change from the swamps of the "malarious [sic] Chickahominy" and that he and those of his company would do their part in assisting Jackson. B stated that the manner in which Union general Pope's men were destroying the private property of many of the Gordonsville residents had jammed local roads with the region's farmers and their livestock. These refugees were en route to mountain hideouts not easily entered by the enemy. Clover, corn, sheep, and wild berries filled the valley and easily satisfied the hunger of the men whose health had been largely diminished from the "long subsistence upon bread and soldier meat." Most interesting to B appeared to be the potential the large herds of cattle had of providing "abundant milk … golden butter … and tooth-some beefsteaks." The mountain range bordering the valley was filled with springs and yielded a supply of fresh, pure water for the soldiers. Two daughters of a local doctor/farmer lived within sight of B's Gordonsville quarters. Their physical beauty was greatly appreciated by B, and he referred to their fondness for horseback riding. B concluded his letter to the *Courier* with updates of the health and well-being of his comrades. Diarrhea had evidently worn down several members of the Nineteenth Georgia; Sgt. Adams of Gordon County, Georgia was said to be in a doubtful state of recovery, and Dr. Pinson was being dismissed to return home after battling chronic dysentery for months.[3] The boredom B felt in Gordonsville would last only days after his composition of his letter to the *Courier*.

On the morning of August 9, 1862, Jackson's "Stonewall Brigade" and a detachment of cavalry crossed the Rapidan to engage Pope's army. Jackson's camp had been raided hours before, at three o'clock in the morning; the Yankee culprits lay ahead. Jackson soon encountered the Union army, and the resulting sound of distant cannon signaled those units trailing Jackson that the battle had begun.[4]

Hill's division was stretched out for some ten miles along dusty roads, further encumbered by heat that approached one hundred degrees. Encountering strong Union fire, Jackson sent a message to Hill, urging him to advance with haste. Hill's troops responded rapidly to Jackson's request, overcoming the heat that was described as being "almost suffocating." Contributing to the troops' motivation was the sound of increasing artillery fire and the conclusion that intense fighting lay ahead. In his official report, Maj. Gen. A.P. Hill explained he heard the heavy firing approximately six miles from Culpepper Courthouse and received Jackson's order to send a brigade forward to reinforce Taliaferro. Gen. Thomas responded to Hill's command to progress with haste and formed immediately behind Taliaferro.[5]

As successive brigades of Hill's division moved forward, the extreme heat quickly decimated their ranks. On the morning of the ninth, Archer's Brigade left their camp with some 1,200 men. Having crossed the Rapidan while "holding ... guns and cartridge boxes above the water," the brigade advanced with Col. Peter Turney's First Tennessee in front. H.T. Childs recalled the ensuing events:

> It was the hottest day I ever saw, the big men continually falling by the wayside, worn out by fatigue and oppressive heat ... When the 1st Tennessee came up, General Pender's North Carolina troops had laid off their knapsacks, and we followed suit. Here I saw two of Pender's boys faint away from excessive heat. Colonel Turney caught each one and eased him down, calling for the surgeon. Colonel Turney then looked around for his own men. I heard him ask: 'Where are my big men?' We answered: 'Colonel, here are your boys. Your big men have broken down.'[6]

Archer's Brigade moved into battle behind and to the southwest of Branch's Brigade and alongside, in angles in a southeasterly direction, Pender's Brigade. These units formed a right angle with the brigades of Taliaferro and Garnett, all of them resting north of Culpepper Road. Branch's Brigade began receiving heavy Union fire and was invaded with fragments of other Confederate commands previously broken apart. Though breaking apart and with a large number of members retreating, Branch's Brigade was ordered forward. Rallying at this critical moment, Branch's North Carolinians pushed the Union soldiers across a wheat field where Federal soldiers were regrouping in woods that bordered the field. Archer's Brigade, assisted by Pender, arrived at the moment of Branch's repulse of the Federals. Archer's troops fired into the enemy as Union dead piled up. With this added Confederate firepower, the Union army entered the aforementioned woods.[7]

Archer's men were receiving heavy fire at this point while Union Brig. Gen. George Gordon's Brigade moved through the woods toward the wheat field. The Tennesseans were positioned some 250 yards from the Union soldiers when a battalion of the First Pennsylvania Cavalry charged down Culpepper Road and into the wheat field. Historian Robert C. Cheeks labeled the charge "as glorious and ineffectual a cavalry effort as any that occurred during the war."[8]

Col. John Fite of the Seventh Tennessee exclaimed the cavalry action was "the grandest sight I ever witnessed" and stated that he felt the Pennsylvanians were unaware of the Confederate's presence in the woods. Closing to within approximately fifty yards of the woods, the Union cavalry was assaulted by volleys from the guns of Archer's men. Men and horses alike fell along the Federal ranks as they attempted to pass Archer's position. Fite overestimated the cavalry number to be 10,000, while in actuality, 164 men of the First Pennsylvania had entered the field. The marksmanship of Archer's Brigade proved highly effective, as 34 of the 164 Pennsylvanians were lost.[9]

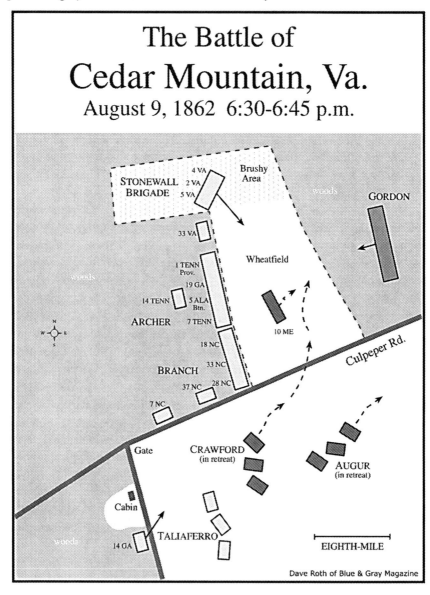

The Battle of
Cedar Mountain, Va.
August 9, 1862 6:30-6:45 p.m.

Dave Roth of Blue & Gray Magazine

Additional Union infantrymen charged into the wheat field, evidently determined to gain revenge for the decimated cavalrymen. The advancing Federals were met with another round of exceptionally accurate fire from the Tennesseans, and the reaction was broken ranks, heavy casualties, and infantrymen attempting to find cover behind the wheat shocks scattered throughout the field. The effectiveness of Confederate muskets added to the Federal panic, as H.T. Childs, 1st TN, recalled that "every boy leveled his gun" and "not a Yankee got out of that wheat field."[10]

Pvt. Henry R. Harkreader, Co. I, 7th TN. Harkreader joined the Confederacy as a private on May 20, 1861. At Cedar Run, on August 9, 1862, he was wounded and served out the war in the Ordnance Department. At Appomattox he was one of only two men from his company to survive to surrender. Following the war, he entered a forty-year marriage that produced five children and passed away in 1926. Courtesy of The Gregory A. Coco Collection.

Across the wheat field stood a fence that fronted yet another group of Gordon's Federals waiting for the Confederate attack. Archer's Brigade led a push toward the Union location, while Pender's North Carolinians and the Stonewall Brigade followed. H.T. Childs recorded the events: "The order rang down our line: 'Forward! Guide, center!' And when we reached the fence it was turned bottom side up, and on we moved, while bullets whistled by our ears … crossing a ravine in the field our company officers told us to hold our fire until we reached the line of Yankees at the fence. When we reached the brow of the ridge … with fixed bayonets and the wild Rebel yell, we made a terrific dash for the fence. While making this dash Paul Boyce, who was by my side, was wounded in the leg, causing the loss of it … In making this charge two of the Fayetteville company lost an arm each, Jim Kelso and Jim Cashion."[11]

Col. John Fite was another brigade member wounded in the charge over the ground of the wheat field. As he reached the midway point of the field, a bullet hit his left leg, breaking it in such a manner that an early prognosis of the wound required the amputation of the limb. The leg was not removed, and Fite was sent to the rear for more medical care.[12]

The remainder of Archer's men reached the fence line, and the Federal soldiers retreated in haste. A member recollected, "When we reached the fence the line of Yankee soldiers was not there. They had retreated into a dense thicket … we followed … picked up prisoners and sent them to the rear. When we emerged from the jungle, a distance of half a mile, we were in another field."[13]

The Confederates pursued the retreating Federals through woods and darkness, in an attempt to gain additional prisoners. H.T. Childs recorded another event of this phase of the battle in writing, "…While we were dressing up our lines two men rode in our front. One of them said,: 'Boys, I want to introduce you to Gen. Stonewall Jackson.' Jackson took off his hat. Every boy snatched off his hat and with the wild Rebel yell saluted the General. Jackson then called for fifty volunteers as skirmishers to go in front. The whole line stepped forward. The company leaders called us back and designated who should go. I was sent from my company."[14]

Many of the brigade's members worked into the night, rounding up prisoners and acquiring control of Union ambulances and medical supplies. Peter Turney's big men of the First Tennessee, several of whom were incapacitated by the heat prior to the battle, erupted in panic at the sight of one such group of captured Federals. Approximately one hundred Yankee soldiers marched into the group of recuperating men from the First Tennessee, causing some of the near-delirious Confederates to run half-naked through a mile or more of woods before being convinced that the enemy troops they had encountered were actually captives.[15]

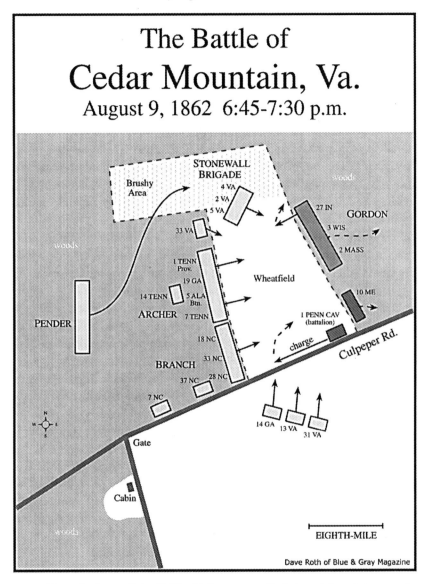

The Battle of
Cedar Mountain, Va.
August 9, 1862 6:45-7:30 p.m.

Dave Roth of Blue & Gray Magazine

William Fulton of the Fifth Alabama recalled the night of August 9 as being filled with the sound of shells passing overhead, toward and occasionally from the retreating Union army. Longing for rest, Fulton's thoughts were of his home and the feather bed in which he longed to rest.[16] Certainly others in the Tennessee Brigade pondered upon such comforts of home that, for many, were now year-old memories.

John Fite, 7th TN, escaped the Cedar Mountain battlefield covered with the dead and wounded as two men of his regiment carried him to safety while he straddled a rifle. Lt. Rufus Doak, recently returned from a furlough, told Fite he would gladly pay him fifty dollars for his wound, evidently realizing that the colonel's injury equaled a significant break from fighting. Fite jokingly acknowledged that he'd sell the wound for far less money than Doak offered.[17] This conversation would prove ironic for Doak during the battle of Second Manassas, as he would meet his death on the field.

In addition to Fite, the Seventh Tennessee suffered thirty-three casualties compared to twenty-four inflicted upon the First Tennessee during the action around Cedar Run. Among the wounded of the First Tennessee was twenty-one-year-old Capt. Joseph Lusk. Lusk's left arm was so severely wounded that it had to be amputated. The Fourteenth Tennessee had 135 casualties, 19 fatal, including Lt. Col. George Harrell of Company A. The Fifth Alabama had light casualties, with one killed and eight wounded.[18]

Heavy rains on the following day provided relief from the heat for those wounded and unhurt alike. On August 11, the Tennessee Brigade moved away from Cedar Mountain with "the smell of putrefying flesh heavy in the Virginia air."[19]

The Tennessee Brigade had played a significant role in Jackson's fulfillment of his objective to limit Pope's progress. The brigade moved to Gordonsville, where Lee's Army of Northern Virginia developed a plan to again attack Pope. The Union general was camped between the Rappahannock and the Rapidan rivers; Lee saw an attack upon this position, with Pope having to cross the Rappahannock, as being full of opportunity to destroy Pope's army.[20]

Pope grew aware of his dangerous position and on August 18 moved his army north, across the Rappahannock. Lee perceived this move as cause to change his plans. Jackson's corps, including Hill's division, was then ordered to cross the Rappahannock, proceed behind the Bull Run Mountains, and advance to Manassas Junction, where the Confederates would destroy Pope's supply base. The Tennessee Brigade remained in reserve near Warrenton Spring Ford until August 24, at which time they were relieved.[21]

The Tennessee Brigade marched twenty-five miles under intensely hot conditions on the twenty-fifth, camping that night at Salem White Plains. Capt. W.F. Fulton, 5th AL, noted that he and others under "Generals Lee and Jackson had been playing hide and seek for some days" with General Pope and that they fully "expected something to happen at any hour." The next day, the Tennesseans passed through Thoroughfare Gap, described as "a narrow passageway worn in the course of years by the water currents forcing their way down the mountain side, just wide enough to permit the passage of an army line … That night the brigade moved within four miles of Pope's supply base."22

Fulton wrote sixty years later that "at a swinging gait we moved out, and all day, until late at night, we pushed on." He stressed that he exhibited the confidence of so many other Confederates in their leadership, noting, "No one knew whither or for what purpose, but all were content, as 'Old Jack' was at the helm." The men of the brigade had been largely oblivious to their destination until this point, yet with the objective now becoming clear, they responded in kind. A brigade member explained, "We soon became aware that we were getting between General Pope and Washington City, and what a stimulus this was to our weary bodies … and we forgot our weariness in contemplating the unique status of affairs. Here we were marching straight toward Washington … with Longstreet and General Lee bringing up the rear, hurrying to keep up with Pope."23

The Tennessee Brigade marched approximately fifty miles with few supplies. Green corn constituted the majority of nutrition for the soldiers during their advancement toward Pope's position, yet that obstacle was to be largely eliminated upon the brigade's arrival at Manassas Junction. J.H. Moore, 7th TN, remembered the Tennessee Brigade leading Hill's division into Manassas Junction and that other troops who had arrived earlier had captured large amounts of supplies capable of fulfilling the hunger of each member of the brigade.24

Another soldier added, "General Pope's army stores fell into our hands, great piles of crackers, bacon, etc., in abundance. A soldier would stick his bayonet in a big chunk of bacon and start off with it, but soon he would take out his knife and cut it in half—too heavy for a tired man—and when he got to the stopping place, there was wasn't much left."25

While the men of Hill's division looted the sutlers' houses and other supply agencies, Gen. Issac Trimble, who had been among the first Confederates to enter Manassas, watched in a state of shame. Gen. Jackson was evidently not as concerned over the pillaging of his troops as he was about one of the items his men had uncovered in a rather large quantity. Capt. W.F. Fulton described the incident: "General Jackson sent to A.P. Hill an order for an officer with a detail of men—the officer must be, according to the order, a strictly sober man, and also the detail. When they reported, Jackson told them he was informed that there were barrels of whiskey in the captured commissaries, and he wanted them to take charge of it, to knock the heads out of those barrels, and see that it was all poured out on the ground. 'For,' said he, 'I fear that whisky more than I do Pope's army.' This was a wonderful prohibition speech indeed by the immortal Stonewall. He knew that many of the men would indulge to excess, and would be in no condition to meet the events soon to follow."[26]

The festivities and merriment of the morning proved to be short-lived, as the Tennessee Brigade received orders to fall in. As the command was issued, members of the brigade were helping themselves to the bounty of the captured Union supply houses and attempting to fill their haversacks.[27]

The brigade moved forward from their position to the left of the Manassas Junction depot toward a retreating artillery piece. The men advanced approximately half a mile when the Union infantry came within sight, one mile to the north. Gen. Jackson ordered Archer to support an artillery battery in taking the Union position.[28]

J.H. Moore, 7th TN, recalled a sudden Confederate advance toward the enemy, yet W.F. Fulton, 5th AL, submitted a slightly different version of the opening action in writing, "Now, as we moved on up into the old field encompassing Manassas, looking off toward Washington, we saw a great blue line of men with guns, marching in line of battle, with the Stars and Stripes floating out on the breeze, coming straight toward us. We were drawn up in line to await their coming. Archer's Brigade was here alone; the rest of our division had gone in another direction. As the blue line approached nearer and nearer, the officers of our command were persistent in their orders: 'Don't shoot, men. Stand steady and let them come on.' And they came briskly on, making right for us, and it seemed that they would walk right over us. Our men began to get nervous and would raise their guns, but the officers were sharp in the command not to shoot: 'Put down your guns, and stand steady.'"[29]

Gen. Archer noted that Jackson's order was followed and effectively carried out, breaking the Union infantry line and resulting in the pursuit of the retreating Federals as far as the terrain allowed the rapid transporting of the artillery. J.H. Moore stated he heard Gen. Archer explain that the time had arrived to test the two armies' fighting skills and that victory would depend upon fighting alone.[30]

W.F. Fulton recalled hearing neither Gen. Archer's proclamation nor Jackson's orders, yet his respect for the latter and pride in the performance of his fellow brigade members were clearly documented in his statement of the events: "Just to our rear, on a little elevation, a battery of artillery unlimbered. Who they were or where they came from I never knew, but I saw General Jackson sitting on old Sorrel as stiff as a board, with his eyes intent on that blue line … and suddenly every one of those guns blazed away, right over our heads, sending their missiles into that blue line, which by this time was within a stone's throw. As the artillery fired we raised a yell and made a dash forward, our guns blazing away. That line of Yanks melted away like wax in a blaze of fire, and it became a fox and dog chase for quite a distance. They broke without firing a gun. Archer's men were running at good speed, firing as they ran. In passing a house on the way, many of the Yanks entered and began throwing their guns out of the windows, as much as to say: 'We surrender.' The officer in command of this body of men was killed among the first shots. It was said these men were sent out from Washington to drive off the cavalry which they supposed were the only troops at Manassas. Anyway, this was one of the remarkable incidents of the war that I was to witness."[31]

The Nineteenth Georgia was sent in pursuit of the retreating enemy while Archer led the remaining brigade regiments along a railroad track. Near the railroad bridge, Archer's Brigade encountered the enemy making a stand on the opposite side of Bull Run. The Tennessee Brigade exchanged fire with the Federals for half an hour and advanced a half a mile after carrying the Union position.[32]

F.S. Harris recalled adjutant George A. Howard calling Archer's attention to a body of Federal troops in his front. Archer knew his troops must take action and ordered Shoemaker's battery to turn loose on the enemy. Shoemaker's aim was deadly, an accomplishment in itself due to the distance of one hundred yards or less existing between the lines and Shoemaker possessing only long fuse for the cannon. His grapeshot and shell had "killed nearly all of them."[33]

Archer's Brigade had assisted in taking the Union line and inflicting a great number of casualties. Union general George Taylor and several of his men were killed and many more captured. An even higher number dispersed, supposedly heading toward Washington. Archer's Brigade ceased their pursuit and re-crossed Bull Run. Archer took a strategic position on a hill overlooking the bridge, where he remained until approximately ten o'clock that night, when orders were given to return to the railroad junction.[34]

Archer's entire brigade suffered minor casualties in this phase of the second Manassas battle, with four killed and only seventeen wounded. Company H, Seventh Tennessee, entered the contest with a dozen men. All of them were killed or wounded in the early action, a number of casualties greater than the remaining regimental companies combined.[35]

Col. Peter Turney commanded the First Tennessee Regiment at this point of the war, while Maj. S.G. Shepard led the Seventh Tennessee and Col. W.A. Forbes headed up the Fourteenth Tennessee. Capt. F.M. Johnston was at the helm of the Nineteenth Georgia; Capt. Thomas Bush led the Fifth Alabama Battalion.

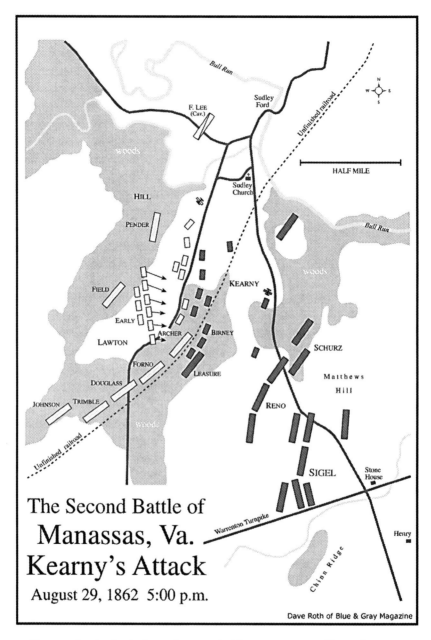

The Second Battle of
Manassas, Va.
Kearny's Attack
August 29, 1862 5:00 p.m.

Dave Roth of Blue & Gray Magazine

That night Archer's Brigade joined other units in Hill's Light Division in leaving the area of recently captured Union supply warehouses, sutlers' stores, and trains. The stores were set afire, and the light from their flames illuminated the paths of Hill's men heading toward Centreville. The brigade moved up the Warrenton Turnpike, crossed Bull Run and at daylight on

August 28 turned south to align themselves with the remaining divisions of Jackson's corps.[36]

Branch's Brigade formed to Archer's rear with Field positioned on Archer's right. Federal soldiers under Pope, progressing to the rear in an effort to reconstitute communication, hit this arrangement around five o'clock in the afternoon. Archer moved forward in an effort to support two batteries situated in an open field three hundred yards ahead. Federal artillery on Archer's left and front propelled heavy shell and round-shot fire toward Archer, yet no losses were inflicted and the Tennesseans were never actually engaged in this phase of the battle.[37]

Capt. W.F. Fulton of the Fifth Alabama documented the events of the afternoon, emphasizing the bravery and action of his brigade commander in writing, "we came out into an old field and were drawn up in line of battle … in the distance a battery of artillery, accompanied by infantry … began firing on us … General Archer continued to ride up and down our line as we lay sprawled on the ground. The men at last appealed to him to dismount, as he evidently provoked their fire. A piece of shell came ricocheting along the ground right in line with me as I lay prostrate. It finally reached me, almost spent, and struck me on the head, doing no damage, but affording me the privilege of saying I was wounded by a piece of shell at Second Manassas."[38]

Late that night, the weary and haggard members of Archer's Brigade moved into a railroad cut located in a section of woods. They remained there until the next morning, when they were assigned to the left side of the division and shared that position with Braxton's battery.[39]

At three o'clock in the afternoon, Hill ordered Archer to move to his right. Archer's men on the extreme right then rested on a road that formed a right angle with the railroad. From this point Archer could support the various brigades of Hill's Division that were becoming fatigued from earlier action. By this time most of Jackson's corps had been engaged with Federal troops for four days with little or no rest; many were half-starved.[40]

An hour later Archer received a request via Gen. Pender's aide-de-camp to relieve Pender. Archer was presently located near Gen. Hill, who quickly agreed to allow Archer's repositioning. Archer's Brigade began moving into the railroad cut when Archer realized Federal troops were filing into the cut from the opposite direction. Archer felt it best to wait until his men were properly aligned before issuing the order to attack.

As half of Turney's First Tennessee Regiment, the last of the brigade's units to enter the cut, took position, Archer pointed to his left, noting the enemy's position, and ordered Turney's regiment to fire. Turney's men poured lead into the oncoming Federals to the extent that Gen. Archer wrote that the firing was exercised "with great effect." The Union response was furious as an assault began along Archer's entire front. Archer's men held firmly to their position for more than twenty minutes, an amazing accomplishment due to the fact each man averaged only two cartridges at this point.[41]

As the sun set on the twenty-ninth, Archer's soldiers reentered their posts left during the countercharge against the third Union assault. Many brigade members lay on their guns that night in an attempt to lessen the effect of a surprise attack. Each company of the Fourteenth Tennessee sent out soldiers to retrieve cartridge boxes from dead and wounded men of Pope's Federal troops that night, and by the end of the next day, a large number of Union soldiers would ironically suffer from wounds this ammunition inflicted.[42]

On the morning of the thirtieth, Archer's Brigade changed places with Early's Brigade, located on Archer's left. Lt. Col. N.J. George, 1st TN, a man whom Archer noted was "always ready and anxious for the most daring service," was given command of 130 men to relieve Gen. Early's pickets. The pickets soon began a rapid exchange of fire with the Union skirmishers located in woods along the Confederate front. Archer sent Lt. O.H. Thomas, his aide-de-camp, to ascertain the cause of the shooting and to caution George's men against depleting the already low ammunition supply. Thomas crisscrossed the entire picket line, noted its exposure to the Yankee sharpshooters, and reported the Confederate fire was essential to holding their location.[43]

Serving with Lt. Col. George as a picket that night was Theodore Hartman, Co. A, 14th TN. Hartman recalled years later the unique wound he inflicted upon a Yankee soldier and an encounter with the legendary Stonewall Jackson. "I was on picket duty covering the front of our regiment … Our position was on the extreme left of our army, and we were engaged in sharpshooting with the enemy's pickets, some fifty or sixty yards away … My post was at the left of our line, and I had fortified it by placing a large tree immediately in front of me … It was about 3 p.m. when I heard a horse approaching from my right along the graded roadbed. Upon looking around I saw General Jackson on his old claybank, unattended by an aid or courier. As he neared me and was about to pass on I halted him, saluted, and said: 'General, this is our extreme left; the enemy is right out there.' He returned my salute and asked: 'To what command do you belong, and where is your colonel?' I told him, he again saluted and rode off in the direction I pointed. On resuming my watch my next tree comrade, Cornelius Mehigan … said ' … some … bluecoat has found my position and shot at me several times, but I can't locate him.' … I then told him to put his cap on the end of his gun and let it show at the side of the tree; and if he bites at it, I may be able to locate him. He did so, and the fellow bit all right. He was behind a tree just large enough to cover him when he stood erect, but in stooping over to shoot he exposed a portion of his body most serviceable in a sitting position. As he ... proceeded to draw a bead on Mehigan's cap, I trained my rifle on the exposed portion of his anatomy ... and sent a bullet through it. He dropped his gun and made a record jump, both for height and distance, and lit running."[44]

Around four o'clock that afternoon, Archer received orders from Gen. Hill to move to the right and support the soldiers now becoming heavily engaged. As Archer received his order, his pickets were being pushed back and his brigade fell under attack. Lt. Thomas Herndon saw three Federal lines, spaced one hundred yards apart, approach and push back his company's skirmish line.[45]

Intense fighting ensued and lasted ten to thirty minutes, ending only with Archer's troops charging through the railroad cut and forcing the Union soldiers into the woods from which they'd charged. The front Federal line was pushed backward into the second, and it into the third. The Tennessee Brigade acted largely alone in this charge, joined only by Col. Smith's regiment of Early's Brigade. Early recalled that Col. Turney's First Tennessee, on Archer's right, retired with Smith's troops. Again members of Archer's Brigade raided the dead Union soldiers for additional ammunition.[46]

Confederate general Pender issued an order for a general advance at five o'clock on the afternoon of the thirtieth. Archer's Brigade, located on Pender's left, moved forward and proceeded through woods. The brigades entered an open field near the Federal battalions. Six large Union cannon were located to Archer's left and at a distance of about three hundred yards. Archer sent his regiments toward them.[47]

Pvt. Theodore Hartman, Co. A, 14th TN, participated in the charge toward the battery and wrote of its events. He stated, "Came into an open field and about one hundred yards from another body of woods on our left ... In front of us on the summit of a gentle slope, was a light field battery, which promptly saluted us with grape and canister. We started for that battery on a run, and ... to our left a full regiment of bluecoats, and they started to take us in on the flank. We were in a very critical position surely—a battery in front and a fresh full regiment on our flank. We were 'ambushed.'"[48]

Archer reported that the circumstances that Hartman noted as an "ambush" failed to cause his brigade to waver despite exposure to fire from two batteries. The Union cannon continued pelting Archer's and Pender's brigades until the dogged Confederates moved within seventy-five yards of their guns. Sensing the Confederates' tenacity, the Union battery men retreated without their cannon. The six large guns fell evenly to Archer and Pender.[49]

Pvt. Hartman described the subsequent events: "After the capture of the battery, our lines re-formed, and we proceeded cautiously, meeting no opposition until dark. We were ... going up a sharp incline, when we saw a dark line come between us and the horizon just over the crown of the ridge. We halted ... The dark line was allowed to come to the top of the ridge, within easy gunshot, before they were challenged ... General Thomas ... rode close enough to satisfy himself that they were Federal troops and shouted: 'Men, they are enemies!' There was no time to say 'Fire!' Two thousand rifles spit fire and sent as many bullets at the dark line on the ridge."[50]

The trek through the woods led to Pender's and Archer's Brigades crossing one another's direction, with Archer now positioned on Pender's right. Order was restored to both units when they then moved forward. Near the Lewis house, the Confederates encountered an undetermined number of Federal infantrymen whose members called out, "For the Union." With this verbal challenge, Archer's men sent a single volley in the direction of the voices, whose owners were now somewhat sheltered by the increasing darkness.[51]

A brigade member recalled, "our commanders formed us in a hollow square and ordered us to sleep on our arms. We were not easily wooed to dreamland by the groans of the poor fellows in the big house near by ... I was awakened by a gentle rain. As soon as it was light I walked out to see how many Yanks we had killed ... I found the place where they had stood marked by a thousand new Belgian rifles loaded, but not a single dead or wounded soldier. Well, a bullet is a small thing, after all, and I am now glad we did not kill any of those raw Dutchmen. Quite a number came out of the numerous little thickets after it was broad daylight, jabbering any and everything but English, and surrendered. Our interpreter said they told him they ... were substitutes ... hired by loyal patriots ... who did not believe in fighting for their country." [52]

Archer reported an undetermined number of Union prisoners and arms were collected during that night and the next morning. Thomas Herndon of the Fourteenth Tennessee estimated thirty thousand rifles and prisoners were taken in addition to an impressive variety of supplies.[53]

The cost of achieving victory had been high. As in previous engagements, the losses to the brigade would largely remain un-replenished. Col. William A. Forbes of the Fourteenth Tennessee, who had been commissioned on June 6, 1861 at the age of thirty-six, was mortally wounded on the thirtieth while leading the capture of the Federal battery. Capt. Thomas Bush, 5th AL[54], was wounded on the thirtieth and died September 4.

Bush was immortalized in the words of A.N. Porter, Co. B, 5th AL, who explained that Bush's friends openly desired that his life had been extended. Bush's bravery, leadership, and virtues, Porter stated, would have undoubtedly resulted in his name being eternally revered in the pages of history rather than serving as the subject of campfire memoriams. Bush's servant, a young man named Charles, carried Bush's sword home to Mrs. Harriet Bush Jenkins, the captain's mother.[55]

Thomas Herndon, 14th TN, spent eighteen days in a field hospital before being moved to Warrenton. When the hospital and other available buildings became occupied, a one-hundred-acre field was filled with tents to be used as hospital sites. Herndon and his tent mates, John Wiking and Ephriam Manson, both of Company L, Fourteenth Tennessee, were taken to a nearby mansion where "some splendid ladies" provided them with care.[56]

Col. William A. Forbes, 14th TN. Forbes was wounded at the Battle of Second Manassas and died at a field hospital on September 2, 1862. Courtesy of Virginia Military Institute.

Lt. Charles M. Hooper replaced Capt. Bush as commander of the Fifth Alabama following the latter's death. Col. Forbes's mortal wound necessitated the leadership of the Fourteenth Tennessee going to Major James W. Lockert. Throughout the events of Second Manassas, the First and Seventh Tennessee infantry regiments and Nineteenth Georgia experienced consistency in regimental command under Col. Peter Turney, Maj. Samuel G. Shepard, and Capt. F.M. Johnston respectively.[57]

Rufus Doak, Co. H, 7ʰ TN. The first lieutenant was wounded at Second Manassas and died in September 1862. Courtesy of Paul Gibson.

The activities of Second Manassas had resulted in 21 members of the Tennessee Brigade being killed and some 213 wounded. The First Tennessee suffered fifty-seven casualties, including the wounded James Turney, C.M.M. Tuley, and J.W. Cunningham. N.G. Norvill of Company D was one of the battle's fatalities. The level of casualties had temporarily lowered the number of effectives in the Seventh Tennessee to less than one hundred.[58]

Lt. William M. Harkreader, 7th TN. Harkreader lost his left arm at Second Manassas and was captured later in the war at Marietta, Georgia. After the war, Harkreader served as president of Union Bank and Trust Company in Nashville and was an active Mason and a member of the Methodist Church. Having served as an officer in Confederate veteran organizations, Harkreader was buried in Lebanon, Tennessee with comrades serving as pallbearers. He was seventy-four. Courtesy of Confederate Veteran.

Archer consistently held the characteristic of recognizing the contributions of those around him rather than seeking personal accolades. An example of this is found in Archer's official report relating to Second Manassas. In the conclusion of his report dated March 1, 1863, Gen. Archer specifically recognized the gallantry of Lt. Col. N.J. George of the First Tennessee, largely for his leadership of the Confederate pickets on the last night of Second Manassas. Lt. Hooper, 5th AL, and Dr. J.H.G. Turkett were noticed as well, the latter for "conspicuous valor" noted while fighting effectively though his horse had been shot from under him and for serving as Gen. Archer's courier. Pvt. Francis M. Barnes, Co. A, 14th TN, also received Archer's highest remarks for his rescue of the regimental flag "from the hands of the wounded color-bearer" and subsequently carrying it as he charged the Federal battery. O.H. Thomas, Archer's aide-de-camp, was the only of Archer's staff officers present and thus also received the general's grateful recognition.[59]

This is a payroll voucher from the Thirteenth Alabama issued to W.L. Adams. For five months service, from April to September 1862, Adams received fifty-five dollars. Courtesy of Shiloh Relics.

September 1, 1862 saw the Tennessee Brigade held in a reserve capacity while generals Gregg and Thomas and Pender's Brigades met the retreating armies of Pope, bound for Washington at Chantilly or Ox Hill.

One soldier recalled that in the midst of a rainstorm, "General Jackson ... moved rapidly around to a place called 'Ox Hill,' where he struck the retreating army of Pope ... and produced confusion in their ranks ... This encounter with the retreating foe occurred amid rain and a thunderstorm, and it was here that an aide from General Hill rode up and reported that the ammunition was wet and on that account they wished to retire. General Jackson is said to have replied, 'Give my compliments to General Hill and tell him the Yankee ammunition is as wet as his; to stay where he is.'"[60]

CHAPTER TEN

The Maryland Campaign Harper's Ferry, Antietam, and Sheperdstown

Following the Confederate success at Second Manassas, Gen. Lee developed a plan to move into Maryland. Historian C. Wallace Cross Jr. has explained the idea behind Lee's movement was multifaceted. Aggression in Maryland and eventually Pennsylvania, under Lee's deductions, might have lowered the Union defenses at Washington. In addition, the heavy pro-Confederate element in Maryland could have grown and thus benefited Lee's underfed and tattered army while allowing Virginia farmers to gather their crops free of Yankee harassment. Ultimately Lee felt that in Maryland he might destroy Pope's Army of the Potomac. In the early stages of planning his tactics, Lee discovered that Pope had lost his command to George McClellan. This information was disturbing to Lee, who held the highest respect for McClellan's abilities.[1] Nonetheless, Gen. Lee's plans were implemented.

The condition of the members of the Tennessee Brigade differed little from those of other brigades in the Army of Northern Virginia. It has been recorded that a large number of Archer's soldiers were barefooted and lacked proper clothing.[2] Perhaps the motivation to reach and control the supply houses of the North somehow motivated Lee's army toward its boldest move to date.

The Tennessee Brigade crossed the broad Potomac River at the Point of Rocks on September 6, 1862. That night, with orders to rendezvous at Frederick, Maryland, Archer's men ate green corn cooked on fires of fence rails that had encircled the cornfields earlier in the day.[3] Those individuals attempting to rejoin their commands within the Army of Northern Virginia fared similarly.

Capt. Will J. Muse, 1st TN, was leading one hundred men returning to service from Richmond area hospitals. These men headed toward Frederick, Maryland with three days' worth of rations that ran out approximately one hundred miles from the Confederate army. Muse's plight was worsened by the fact that most of the countryside he and his "followers" traversed had already been raided of supplies. Muse placed his men into squads of ten men with the understanding that they would fend for themselves. Muse's near-famished squad encountered a hog during their march, and Muse's order to kill it was immediately carried out. The hog was shot and carried to a stream, where it was dressed. The carcass was removed from the water and covered with grass. Muse's group set fire to the grass, and when the fire had extinguished itself, the men divided the hog and ate it with no bread or any form of seasoning. The next day the same group feasted upon a farmer's ripe tomatoes before reaching the Tennessee Brigade in Frederick.[4]

The Tennessee Brigade remained in Frederick until September 10, 1862, a period of approximately four days. On the tenth, Gen. Archer led his men back across the Potomac, spending the night seven miles northwest of Martinsburg, near the depot. The brigade then advanced to Harper's Ferry, reaching the garrison on the thirteenth. Hill's division, including the Tennessee Brigade, led the advance upon the city and bivouacked that night at Halltown, approximately two miles from the Union defenses. Gen. Lee intended to eliminate the Federal stronghold at Harper's Ferry before probing more deeply into Northern soil. Gen. Jackson was in charge of the two divisions assigned to attack the garrison while Gen. Lee took a position intended to negate any attempted retreat.[5]

The Tennessee Brigade spent most of the day of September 14 establishing communication with other Confederate units that, combined with Archer's Brigade, surrounded Harper's Ferry. The establishment of effective communication would enable Gen. Jackson to determine if the various Confederate divisions were in the proper position to begin the attack upon Harper's Ferry. The use of signals proved ineffective, and Jackson sent forth a courier to each point where he deemed necessary.[6]

The brigades of Archer, Pender, Field, Branch, and Gregg, along with batteries under Lt. Col. R.L. Walker, comprised A.P. Hill's division at this point of the war. Regiments of Archer's Brigade and their respective commanders were the First Tennessee, with Col. Peter Turney leading; the Seventh Tennessee, under Maj. Shepard; and the Fourteenth Tennessee, under the command of Lt. Col. James Lockert, who had replaced Forbes following his mortal wounding. The Nineteenth Georgia, under the command of Maj. J.H. Neal and Capt. Hooper, led the Fifth Alabama Infantry Battalion.[7]

Archer's Brigade stood with the Shenandoah River to their rear and facing northeast toward the Union position of Bolivar Heights. Field's and Pender's brigades joined Archer as the time drew closer to attempt to secure possession of the Federal garrison.[8]

As evening approached on September 14, the brigades of Archer, Fields, and Pender left their positions along the Winchester and Potomac Railroad and used a back road to advance toward the southern portion of the Federal defenses located on Bolivar Heights. The more lengthy Federal detachment under Col. D.S. Miles faced northwest; the lesser line faced southwest. From the latter direction, Archer, Field, and Pender moved in. Hill's division obliqued right until his men made contact with the waters of the Shenandoah River. Jackson noticed Federal infantry lacking artillery support occupying a high point on the extreme Federal left, protected only by fallen timber. The brigades of Archer, Pender and Field were directed to gain control of the hill while Branch and Gregg moved along the river to gain a new position to the left and rear of the Union defenses.[9]

Archer's skirmishers to the right of the road being used for their approach soon established contact with enemy skirmishers. Gen. Archer quickly formed a line of battle and advanced at an even pace with the left side of the brigade tracing the road. The Union pickets steadily retreated under Archer's advance, offering limited resistance, until the Tennesseans neared their objective at the crest of the hill and were coming within clear sight and easy range of the Union batteries. Archer's troops moved from an open field into woods on his right in an attempt to flank the Union guns. The Tennesseans moved as rapidly as possible, yet the rough ground and entanglement of the cut timber proved largely impenetrable. Darkness drew heavy and combined with the slow progress of the brigade in the rugged terrain to cause Archer to halt for the night. Archer had his men within four hundred yards of the Union cannon as the Tennesseans, Alabamians, and Georgians of his brigade spent the night laying upon their arms. From this proximity the soldiers of the Tennessee Brigade would move forward the next morning.[10]

Confederate artillery began firing upon Harper's Ferry soon after sunrise on the morning of the fifteenth. Lt. Col. R.L. Walker bombarded the Harper's Ferry area with his entire battery from one thousand yards to the southeast, along Loudoun Heights. Maj. Gen. McLaws provided minor artillery support from Maryland Heights, across the Potomac from the Federal defenses. Col.

Douglas, commanding a detachment of Lawton's Brigade, moved into the bottomland situated to the southeast of School House Ridge and slightly northwest of Bolivar Heights. From here Lawton's troops were to support A.P. Hill's advance.[11]

Following an hour of intense Confederate cannonade, the Federal guns ceased all return fire, and the resulting order for the termination of Confederate battery fire signaled the moment for attacking the town. Gen. Pender began his advance, resulting in the reopening of Federal battery fire. Captains Pegram and Crenshaw of Hill's artillery division responded to the renewal of the Federal battery with rapid fire into their position. Meanwhile, Archer's men struggled to negotiate the abates that so effectively hampered their efforts to relocate to the rear of the Federal guns, as Gen. Hill had ordered. Finally clearing the twisted timber and positioning themselves to charge the Union front, Archer's men saw the white flag of surrender appear.[12]

Capt. W.J. Muse had returned to the First Tennessee only five days earlier and had been placed in charge of a skirmish line at Harper's Ferry. He held his men there in a relatively safe position at the base of a cedar-studded hill. Joining the Tennessee Brigade during its advance through the cut timber, Muse and his skirmishers "sprang up and over the timber as though it was only sage grass" at the command of "Forward Tennesseans." Muse's enthusiastic charge up the hill overlooking the Federal garrison was greatly lessened at the sight of the flag of surrender flying over the fort.[13]

Archer's Brigade and the other units of A.P. Hill's division were given the task of accepting the surrender of the garrison's eleven thousand defenders and securing the captured munitions and stores. Seventy-three artillery pieces and thirteen thousand small arms were taken in addition to the extensive number of prisoners. Captured supplies included shoes, blankets, coffee, and sugar.[14]

The captured Federal officers and enlisted men were duly paroled, and the former were given permission to hold fixed their personal baggage, swords, and pistols. Jackson later explained that the liberal terms extended to the Federal prisoners were regrettably never appreciated among US government officials. Per Gen. Lee's command, Jackson advanced toward Sharpsburg, Maryland while Hill's division safeguarded the cache.[15]

The capture of Harper's Ferry as well as its numerous defenders and supplies had cost Archer's Brigade one man killed and twenty-two wounded.[16] The immediate days ahead would prove to be much more devastating to the ranks of the brigade.

Jackson's departure to join Lee at Sharpsburg created an extensive workload for A.P. Hill's men. Felix Motlow wrote, "It was indeed a show for the private soldier to see. We believed there would be no more fighting, at least for several months."[17]

J.H. Moore, 7th TN, looked forward to the prospect of several days filled with rest; his feelings were widely shared throughout his regiment. Scarcely had Moore and his comrades finished caring for the conquered supplies when the Tennessee Brigade received orders to move to Sharpsburg. This command was actually followed before Hill's men completed the task of paroling all Union prisoners from Harper's Ferry.[18]

Archer's Brigade left Harper's Ferry at sunrise on September 17 with the appearance of a newly raised Union brigade. This was attributed to the fact that new blue uniforms that adorned most of the soldiers. The tattered battle flags gave clarification that the brigade was neither new nor Federal. However, the fast pace of the forced eighteen-mile march rapidly caused the shedding of the new attire.[19]

The Fifth Alabama had remained in Harper's Ferry to safeguard the captured Federal artillery and ensure its safe arrival in Richmond. The remaining units of the Tennessee Brigade, Turney's First Tennessee, the Seventh and Fourteenth Tennessee, and the Nineteenth Georgia moved toward Sharpsburg as the second brigade in Hill's procession. Gregg's South Carolinians led the way.[20]

Gen. Archer was, in his own words, "too unwell for duty" and turned command of the brigade over to Col. Peter Turney of the First Tennessee. Archer, moving toward the battlefield aboard an ambulance, followed the brigade. The pace of the march and the high level of heat caused a large number of Archer's men to withdraw in states of exhaustion. When the four regiments of the brigade reached Sharpsburg, only 350 men of its enrollment were capable of performing their duties.[21]

Having waded the Potomac, the Tennessee Brigade moved atop hills overlooking the valley of Antietam Creek. Here the Tennesseans heard Union soldiers cheering, signaling the retreat of fellow Confederates from a portion of the battlefield. Union general Ambrose Burnside had driven Confederates under Jones and Toombs from their positions and was threatening to take control of one of the remaining roads by which the broken Confederates could retreat.[22]

Gen. Archer resumed command of the brigade from Col. Turney as the men aligned for battle. It has been proposed that Archer made this move only because he was fighting on the soil of his native state.[23]

The Tennesseans stood on the extreme left of Hill's division, true to Hill's orders, yet were unable to see another brigade of Hill's Division from this post. Flanking right in front along the Sharpsburg Road, the Tennessee Brigade stopped and faced to the right.[24] Archer's Brigade joined others in Hill's division to bring the group's total strength to approximately two thousand. These men faced fourteen thousand troops of Gen. Ambrose Burnsides who were now highly motivated from the dislodging of Toombs' men previously defending the infamous Burnsides Bridge spanning Antietam Creek.

One of Lee's officers noticed Hill's arrival and noted the line of men descending from the surrounding hills. Lee inquired as to what flag the men were flying, and Lt. John Ramsey informed him that the troops belonged to Hill's Light Division. The arrival of Hill's division has been proclaimed "a great moment in Confederate military annals."[25]

At three o'clock in the afternoon, Archer stood to the left of troops in Branch's and Gregg's brigades, and on his right Toombs' rallied brigade waited. About six hundred yards ahead lay a stone wall that offered a strong defensive position for the Federal soldiers behind it. Between Archer and the wall, a cornfield and a freshly plowed field awaited the Confederates.[26]

Felix Motlow recorded the action of that and the following minutes. He wrote, "I distinctly remember Archer's Brigade advancing rapidly in line of battle right under the fire of their powerful artillery, until we came to a road running north and south, where we were ordered to lie down along a cornfield fence, not to be 'too impetuous,' to wait for our supports; how the enemy's sharpshooters killed some of our men through the fence cracks, they could shoot with wonderful accuracy when the fire was not returned; how after awhile 'Old Pete' ... towered up above that fence as bold as a lion it is a wonder they did not kill him, and gave the command, 'Hog drivers, advance!' how we leaped over the fence and advanced through the tangled corn."[27]

Archer wrote his mother that he had been confined to his bed the day before moving to Sharpsburg and that he was too weak to mount his horse as his brigade proceeded toward the battlefield. The sound of battle and the thought of his men entering it without him caused Archer to muster the strength to mount his horse and rejoin his troops. The general informed his mother that he never felt stronger than he did during the Battle of Antietam, but he quickly added that, upon the conclusion of the fighting, he found himself completely prostrate for two days.[28]

When Archer emerged from the cornfield, he noticed that only the Fourteenth Tennessee was with him; the other units fell back after hearing an order to do so and assuming the command had come from Archer. The Tennessee Brigade was reformed and again charged toward the stone fence that formed the western line of the forty-acre cornfield.[29]

Felix Motlow recorded the charge toward the stone fence: "We ... then beheld the enemy posted in a heavy, dark line behind a rock fence; how 'Old Pete' still led forward right in the face of their fire, and of course we went with him. These were the most accommodating Yankees we had met. They actually moved back and let the Tennessee riflemen use that rock fence for a breastwork ... the Tennessee marksmen had already exchanged the old smooth-bore musket, on the battlefield of Manassas, for the long-ranged and otherwise improved rifles … they picked them off with unerring aim by the score before they got out of range of these guns. Even their powerful artillery, that had been annoying us so grievously, had to limber up and hustle to the rear to prevent being captured."[30]

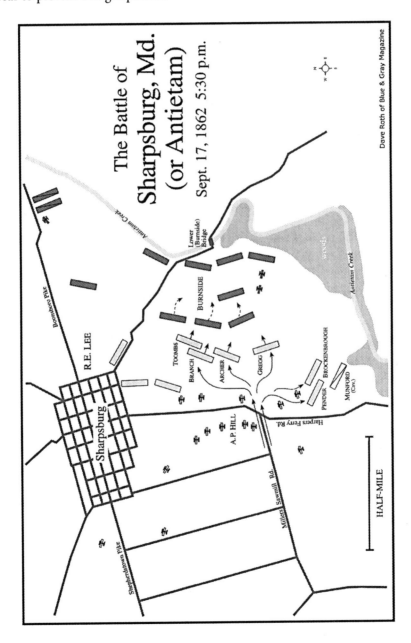

The Battle of Sharpsburg, Md. (or Antietam) Sept. 17, 1862 5:30 p.m.

Archer noted that almost one-third of his command, already reduced from illness and straggling, was lost while crossing the plowed ground yet moved forward double quick. Archer was able, with assistance from Gregg on his right, to dislodge the Twenty-third and Thirtieth Ohio regiments before stopping at the stone fence.

Maj. Gen. George H. Hildt of the Thirtieth Ohio stated that his exhausted men received erratic fire from the Confederates until posting their regimental colors atop the wall. At that point, "a withering fire was directed upon us from our left flank."[31] The Union defenders were unaware of the small number of Confederate attackers and left the wall to the Southern advantage.

A number of Archer's men reached the stone fence as the Ohioans were leaving it. Archer's left wing crossed the fence before the left side of the defenders left, resulting in the capture of Lt. Col. Jones, commander of the Thirtieth Ohio. Archer arrived momentarily, sending the remainder of his men forward. The response from the six companies of the Thirtieth Ohio, assisted by a group of rallied Connecticut soldiers, was a series of volleys that necessitated Archer's men to seek cover behind the stone fence. It is highly likely that friendly fire was a major cause of the casualties Archer's men suffered at this point of the battle. The Twelfth South Carolina was unaware the Twenty-third and Thirtieth Ohio had retreated and thus fired in the direction of the wall.[32]

Sunset approached as Branch's Brigade joined Archer's at the stone wall, thirty minutes after the Tennesseans had helped gain possession of the defensive position. McIntosh's Confederate guns, captured earlier, had now been recaptured, and Braxton's battery also opened up on the Union soldiers. Brig. Gen. Branch, whose command had worked so effectively with Archer's Brigade, was killed by a Union sharpshooter.

It has been observed in numerous accounts of the battle of Antietam that Hill's arrival saved the day for the Confederacy. Both armies claimed victory; neither admitted defeat. R.T. Mockbee, 14th TN, wrote an article on the debate forty-six years later. In it he stated, "General Lee's position would have been untenable in a very short time in view of Burnside's victorious advance, cutting Lee's line of communication by the Shepherdstown road, and … continued his advance, and completely turning Lee's right, compelling him to yield the position he had with such obstinacy held in the face of more than double his own army, with a loss unprecedented in any battle of the same duration. Lee had no men to spare from his already hard-pressed and thin lines of his left and center to meet and check Burnside's advance; and I believe that but for the timely arrival of A.P. Hill's Division and the promptness with which he, his subordinates, and the brave men under them hurled back Burnside's hosts of Lee's right Sharpsburg could not be called a drawn battle

... A.P. Hill's Division lay behind that stone fence all day, at first expecting a renewal of the contest, and then praying that Burnside would try to do for us what we had done for them—to drive us from behind that stone fence."[33]

Felix Motlow added, "How a few fresh men might have turned this rout of Burnside into a complete rout of McClellan's whole army. But, alas! Lee had put in his last man, and had no more reinforcements. We stayed at that rock fence all that night and all the next day waiting for McClellan to attack. He did not attack, but was preparing for it and receiving heavy reinforcements. As rapidly as steam could rush them from the North, they were hurrying to that battlefield; therefore when night came we silently moved out under orders, and had the pleasure of another cool bath crossing back to the Old Virginia shore. It reminded us of what we had read of some of Washington's masterly retreats from the presence of an overwhelming foe."[34]

At nine o'clock on the morning of the eighteenth, Gen. Archer again transferred his brigade's command to Col. Peter Turney. Gen. Archer was completely exhausted from the action of the seventeenth and retired from the field. As the Army of Northern Virginia re-crossed the Potomac at Shepherdstown, Archer's Brigade served with the brigades of Branch and Gregg as the army's rearguards. The casualties inflicted upon the Tennessee Brigade were rather high, especially when viewed as a percentage of men actually capable of serving. Fifteen deaths and ninety wounded men were the result of the short period of intense fighting for the 350 members who saw action. The Seventh Tennessee had been reduced to less than one hundred able-bodied men prior to the battle at Antietam; more than thirty of its officers and men were killed or wounded there.[35]

The wounded of the First Tennessee included Neil Hedgepeth, J. George, and W. M. Finley. Those killed at Sharpsburg from the First Tennessee included T.B. Gunter, Henry W. Minor, and J.W. Stockstill. Connected with the surgical unit of the army, A.G. Emory remarked that his report of the dead of the Fourteenth Tennessee was deficient due to the regiment's movement and the "impracticability of sick calls under such circumstances." He did note the deaths of four privates of the Fourteenth Tennessee. These were Belfield Marshall (Co. B), Leonidus Lynn (Co. B), James Horn (Co. B), and John Fields (Co. A).[36] These statistics, reflected in similar and oftentimes greater proportions among other units, North and South alike, contributed to Antietam becoming the bloodiest single day of the war.

Lee's crossing of the Potomac resulted in many of the wounded Confederates being left in the town of Sharpsburg. The surgeon of the Fourteenth Tennessee, Dr. Daniel F. Wright, had remained with the wounded and was in charge of the field hospital. Stephen Turner Rives of the Fourteenth Tennessee was among Wright's patients and was sent temporarily to Johnson's

Island before being released prior to the war's end. Col. William McComb, himself wounded at Antietam, wrote of Pvt. Rives, "Comrade S.T. Rives was an ideal soldier, and I always depended on him in any emergency."[37]

Stephen Turner Rives, 14th TN. Rives was wounded and captured at Antietam and served time as a prisoner of war at Johnson's Island. He died at the age of eighty-three and was buried in Hopkinsville, Kentucky. Courtesy of Confederate Veteran.

Capt. Will Muse also suffered a wound at Antietam, his first battle following a lengthy hospital stay for a previous injury. Muse was shot in the left side as his regiment left the cornfield following the brigade's regrouping. He continued across the plowed field until hit again, this time by a minié ball that passed through his left thigh. Muse was carried to the safety of a field hospital by Capt. Daniel, who later received a shoulder wound in the battle. Unable to be moved, Muse, like Rives, remained behind when the Potomac was crossed. Muse remained in a field hospital for six weeks as a prisoner of war. Exchanged in November of 1862, Muse rejoined his company in February of 1863.[38]

Those members of the Tennessee Brigade not wounded or too fatigued to march moved toward Shepherdstown to drive back the Union army that was crossing the Potomac near the ferry. Three-quarters of a mile from the ferry, a line of battle was formed in a cornfield. Pender's Brigade moved toward the ferry while troops of Gen. Gregg and Col. Thomas moved farther right.[39]

Archer received orders from Gen. Hill to assume command of three other brigades present: his own, with Col. Turney leading; Lane's; and Fields's; lined up respectively left to right. These three brigades were to support Pender in his advance. Pender sent word to Archer regarding an attempt from the Federals to flank Archer's command; Archer responded with flanking moves himself and moved in the direction of the enemy. Archer noted that the advance his men made toward the Union lines was done under the heaviest artillery fire he had personally seen up to that time.[40]

Felix Motlow recalled, "McClellan ... under the fire of his powerful artillery ... did cross over a number of brigades, intending, no doubt, to cross over his whole army. He had positive orders from his superiors to do so. Lee believed it. He had halted Longstreet's corps, that had proceeded a considerable distance, and ordered him to countermarch, intending to give McClellan battle again. But Stonewall Jackson, who had charge of the rear, hurled A.P. Hill's division against those brigades before too many of them got over, and drove them right under the fire of their powerful artillery back into the river, without using a single cannon. Then again did the Tennesseans pick them off, as they struggled through the waters of the sparkling Potomac. The broad surface of the river was black with dead bodies floating down."[41]

About that time, a courier came from Lee in hot haste for Jackson— hunting for his 'right arm' with which to strike. It had already struck. Jackson quietly sat on his horse, under the fire of shot and shell, watching his men repulse the enemy, and remarked, "Tell Gen. Lee that by the blessing of Providence they will soon be driven back." The Union acknowledged a loss of three thousand killed and drowned in this affair and two hundred prisoners. The Confederate loss was 31 killed and 231 wounded.[42]

Archer again revealed his tendency to readily praise the efforts and contributions of others as he wrote that it was impossible to award too much praise to the men and officers of his brigade for their conduct in the battle at Shepherdstown. Holding their position until dark, the brigade began a late-night march to Martinsburg while mourning the brigade casualties of the six killed and forty-nine wounded at the river.[43]

The Tennessee Brigade moved to the area between Winchester and Harper's Ferry. With other brigades of Hill's division, a much-needed rest was received, and the number of effectives grew as stragglers returned and the condition of the sick and wounded improved. John Fite was among the wounded returning to the brigade. He had been wounded in the August battle at Cedar Mountain and had received a furlough in the process. He later recorded that on his return to Virginia from Tennessee, he shared a brief train ride with Stonewall Jackson.[44]

According to Fite, as the train stopped in Farmville, Virginia, a gentleman dispersed red clay pipes to a large number of passengers. He, Gen. Jackson, and others shared a cup-sized pipe full of tobacco as "we all took a few whiffs of it." Upon reaching Richmond, Fite learned of his company's location and returned to them just outside of Winchester.[45]

During Fite's recuperation, the Tennessee Brigade surgeons were able to accurately assess the damage inflicted upon the troops during the recent engagements. The October 1862 report of C.B. McGuire, a surgeon of the Confederate army, noted that the First Tennessee had sixty-four men sick, nine of whom were sent to the hospital. One man, Sgt. Thomas J. Denson, had been discharged with chronic diarrhea. Thirty-nine men with various afflictions had returned to duty. These figures were from an aggregate strength of forty-eight officers and four hundred men. The most frequent ailment was varying forms of diarrhea, with some eighteen cases being reported. Eleven men suffered from fevers of various types with ulcers. Respiratory and nervous-system diseases accounted for most of the remaining complaints.[46]

Similar numbers came from the report on the 10 officers and 225 men of the Seventh Tennessee. Some sixty-five men had reported illnesses, with two privates being discharged and fifty men being sent to the hospital. Most common among these men was diarrhea and fevers, with seven men suffering from abscesses and ulcers. Hernias and diseases of the urinary and genital organs also accounted for a large number of illnesses.[47]

Among the 19 officers and 245 enlisted men of the Fourteenth Tennessee, some 79 had fallen ill, with 8 being sent to the general hospital. Diarrhea and constipation made up the majority of complaints, yet circulatory diseases accounted for a large number of health issues as well. Five men of the Fourteenth, among them Lt. R.A. Barnes and Pvt. F.M. Gavin, received a surgeon's discharge.[48]

One task the Tennesseans performed was destroying an area railroad, the Baltimore and Ohio, the most direct link between the west and Washington. Aside from this activity, the only action the brigade saw was the repulse of a Union detachment passing through Snickers Gap toward Castleman's Ferry on the Shenandoah River. This skirmish on November 6 was a minor interruption of the men's time filled largely with rest and relaxation.[49]

During this period the Army of the Potomac gained a new commander in Ambrose Burnside, replacing George McClellan. Burnside began gathering his army in the vicinity of Fredericksburg on the Rappahannock River. Gen. Jackson received orders to move his men to Fredericksburg[50] and began marching to the town on November 22.

On Saturday, November 29, Archibald Debow Norris, 7th TN, rejoined his regiment following a three-week sojourn. Norris recorded the events of the following days as the Tennessee Brigade moved toward Fredericksburg. Norris wrote, "Joined the regiment ... We camped near Orange, C.H. The clothing for the regiment was brought up and distributed ... which most boys truly appreciated, edibles were also sent to some ... on the march they could not enjoy them."[51]

The following day, Norris continued, "The march was resumed at an early hour this morning. I took a severe cold last night ... Our course for a time lay along the same route we traveled over to Cedar Run last summer. We left the plank road a few miles from Orange ... procuring forage. Our wagons were late in getting to camp ... ten or eleven p.m. when we got supper." Over the next week, Norris continued to describe the march toward Fredericksburg and the conditions encountered in its fulfillment. He described the events: "Struck shelters, not tents, early this morning and formed along the road ... After a hard march, we came to within five miles of Fredericksburg and camped ... Marched about 6 miles around Fredericksburg and camped in a dense forest about 5 miles from town on the railroad to Richmond. In the scramble for tents I failed to get one. Our mess put up a 'bunk' whilst I went to the depot bought coffee, Confederate sugar, cigars, etc ... no supper till 9 p.m. having had nothing since sunrise."[52]

The arrival of the Tennessee Brigade in Fredericksburg area on December 3 took place after approximately 175 miles had been covered in 12 hard days of marching. In the following days, brigade members cut wood and secured a shipment of supplies such as tents and blankets that made them "decidedly more comfortable than before."[53]

CHAPTER ELEVEN

Fredericksburg

The battle of Fredericksburg is etched into the minds of most Civil War students. The scene of Confederate troops standing behind the stone wall at the base of Marye's Heights, repelling numerous Federal assaults and the photograph of dropped weapons and dead soldiers behind the same wall are military classics. The interest in Kirkland, the "angel of the battlefield," continues to grow as individuals become more interested in the humanitarian efforts of the great conflict. Though not involved in these events, the Tennessee Brigade did play an important role in a pivotal part of another section of the battlefield.

On November 21, 1862, Gen. Lee noted the apparent concentration of Gen. Burnside's entire Federal army on the north side of the Rappahannock River. With the Union threat to bombard the city and the inevitable clash of two mighty armies upon their city, the citizens of Fredericksburg left their homes. Meanwhile, Gen. Jackson had relocated to the Fredericksburg area by early December.[1]

Reverend Nathaniel D. Renfroe, a lieutenant in the Fifth Alabama, had recently returned from a near-death bout with typhoid fever to make the march to Fredericksburg at the head of his company. His self-fulfilling prophecy was written in a letter to his brother, J.J.D. Renfroe, as he stated:

> We have just completed another march of one hundred and seventy miles, crossing two awful mountains in the time. We were twelve days on the march. I had no wagon, or horse, or any other means of transportation, except my feet for myself and baggage; we

139

rested, only at night—rising at 4 ½ in the morning and marching until sunset. I suffered much—frequently thinking that I would fall out and rest, but when I would look through the company and see several men barefooted and still keeping up, it would stimulate me, and I would press on. The tramp finished my boots, and both my feet are on the ground, and but little prospect of getting any shoes soon. But it is my duty to bear a little hardness as a good soldier of Jesus Christ, and submit to it cheerfully, and without a murmur in view of my country's freedom and the honor of my religion. We are certainly on the eve of a great battle here—it will be a grand affair—I may not survive the conflict, but, brother, if I die, I shall fall at my post, and I am ready to go.[2]

With Stafford Heights completely commanding the north side of the Rappahannock, the inability of the Confederates to erect a bridge without risk of fire from a large number of well-entrenched Federal batteries became apparent. Lee's decision centered on the selection of a force large enough to check a Federal advance and firmly resist the enemy upon crossing the river. The Union army's opportunity to more freely construct bridges without Confederate intervention was greatly aided by the Rappahannock's narrowness, winding course, and deep bed, in addition to the superior geographical location the Federals held. [3]

In the early-morning hours of December 11, Confederate signal guns proclaimed the movement of Burnside's army. Over the course of several hours, a series of points were probed as possible sites for the construction of a Federal pontoon bridge; this task was completed at approximately 1:00 p.m. on the eleventh.[4]

A.D. Norris recorded the events of the morning of the eleventh in writing: "Was awakened this morning about three o'clock by the rapid and continued discharge of heavy artillery. The cannonading was rapid and continued till about noon. Several houses in Fredericksburg were battered down or set on fire, but fortunately no general conflagration took place. It was afterwards ascertained that the enemy tried to force a passage across the Rappahannock River at three points, Knox Mill above town, at the railroad bridge and at deep run about two miles below town and nearly opposite our camp. They failed at the first two places but succeeded at the last under cover of their cannons. Their pontoon bridges once across, they came over by thousands and by night there were probably 50,000 on this side. No collision with small arms occurred during the day. In our camp everybody was restless … rumors floated, the sounds tending to increase the excitement. At 8 a.m. orders came to hold ourselves in readiness to move at a moments warning. This was by another order to cook up what rations we had and to draw more from the commissary as soon as practicable. The sure precursors of a movement, guns were cleaned up, ammunition distributed and sick lists made out. No move was ordered during the day. At night an order was brought round to be ready to move at 6 ½ in the morning. Expecting the great battle of Fredericksburg to come off in the morning, we lay down to sleep and dream of charges and repulses."[5]

Late that night Gen. Lee ordered Hill to move his Light Division at dawn on the twelfth to relieve Hood. Meanwhile, large numbers of the Union army crossed the Rappahannock during the night of the eleventh and on the morning of the twelfth, aided largely by the presence of a thick fog. Confederate artillery effectiveness was minimized with the combination of fog and regular-interval firing of Federal batteries located on Stafford Heights.[6]

A.D. Norris entered the day's events in his journal: "We marched off briskly and cheerily passed Hamilton's crossing on the Richmond Fredericksburg and Potomac Railroad, turned to the left, marched half a mile, halted, fronted to the rear facing Fredericksburg, loaded guns, then marched about three-quarters of a mile through a dense forest and took our position in line of battle behind a ditch cut for a fence along the edge of the forest next to the Rappahannock, and about a mile and a half from the river. In front of us lay a cleared plane reaching to the river, behind us lay the forest which offered excellent shelter for bringing up supports and supplies, as well as concealing the movements of our troops. After taking our position nothing occurred to vary the monotony of the day, till the appearance about 3 p.m. of the long dark columns of the enemy moving down the river on a road parallel to it. They were first discovered by the glistening of their arms and canteens. They halted about a mile in front of our line and seemed to be making observations. Our skirmishers fell back as they approached without firing on them ... on our left cannonading and skirmishing was kept up during the afternoon with no definite result,"[7]

The morning of Saturday, December 13 dawned with a shroud of a heavy fog. Apprehension over the inevitable clash between the opposing armies surrounding the town of Fredericksburg had led to confusion and contradictions of orders during the night. Orders were given sporadically to soldiers of the Tennessee Brigade to pack cooking vessels and extra blankets and to load two tents per company onto wagons. A radiant sun eventually greeted the men of North and South as the light reflected from the thousands of bayonets the soldiers possessed. J.H. Moore, 7th TN, recalled the sight of officers in brightly colored uniforms, the speed with which artillery pieces were maneuvered into place like a child would move a toy, and the respect each side held for its enemy in what he felt was "the greatest martial scene of the war."[8]

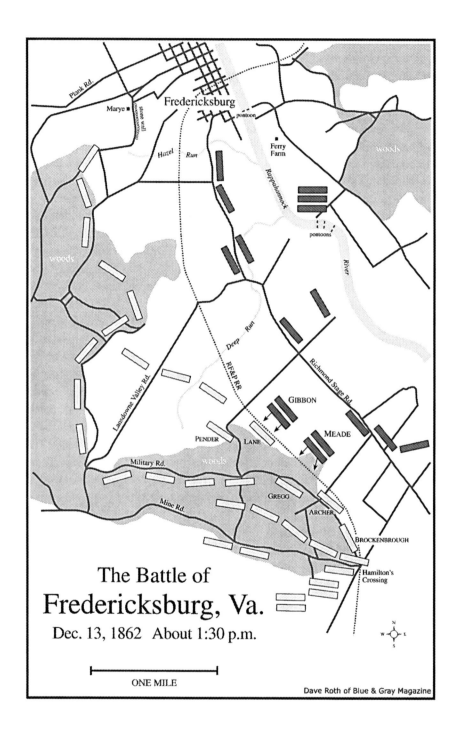

The Battle of

Fredericksburg, Va.

Dec. 13, 1862 About 1:30 p.m.

ONE MILE

Dave Roth of Blue & Gray Magazine

A brigade member added, "About ten … heavy cannonading had already commenced; bombs were falling far in the rear of our lines … Our skirmishers were in the r.r. about 100 yards in front of our line of battle. The sharpshooters of the enemy were about 200 yards beyond them. Continual skirmishing was kept up between them. About 300 yards in rear of the skirmishers, the dark columns of the enemy were drawn up in two lines, in the center of the front line their batteries were placed with which they shelled the woods in rear of our line and replied to our batteries. Our generals and field officers were sure to be fired on whenever they showed themselves."[9]

June Kimble of Co. A, 14th TN, remembered the day as being beautiful but cold. The coolness of the weather was lessened for Kimble, who had received a new gray uniform and a brown overcoat from his mother the day before. His comrades joked with him about his gifts from home, yet the seriousness of the events that lay ahead took over as Kimble responded to the comments with the fact that the new attire might very well serve as his burial clothes.[10]

Gen. Archer arrived from sick leave in Richmond and found the Tennessee Brigade located some 250 yards from the Bernard House at the edge of the woods. From this vantage point, the troops could clearly view Bowling Green Road and Richmond Stage Road, approximately three-fourths of a mile in the distance.[11]

Archer had been hospitalized in Richmond since December 1 and while there received intelligence reports of Union troops gathering to cross the Rappahannock. The general boarded the first available train and arrived at Fredericksburg just prior to sunrise.[12]

Positioned left to right, the units of Hill's division stood as follows: Pender, Lane, Archer, and Field, with Col. Brockenbrough commanding the latter. The left side of the Light Division continued to a point near Deep Run while the extreme right side was on a road that connected Hamilton's Crossing to Port Royal Road. Also to Archer's right stood Lt. Col. R.L. Walker, commanding fourteen light artillery pieces supported by the Fortieth and Fifty-fifth Virginia regiments. Between Archer and Lane lay a gap of six hundred yards where Gregg's Brigade stood to oppose any Union attempt to flank Archer. Gen. Thomas was posted to the rear of the interval between Lane and Pender. In the second Confederate line, left to right, Taliaferro and Early were situated.[13]

With the dissipation of the fog, the Confederates were able to view approximately fifty-five thousand Union soldiers advancing. An artillery exchange between Confederate batteries far to the right of Archer and Federals about one thousand yards from the Tennessee Brigade infrequently threw shell fragments into the woods where Archer stood. Capt. John Keely, 19th

GA, wrote in his diary that the promptness with which the Union artillery had been unlimbered and opened fire "would have done credit to any army on earth."[14]

A return of cannon fire from the Confederates on Marye's Heights poured into the lines of unfaltering Union troops advancing at a steady pace. Despite the volume of the artillery duel, members of Archer's Brigade paid far more attention to "the sequel to come from the barrels of 120,000 muskets" than to the shells exploding around them, an event one Tennessee Brigade member equated to child's play.[15]

Archer noted that the Union infantry formed and rapidly advanced around 11:00 a.m. Gen. Archer sent Lt. George Lemmon to notify Gen. Gregg of massing Yankee infantry to Archer's left near the extension of the woods beyond the railroad. Archer also intended for Gregg, upon the receipt of the message, to move into the gap between the Tennessee Brigade and Lane's Brigade to preclude the Union troops from flanking Archer's position. Archer grew fearful of the possibility that Gregg's arrival would occur too late to close the noticeable gap. At this revelation, Archer ordered the Fifth Alabama Battalion to move from its location on the brigade's right to a point farther left.[16]

The brunt of Archer's troops fired into the advancing Federals with a high degree of accuracy. R.T. Mockbee remembered the storm of lead leaving the ranks of the Tennessee Brigade, melting away the enemy in the same manner the early-morning sun had eliminated the fog. W.H. Johnson, 19th GA, wrote that the brigade's volleys "poured into their ranks" and "made them reel and stagger." Johnson added that the Yankees seemed to be giving way as they "were falling like hay before the mower's blast."[17]

Capt. John Keely, Co. B, 19th GA, reported that the thousands of muskets had caused the entire first line of the three assaulting lines spaced in one-hundred-yard intervals to vanish. The "pop, pop, pop" of the muskets erupted from right to left "while men fell ... shot in every conceivable manner."[18]

A.D. Norris also recorded the harrowing moments of the opening action the Tennessee Brigade encountered at Fredericksburg. He wrote:

> About half an hour after I arrived, a terrific cannonade commenced and continued during an hour. There was then a partial lull when the infantry of the enemy began to advance. They came up in a beautiful line although our batteries played on them from the commencement of their advance. Our skirmishers in the r.r. retired to the ditch. On they came, our fire was random till they came within one hundred and fifty yards of our lines. At that distance they fired a volley. A withering sheet of fire was then poured on them from our lines. Their

front line was scattered and almost annihilated. The fire from their guns set broomsage, with which the field was covered, on fire. One of their colors, a dark blue flag with white borders, was burned up. Another had its bearer shot down several times. The second line now came up to our left however, a gap had been left open between the 19th Georgia of our brigade and Co. Lane's Brigade which the enemy was not slow to discover. Through this gap they poured a strong flanking party capturing some of the Georgians. They now directed their whole force to this point.[19]

J.H. Moore explained that the spaces and gaps that developed foretold of a deadly battle. Moore felt that the Federal troops easily entered the swampy area to Archer's left because Gregg's Brigade was too far behind its assigned position. The wet, marshy ground was a difficult area in which to wait for the advancing Yankees.[20]

In the early phase of the attack, a bullet entered the mouth of Col. Peter Turney, 1st TN, just below his nose and tore a gap in the roof of his mouth. Turney fell from his horse when the slug struck, as the lead removed half of the officer's tongue and a large number of teeth before lodging in the left side of his neck, narrowly missing his jugular vein.[21]

Four soldiers placed Turney into a blanket and began carrying the severely wounded officer to safety when a shell exploded in their vicinity, killing or wounding all four. Turney was dropped heavily to the ground, which added greatly to his worsening condition. An order was issued to abandon additional attempts to assist Turney, whom many feared was mortally wounded. A strong Union attack had begun, resulting in a retreat along a large portion of the Tennessee Brigade's position, and any attempt to rescue Turney could have likely resulted in the rescuer's death or capture. Archer's men, obviously affected by Turney's apparently declining condition, began falling back.[22]

Sam Estill of Winchester, Tennessee, Turney's hometown, ignored the order to avoid an attempt to rescue his regimental commander and crawled through a hail of gunfire to Turney's now still form. Estill turned the colonel over, preventing Turney from choking on his teeth, flesh fragments, and blood.[23] It is highly probable that Estill's actions saved Turney's life.

In addition to Estill, another of Turney's close associates performed heroically at a pivotal juncture of the battle. Tom, Turney's horse, had joined in the retreat of many members of the Tennessee Brigade. As if motivated by some strange sense, Tom suddenly ceased his flight, neighed loudly, and returned to stand near Turney's wounded body. The Tennesseans saw Tom's unusual response and acted accordingly, mounting a counthe he coun-charge that pushed the Union attackers toward their lines.[24]

The devastating fire from the Tennessee Brigade had caused the advancing Union troops to take cover in the railroad bed. From there the Yankees sent erratic fire into the line of Archer's Brigade. The Nineteenth Georgia and Fourteenth Tennessee regiments of the brigade had been successfully flanked and lost some 160 prisoners to the Union attackers.[25]

Lt. Col. Andrew J. Hutchins, 19th GA, reported that his unit had maintained its ground fifteen to twenty minutes before being forced to retire, leaving behind fellow regiment members to fall into enemy hands.

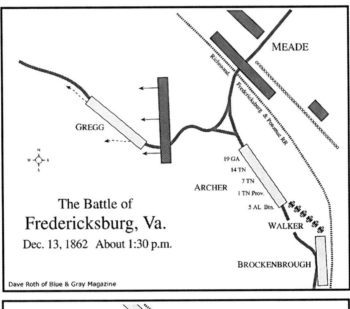

The Battle of
Fredericksburg, Va.
Dec. 13, 1862 About 1:30 p.m.

Dave Roth of Blue & Gray Magazine

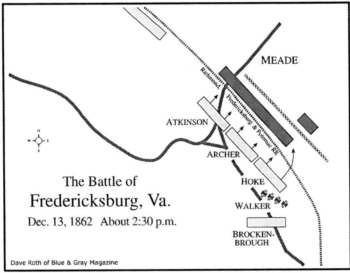

The Battle of
Fredericksburg, Va.
Dec. 13, 1862 About 2:30 p.m.

Dave Roth of Blue & Gray Magazine

Lt. George Boyd Hutcheson, Co. C, 14th TN, who had been promoted to first lieutenant less than four months earlier, informed Lt. Col. James W. Lockert, commander of the Fourteenth Tennessee, that the retreat of the Nineteenth Georgia was necessitated by the Union's flanking of the brigade's position. Lockert had seen the Georgians giving way, yet assumed their ammunition had been depleted, as had that of his own regiment.[26]

Lockert's determination to maintain his position lessened when he saw a Union line advancing through pines to his left. Lockert then ordered a retreat; the Fourteenth Tennessee "fell back in disorder to the open field" located to the regiment's rear.[27]

June Kimble proposed that he and fellow members of the Fourteenth Tennessee were unaware of the Union penetration of the gap between Archer's and Gregg's brigades until shots from their left gained their attention. Kimble and his comrades began dividing their attention and firepower in two directions when a member of the Fourteenth Tennessee made a desperate attempt to escape the stress of army life. Kimble stated that the young man raised his hand above the ditch bank where he was crouched and shouted that he would now attempt to gain a thirty-day furlough. Moments after lifting his hand, the young soldier accomplished his goal when a bullet smashed into his hand.[28]

Kimble also recalled how T.D. Johnson paused to curse his fellow regiment members for firing a series of shots in the area around him, the last of which landed close to his right knee. Turning to his rear, Johnson saw a line of Federal soldiers advancing in his direction. This angered Johnson to an even higher degree, and Kimble felt no one fired more effectively in the ensuing battle than did the agitated Johnson.[29]

The retreat of the Fourteenth Tennessee and the Nineteenth Georgia was seen among the ranks of the Seventh Tennessee, located at the brigade's center and to the right of the Nineteenth Georgia and Fourteenth Tennessee. Most members of the Seventh possessed no ammunition at this stage of the conflict, though Col. John Goodner noted that some still had two or three rounds. The level of ammunition, the onslaught by superior Federal numbers, and the collapse of the regiments to the left resulted in a withdrawal of a large number of the men of the Seventh Tennessee from the line, yet not before a group of five of its members on the extreme left were captured.[30]

Lt. W.M. McCall, Co. E, 7th TN, remembered the heroism and bravery of Gen. Archer and the men of the Fifth Alabama while the situation seemed hopeless. He wrote:

> The Federals, four lines deep, had broken our lines, and as I went
> out, making about thirty miles an hour, I met Archer going in with
> that band of heroes, the Fifth Alabama Battalion, numbering about

one hundred and fifty men. In attempting to rally my company on the hill, I saw Archer and the Fifth Battalion surrounded by Federals; yet standing like a rock they held the Yankees at bay until D.H. Hill's division came up. The last thing I saw of Archer at that time, he was on his little black, a Federal soldier had the mare by the bridle-bit, the mare was rearing straight up, and Archer's heavy cavalry saber was poised above his head. I never learned what the fate of that one yankee was, only surmised.[31]

One soldier witnessed the events from his position and noted that the Fourteenth fell back to prevent being captured, as did a portion of the Seventh Tennessee. Capt. H.J. Hankins of the First Tennessee recalled that a heavy Union cannonade began then, killing Lt. C.N. McGuire of Company K and causing his regiment to hold its ground for an estimated three hours. Hankins had gained command of the First Tennessee following the successive wounding of Turney, Maj. Felix Buchanan, Col. N.J. George, and Capt. M. Turney.[32]

J.H. Moore remembered that the brigade members located on the right side were confused by the retreat, as they saw only the routing of the enemy to their front, not those flanking from the extreme left. Enraged at the withdrawal by men they perceived as cowards, officers and men of the right shouted and threatened their comrades. Officers and a large number of enlisted men reportedly leveled their guns and fired into the fleeing brigade members. Another brigade member reported brigade members being shot in the back, yet he believed the shots came from the enemy.[33]

Gen. Archer praised the First Tennessee for its gallantry in holding steady throughout the Union attack. In addition to the First Tennessee, Archer noted how the Seventh Tennessee companies led by lieutenants Timberlake, Foster, Wilmouth, and Baird stood strong while the chaos negatively affected those around them.[34]

Lt. W.H. Johnson, 19th GA, explained that he was unable to say whose fault it was that the gap had existed, yet he was quick to add, "I do know that men never fought more bravely." He also noted that he had received word of the Union flanking of Archer's left side from a Lt. Simms and immediately notified Lt. Col. Hutchins of the situation. Hutchins urged Johnson to go to Gen. Archer and ask for support. Upon Johnson's return to his regiment, he saw the success of the Federals' intention to encircle the Tennessee Brigade's position.[35]

An attempt to fill the gap was led by Lt. Nathaniel Renfroe of the Fifth Alabama. Renfroe had written his brother upon his arrival in Fredericksburg, explaining that, should he die, he would do so while maintaining his position.

His brother detailed the following moments, based upon firsthand accounts from his brother's comrades:

> About three o'clock in the afternoon three regiments of his brigade gave way and retired, leaving a gap through which the enemy was moving rapidly to flank their position. Gen. Archer threw the Battalion and First Tennessee regiment—who alone remained in the battle at that point—into the breech to hold the enemy in check until another brigade could be brought up. The enemy rushed on and were too strong. An order came to retreat. It is supposed by his comrades that brother did not hear the order. The first Tennessee retreated, and the battalion retreated, except for a few of his company who stood by him. The enemy coming up a few steps ordered a surrender. He turned to his few men, with a gentle smile, and said: 'Boys, this is a pretty hot place, and you must get out the best you can.' Then turning to the enemy with his Repeater in hand he began to fire, and was unhurt, and firing his piece with cool deliberation, when his 'boys' left him! And here he was found dead. No friend saw him die. I do not say that he acted with the best discretion, but I do claim for him that, in the last moments he stood *alone* on that part of the field of carnage with his face to the enemy giving him battle.[36]

Renfroe's remains were carried home with the accompaniment of his close friend, Lt. Mattison, who arrived with his battalion mate's body on New Year's day, 1863. The deceased officer, viewed among others as being "a walking example of Christianity," was buried with full military honors in a Talladega, Alabama cemetery.[37]

Archer had sent Lt. O.H. Howard, preceded closely by Lt. George Lemmon, to Gen. Gregg for the purpose of explaining the urgency of the Tennessee Brigade's situation. Archer's own Fifth Alabama Battalion was joined by the brigades of Gregg and Lawton and began pushing back the Union attackers. A.D. Norris added, "At this juncture a portion of Ewell's Division came up and charged the impudent foe, capturing about one thousand and driving them back to their first position with terrible loss. Our troops reoccupied the ditch and our skirmishers the r.r. The enemy sullenly retired behind their batteries and resumed the cannonade. The repulse was … complete."[38]

When Lemmon got to Gregg's position, he found the guns of the men stacked, with Federal bullets rattling the stacks. Archer was vindicated by A.P. Hill for any responsibility for the Union breakthrough.[39] Gregg was mortally wounded in the attack, possibly creating for himself the ability to become the scapegoat. Many of those holding their positions saw defeat or capture as their only options and were unaware that reserves were near. Exclaiming that "Old Jubal's boys" were once again getting Hill's men out of trouble, Early's men entered the area of Archer's retreating regiments, saving them from defeat or death.

Brig. Gen. Robert F. Hoke commanded Trimble's brigade and assisted in the charge that drove back the Federals. He explained that upon discovering Archer's left side had been driven back, he saw that the Union troops were quickly pushed from Archer's previous position. Not satisfied simply with the dislodging of the enemy, Hoke entered the entrenchments at the edge of the woods where he sighted the Union troops in the railroad where reserves had joined the retreating Federals. He also perceived the position the Yankees held at the railroad provided an excellent point from which their sharpshooters could administer a high rate of casualties among the Confederates. Hoke and his brigade immediately charged the position, capturing one hundred Federals and killing an estimated two hundred. Hoke had passed Archer's original position, which the latter maintained with the right side of his brigade, though this was accomplished with empty rifles and cartridge boxes. Archer's remaining troops joined Hoke's in pushing the Yankees through the railroad. Returning to woods, Archer drew back his men some thirty yards and reformed the brigade.[40]

Col. John Goodner, 7th TN, and Lt. Col. James W. Lockert, 14th TN, wrote in their respective official reports that the retreating members of their regiments made their way to the rear and replenished themselves with ammunition. Lockert noted that upon his return to the front, he found the enemy already driven back by other troops.[41]

Capt. John Keely, Co. B, 19th GA, wrote that the scene that followed "was sickening in the extreme," as the sage grass covering the area between the two armies erupted in flames caused by the exploding shells. The inferno caused the incineration of the dead and wounded alike. Keely recalled that the Federal grape and canister shot prevented the rescue of any of his comrades. An unforgettable incident from this phase of the battle occurred when Keely saw a young wounded man bravely fighting the advancing fire with his ramrod. Unable to rise, the youth attempted to preserve his life until the moment his cartridge box exploded, tearing him to pieces.[42] As night fell, the screams of the dead and wounded in unburned areas of the fields filled the air. In addition, the stench of gunpowder created an almost unquenchable thirst throughout the ranks of survivors.

A.D. Norris recorded the post-battle atmosphere in the camp of the Seventh Tennessee Infantry. "The proximity of the river and the heavy guns of the enemy on the other side prevented us from following up our victory. The enemy's dead and wounded and singular enough unhurt in the battlefield before us. The last seemed glad enough to give up and thus escape the dangers of another charge. Guns of the best pattern lay thick on the ground, along with them many old buck and ball muskets. Many of the dead were charred and the wounded severely burnt by the sage." J.H. Moore also recalled the unceasing fire from Union artillery and proposed that it ended any plans of a Confederate night attack upon the Union camps. The sight of the dead and mortally wounded with their clothes and hair burned caused Moore to become heartsick.[43]

The grim task of gathering the dead and wounded then began. The official numbers by unit were: the Fifth Alabama Battalion, three killed, eighteen wounded; Nineteenth Georgia, fifteen killed, thirty-nine wounded; First Tennessee, five killed, fifty-two wounded; Seventh Tennessee, five killed, and thirty-three wounded; and the Fourteenth Tennessee, four killed, fifty-five wounded. Gen. Archer reported 166 soldiers from the Tennessee Brigade as missing and presumed captured. J.H. Moore wrote that the enemy's dead covered the ground for almost a mile in front of his regiment's position.[44]

Michael Ashley, Co. F; Amos Small, Co. G; and C.N. McGuire, Co. K, were among the members of Turney's First Tennessee to be killed at Fredericksburg. M.B. Hill and G.W. Sawyers were included in the wounded of Company K of the regiment.[45]

The accolades for bravery were numerous in the official reports of the brigade. Archer himself was quick to explain that not a single Union soldier moved within fifty yards of his front and that the enemy refused to attempt to regain Archer's flank following its sharp repulse.[46] Numerous reports noted the coolness with which those not retreating performed their duties.

Col. John Goodner explained, "I did not observe any misconduct in my regiment," while Col. James Lockert, 14th TN, added that during the battle his men "showed great courage and coolness" and that he "never saw shots better aimed or more effective." Capt. H.J. Hawkins expressed how his troops held their ground, despite heavy enemy fire, until moving, only when ordered to do so.[47]

Lt. Col. Andrew J. Hutchins, 19th GA, singled out the actions of five men of his command: Lt. W.H. Johnson, Lt. Miles Edwards (Co. H), Capt. C.W. Mabry (Co. E), Sgt. Shell (Co. D), and Cpl. Rogan (Co. B). Johnson was commended for his bravery during multiple trips to and from Gen. Archer, all of which were made "through a terrible volley of musketry." Edwards gained Hutchins's praise after passing along the ranks of his men throughout the action, directing individuals how to shoot. Mabry received the same notice, once taking a gun from a member of his company and modeling the manner in which to shoot. Shell and Rogan had joined Hutchins in attempting to rally the men of the Nineteenth Georgia, faltering under the threat of the advancing enemy.[48]

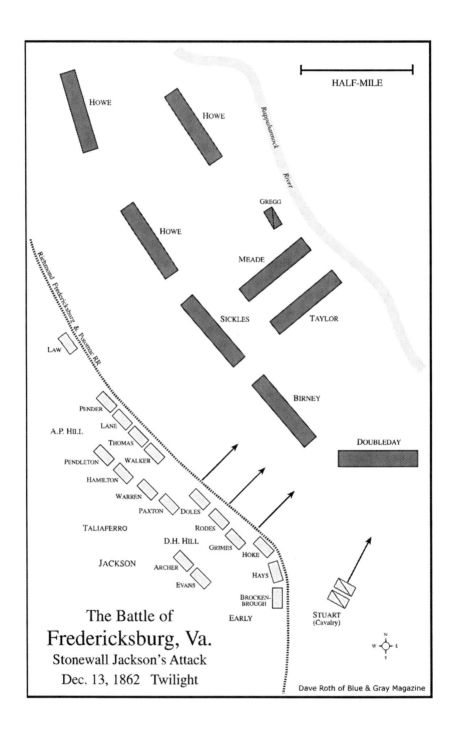

Compliments were not always reserved for official reports. June Kimble wrote in his memoirs that he stood eight feet from Gen. Jackson and saw firsthand how the officer's spirit and sense of invincibility spread to his men. With Federal shells bursting overhead and removing tree limbs that crashed to the ground, Jackson sat upon his horse, surveying the enemy's position. Jackson made his observations while appearing "calm, deliberate, but alert and seemingly unconscious of danger."[49]

Besides the fatalities, many of the wounded of the brigade had seen their last action of the war in the Battle of Fredericksburg. Among those was Col. Peter Turney, the man responsible for the formation of the First Tennessee Infantry Regiment. A Federal bullet had shattered Turney's mouth and neck, leaving him near death. Turney had gained a reputation through the ranks of the Tennessee Brigade as an outstanding leader and fighter. His large frame contributed to the respect he received, yet he also insisted that death awaited him at the onset of every battle.

On the morning of Saturday, December 17, 1862, Turney had bet John Fite a gallon of whiskey that one of them would die that day. Turney joked years later that Fite had stated to him as he lay wounded that it appeared Turney had won the bet. Fite denied such a statement, though; he said he felt Turney was near death when he saw him. J.H. Moore remembered seeing Turney lying on the battlefield and assumed he was dead, as blood literally covered him, oozing from his head and ending virtually all chances of recognition.[50]

Turney survived the wound, yet army surgeons refused to remove the lead bullet due to its close proximity to Turney's jugular vein. When he recovered enough to be moved, he returned by train to Winchester, Tennessee, where his wife and mother cared for their loved one. Using a sterilized kitchen knife, Turney's wife removed the bullet from Turney's neck, and his condition rapidly improved.[51]

John W. King, Co. A, 14th TN, was wounded in the battle and died on Christmas Day, 1862. Thomas Herndon, King's best friend, took King's body to Bristol, Tennessee for burial. Capt. J.P. Brown and Lt. Z.G. Gunn were also fatalities from the Fourteenth Tennessee, both killed while performing their duties.[52]

Families and friends of many of the dead or wounded received the news of their loved ones from local newspapers, often weeks after the battle. On December 30, 1862, the casualties of the Nineteenth Georgia appeared in an Atlanta newspaper. Among the names were Sgt. J.J. McCarley and Pvt. B.F. Wilkerson, killed, and corporals W.J. Harris and S.R. Watson, wounded. Sgt. John Sherwood was wounded in the bowels and died soon after the battle. Lt. Peter Felon, Nineteenth Georgia, suffered a broken leg at Fredericksburg, and the severity of the wound resulted in the leg's amputation. A comrade recalled Felon "died of mortification" along with "seven-eighths" of the company he served.[53]

Gen. Archer detailed the mortal wounding of Mr. Frank Wootten, a volunteer aide on his staff, who had accompanied Archer as the general rode down his lines, following the Union breakthrough. When the cannonade began, a shell struck the aide and inflicted the deadly wound. Archer wrote that Wootten was a volunteer on A.P. Hill's staff but became separated from Hill during the action. Archer readily accepted Wootten's offer of his services during the battle, as many of his own staff were absent. The volunteer received his head wound less than two minutes after Archer's acceptance.[54]

Archer explained the cause of his missing staff members. At least one, he wrote, "got tight both evenings while in Richmond." Archer also proclaimed his disgust with alcohol by writing, "I wish all the liquor in the universe was poured out."[55]

Aside from the wounds and deaths, veterans noted a variety of points arising from the battle. June Kimble made the statement that Burnside's unfitness for leadership and Robert E. Lee's illustrious leadership skills were the two major points to arise from the carnage at Fredericksburg.[56] While these statements are easily defended, they also offer insight into the events that lay ahead for the Tennessee Brigade and the entire Army of Northern Virginia at Chancellorsville.

CHAPTER TWELVE

Chancellorsville

After participating in the battle of Fredericksburg, the Tennessee Brigade moved approximately ten miles to the area of Guinea Station, where it established its winter camp. Sgt. Robert T. Mockbee recalled that at Guinea Station, which also bore the designation of Camp Gregg, most of the soldiers resided in cabins or had good chimneys incorporated into their tents. Routine picket duty constituted the majority of the activities of the brigade members in the early days of the occupation of the area.[1]

From this camp Gen. Archer wrote his brother on January 2, 1863. In a short and direct letter, with no additional insight, Gen. Archer told Bob Archer that he felt the prospects of peace looked good since Fredericksburg and that a victory in the west would end the conflict entirely. Ten days later, in a letter to his mother, Gen. Archer explained that the road taken during the war had been difficult but that it led to "liberty and honor and happiness and home and friends" and that soon he would be home.[2] One may only wonder what revelations Archer was experiencing to cause such comments.

The Confederate War Department requested that a member of each company from the three Tennessee regiments in the Tennessee Brigade journey home for the purpose of recruiting men to join the ranks of the brigade. A detail was formed in January 1863 with Robert Mockbee designated to represent Company B of the Fourteenth Tennessee. Mockbee's absence from January 29 to May 7, 1863 was for this purpose, and he later referred to the mission as fruitless. The Union occupation of most of the area from which the Fourteenth had been raised, along with the fall of Ft. Donelson, had caused the majority of men from the area interested in Confederate service to join the army of Gen. Bragg or another whose service was to be spent in the area near the volunteers' homes.[3]

The brigade also received a change in membership during this period when the Nineteenth Georgia was transferred to Colquitt's brigade and the Thirteenth Alabama Infantry Regiment, under the command of Col. Birkett D. Fry, joined the Tennessee Brigade. Fry was a forty-year-old Mexican War veteran who had left civilian life at the Civil War's outbreak to join the Thirteenth Alabama as a colonel. Fry was in a Richmond hospital nursing a shattered arm injured at Antietam when his Alabamians joined the Tennessee Brigade.[4]

The Thirteenth Alabama Infantry Regiment had been organized at Montgomery in July of 1861. Ten companies originally comprised the regiment, with the members coming largely from Randolph, Coosa, Butler, Macon, Wilcox, and Tallapoosa counties. Randolph residents composed Company D, the Randolph Mountaineers; Company E, Randolph Rangers; Company I, Roanoke Mitchell Invincibles; and Company K, Stephens Guards. Coosa County residents made up Company C, Alabama Borderers; and Company H, Coosa Mountaineers. Company A, the Camden Rifles, was raised in Wilcox County; Company B, Southern Stars, came from Macon County; Company F, Tallassee Guards, hailed from Tallapoosa County; while the members of Company G, Yancey Guards, called Butler County home.[5]

Gen. Archer wrote of the realignment that the Georgians were highly dissatisfied over their transfer and the Alabamians were delighted with the change. Special Order 19, dated January 19, 1863, called for the transfer of the Thirteenth Alabama from Colquitt's brigade to the Tennessee Brigade and was issued two weeks prior to Archer's letter expressing the delight of the Alabamians.[6]

However, in a January 22, 1863 letter, Capt. John T. Smith, Co. I, Thirteenth Alabama, wrote to his mother, noting that the transfer to Archer's command was widely unpopular and that a request had been made to reverse the order, thus placing the regiment in an Alabama brigade. That same day, Smith reluctantly tendered the regiment to Gen. Archer. The next day the Thirteenth entered the Tennessee Brigade's camp.[7]

Gen. Archer and Capt. Smith did agree on one point—that neither anticipated an immediate Federal crossing of the Rappahannock, near which the Tennessee Brigade performed picket duty. Each wrote his respective mother, three days apart, with Smith stating the unwillingness of the Union army to face another defeat at the hands of the Army of Northern Virginia; Archer noted the poor conditions of roads in the area that would certainly limit the Federals' maneuverability. Smith proposed that as long as the Confederates had Robert E. Lee in charge, the Union army would meet defeat, even when numbering three times the forces of the Confederacy. Perhaps the confidence Smith had, one that was undoubtedly shared by others, is summed up in a sentence from his February 1, 1863 letter to his mother. Smith wrote, "This army is invincible by any force the enemy can possibly bring to bear against it."[8]

The battle flag of the Thirteenth Alabama Infantry Regiment. Courtesy of the Alabama Department of Archives and History.

Smith also shared Gen. Archer's contempt for alcohol, explaining to his mother how one man, willing to give any amount for a drink of whiskey, paid forty-two dollars for a canteen full. In addition to high prices charged for alcohol, sutlers in camp also charged the men of the Tennessee Brigade three dollars for a chicken and one dollar for a ginger cake. The exposure of a variety of morals, social classes, and lifestyles appeared to harden Smith to those less fortunate than he, for he wrote, "The bad are not reformed, while the good are made bad."[9]

June Kimble held the opposite view of Smith in relation to the moral condition of the Army of Northern Virginia. During what Kimble recalled as "the most quiet and undisturbed winter season" Lee's army encountered during the war, Kimble fondly remembered the zeal of religious leaders from all denominations as they successfully demonstrated the Gospel power. The unity of these men of God resulted not only in an overall improvement in morale but more significantly in a religious revival in which thousands of conversions took place, according to Kimble's estimation.[10]

The winter of 1863 enhanced Archer's idea of a peaceful season. He wrote his brother in late February of his hope that the violent snow storm that had lasted for days and stranded the Confederates in camp would also wreck all plans of the enemy in relation to attacking. As mid-March arrived, Archer was excited for his own health, which was "better than ever," he noted, aside from an occasional cold, commonplace in winter encampments.[11]

John T. Smith also exclaimed that his health and that of the Thirteen Alabama was as good as ever. The Army of Northern Virginia's medical director had informed the brigade that his sick list was at an all-time low. Smith noted the latter fact was a true godsend, as medical supplies had also recently been depleted.[12]

Conditions on the Federal side had also improved as a reorganization occurred, placing "Fighting" Joe Hooker in command of the Army of the Potomac and relieving Gen. Ambrose Burnside of his command.[13] The hopes of a potential end to the fighting were dashed with the arrival of this news in the camp of the Tennesseans.

A.D. Norris's journal entry of April 29, 1863 clearly explained the advent of the long-feared Union offensive that would take place. Norris wrote, "About eight o'clock orders came to pack up and be ready to move at a moments warning. We were not expecting however to leave right away and did not hurry, in about half an hour we were ordered to fall in, without cooked rations ... Leaving our tents and cooking vessels to be packed up and put in the wagons by those who were unable to march, we hastened to the fortifications near Fredericksburg and took our position. The Federals had crossed below Fredericksburg and several miles above at the same time. Two balloons were kept constantly up in the air by them. One opposite the mouth of deep run 2 miles below and the other at Kelly's Ford about 15 miles above the town."[14]

The Tennessee Brigade's march to Chancellorsville was undertaken largely through night travel, with few men aware of the unit's destination. The moon shone almost as bright as the sun on one particularly beautiful night as the brigade passed cornfields that turned the thoughts of the brigade's members homeward. At one o'clock in the morning, a surgeon of the Fourteenth Tennessee pulled his flute from his saddlebag and began to play "Home Sweet Home." Other members of the Fourteenth Tennessee Glee Club joined in and performed a series of songs, climaxing in "Dixie Land." The positive effect of the performance was said to be unequaled throughout the war.[15]

The artillery fire and subsequent troop movements of the Union army signaled to the Confederates that Hooker intended to attack. Union general Sedgwick crossed a large number of troops from the left side of Hooker's army and positioned the men at Jackson's front as a decoy. A veteran recalled, "On the evening of the 30th it became evident that Hooker designed the crossing at Deep Run as a feint. Up to that time not more than a brigade had crossed and there seemed to be not more than a division on the other side of the river. They were crossing rapidly ... at Kelly's Ford and had driven back the force we had left at that point."[16]

It has been proposed that Hooker's intention in establishing lines on Gen. Lee's rear and left was to force the Confederate general to retreat to the safety of Richmond. Rather than erupting in a generous withdrawal, Lee's Army of Northern Virginia aligned itself in Hooker's front, impeding the Union progression.[17] Hooker's sudden and forceful movements largely ground to a halt as the shifting of regiments, likes pawns in a chess match, began.

On May 1, 1863 a member of the Seventh Tennessee wrote, "We were aroused from our sleep and started to march. Our course was up the river and movements rapid for infantry ... halted about one o'clock, formed a line of battle and rested about two hours then resumed the march ... At length we came upon the enemy's lines in a perfect wilderness. It was so near night however that no fighting occurred except skirmishing. My company was ordered out as skirmishers on the night of the first and consequently did not sleep much ... The hooting of the owls grated harshly on the night air. Back in our rear commands indicated the fresh arrival of troops during the entire night. The incessant chopping in our front and the occasional fall of a tree indicated the presence and activity of the enemy."[18]

H.T. Childs, 1st TN, recorded the widespread anticipation of the battle that quickly approached: "My company was sent forward on picket duty, and we were stationed, two on a post, thirty or forty steps from the Yankee pickets. The boy who stood with me was messmate, R.H. Anthony, as noble a boy as Franklin County ever produced. He was sick and wanted to lie down; but though it was very cold, no man was allowed to unroll his blanket. About midnight I told him to lie down and go to sleep, and I unrolled my blanket and spread it over him. Occasionally during the night some Yank or

Johnny would expose himself and then there would be a general fusillade of musketry."[19]

Childs continued, "Just before [the] break of day every band ... along the Confederate lines struck up 'Dixie.' It was grand! As our music died away, every band along the Federal lines struck up 'Rally Round the Flag, Boys,' and it too was grand. Then both sides struck up 'Home, Sweet Home.' As this music died away, with thoughts of home and tears in my eyes, I kicked Bob and told him to get up, and then the rattle of musketry began. We were expecting the Yanks to drive us in, and they were expecting us to drive them in. When our line reached the brow of the hill we found our boys in line beginning temporary breastworks in breathless expectation of a heavy column of blue to be right after us; but the Yankees did not come."[20]

One man of the brigade recalled the early-morning events of the next day when writing, "Contrary to our expectations, day dawned and the sun rose without any indications of a attack on either side. We were relieved about half an hour by sun and returned to the brigade. The troops then commenced to withdraw ... the entire army was in motion. Gen. Hooker's aeronaut saw the movement and telegraphed to him that the Rebel army was in full retreat. He immediately began to shell our trains and some cavalry and infantry, made a dash at one point but were repulsed by our infantry."[21]

Gen. A.P. Hill ordered Archer to move his brigade from its frontal position on Plank Road around eleven o'clock on the morning of May 2. Archer did, and proceeded to follow the other brigades of the division, which, except Thomas's, had gone by the Welford Furnace road. Archer had moved two miles beyond the furnace when he received information that caused him to retrace his steps with his own brigade and that of Thomas. The latter was following Archer to meet an attack on the trains that were passing at that point. Arriving at the furnace, Archer found that Lt. Col. Thompson Brown, of the artillery, and some infantry had repelled the enemy. Among those infantry companies participating in pushing back the Federals were companies L and H of the Fourteenth Tennessee, commanded by Capt. Moore.[22]

A.D. Norris made the following addition: "We made a rapid march round the Yankee Army passing from its left to its right flank. A portion of the army attacked the right flank of the enemy driving them in and demoralizing one corps completely, capturing several cannon and many prisoners. Archer's Brigade and Gen. Thomas were sent back to guard the trains threatened by the enemy."[23]

Thomas Herndon, Co. L, 14th TN, shared command of his company with Lt. Alexander Collins; Capt. Moore led Company H while the two units defended the Confederate wagon train. The 125 muskets of the companies supported two batteries of artillery for more than an hour to keep a series of cavalry charges in check until the wagon train was safely past. John Hurst remembered that Col. Moore had formed "a line of battle with the 23rd Georgia Regiment ... this force hotly contested with a large force of the enemy for at least twenty minutes ... With the resistance given by this force the train was able to get by with the exception of one caisson, which was broken down."[24]

George Lemmon, ordnance officer of Archer's Tennessee Brigade, recalled Hooker's attempt to cut Jackson's supply column at Chancellorsville and in doing so noted the highest admiration for Capt. Moore. As the ordnance train neared the sharp left and downhill turn at Catherine Furnace, Lemmon noticed bullets piercing the wagons. Lemmon asked Moore for assistance. Moore's only reservation about assisting the train was the fact that he had not been given Archer's permission to do so. Lemmon wrote "Captain Moore's brilliant dash ... accomplished all needed."[25]

Archer's maneuvers delayed the brigade's ability to rejoin Hill's Light Division for several hours, at which time the Tennessee Brigade formed on the division's extreme right with Gen. McGowan's Brigade to its left. As dark arrived, the Tennessee Brigade was given the command, "By company file left!"

The ruins of the Chancellor house, the structure from which the battle gained its name. Photo by author.

This moved the men into the bushes and undergrowth, where they received the additional orders, "Halt, front, stack arms! Lie down, boys, and go to sleep!" Another brigade member recalled going into bivouac about nine o'clock and gaining much-needed rest. At two o'clock, the men started marching again, covering five miles before reaching their position in the line of battle, a few hundred yards from the enemy.[26]

During the few hours Archer's men rested, many of his members took time to write loved ones, prepare for battle, or aid a sick comrade. H.T. Childs was among the latter group and recorded his adventures of the night: "Bob Anthony asked me to get him a canteen of water, and other boys came with their canteens. Taking eight of them, I slipped back into the road, examining the boughs of the trees as I went along so I would know the place when I got back. Passing forward, for I knew there was no water on the road we had come over, I soon came to the plank road ... The road was full of Confederates and Yankee prisoners. As I turned to the left I met an artilleryman who had been to water his horses. He pointed to a big light in the distance as the place where General Hill's wounded had been gathered and said I would find plenty of good water there. It was a mile away, but I got there, and after drinking all I wanted I sat down to rest and watched the army surgeons amputate arms and legs. It was frightful to see them grab up a boy and lay him down upon a scaffold, while he begged for his arm or leg. I soon got tired of this barbarity, filled my canteens, and started back. On getting back to my starting point I was perplexed, for there were no stacks of arms there and no boys sleeping on the ground. Feeling that Bob would not leave me, I began calling for him. He answered, saying the brigade had moved ... The brigade had moved only a short distance, and we were soon with the company ... General Archer dashed in among us. He had spread his blanket just in rear of our company and, hearing the racket about the canteens, came to see if he could get a drink. I handed him my canteen, and he almost emptied it."[27]

"We were in a dense wilderness," A. D. Norris wrote, "with pines blown and chopped down in every conceivable direction. Day was now breaking. Many overcome by fatigue dropped down asleep but about sunrise were aroused with the command 'forward march.' We met no resistance from the enemy, for some time, our skirmishers advanced rapidly in them, taking them completely by surprise capturing several pieces of artillery."[28]

H.T. Childs added, "As we moved ... we could see the dead Yankees and dead horses left upon the field the evening before. When we began to get near the Federal lines our officers cautioned us to make no noise. Filing to the right in a dense jungle, we got in position and were told to lie down with guns in hand and sleep if we could ... At the first streak of day the company officers aroused us, and we moved forward some fifty yards and halted to dress our lines. Then General Archer's shrill, clear voice was heard along the line: 'Fix bayonets! Forward, guide center! Charge 'em boys!' With an onward bound and the terrific whoop of the wild Rebel yell, we dashed forward through the dense jungle ... Soon we struck a steep little hill, and right up it we went. Along the brow of this hill the Yankees had thrown up temporary breastworks. They were taken by surprise. Over these works we poked our guns and poured a volley into them as they were getting up. A battalion of artillery was standing there. We killed every horse and, I suppose, every artilleryman. How General Archer got there on his big gray horse I do not know, but he commanded, 'Right over, boys!' and, spurring his horse, he scaled the works. Then he waved his sword and commanded, 'Halt!' He wanted to re-form his lines."[29]

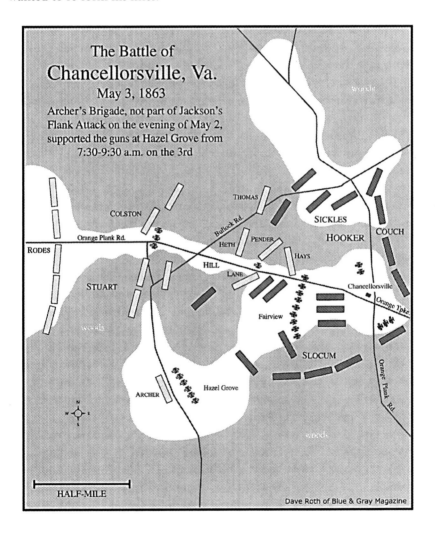

The Battle of
Chancellorsville, Va.
May 3, 1863

Archer's Brigade, not part of Jackson's
Flank Attack on the evening of May 2,
supported the guns at Hazel Grove from
7:30-9:30 a.m. on the 3rd

Woods

THOMAS

COLSTON

SICKLES

Orange Plank Rd.

Bullock Rd.

HETH   PENDER

HOOKER   COUCH

RODES

HAYS

HILL

LANE

Chancellorsville

STUART

Fairview

Orange Tpke.

woods

SLOCUM

Orange Plank Rd.

ARCHER   Hazel Grove

N
W—E
S

HALF-MILE

Dave Roth of Blue & Gray Magazine

Archer had moved forward as the Federal Third Army Corps under Maj. Gen. Daniel E. Sickles was evacuating its position at Hazel Grove. Archer's ability to closely press the retreating troops had enabled him to not only gain control of four artillery pieces but also capture approximately one hundred prisoners.[30]

Failing to sense Archer's order to halt as a desire to reform the brigade, A.D. Norris saw the situation of May 3 evolve into abounding chaos. He wrote, "We were thrown into great confusion … The enemy feebly graped us but did no damage. Soon we entered into an open field where the 2nd line of the enemy's works were plainly visible. Without waiting to form our ranks in order and without connecting with the main line which we passed either on the right or left, Gen. Archer ordered a charge. The line advanced boldly to within a short distance of the trenches, then finding them much stronger than we first thought, the men fell back a few hundred yards, formed again and strange to say were ordered right back by Gen. Archer. The order was obeyed and with the same result as before. Our brigadier now thought it best to wait for help."[31]

H.T. Childs indicated that the failure to halt and reorganize rested not on Archer but with the members of the brigade who had become totally entranced by the battle. He wrote, "They would not halt. When on a charge Tennesseans haven't got a bit of sense. On they rushed, the Yankees in their confusion shooting back at us. I was just as afraid of being shot by our men from behind as I was of being shot by the Yankees in front. On we swept in a southeast direction … within two hundred yards of their second line we met a volley of Yankee bullets. Then we began to touch elbows and move steadily in a good line up the hill to a kind of bench, where we could lie down and load, then rise and fire. From this position I fired three times and began loading again. I could see comrades falling around me. One boy from the Fourteenth Tennessee Regiment fell right across me. George Jones, who had kept with me, had a breech-loading gun, and he was loading and firing rapidly. As he was getting down to reload it seemed to me that I saw a bullet whistle through his mouth, and at the same time he was shot in the knee. When my gun was loaded I hesitated, then I thought, 'That is what I am here for,' and as I made my spring to rise I was shot through the left thigh."[32]

The help Norris proposed and Gen. Archer desired soon arrived. John Hurst explained, "The Confederate artillery moved in and occupied the elevation at Hazel Grove, and three regiments of Doles' Brigade, under the command of Col. John T. Mercer, came up on Archer's left, and the troops of Maj. Gen. R.H. Anderson joined his right. Soon … Lee rode up and directed Archer to move forward with his own brigade and the three regiments of Doles' … After he advanced four hundred or five hundred yards a short halt was made to distribute ammunition to the regiments of Doles'. Though he had received an order through a staff officer of General Stuart, then in command of Jackson's Corps, not to advance farther until he received orders from him … moved slowly forward and soon came to the ascending hill in front of Chancellorsville in full view of the enemy's cannon, which opened fire on the advancing line. General Archer had difficulty distinguishing his brigade, as members of other brigades had become integrated into its ranks in the advance. Archer 'feared it had fallen back' but grew relieved and pleased upon finding that the Tennessee Brigade 'had moved promptly forward and had driven the enemy from that part of the trenches to the left and nearest' to the location of the Chancellor's house."[33]

Capt. Fergus S. Harris, Co. H, 7th TN, gave this thrilling rendition: "After driving the enemy some distance, they ran against a heavy line behind splendid works. Retiring behind a low ridge, we rested while Pelham peppered them with his horse artillery. When the artillery duel was over, Capt. Oliver Foster and I were standing off to the right, when Gen. Lee approached and asked whose troops these were. Capt. Foster answered that it was Archer's brigade, and pointed out the General. With a soldier's curiosity, we followed to hear what he would say to Gen. Archer. After salutations, Gen. Archer explained how his troops had driven the enemy for a mile until they struck the strong entrenched line on the hill, which they did not carry. Gen. Lee looked steadily for some minutes at the strong line on the hill, then turning to Gen. Archer, said in a businesslike way, 'General, if you will move your brigade to the front about half way to that ravine, then make a left wheel move in that direction until your right is opposite that clump of trees, then right wheel again and strike those people in front, you will drive them out. They will not bother you much until your last movement.'"[34]

Harris continued, "Archer maneuvered his little brigade beautifully and everything moved like clock work until the right wheel came. The Seventh Tennessee on the right, instead of wheeling, went into their works 'on right into line.' Hal Manson … was the first man I saw go in. He never stopped until he stood on top of their works on the other side, waving his hat to the boys to come on. In five minutes he was worrying John Henlin for some of his rations. 'Old Bones' knew who carried the biggest haversack. How the other regiments got in I never knew, but it is told that when Col. Newt George, commanding the First Tennessee, and on the extreme left, saw the other regiments going in and driving the Yankees pell-mell from their front, he could not wait for the regular right wheel, but yelled out, 'Get in there endways, if you can't get in any other way. Don't you see the other regiments all going in.' No man ever accused Col. George of timidity in battle. The enemy fired but few rounds when the Tennesseans commenced to pour in on them, but their few rounds cost some of the best blood of the South."[35]

James H. McClain, Co. H, 7ʰ TN. Following a severe wound at Chancellorsville, McClain's right leg was amputated at the knee. A request was made for the receipt of a wooden leg, but no records indicate if this was ever granted. McClain died of fever on July 22, 1864 in Alabama. Courtesy of Paul Gibson.

June Kimble later wrote that the importance of the ground that Archer's soldiers captured was quickly realized by Gen. Lee, who rushed the Confederate artillery into position in order to impose deadly fire upon the Union lines. Archer had defeated two lines of Federal defenses and advanced upon the open hill at a high cost of casualties.[36]

There is a claim that Gen. A.P. Hill declared the Tennessee Brigade as the heroes of Chancellorsville after the men gained possession of the ground around the Chancellor house. In his official report, Hill did credit Archer's men for the capture of the four cannon, yet further accolades appear as nonexistent. Archer wrote his sister on June 14, 1863 that both Generals Lee and Hill had expressed congratulations to him for the Tennessee Brigade's performance. Archer also rationalized the loss of more than a fourth of his brigade, as he felt satisfied that gaining the key position of the battlefield had created a much greater loss to the Yankees.[37]

The respect Archer's men gained among the Northern soldiers at Chancellorsville is epitomized in a letter to Capt. F.S. Harris from Lt. Col. William Fox of the 107th New York Volunteers. Fox penned, "It is unnecessary for you to remind me of the fighting qualities of your old brigade. I was in the Twelfth Corps at Chancellorsville, where we were confronted by Archer's and McGowan's men, and where we courteously vacated our position in acknowledgment of their claims."[38]

H.T. Childs, 1st TN, wounded during the early charge of the day, experienced fear and exaltation at the battle's closing events. He penned this passage: "Our line began to retreat, leaving us wounded boys within forty yards of the enemy's works. Coming over their works, the Yankees in perfect line began to advance … We thought they would pin us to the earth with their bayonets as they came over us. On they came, making the earth tremble, but just before reaching us I heard the command, 'Right about!' and the line moved back behind their works. The battalion of artillery which we captured in running over their first line now turned on the Yankees in their second line … grape and canister fell all over us wounded boys. At the first volley that fell among us I was on my hands and knees trying to crawl down the hill. A grapeshot glanced my left hand, rendering it useless for a long time. Finally I managed to crawl down to the creek and got right in it … While lying in the creek I looked back and saw General Archer coming over the hill; then the flags came in sight, then the bayonets, then the boys. My company came within ten steps of me. The first man to get to me was Maj. F.G. Buchanan, who pulled me out … It was the last time I ever saw the 1st Tennessee Regiment. Soon I was carried by the litter bearers to the field hospital, where my wounds were dressed."[39]

A.D. Norris explained, "We charged that position also and after an obstinate conflict, drove them back, by this move we got possession of the plank road and forced them directly toward the river. This terminated the battle for the day, our victory was complete, though dearly won by the wound of Gen. Jackson and the loss of many of our bravest men."[40]

H.T. Childs, Turney's First Tennessee Regiment. Childs joined the Confederate army as a self-described "beardless boy, a high private in the rear rank." He would be one of the last survivors of the First Tennessee in post-war years, serving as a representative to the Tennessee General Assembly. His recordings of the war's events serve as a major source for this text. Photo courtesy of Confederate Veteran.

Archer was constantly exposed to Union fire while commanding the entire right side of A.P. Hill's Light Division. J.H. Moore, 7th TN, felt that the brigadier showcased bravery seldom seen in any other phase of the war. Archer's ability to escape wounds or death during the battle even while leading a series of charges on horseback was "one of the inexplicable enigmas of war."[41]

June Kimble, 14th TN, exclaimed that this battle fully illustrated that valor, not necessarily numbers and equipment, could achieve victory. Lee's army of approximately 49,000 had defeated Hooker's 120,000 men.[42] History has duly recorded the fact that this victory was extremely costly for Lee, the Confederate army, and the entire Confederacy, as it had cost the nation an unequaled leader in the mortal wounding of Gen. Jackson during the night of May 2.

Andrew F. Paul, Co. K, 7th TN. The native Texan joined his Cumberland University classmates as a member of the Wilson Blues. Paul attained the rank of 2nd Lieutenant before being killed at Chancellorsville on May 3, 1863. Courtesy of Paul Gibson.

Archer reported his loss at 14 killed and 317 wounded. As he carried 1,400 men into battle that morning, this shows a loss of over 25.5 percent.

The tabulated statement, however, varies slightly: Fifth Alabama Battalion: 3 killed, 32 wounded, 1 missing, aggregate 36; officers killed, Capt. S.D. Stewart and Lt. W.B. Hutton. Thirteenth Alabama Regiment: 15 killed, 117 wounded and missing, aggregate 140; officers killed, Maj. John T. Smith and Lt. J.J. Pendergrass. First Tennessee Regiment: 9 killed, 51 wounded, 1 missing, aggregate 61. Seventh Tennessee Regiment: 10 killed, 51 wounded, missing, aggregate 64; officer killed, Lt. Andrew F. Paul. Fourteenth Tennessee Regiment: 7 killed, 56 wounded, missing, aggregate 66; officer killed, Capt. W.W. Thompson for an aggregate loss, including missing, of 367. Col. William McComb, commanding the Fourteenth Tennessee, was severely wounded.[43]

Among the officer casualties of the brigade was William Bryan Hutton of Co. A, 5[th]AL. The fifth child of an Alabama doctor, William had attended the University of Virginia, received diplomas in several languages, and intended to travel to Germany to complete his studies. Hutton's plans were forever altered when Alabama seceded, and the young man returned home to enlist in the North Sumter Rifles. Hutton was given several promotions during his service, during which time he fought in thirteen battles.[44]

A friend noted that, "In all of these he had been so conspicuous and faithful that he was commissioned as third lieutenant. He met his death … leading the battalion. About sunrise Sunday morning, May 3, 1863, he was mortally wounded in the breast, and fell. He was shot again in the arm, on the way to the division hospital." Hutton's sister, Eugenia Williams, placed a tombstone over her brother's grave in the Spotsylvania Court House Virginia cemetery on July 4, 1868. She paid for this with coins, which had been received from time to time at the ferry and which her husband habitually gave her as pin money.[45]

Another tragedy of the battle of Chancellorsville was Gus Thompkins of Co. A, 14th TN. Wounded severely in the left shoulder during the battle of Fredericksburg, Pvt. Thompkins had been given an indefinite furlough to allow his wound to properly heal. Thompkins sought recuperation in the home of his uncle in Spotsylvania County, Virginia yet had to leave the home, as the actions of Union scouts made the sanctuary less hospitable with the battle of Chancellorsville approaching. Thompkins located his company and shared with his comrades that he was engaged to a lovely Virginia lady; his friends marveled at his elation. However, on the afternoon of May 3, 1863, Thompkins fell with a shot and shell wound to both legs. His legs were amputated and the shock proved too much for the soldier. Thompkins's last request was for June Kimble to deliver his personal items to his fiancée. This act was carried out and Thompkins's body, buried for a short time in the field hospital cemetery, was reburied in his uncle's family cemetery in Spotsylvania County.[46]

William Bryan Hutton was the son of a doctor and was himself a college graduate with diplomas in several languages. A veteran of more than a dozen battles, the twenty-two-year-old lieutenant was shot in the chest and arm at Chancellorsville and died soon after. Following the war's end, his body was moved from the base of an apple tree on that battlefield to Spotsylvania. Courtesy of Confederate Veteran.

Prior to the battle, Maj. John T. Smith, 13th Alabama, had written his loved ones, relating his unhappiness over the transfer of his regiment to Archer's command, yet he also noted the need to carry out his duties to his country. Smith, in his mid-twenties, died in the charge upon the Union breastworks. Col. B. D. Fry appointed a four-member committee to pay the proper respect to the popular officer and Mason.[47]

One action of the committee that consisted of Capt. A. Sidney Reaves, Capt. W.J. Taylor, Lt. William H. Burton, and Lt. C.C. Sellers of companies D, C, K, and A respectively was the adoption of a set of resolutions. These were developed at Camp Gregg, Virginia on May 11, 1863 and sent to the major's family along with a trio of papers that circulated in and around his home in Randolph County, Alabama.[48] They stated:

> Tribute of respect to the memory of Maj. John T. Smith, 13th Regiment Ala. Vol., who fell in the battle at Chancellorsville, Va., on the 3rd inst.
>
> Whereas, It has pleased Almighty God to remove from our midst our much esteemed, and brave Major, John T. Smith, by death while engaged in front of our common enemy at the battle of Chancellorsville, Va, on Sunday the 3rd inst. Therefore, Resolved,
>
> 1st. That by the death of Major Smith our beloved country has been deprived of one of its noblest and bravest sons, our State of a true patriot, and our regiment of one of its most gallant officers. By his gallant and unflinching conduct exhibited in every battle in which he was a participant, he gave promise of much future usefulness to his country, and his memory will ever be cherished by his brother soldiers, and his name gratefully remembered by his fellow-citizens at home.
>
> 2nd. That the Regiment deeply sympathizes with the family, and friends of the young hero, and while we admit that the circumstances of his death render this affliction most severe, yet in bowing submissively to the will of God, we remember that he doeth all things well, and all things work together for good to them that love Him.
>
> 3rd. That this Regiment well remembers the many gallant and praiseworthy acts displayed by Major Smith on the memorable battlefields of Cold Harbor and Malvern Hill, while then Captain, and in command of our Regiment.[49]

On the night of May 3, the Tennessee Brigade joined others in constructing temporary breastworks and establishing a picket line. The thick undergrowth in front of the picket line concealed the Union army that lay nearby. John Fite, 7th TN, remembered taking shots at anything that moved in the thicket as well as being the recipient of a late-night visit from Gen. Pender. Pender asked Fite where the enemy was located, and Fite responded that they were positioned just to his front. Pender jumped atop the breastworks for a better view. Fite exclaimed that Pender had placed himself in a dangerous position and could now easily be picked off, standing in his current location. Pender reportedly stated, "No, I guess not," and a shot rang out almost immediately from the Union lines, striking the general in the hand. Pender climbed down and walked away, slinging his hand and offering statements that he was not hurt. Gen. Archer sent for Fite to come to his tent in order to provide a firsthand account of the incident involving Gen. Pender's wound. Fite explained the incident to Archer, who expressed his dislike for Gen. Pender by saying that he wished the enemy had shot Pender in the head rather than the hand.[50]

June Kimble held the rank of sergeant at Chancellorsville and was given the responsibility of commanding and posting a portion of the picket line. Kimble informed the hungry members of his picket that he would take a few haversacks a half-mile to the rear, to the main line, and gather rations for them if they would assure him they would stay awake and be careful. Pushing his way through tangled undergrowth, Kimble sensed he was approaching a dead body as the stench became more offensive with each step. Reaching the corpse of a Confederate soldier in his mid-twenties shocked Kimble, for a light instantly flashed from the face of the corpse, an event Kimble noted as shocking to him forty years later. A doctor explained to Sgt. Kimble that the humidity of the area and the body's level of decomposition could possibly have initiated an electrical passage between the corpse and Kimble, creating the instantaneous glow that Kimble saw. Regardless of the cause of the event, Kimble returned to the body the next day and buried the young soldier whose identity and exact cause of death in the lonely section of woods remained a mystery. Kimble lamented the realization that the sorrow, grief, and unfulfilled hopes of return felt by the young man's family was undoubtedly relived in an almost infinite number of families[51] of the North and South. Neither army could fully comprehend that the casualties suffered at Chancellorsville were but a prelude to those awaiting them at a small Pennsylvania town named Gettysburg.

CHAPTER THIRTEEN

Gettysburg: Day One

Following the costly Southern victory at Chancellorsville, the Tennessee Brigade joined the remainder of the Light Division in returning to their camp near Fredericksburg. Jackson's former corps was then reorganized, with Gen. Ewell taking charge of the Second Corps and A.P. Hill assuming command of the Third Corps. Into the latter corps were placed the divisions of generals Pender, Anderson, and Heth. The Tennessee Brigade joined Gen. Davis's Mississippi Brigade, Pettigrew's North Carolinians, and Buckenburgh's Virginia Brigade in rounding out Heth's division.[1]

In the meantime, the First Corps under Gen. Longstreet took a path opposite that of Ewell, who was pushing into Maryland and Pennsylvania. Lee and Ewell had captured a large supply of Federal stores, ammunition, and thousands of prisoners at Winchester, while Hill's division, including the Tennessee Brigade, awaited orders to move.[2]

At midday on June 14, 1863, the Tennessee Brigade broke camp near Fredericksburg and began its march to join the main force of Lee's Army of Northern Virginia. The brigade passed through a number of battlefields, including Chancellorsville, before spending a Sunday at Berryville, Virginia. Fording the Potomac at Charlestown Crossing, Archer's soldiers trekked through Sharpsburg and Hagerstown until they reached Fayetteville, Pennsylvania, where they spent their second Sabbath of the march. On June 29, the brigade entered Cashtown,[3] located seven short miles from the town of Gettysburg.

A majority of the members of the Tennessee Brigade enjoyed a rest in Cashtown on the thirtieth. Several of the men washed their clothes and, in the words of a member of the Thirteenth Alabama, prepared to meet "our friends the enemy." E.T. Boland, Co. F, 13th AL, recalled that from his position atop a tall hill on which the Tennessee Brigade was camped that he could dimly see the village of Gettysburg. J.H. Moore was sent from this position to move three miles in the direction of Gettysburg on the morning of June thirtieth for the purpose of guarding the road leading west from Cashtown. With approximately forty men assisting as pickets, Moore sighted a scouting party of Federal cavalry and in turn sent word to Gen. Archer of his observation.[4]

Gen. Archer, aware of Federal scouts in the area, sent John Fite, 7th TN, into Cashtown in order to locate supplies, namely shoes. After a time of unsuccessful searching, Fite and his small detachment were informed that a large supply of shoes was located in the cellar of a specific home. Being told of the intended visit from the Confederate soldiers, the female occupant of the house refused to open the lock on the cellar door. Fite threatened to open the door with an axe and was then given the key. After opening the door, Fite and his party retrieved a large variety of goods and enough men's shoes to satisfy the needs of the men of Archer's command.[5]

Dr. E.B. Spence, Heth's division surgeon, requested permission to ride into Gettysburg to search for medical supplies. Jacuelin Marshall Meredith, chaplain of Heth's division, left camp with Dr. Spence around four o'clock on the afternoon of the thirtieth, assuring the doctor that troops from their division had preceded them into the town, though none were clearly seen at that time. Entering a Gettysburg drugstore at five o'clock, Spence and Meredith were alarmed at the quick march of a group of Confederates from the eastern part of town. The Confederates, one of Gen. Pettigrew's North Carolina regiments, had been informed of an advance by a superior force of Federals into Gettysburg and notified Meredith and Spence of such. The two men joined the North Carolinians in their return to Cashtown, a trip that was carried out free of harassment from the enemy.[6]

On the evening of the thirtieth, the Tennessee Brigade moved to within three miles of Gettysburg, camping near a house and barn. The rain of the evening led some members to the Seventh Tennessee to inquire of the owner of the buildings as to the possibility of using some hay from the barn to make beds, as the wet ground might cause a number of the men to become sick. The owner refused the request, at which point the soldiers began pulling the straw from the barn. The men almost immediately discovered a supply of bacon that the straw had been concealing. The find was reported to the Confederate headquarters. Wagons were quickly sent to remove the bacon for use by the Southern soldiers.[7]

The next morning, July 1, 1863, pickets of the Tennessee Brigade enjoyed breakfast from the previous night's confiscated pork. For the second consecutive day, J.H. Moore observed Federal cavalry movements in the direction of Gettysburg and began preparing to send a report noting such. W.H. Bird, Co. C, 13th AL, and a comrade, Sam Biekly, each carried five canteens and haversacks in a quest to help themselves and others of their regiment in obtaining food and drink. The gentlemen filled the canteens with cherry wine and were eating cherries straight from a tree when they heard a long drum roll that signaled the need for the troops to fall in. Likewise, Moore received order to rejoin his regiment, and Fite and his pickets were called in.[8]

Archer's Tennessee Brigade joined Pettigrew's in an expedition at approximately five o'clock in the morning of July 1. The purpose of the expedition was to complete Pettigrew's unsuccessful search of the previous day. Gen. Heth notified Gen. A.P. Hill of his intention to ride into Gettysburg that morning and, if there was no objection, he would "get those shoes." Hill replied to Heth that there was no objection.[9]

Pvt. E.T. Boland, 13thAL, remembered the subsequent march: "Broke camp at Cashtown ... the 13th Alabama in advance. We passed Anderson's Division in camps; and when within about four miles of Gettysburg, we passed through a small village of a few brick houses. About one-half mile above the village the turnpike enters a thick woodland or swamp. Here we halted. A misty rain had begun to fall."[10]

J.H. Moore, 7th TN, summoned from his picket post earlier on the morning of July 1, rejoined his regiment after the march into Gettysburg had begun. Archer's Tennessee Brigade was in the advance of Heth's division as it approached the town and the presence of a force of Federal troops in the town became more evident.[11]

E.T. Boland recorded the preparations of the moments before the opening of the largest battle of the war: "Col. B.D. Fry, of our regiment, rode back to the color bearer and ordered him to uncase the colors, the first intimation that we had that we were about to engage the enemy. We discovered about this time a squad of Federal cavalry up to our right in an old field, holding their horses. We were then ordered to file to the right into an apple orchard and to load our guns at will. Companies B, C, and G of the 13th Alabama, and the 5th Alabama Battalion were ordered out and deployed as a skirmish line. After the line of the brigade was formed, the command, 'Forward, march!' was given. As soon as the skirmish line entered the swamp a shot rang out, it being the first gun fired in the great battle of Gettysburg."[12]

A debate still exists regarding who fired the first shot at Gettysburg. The shots Archer's command encountered most likely came from Brig. Gen.

John Buford's First Cavalry Division. An advance Union picket member was Corp. Alponse Hodges, Co. F, 9th NY Cav., who had moved into the area of the advancing Confederate troops on the Chambersburg Pike. Due to the fact that Cyrus W. James from Company G of Hodges's cavalry regiment is usually named as the first Union soldier killed in the battle of Gettysburg, Hodges's claim is somewhat reliable. Sgt. Marcellus E. Jones, Co. E, Eighth Illinois Cav., reportedly asked a fellow sergeant for his carbine and took aim at an officer atop a horse in the Marsh Creek area. Many historians agree with Jones's claim and cite him as the individual who fired the opening shot of the battle.[13]

Capt. W.F. Fulton, 5th AL, recalled this action in an article written forty years later. He stated, "The 5th Alabama Battalion of Archer's Brigade was detached to drive in this cavalry, and the inference is conclusive that my contention is correct—namely, that Archer was the man who brought on the battle of the 1st of July, and the 5th Alabama Battalion fired the first shot on the Southern side."[14]

Lt. Will Crawford commanded the Thirteenth Alabama detachment that joined the Fifth Alabama Battalion, recently removed from provost duty, as the column slowly advanced along the road. W.H. Bird and Sam Biekly, arriving from their quest for provisions and distributing canteens of cherry wine among the members of their company, reached the regiment as it was forming into a line of battle.[15]

Dr. W.H. Moon recalled, "In column formation we continued to advance … when Davis's Brigade came up, we filed right into a body of woods, Davis's Brigade taking position on the left of the road. Confederate battery of three guns came up and took position on the right front of my regiment, the 13th Alabama, in the edge of an open field which extended down to and across Willoughby Run. So we had an unobstructed view of the blue coats on Seminary Ridge in our front."[16]

Pvt. E.T. Boland added, "I will say here that the cavalry we encountered was Buford's Division, which was easily driven back … one mile of Gettysburg we came in plain view of the town and also a long string of bluecoats marching. We learned it was the first Federal Army Corps, commanded by Major General Reynolds. When we started across this field, the enemy's artillery, which was located in the edge of town, opened up on us with shot and shell. We were then ordered to doublequick. Just before reaching Willoughby's Run, the cavalry began to get stubborn, and our line passed the skirmish line. Then we drove then back until we crossed the Run and went up a short hill."[17]

Buford's technique of mounting, dismounting, and remounting his cavalry was a technique learned in fighting Indians and in earlier Virginia operations. The threat of a massive cavalry assault ground the advance of the Confederates to a minimum.[18]

As the column from the Tennessee Brigade advanced, the two companies on the right of the Thirteenth Alabama were faced with passing a house in which "an old lady and a large yellow dog" resided. The dog evidently intended to end the trespassing and advancement of the Thirteenth, and began barking at and attempting to bite a number of the soldiers. Several of the Alabamians opened fire on the dog, killing it where it stood and opening up several of Archer's men to receive the verbal wrath of the woman, who wholeheartedly regarded the Confederates as "terrible fellows."[19]

Capt. W.F. Fulton remembered a similar situation with a slightly different outcome. He wrote, "As our skirmish line neared Willoughby Run ... in passing an occupied residence a large watchdog bounded out and set up a determined protest to our passing his master's premises; and directly a man emerged from the cellar, bareheaded, with spectacles pushed up on his forehead, in his shirt sleeves, with a shoe knife in his hand and a leather apron on, and he appeared much surprised at sight of men around and in his yard with guns in their hands, and at one demanded what it meant. When one of the boys told him that General Hill sent us to drive back the cavalry, and that there would soon be some hot fighting nearby, judging from appearances, he at once became greatly excited and exclaimed: 'Tell General Hill to hold up a little, as I turned my ... cow out this morning, and I wish to get her up before the fighting begins.'"[20]

Fulton recollected that Archer's skirmishers drove back Buford's cavalry "in gallant style" and "that the distance over which they drove this cavalry was some three or four miles, maybe more, hardly any less." John Purifoy wrote that the cavalrymen "were pressed back slowly for about three miles."[21]

The ease with which the Confederate skirmishers advanced upon their enemy hid the fact that a much superior Federal force awaited them nearer Gettysburg. By his own admission, Maj. Gen. Heth "was ignorant what force was at or near Gettysburg" and felt those present were largely cavalry with one or two infantry brigades in support.[22] Heth's proclamation of his lack of knowledge was supported among his subordinates.

John Purifoy elaborated, "Heth was ignorant of the character and magnitude of the force in his front. Archer's Brigade, numbering about eight hundred effectives, was deployed on the right of the Cashtown, road, and Davis's Brigade was deployed on the left of the same road. Davis had three of his four regiments with him, the fourth having been left as a guard for the division wagon train. The two brigades, Archer's and Davis's, numbered less than two thousand effectives when they entered the battle."[23]

Dr. W.H. Moon concurred with Purifoy's explanation in stating, "Here were Archer's and Davis's brigades confronted by Reynolds's corps and Buford's Division of cavalry. When we came in contact with the cavalry, General Heth dispatched to General Lee this fact. Lee's reply, 'Develop the infantry, but don't bring on a battle if it can be avoided,' is well known history. Why Heth did force the battle with such odds against him and in the face of Lee's orders and without support has ever been an unsolved problem to me."[24]

Pvt. Elihu H. Griffin, Co. B, 5th AL. Courtesy of Don Griffin.

In addition to the deployment of Archer and Davis, Heth's entire division was soon thrown into line. Now within a mile of Gettysburg, Archer's troops stood to the right of the pike; Davis to the left, with the brigades of Pettigrew and Brockenbrough in reserve. Federal infantry, cavalry, and artillery had been fully detected in and around the town; in response, Heth ordered Pegram's battalion, Marye's battery, to open fire. Archer and Davis were now formed and received orders to advance, making a forced reconnaissance to evaluate the number of Federal troops and determine if a massing of the enemy forces was being conducted at Gettysburg. Upon advancing, both brigades contacted heavy Union columns.[25]

Dr. Moon recalled the circumstances: "We had been in line of battle but a short time after our battery took position until the order was given: 'Forward!' As we debouched into the open field, a Federal battery, located about one hundred yards south of where the Reynolds monument now stands, saluted us with a shower of shells. Our line of advance placed the 13th on a direct line between the Federal and Confederate batteries. The descent to Willoughby Run is a gradual slope with a dip about one hundred and fifty yards from the Run, so our battery could not engage the Federal guns until we had gone about a half mile down the slope. As soon as we were below the range of our guns, they fired a volley at the Federal battery, and I thought it the sweetest music I had ever heard as the balls went whizzing just above our heads. At the second volley from our battery, I saw one of the Federal guns topple and fall to the ground. This raised a terrible Rebel yell all along the line. I was color guard on the left of the color bearer, Tom Grant. He was a big, double-jointed six-footer, and, having that morning [partaken] freely of Pennsylvania rye or apple joice [sic], he was waving the flag and holloaing [sic] at the top of his voice, making a fine target while the shells were flying thick around us. I said: 'Tom, if you don't stop that I will use my bayonet on you.' Just then a fusillade of rifle balls from the Federals greeted us, and Tom needed no further admonition from me."[26]

Moon continued, "We were now in easy range of the Federals across the Run, who were firing on us, but not advancing. We continued to advance, but in a walk, loading and firing as we went, until we reached a strip of low land along the Run. There we were protected from the fire of the enemy by an abrupt rise across the Run in our front. We halted to reform, reload, catch our breath, and cool off a little. It was but nine o'clock in the morning and hot, hotter, hottest! While we were engaged, the Tennesseans on our left advanced through a copse which ran up a ravine, spreading out into a fan shape as it neared the top of the ridge. They were hotly engaged at close quarters, the Yanks charging them in column, the Tennesseans lying on their backs to load and whirling over to fire. At this stage, Colonel George ... rode down the line to the right and requested General Archer or Colonel Akin—they were close together—to left wheel the 13th Alabama Regiment so as to cross fire on the Federals in front of the Tennesseans. This move placed the right of our regiment on or near the crest of the ridge and about seventy-five yards from the blue coats, into whom we were pouring volley after volley as fast as we could load and shoot. We were rather enjoying the fray when the order was given to 'fall back to Willoughby Run.' We could see no reason for the order, as the Tennesseans were keeping the 'blue boys' busy, and things seemed … pretty well for us, as we had only a skirmish line to our right, to which we gave little attention."[27]

As the Tennesseans advanced and forcibly reached a standstill, the number of casualties began to rise. All three of the first Confederates wounded in the battle of Gettysburg were members of the Fifth Alabama Battalion. Among them was Company B's Elihu H. Griffin of Jacksonville, Alabama. The twenty-four-year-old Griffin was seriously wounded and taken prisoner by the Union troops.[28]

Henry Raison, Co. B, 7th TN, became the first man killed in the Battle of Gettysburg, being shot just after crossing the branch as the brigade climbed a small hill. Across the field, Capt. John Dowell, Co. A., 7th TN, was shot through the breast.[29]

Archer's crossing of Willoughby Run, though protected by artillery fire, quickly grew disastrous. The Federal units had been pushed into a skirt of woods where the Confederates, continuously firing, again attacked.[30]

John Purifoy recalled, "Information reached Reynolds that the Confederates were approaching from … Cashtown. He deflected the head of his column to the left, and approached the Cashtown road about three-quarters of a mile from Gettysburg at about 10 a.m. Cutler's Brigade, leading the column, was deployed in line of battle north of the Cashtown road, and Hall's Battery was placed in position near the road. Meredith's Brigade, which followed Cutler, was … placed in line of battle south of the Cashtown road. Both brigades held position on the east side of Willoughby Run and near McPherson's farm house and barn … Cutler became sharply engaged before his line was formed, and while supervising the formation of Cutler's line, Reynolds was mortally wounded … by the bullet of a Confederate sharpshooter … As Cutler fell back, pursued by Davis, Doubleday, commanding the First Corps, hurried his reserves to the relief of Cutlers retreating forces. These new troops made a charge … Meredith confronted Archer's Brigade and during the desperate fighting which followed, it charged across the run, forcing Archer back."[31]

Reynolds's death was a tragedy for the Federal army. The young general had only recently declined an offer to lead the Union army, a position then offered to and accepted by Meade. The identity and uncertainty of Reynolds's assassin is still in dispute, yet a large number of possibilities exist.

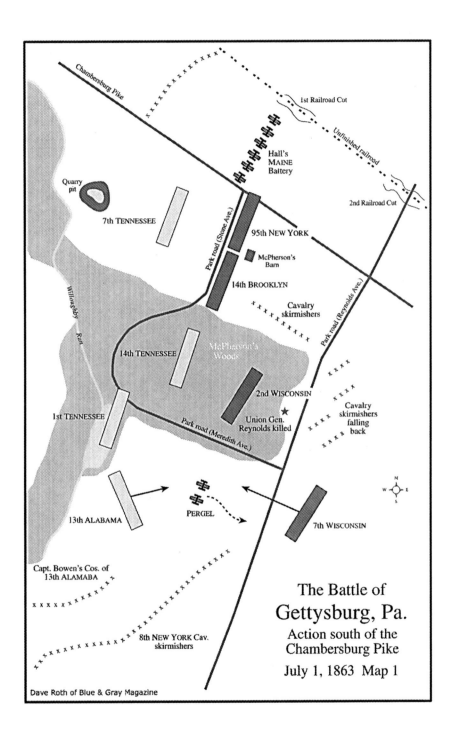

The Battle of
Gettysburg, Pa.
Action south of the
Chambersburg Pike
July 1, 1863 Map 1

During an 1899 visit to the battlefield, F.S. Harris, formerly of the Seventh Tennessee, toured the grounds with a group of battlefield commissioners. When Harris inquired of the men as to the validity of a decades-old rumor that a member of Company B of the Seventh Tennessee shot the young Federal officer, the men agreed that the fact was certain. One of the commissioners stated to Harris that is was "the singular feature ... that the same company lost the first man and killed Gen. Reynolds." There resided, according to Harris's story, an unidentified Nashville man who claimed to hold the distinction of being Reynolds's killer.[32]

Union Gen. John Reynolds—killed in the early stages of the battle of Gettysburg, perhaps by a member of the Tennessee Brigade. Courtesy of the Urigen Collection.

Harris was commanding the Tennessee skirmishers during the early action and at the turn of the twentieth century. He maintained that the

Nashville resident claiming to be the man who killed Reynolds had also been in the advance skirmish line that drove the Federal army back. The man informed his company lieutenant, soon after being driven back by the Iron Brigade, that "I have just shot a general!"[33]

The killing of Reynolds brought a different story to the mind of Dr. W.H. Moon who explained, "General Reynolds was shot from his horse by a member of Company F, 13th Alabama Regiment. This company was on the left, joining a Tennessee regiment, which placed them in much closer contact with the Federals than the right. I had been under the impression that General Reynolds was shot by a Tennessean until I met Captain Simpson ... at Gettysburg in 1913, and we went to the Reynolds monument, when he pointed to the place where he and his men were standing when he ordered one of them to 'shoot the man on the horse,' only about thirty yards distant, which was promptly done."[34]

W.H. Swallow, in his account of the incident, remembered Reynolds brandishing his sword and issuing orders when one of Heth's sharpshooters spotted the general. Working from a tree, the sharpshooter raised his rifle and fired at the officer, killing him instantly. One historian added that when Reynolds turned his head, as he had frequently done in battle, he was hit by a sharpshooter's bullet that exited near the general's eye.[35]

Historian Edwin B. Coddington noted that Reynolds had shouted to members of the Second Wisconsin to push "those fellows out of those woods" and turned in his saddle to look for support. A heavy exchange of fire between the Second and a section of Archer's troops resulted, during which time Reynolds fell from his horse, shot by a ball behind his right ear.[36]

Reynolds's Iron Brigade, known for its trademark black hats and bravery under fire, was quickly recognized. With one Tennessee Brigade member explaining that the group wasn't militia but was in fact part of the Army of the Potomac, the Tennesseans prepared for the onslaught. Just before twelve o'clock[37], as one side of Archer's brigade began crossing Willoughby Run, a series of events transpired that would forever affect its numerical strength. The underestimation of Heth in believing Archer and Davis to only be confronting militia or the motivation of Reynolds's troops to avenge their leader's death brought about a catastrophic series of events.

The left side of the Tennessee Brigade began successfully pushing back a portion of Reynolds's corps, yet in minutes it became clear that Reynolds's troops were beginning to flank the Tennesseans's right side. The ability of the Federals to maneuver so quickly around Archer's right was maximized in the fact that a strip of woods on the Tennessee Brigade's right concealed the enemy's flanking movement.[38]

Capt. June Kimble of the Fourteenth Tennessee added, "We crossed the run and advanced rapidly into a field densely covered with tall wheat, when suddenly a heavy line of battle confronted the brigade at close quarters and delivered a deadly volley into our very faces. Instant confusion and retreat followed, with many killed, wounded, and a number captured."[39]

W.H. Bird described the action: "Our regiment was on the right of the Brigade, and I believe our Brigade was on the right of the division. So we went on down the slope to a ravine, but before we reached it, Capt. B. A. Bowen was detailed off with fifteen or twenty men to watch a flank movement and to try to prevent it. So on we went down the hill with Lieut. H.W. Pond in command of the remainder of the company. We finally arrived at the ravine, crossed the clearest stream; pebbles in bottom nearly knee deep. Rose a rugged steep bluff, and entered a wheat field about a half mile west of Gettysburg. When we got up on the hill we seen a line of skirmishers some one hundred yards in front; the field officers were cheering their men and urging them forward. Lieut. H. W. Pond … was there urging on his Company; when all of a sudden a heavy line of battle rose up out of the wheat, and poured a volley into our ranks, it wavered and they charged us, and we fell back to the ravine again, and before we could possibly rally, it seemed to me there were 20,000 Yanks down in among us hollowing [sic] surrender."[40]

Bird's fellow regiment member, Pvt. E.T. Boland, described the hopelessness of the situation he and his comrades had entered into. He wrote, "About one-fourth of a mile from the town we discovered that we had tackled a hard proposition, for there were Federal soldiers to the right and to the left … 'We had Yankees on the front, Yankees on the flanks, and soon Yankees behind us.' For as soon as we engaged them in front the cavalry passed around and came in our rear. Here occurred one of the most unequal and hardest fought battles, considering the number of men engaged on either side, that I ever saw or heard of. The 13th Alabama was on the right of the two brigades, and had struck the Federal line in or about its center, so all they had to do was to wind themselves around us. After a short, furious fight, surrounded by infantry and cavalry, nothing was left for us to do but lie down in the field and allow the enemy to come on or surrender, which we did. General Archer had gone in on foot; and when the writer arose, two or three other comrades got up also. I cannot say how many were taken prisoners; but all who had not grasped time by the forelock and left when they realized what a deadly trap we were in surrendered."[41]

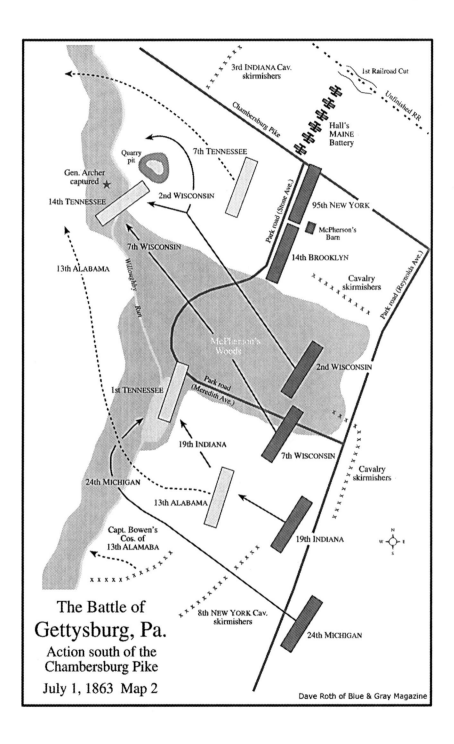

3rd INDIANA Cav. skirmishers

1st Railroad Cut

Unfinished RR

Chambersburg Pike

Hall's MAINE Battery

7th TENNESSEE

Quarry pit

Gen. Archer captured ★

14th TENNESSEE

2nd WISCONSIN

Park road (Stone Ave.)

95th NEW YORK

McPherson's Barn

7th WISCONSIN

14th BROOKLYN

13th ALABAMA

Willoughby Run

Cavalry skirmishers

Park road (Reynolds Ave.)

McPherson's Woods

2nd WISCONSIN

1st TENNESSEE

Park road (Meredith Ave.)

7th WISCONSIN

19th INDIANA

Cavalry skirmishers

24th MICHIGAN

13th ALABAMA

19th INDIANA

N
W ◇ E
S

Capt. Bowen's Cos. of 13th ALAMABA

The Battle of Gettysburg, Pa.
Action south of the Chambersburg Pike

July 1, 1863 Map 2

8th NEW YORK Cav. skirmishers

24th MICHIGAN

Dave Roth of Blue & Gray Magazine

Dr. W.H. Moon provided a similar account of the brigade's entrapment: "I suppose the order to fall back to Willoughby Run was prompted by Buford's Cavalry driving our skirmishers back and forming a line of battle in the open field in our rear, through which we had passed. When we reached the Run, order was given to 'lie down.' The blue coats soon covered the hillside in our front, ordering us to surrender. Our only hope now was that a supporting line would come up, drive the cavalry from our rear, fall in line with us, and drive the Federals from Seminary Ridge. But, alas! Our support did not materialize, so we were forced to surrender, General Archer and Colonel Akin with the 13th Alabama Regiment only a few steps to the left of Company I, of which I was a member."[42]

Thomas Herndon, 14th TN. Courtesy of Tennessee State Library and Archives.

Thomas Herndon, Co. L, 14th TN, also became a Union prisoner of war near Willoughby Run. He stated that the ease with which the brigade advanced into the Union center allowed the Federals to extend their "long wings" with little detection. The men attempted to fight their way out of the Union snare; those who were unable to do so were easily captured.[43]

Meredith, Heth's division chaplain, recorded a slightly different account. He explained that a majority of Archer's men, numbering less than one thousand, were suddenly charged by 2,500 Federal cavalrymen under Buford. The abrupt charge and capture were so efficiently carried out that Meredith recalled seeing "General Archer and two-thirds of his brigade captured with only a few pistol shots from the cavalry."[44]

John T. McCall proposed that the enemy's quick appearance was accompanied with a crossfire and that the brigade's left flank also came under attack. R.E. McCulloch, 14th TN, substantiated McCall's claim in writing, "At one time the regiment was almost entirely surrounded by the enemy, and some of our best men were captured." McCulloch also recalled that the regimental flag of the Fourteenth Tennessee was shot down twice yet triumphantly raised each time and waved before the faces of the advancing Union troops.[45] The bravery of the men who served as color bearers was reflected in the leadership of Gen. Archer.

This photo shows the location of Archer's capture during the fighting on the first day at Gettysburg. Courtesy of Dave Roth, Blue and Gray.

Capt. W.F. Fulton remembered Gen. Archer closely following the skirmish line and pushing the brigade past the skirmish line before being flanked. J.B. Smith added that Archer's fashion was to lead his men into battle while cheering and encouraging them. Smith explained that Archer surrendered, along with two hundred of his men, rather than sacrifice them in a futile escape attempt.[46]

A member of the Thirteenth Alabama, writing under the initials of A.S.R., explained that while the brigade was surrounded "on nearly all sides," Archer ordered his men to fight to the last. A.S.R. proclaimed that Archer's command was largely followed, as none of the brigade's members surrendered until Federal troops were within ten to fifteen steps of the general. A.S.R.'s report can be taken lightly, though, as he also claimed to see Archer fall wounded, perhaps mortally, amid a hail of shot and a cloud of smoke.[47]

F.S. Harris, 7th TN, stood near Gen. Archer and offered to assist the general in an effort to avoid capture. Harris stated that Gen. Archer chose to hide in the bushes along Willoughby Run, yet he was found and captured. Harris waded across the Run moments before a number of his regiment fell captive.[48]

The respect Archer had among his men showed not only in the actions of those who urged him to escape but in their attitudes as well. Sgt. Robert T. Mockbee, 14th TN, said that the capture of Archer "caused deep regret" among the brigade members. The general maintained his concern for others to the moment of his capture, urging W.A. Castleberry, a member of Co. F and the color bearer of the 13th AL, to drop his flag to possibly keep it from falling into Union hands or to eliminate bringing harm to its bearer. Castleberry reportedly witnessed Archer break his own sword in the ground to avoid it being taken as well.[49]

In an article written fifty years after the event, W.H. Harries of Company B., Second Wisconsin Infantry, reported on the action of his regiment capturing Archer. He also disputed Castleberry's report of Archer breaking his sword, noting its value as a relic. Harries explained, "As we charged into the woods Archer's Brigade gave way, and it appeared to me that General Archer refused to be borne to the rear with his retreating men, some of whom remained with him and became prisoners. I came up directly opposite General Archer and a few feet from him, and while I was getting the prisoners to the rear of our troops Lieutenant Dailey stepped up to General Archer and said, 'I will relieve you of that sword,' and he did so. He then threw away his own sword and buckled on the Archer sword. On the afternoon of July 1 we were driven back through the town of Gettysburg, and Lieutenant Dailey, seeing that he would probably be taken prisoner, rushed into a house and gave the sword to a Miss McAllister, who resided there. When I was in Gettysburg twenty years ago, I saw and conversed with her in relation to the sword. She said that she concealed in a wood box the sword Lieutenant Dailey gave her, throwing a newspaper and some wood over it. General Archer did not break his sword in the ground or anywhere else that day. Lieutenant Dailey was taken prisoner about 4 p.m. on July 1. He escaped in the dark July 5, and went back to Gettysburg and got the sword from Miss McAllister."[50]

Maj. Mansfield, commanding the Second Wisconsin Infantry, noted in his official report that he personally gave Archer's sword to Lt. D.B. Bailey, acting aide-de-camp on the brigade staff. The sword and Archer had been brought to Mansfield under the guard of Pvt. Patrick Mahoney, Co. G., 2nd WI. Mahoney is generally credited with capturing Gen. Archer. Mahoney's ability to revel in his act would be limited, as he would be killed in action later that day; his body was never recovered.[51]

Gen. Abner Doubleday. The Union officer greeted the captured Archer at Gettysburg. Courtesy of the Urigen Collection.

Gen. Archer was embarrassed at the fact he was the first Confederate general in more than a year to be captured on the field. Following his surrender, Archer was taken to Gen. Abner Doubleday, who had assumed command upon Reynolds's death. Having been a West Point cadet with Archer, Doubleday greeted the Confederate general and declared he was glad to see Archer again. Archer's reply, laced with profanity, informed Doubleday that his captive was far less joyful over their reunion.[52]

Near the time of Archer's capture, Maj. Gen. Henry Heth escaped serious injury. Though his wound would render him incapacitated for several hours, Heth's life was saved by an unusual event. That day Heth wore a new hat, one that was too large for his head. Heth's clerk had lined the hat with thick folds of paper to compensate for the improper fit. These folds of paper prevented the mortal wounding of Heth, who was struck in the head yet miraculously survived[53] despite the best efforts of a Federal soldier.

W.A. Castleberry found the concept of captivity unbearable. Implementing a quickly rationalized plan, Castleberry escaped, evading prison and surviving the war. His recollection showed the respect others in command had for their leader, Gen. James J. Archer: "As General Longstreet was to support General Archer, I knew he must be near; so I crawled along in the wheat. Sure enough, General Longstreet's men came firing, and right there I offered up my check and stretched myself out, for the wheat was being cut down by Minie balls. General Longstreet charged, as usual; and as the men jumped over me they would say: 'Here is one of our men dead out here.' As they drove the enemy I made my way to a skirt of timber and got behind a cord of wood to watch the battle, for I could see both armies concentrating. About the time I was well fixed a fellow came galloping up and asked: 'To what command do you belong?' I answered of course: 'Archer's Brigade.' ... he ... told me that General Lee said for me to come down there. Of course I felt very strange, because I thought I would be put under guard. General Lee asked me if I belonged to General Archer's brigade, and upon my replying that I was he asked if General Archer was killed I told him no, and he said: 'Are you certain that he is not killed?' I told him that I was certain, as I saw him breaking his sword in the ground. He asked how far away it was to where he was captured, and I pointed to the timber where he surrendered. General Lee seemed very glad to know that General Archer had not been killed ... He rubbed the tears from his eyes and said: 'Go on.'"[54]

W.H. Bird saw surrender as the only option, as he advised a superior of his opinion after becoming surrounded by a group of Union privates. Thomas Herndon felt that he and those around him would have avoided capture had the other brigades of Heth's division come to the aid of Archer. Herndon backed his proposal in that once the trailing brigades joined and rallied the escaped members of the Tennessee Brigade, the circumstances changed in the Confederate's favor. R.T. Mockbee, also of the Fourteenth Tennessee, had avoided capture when his regiment became almost totally surrounded, and he cited the failure of the supporting brigades to keep up with Archer as the cause of the capture of such a large number of his fellow brigade members. An estimate of the number of officers and enlisted men captured with Archer on the morning of July 1 places the figure at nearly 350.[55]

Gen. Henry Heth, division commander of the Tennessee Brigade at Gettysburg. Courtesy of Blue and Gray.

Historian Gary Kross explained that several factors contributed to the failure of the defense initially offered on the part of Tennessee Brigade. The withdrawal of the Seventh Tennessee and the Thirteenth Alabama's inability to overcome the large number of soldiers of the Twenty-fourth Michigan caused several of the Alabamians to retreat to the rear. When the Second Wisconsin gained a point along the quarry pit, overlooking the Fourteenth Tennessee's left, the rear of Archer's position became exposed.[56]

Gen. Heth's chaplain recalled seeing a great deal of Archer's men fleeing toward a line being established within the ranks of Brockenbrough's Virginians. Brockenbrough's opportunity to fire into the Federal position was negated with the presence of a large number of "flying Tennesseans" rallying to his brigade's rear.[57]

Capt. J.B. Turney, Co. K, 1st TN, was among those eluding capture. He reported, "During the excitement attending the capture of General Archer, I succeeded in escaping with the major part of my company, falling back some two hundred yards to the skirt of timber. The Federals deployed; and, Heth having arrived, the battle was on in earnest. Archer's Brigade, under command of Colonel ... Fry ... was then withdrawn to the right of Lee's army. There we were deployed as a body of observation. My company was ordered as far in the advance as it was safe to go. I ventured near to the Emmettsburg road, where I saw the enemy moving its transportation to the rear. In my effort to report to my commander, I encountered General Lee, who asked what I found in front. When I reported, he remarked to his staff officers: 'I am afraid they will get away.' From this I concluded that he thought we had only encountered the enemy's advance."[58]

Dr. W.H. Moon noted, "All firing ceased in a few minutes after our surrender, and, as I remember, it was at least two hours before the fight was resumed. Quite a number of the 13th Alabama made their escape as we fell back to the Run by remembering the old adage: 'He who fights and runs away may live to fight another day.' Those who escaped were mostly from the left of the regiment and near the woods, occupied by the Tennesseans, which afforded considerable protection from the Federal rifle."[59]

John Purifoy noted the action: "Heth now decided that the enemy had 'been felt and found in heavy force in and around Gettysburg.' He proceeded to form his line of battle between the Cashtown and Fairfield roads. Archer's Brigade, Col. B.D. Fry, 13th Alabama Regiment, commanding, on the right, Pettigrew in the center, and Brockenbrough on the left. Davis's Brigade was allowed to remain on the left of the road to gather its stragglers. After resting an hour or more, one witness says two or three hours, Heth received orders to attack the enemy in his front, advised that Pender's Division would support him ... At first Iverson's Brigade only was deployed by Rodes, but as the conditions were of such character as to admit of cover for a larger opposing force, two other brigades were deployed, Iverson on the right, O'Neal in the center, and Doles on the left. The artillery and two other brigades were moved up closely to the line of battle … the two leading batteries, Carter's and Fry's, were placed in position on an elevated point near the Cashtown road, and fired, with decided effect … which compelled the Federal infantry to take shelter in the railroad cut and change front on their right. The Federal force here was evidently surprised, as no troops were formerly fronting Rode's formation … O'Neal's Brigade, with a wide gap between it and Dole's, guarded by the 5th Alabama Regiment, extended from the plain up the slope of the ridge."[60]

"Heth attacked the brigades of Biddle, Meredith, and Dana. These troops made a stubborn stand, but were gradually forced back, both sides sustaining heavy losses. Gamble's brigade of cavalry was discovered hovering around Heth's right flank, when Col. B.D. Fry … changed front on his right to meet the menace. After breaking through several lines confronting it, and several of Heth's regiments were out of ammunition, Pender, about 4 p.m., ordered an advance of three of his brigades, with instructions to pass Heth if found at a halt, and charge the Federal position on Seminary Ridge. Pender's forward movement was also menaced on his right flank by Gamble's cavalry brigade, causing a delay of Brigadier General Lane, who slowed up to meet it. Though Pender's Division met with a warm reception and suffered considerable loss, it drove the commands of Biddle, Meredith, and Dana, and perhaps other troops, from their position, when they were forced to retreat through the town to Cemetery Hill, south of the town, in a more or less broken condition, notwithstanding the several statements of Federal officers that such a retreat was made in an orderly and compact condition."[61]

Gen. Heth explained in his official report that the "Heroes of Chancellorsville," a name he used for Archer's Tennessee Brigade, performed well under Fry's leadership, maintaining its "hard-won and well-deserved reputation." Unfortunately no one from the brigade was singled out for his efforts in reestablishing the Confederate offensive.[62]

Thousands of Federal prisoners were captured in the town of Gettysburg. Rodes reported that his "division captured about two thousand five hundred— so many as to embarrass its movements materially." Many prisoners were captured in the houses in which they had taken refuge. Early failed to give the number of prisoners his division captured, but also said the number was so great as to embarrass it. Ewell stated that the number captured by the two divisions exceeded four thousand.[63]

Heth's wound, leaving him feeling senseless, failed to prevent his ability to explain that some 2,700 men of his division had been killed or wounded in a twenty-five-minute time frame. Heth's division had lost more men, killed and wounded, than did the remaining Confederate units.[64]

John Purifoy attempted to shed light on the casualty figures when writing, "I have been forcibly impressed with the great exaggeration and erroneous statements made as to the number of Confederates engaged, the captures of prisoners, and deaths inflicted on the Confederate forces. If all the statements were true, the entire Confederate infantry and its accompanying artillery were engaged, whereas but four of the nine divisions constituting the army were engaged, and an equal number of battalions of artillery ... Nearly all the troops engaged on the Confederate side had been in active service nearly two years and had suffered many casualties in battle, besides deaths from sickness. Many brigades numbered less than a thousand effectives. Archer's and Davis's brigades, of Heth's Division, Hill's Corps, bore the brunt of the fighting for a least three or four hours. Both of these were diminutive brigades."[65]

A witness stated, "I reached the battlefield of Gettysburg on July 1, 1863 soon after the fighting began between Hill's Confederate troops and Reynolds's Federal troops, and was a participant in the battle. I was in the pursuing party which followed the shattered Federals into the town of Gettysburg while the sun was high in the western heavens. It was then my deliberate conclusion ... that the first great mistake in the conduct of that battle was made when the Confederates failed to drive the demoralized Federal troops from their lodgment on Cemetery Hill and Ridge ... Though all the Confederates had been engaged, and many of the commands had suffered greatly, they had all just experienced the exhilarating feeling which follows victory ... The battle that had just been fought was an accident, as the commanders of both armies cautioned their advanced troops that if they found their enemy in force not to bring on a general engagement until the remaining commands of the army could be concentrated."[66]

Historian Albert A. Nofi proposed that despite Heth's bungling of the opening action, the Confederacy undisputedly won the first day's fighting at Gettysburg. A.P. Hill's afternoon performance on McPherson's Ridge had preserved a Southern victory. Heth's lack of knowledge related to the size of the Federal army on Cashtown Road could not be helped. If Heth had withdrawn from the field following the initial engagement, Gen. Early would have encountered a force three times his own, with no help within four to five miles. The result would have been a late evening battle with too little time to possibly drive the Federals from their position. Heth's division, including the Tennessee Brigade, deserves all possible honor in pressing the enemy and enabling the men of Pender, Rhodes, and Early to provide the Confederacy with a victory[67] on Gettysburg's first day.

As the second day of the battle began, daybreak on July 2 revealed smoldering campfires and peaceful farmhouses with people emerging, largely unsuspecting of the level of destruction the day would bring. Heth's division was posted on a slight elevation, some two hundred yards from Willoughby Run. The Tennessee Brigade remained in that position all day, provided with a clear view of the day's action of Longstreet and the destruction of the artillery on and around Little Round Top. A member of the Seventh Tennessee explained that the hill seemed at times to be on fire as members of his regiment were amazed at the number of artillery pieces implemented on the small area.

Capt. June Kimble effectively summarized the Tennessee Brigade's participation on the second day of the battle when stating, "Heth's Division … was held in reserve during the whole day of July 2, taking no part in the engagements."[68]

While the members of Archer's Tennessee Brigade present at Gettysburg on July 2 rested and recovered from the action of the previous day, those members captured on the first day were undergoing a day filled with hardships. Undoubtedly scared, confused, and physically fatigued, the men began their trek toward prison camps across the North.

After being paraded to the rear following their capture, the men of Archer's brigade were cursed by women in the town of Gettysburg, ladies who obviously resented their presence in the North. A brigade member named W.G. Martin commented to some of the abusers that he was certain now that they should be satisfied, as "we Southerners have got back in the Union." Throughout the night of July 1, additional captured Confederates joined those captured in the early fighting of the day; eventually the march began toward Chester, Pennsylvania. W.H. Bird recalled, "[We] were marched so hard that General Archer fainted and fell by the roadside, with many others." The members of the Tennessee Brigade were eventually separated in Baltimore, with the officers being sent to Johnson's Island, the privates to Ft. Delaware. Dr. W.H. Moon added, "After being captured, we were assigned headquarters at Fort Delaware, where many of our bravest and most noble comrades lost their lives on account of the treatment received."[69]

Thomas Herndon noted that he and other prisoners from the brigades of Archer and Davis remained on Round Top Mountain, where they had a clear view of the day's action. A forty-to-fifty-mile march was started at midnight, intended to carry the prisoners to a railroad to Baltimore. A potential problem for the new prisoners was unknowingly eliminated when Archer's men had earlier cooked five days' rations prior to departing Cashtown on June 30. Herndon and his fellow prisoners marched throughout the night of July 1 and under a torching July sun until three o'clock in the afternoon of July 2. Many of the men were exhausted and starved for water. Herndon, having perfect health at the time, divided his rations with Gen. Archer in order to relieve his commander's suffering.[70]

A young West Point lieutenant whom Thomas Herndon cited as being "without experience or judgment as to marching men" ordered the Federal guards to use their bayonets at will on the worn and disoriented Confederates. Several Yankees obeyed the command, seriously wounding a number of their captives. This continued until approximately four o'clock in the afternoon of the second of July when the Confederates boarded a train for Baltimore, reaching the city late that night.[71]

The Battle of Gettysburg and the Civil War were over for many of the men of the Tennessee Brigade, at least in the respect of fighting. Yet a new kind of war would emerge for many of them, as they struggled daily to maintain a grasp on their sanity and to dispel the growing doubt of self-worth. For their comrades waiting in Gettysburg, an all-too-familiar carnage, yet one unforeseen to that point of the war, lay ahead.

CHAPTER FOURTEEN

Gettysburg: The Third Day

July 3, 1863

On the night of July 2, Gen. Lee devised a plan for the following day. Meade's strength on his right and left sides had been tested; upon the plan to attack the center, Lee placed the success or failure of his campaign of invasion. The troops of Gen. Longstreet would move from the Peach Orchard and the Devil's Den, while Gen. Ewell struck southward from the recently captured trenches on Culp's Hill, to the right. The Federal center would receive the assault of Gen. Pickett's three brigades, intended to reinforce Longstreet.

The thirty-eight-year-old Pickett was known for his trimmed and perfumed hair that grew in ringlets to his shoulders. Containing six thousand men in fifteen regiments, Pickett's Virginia Division was one of the smallest in Lee's Army of Northern Virginia. Held in reserve at Fredericksburg and absent from the battle at Chancellorsville, the group also had little fighting experience. Despite having been serving as guards for the supply wagons at Chambersburg when the action had erupted at Gettysburg, the unit had moved to Gettysburg, eager for battle. As such, Pickett's division was the only one of Lee's Army that had yet to take part in the fighting at Gettysburg.[1]

As Pickett's division approached the battlefield on the morning of July 3, the sound of gunfire notified Gen. Lee that Ewell was engaged with the Federal army. The day soon went badly in regard to Lee's plan when Ewell was driven from Culp's Hill. In addition, Jeb Stuart's attempt to place his cavalry for an attack upon the Union rear had been ruined by a series of charges led by the young Union general George Armstrong Custer.[2]

The effectiveness of Lee's plan now depended upon the attack at the Federal center on Cemetery Ridge. Longstreet objected to the attack, recalling the futile Union attempts to dislodge the Confederates from a similar position at Fredericksburg.[3] Longstreet verbally objected to Gen. Lee's plans to use Hood's and Law's divisions in the attacks, as these two had suffered heavily in the previous day's fighting. Lee agreed to change his strategy on the deployment of these two divisions.

Pickett's division was chosen to replace Hood and Law with assistance from a combination of four brigades from the divisions of Gen. Dorsey Pender and Gen. Richard Anderson. Henry Heth's division, including the remnants of the Tennessee Brigade, would also participate in the assault. Gen. James Pettigrew, the lone uninjured brigade commander of Heth's division, would assume command of Heth's troops. Longstreet inquired of Lee as to the number of men who would attack the Federal stronghold. Lee answered that about fifteen thousand would make the charge, to which Longstreet replied that the position the Federal army held could never be taken by any fifteen thousand men. In addition to Longstreet's analysis, Lee's number was exaggerated by some twenty percent. Between nine and ten o'clock on the morning of July 3, the opposing armies began gathering, each on an elevated ridge almost parallel to that of the enemy. Heth's division reported to Longstreet and formed to the left of Pickett's division. Here the Tennessee Brigade was given orders to rest at ease in the line of battle.[4]

Pickett's division would hold the southernmost portion of the advance with Kemper's brigade on the extreme right. To his left was Brig. Gen. Richard Garnett's brigade. Serving as Pickett's left anchor and holding a position to the rear of Garnett was Armistead's brigade. To the east of Kemper's brigade was situated Perry's Florida Brigade with Col. David Lang commanding; to Lang's right, the Alabama regiment of Brig. Gen. Cadmus M. Wilcox. The position of these two brigades from Anderson's division gave the visionary effect that they were disconnected from the main body.

Archer's Tennessee Brigade, with Col. B.D. Fry leading, formed the extreme right of Heth's division, now under Pettigrew's command.

Pettigrew's North Carolinians were to Archer's left and under the command of Col. J.K. Marshall. Davis's Mississippi Brigade and Brockenbrough's brigade completed the right-to-left alignment of Heth's division, standing 325 yards to Armistead's left. Behind the Tennessee Brigade and Pettigrew's North Carolinians stood Scales's Brigade of North Carolina troops and, to the extreme north, Lane's North Carolina Brigade.

As the temperature approached ninety degrees, troops did their best to rest for the looming offensive. Some napped, others ate. Water was becoming scarce, as the wells in town had been drained of their supplies due to the usage of the 150,000 soldiers. Fresh fruit, particularly early apples, was ripening, though an overindulgence often led to diarrhea. It has been proposed that Gen. Lee was suffering from this ailment at Gettysburg, perhaps increasing his level of agitation and affecting his overall vigor.[5]

June Kimble recalled the formation and period of waiting for the assault amid the hot weather of the day: "Early on the morning of July 3 Heth's Division was moved to the right and formed a line on Seminary Ridge opposite and about a mile from the center and crest of Cemetery Ridge, upon which the enemy were strongly posted behind works, with parks of artillery covering their entire front. An open plain with a slight incline to the foot of Cemetery Ridge extended from Seminary Ridge with no obstructions between except three fences, two rail or worm fences, and one slab fence nearest to the enemy's front. For about four hours or more all this was under the eye and scrutiny of every veteran in Heth's Division as they stood in line, each knowing what the ominous silence pervading the whole field meant and each counting the probable results."[6]

Kimble continued, "During the lull, already oppressive, I walked out alone to the edge of the open some fifty yards in advance of the line then lying in the timber, and there deliberately surveyed the field from Round Top Mountain on our right to the suburbs and spires of Gettysburg on the left. I sought to locate the point on Cemetery Ridge about which our brigade and regiment would strike the enemy, provided our advance be made in a straight line. Realizing just what was before me and the brave boys with me, and at one of the most serious moments in life, I asked aloud the question: 'June Kimble, are you going to do your duty today?' The audible answer was: 'I'll do it, so help me God.' I turned and walked back to the line. 'How does it look, June?' said Lieutenant Waters. I replied: 'Boys, if we have to go, it will be hot for us, and we will have to do our best.' When I responded to my own question as to doing my duty, a change of feeling immediately took possession of me; all dread even passed away, and from that moment to the close of that disastrous struggle I retained my nerve, and my action was as calm and deliberate as if upon dress parade. It was different from all other experiences, many and various, in my four years of unbroken service."[7]

A member of the Seventh Tennessee recalled feeling as though he and those around him were facing certain death. The individual explained that by eleven o'clock the mood was prepared for the command to advance upon the Federal position, then in full view. The apprehension of the impending carnage was widespread as the danger of the task before the Confederates became increasingly evident. He added that at least three times after the Confederate battle line had been formed, Pickett, Lee, and Longstreet rode back and forth in front of the line, evidently discussing the assignment of the attack. Using field glasses, the trio noted the Federal positions and movements, as they seemed to be growing uncertain about a facet of the assault. At this point, the generals rode to the rear of the line and "engaged in earnest conversation."[8]

June Kimble, 14th TN. Kimble's records of the exploits of the Tennessee Brigade are among the most insightful of any of his peers. Courtesy of Confederate Veteran.

Col. Birkett Davenport Fry remembered the generals indulging in conversation while they sat on the trunk of a downed tree less than sixty steps from Fry's position at the right of Heth's division. The commanders carefully examined a map as they held a lengthy discussion. They then again rode up and down the Confederate line, presenting to some of their subordinates their feelings of the hazards of the task at hand.[9]

James Longstreet. Courtesy of Blue and Gray.

Upon the exit of Lee, Longstreet, and Pickett from the Confederate front, couriers and staff officers began circulating around the army. Gen. Pettigrew made his way to Col. Fry and informed him that a heavy cannonade would precede an attack on the area to each regiment's front; a strong Union response to the artillery was certain. Fry was sent to Gen. Pickett, who expressed his confidence in the oncoming Confederate attack and its success after the Union army had been "demoralized by our artillery." Gen. Garnett, of Pickett's left brigade, agreed to dress on Fry's command; this was immediately reported to Gen. Pettigrew. The understanding became widespread that Fry's command, the Tennessee Brigade, would serve as the center of the assaulting Confederate army, the unit by which the assaulting divisions would align. The divisions then moved into a line behind the Confederate batteries and lay down.[10]

The responsibility of coordinating the Confederate artillery bombardment fell to E. Porter Alexander, a twenty-seven-year-old colonel who had proven himself at Fredericksburg and Chancellorsville. Alexander had at his disposal approximately 170 cannon, each with 130 to 150 rounds of ammunition. Seventy-five guns were placed along a 1,300-yard front that ran northward from the peach orchard while eight others covered the attacking infantry to the south. Sixty of A.P. Hill's guns were positioned to the left and rear of the main line with twenty-four guns from Ewell situated beyond Hill's.[11]

Though the total number of cannon present at the battle tends to vary from historian to historian, the recollections of the cannonade they participated in contain similar remarks. Dick Reid explained, "I will never forget that fatal day, as I stood at the last gun, a three-inch rifle, with the lanyard in my hand, awaiting orders to open fire on Cemetery Heights and clear the way for Pickett's charge. We had one hundred and eighty-six pieces of artillery in this line, from ten-pound Parrott's up to thirty-pounders and three-inch rifles. I was at the extreme gun on the left, and opposite Cemetery Heights ... Pickett's Virginia division was laying just in the rear of our long line of artillery, in two lines of battle, with Gen. Heth's Division in supporting distance. In Heth's Division was Gen. Archer's Tennessee brigade, composed of the Thirteenth Alabama, Fifth Alabama Battalion, First Tennessee, Seventh Tennessee, and Fourteenth Tennessee. It was a small brigade, but their loss was terrible ... This terrible loss shows how the sons of old Tennessee immortalized themselves at Gettysburg."[12]

June Kimble, 14th TN, explained his analysis of the events: "At about one o'clock a solitary signal shot was fired far to our right by Longstreet's command. Instantly every battery upon the Confederate line opened on its mission of death and destruction, and was as promptly responded to by every battery, I presume, on the Federal line, and the third and last day of the battle of Gettysburg was on. For about one hour an artillery duel, the equal of which was never fought on this earth, followed this signal gun. The roar and crash of five hundred booming cannon, screaming and bursting shells, and the swish of crashing solid shot brought forth a veritable pandemonium. The very earth shook as from a mighty quake. So intense were its vibrations that loose grass, leaves, and twigs arose from six to eight inches above the ground, hovered and quivered as birds about to drop until the mighty roar ceased. And it did cease almost as suddenly as it began."[13]

Capt. J.B. Turney, Co. K, 1st TN, offered his perspective from farther down the Confederate line: "At about 11 o'clock the fiercest cannonading known to warfare was begun. For two hours the old hills trembled as if affrighted. The limbs and trunks of trees were torn to pieces and sent crashing to the earth to add to the havoc among the gallant boys who waited anxiously an order to charge."[14]

John Fite noted the artillery duel to be "the grandest cannonading of the world." Fite's claim was not completely unfounded, as the event was referred to as the greatest manmade noise to have taken place in North America. The effects of the artillery concussions affected those resting in their distant homes, and windows in Baltimore, Maryland shook during the exchange.[15]

Casualties mounted quickly during the barrage despite most troops finding cover. Kemper's brigade had 15 percent of its men killed or wounded during the event; three hundred casualties were inflicted upon Pickett's division. The confidence felt among the Confederate enlisted men for their officers and the near-worshipful status Gen. Lee held throughout the army overshadowed the prophecy the Federal counter-bombardment presented to those who would soon advance across 1,300 yards of open ground.[16]

John T. McCall personified the cannon as "belching forth their death mission." The shot and shell split the air, tearing horses and men apart as the shrieking and hissing of the shells created a strain on the soldiers' nerves to the point that "none but those who have experienced it have little conception" of its impact.[17]

Col. B.D. Fry recalled the impact of the bombardment with personal pain. Officers and enlisted men of the Tennessee Brigade were being killed or wounded in large numbers. Fry himself was hit by a shell fragment on his right shoulder, a wound that caused him a great deal of pain. J.H. Moore, 7th TN, heard occasional small arms fire amid the thundering cannon as the air grew thick with smoke. Artillery of both sides began targeting barns and houses in the area between them, eliminating their use as shelter for the enemy. Old men, women, and children ran from the homes seemingly oblivious to the danger such action presented. This process, Moore explained, tended to "heighten the scene of terror and dismay."[18]

Panic and fear made themselves known on the Federal side of the cannonade. Lt. L.E. Bicknell of the First Massachusetts Sharpshooters noted that during the heavy cannonading, many regiments sought the shelter of Zeigler's Grove, where he was located with twenty members of the First Company of Massachusetts Sharpshooters.[19]

John Purifoy noted, "General Lee in his report of that assault states: 'About 1 p.m. at a given signal a heavy cannonade was opened and continued for about two hours with marked effect upon the enemy. His batteries replied vigorously at first; but toward the close their fire slackened perceptibly.'" J.H. Moore recorded the cessation of fire to be of "mutual consent" to halt the bombardment. US Maj. Gen. William Scott Hancock estimated the Confederate barrage to have lessened an hour and a half after it began, at which time the Confederate infantry was seen preparing for an assault from the woods near Emmitsburg Road. June Kimble added that he barrage "did cease almost as suddenly as it began."[20]

Hancock's Second Corps sighted the Tennessee Brigade as well as the remainder of Pettigrew's troops as they stepped into the sunlight that bathed Seminary Ridge, three-fourths of a mile to the west of the Federal lines. Hancock estimated the entire Confederate force at fifteen thousand men and stated that their lines "formed with a precision and steadiness that extorted admiration" throughout the Federal ranks.[21]

Though no original Confederate documents listing the order of the attacking regiments within the various brigades exist, there has been little dispute as to the alignment of the Tennessee Brigade. Attacking under the direction of B.D. Fry, the men of Archer's brigade, from right to left, were positioned in the following order: First Tennessee, Thirteenth Alabama, Fourteenth Tennessee, Seventh Tennessee, and the Fifth Alabama Infantry Battalion.

As three o'clock approached on the afternoon of July 3, June Kimble had the opportunity to participate in what was to arguably become the most significant event of the American Civil War. He wrote, "Another ominous lull, and each veteran drew a long breath of relief; then sharply 'Attention!' rang out clear along the line. Instantly fourteen thousand veterans sprang to their feet and awaited the word 'Forward!' which they knew was coming. From Pickett's Division of three brigades came at intervals the command, 'Dress to the left,' and from Heth's, or Pettigrew's, six brigades came, 'Dress to the right,' Archer's Brigade being near the center and the guiding brigade of the assaulting column. It emerged into the open field silent save for the tramp, tramp of the veterans in solid line, with steady nerve ... In my admiration and enthusiasm I rushed some ten paces in advance and cast my eyes right and left. It was magnificent!"[22]

The Tennessee Brigade charged across this field on July 3, 1863.
Photo by author.

Kimble's "ominous lull" was equated to the "interval of comparative quiet" in the statement of J.H. Moore. Moore remarked that there was a prompt response to the order to advance; he and his comrades soon reached the crest of a ridge from which they entered the full view of the Federal batteries atop Cemetery Hill. The rolling hills Moore and his regiment encountered on their march toward their objective were noted as entirely open and offering no shelter from the enemy batteries. John Fite also remarked on the barrenness of the terrain with "not a bush on it."[23]

Several hundred yards remained open between the Tennessee Brigade and Pickett's division. Gradually the parts came together, closing the gap as the halfway mark was reached en route to the Union lines. The color bearers marched some five spaces ahead of their respective units, creating an alignment that John T. McCall remarked "was as good as on dress parade."[24]

Likewise, Dick Reid expressed the coolness of the Confederates as Federal fire erupted in their direction: "Gallant boys, the flower of the South, as they moved forward in that terrible charge with 'guns to the right of them and guns to the left of them, that volleyed and thundered,' they marched as steadily as on dress parade."[25]

In his official report, Union major general Hancock explained that the Union defenders made no attempt to check the Confederate advance until the first line moved within seven hundred yards of the Federal position. The "feeble fire of artillery" had a minimal effect on the "determined advance" as the Southerners pressed forward, well within range of the muskets of the Union defenders.[26]

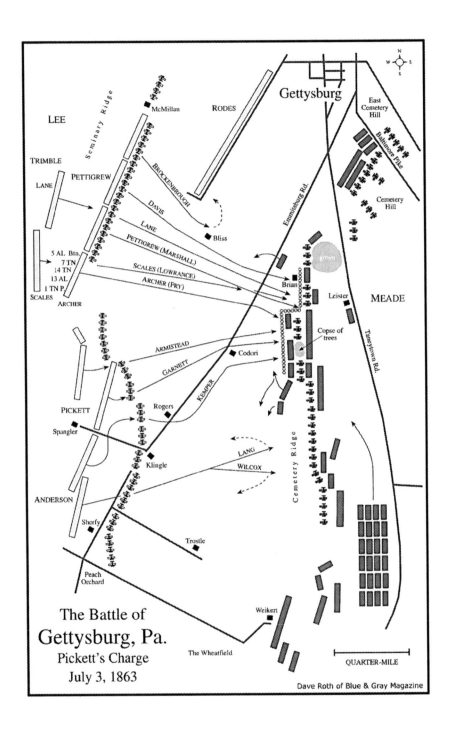

The Battle of
Gettysburg, Pa.
Pickett's Charge
July 3, 1863

Dave Roth of Blue & Gray Magazine

John T. McCall partly agreed with Hancock's comments in that he recalled the Yankees avoiding firing until the Tennessee Brigade and other attacking units moved well within range of the enemy. McCall remarked that the Confederates then encountered "a most galling fire of musketry and artillery that failed to even momentarily check the advance."[27]

John T. McCall, Co. B, 7ᵗʰ TN. Courtesy of Confederate Veteran.

Among the defenders, Major C.A. Richardson of the 126th New York Volunteer Infantry stated that he watched the Confederates advance "through the shower of shell," and the effect was minimal. One exception Richardson noted was the brief staggering of Archer's Tennesseans when the Federal cannon atop Round Top "turned loose on them." Recovering, the brigade proceeded in a renewed perfect line.[28]

June Kimble recalled, "When observed by the enemy, the vicious roar of artillery began its deadly work. Soon shot and shell were plowing through the Confederate ranks; but on, steadily on the line moved without a waver or break save as gaps were rent by solid shot or exploding shell."

R.E. McCulloch, Co. H, 14th TN, called to mind how those around him remained "heedless of the carnage" as grape, canister, and shell sprayed their ranks. B.D. Fry, commanding the Tennessee Brigade in the assault, noted that as the Confederate column advanced, Federal grape, canister, and musket balls created gaps in the line that were quickly closed.[29]

From Stannard's Vermont Brigade, two regiments were placed in a grove, firing at an angle in an attempt to push the Confederates to the left. Their attempts were in vain, and the Southerners moved within three hundred yards of the Union line. The rifled guns of the Union artillery were withdrawn or left unattended as the attackers moved even closer.[30]

J.H. Moore remembered a particularly unique aspect of the charge: "I do recollect that the 'rebel yell' was started on our right, but what was very singular to me in this charge was that previous to this occasion and afterward we never before failed to increase our speed when the 'yell' was started. Moreover, as far as I remember, we never failed to drive the enemy when we raised a lusty 'yell.' I suppose the reason our speed was not increased in front of frowning Cemetery Hill was that the yell was started much farther from the enemy than usual. Generally we raised the 'yell' after infantry firing had begun and near the enemy. On this occasion we marched steadily on, and as soon as the line got closely under way the enemy's batteries opened upon us with a most furious cannonade. Many batteries hurled their missiles of death in our ranks from Cemetery Hill, Round Top, and Little Round Top, in our front and on our right. The ridge we had left and the adjacent spurs belched forth ... smoke of battle that obscured the scent with a dreadful and darkened magnificence and a deepening roar that no exaggeration of language can heighten."[31]

Col. B.D. Fry saw Gen. Garnett give a command, but the deafening level of musketry hindered his comprehension of the order. Garnett turned to Fry, who presented the general with a look of confusion. Garnett called to Fry, "I am dressing on you!" Seconds later Garnett fell dead. Col. George then fell at Fry's side; moments later, Fry himself was shot in the thigh, falling to the ground and unable to walk.[32]

Capt. J.B. Turney remembered the series of events: "We charged in unbroken line, across the fields, through ravines, over fences—on we went, bent on victory or death. The lead rained; the gallant Colonel George, of the First Tennessee, fell wounded; thirty steps farther, and Colonel Fry was checked by an enemy's bullet—wounded in the leg. He called to me and asked for Colonel George, and, when informed of his wound, said to me: 'Captain, take command of the regiment. Proceed with the charge, but don't stop to fire a gun.'"[33]

Capt. J.B. Turney, Co. K, 1ˢᵗ TN. With a flesh wound to his neck, Turney was captured at Gettysburg on July 3, 1863. Confederate Veteran.

The Confederate assaulters now reached fences along Emmitsburg Road. Delayed in negotiating the obstacle, the Tennessee Brigade suffered casualties that were mirrored throughout the Southern ranks.

J.H. Moore, 7th TN, recorded the encounter with the fences in his memoirs: "As the charging column neared the Emmittsburg road volley after volley of small arms aided with dreadful effect in thinning our ranks. We reached the first plank or slab fence, and the column clambered over with a speed as if in stampeded retreat. The time it took to climb to the top of the fence seemed to me an age of suspense. It was not a leaping over; it was rather an insensible tumbling to the ground in the nervous hope of escaping the thickening missiles that buried themselves in falling victims, in the ground, and in the fence, against which they rattled with the distinctness of large rain-drops pattering on a roof. Every man that reached the road, in my view, sunk to the ground—just for a moment, and only for a moment. Right there from our right came two mounted officers, riding at a great speed. One was covered with blood, the other held his head bowed almost to his horse's neck. On they sped to the road at our left. I know not who they were. In an instant one rider, with his horse, tumbled to the ground, and as far as I know was one more victim added to the great number of the unknown slain. Our stay in the road could not be called a halt. In a moment the order to advance was given, and on we pressed across the next fence; but many of our comrades remained in the road and never crossed the second fence, many being wounded in crossing the first and in the road."[34]

John Fite, 7th TN, explained that half of his command fell prior to reaching the first fence they encountered; only fifty climbed the second. John T. McCall also recalled that the two stout post and plank fences became a death trap as the Federal fire "told sadly upon our ranks." June Kimble interpreted the events in a slightly different manner: "The first fence was soon reached and quickly toppled over by hand and upon the points of bayonets. No check, but on we moved. The second fence shared the fate of the first, and without a halt the column went forward as if to victory. The third obstacle appeared, a strong, well-built post or slab fence, too strong to be quickly torn away. Realizing this, over the fence the Confederates sprang, thus pausing for a moment in some confusion; but reforming quickly the line, still unbroken but terribly punished, rushed forward undismayed."[35]

J.B. Turney moved forward with the remnants of his regiment, the First Tennessee. He stated, "By the time I reached my line it was to the first plank fence that inclosed the Emmettsburg road. How like hail upon a roof sounded the patter of the enemy's bullets upon that fence! Onward swept the columns, thinned now and weakened, the dead behind, the foe in front, and no thought of quarter. The second fence was reached and scaled; now no impediment, save the deadly fire of ten thousand rifles that barred our headlong charge. It was one hundred and fifty yards now of open field. Who would live to reach the goal? In wonderful order, at double-quick time, we continued the charge and not until we were within about fifteen steps of the stone wall did I give the command to fire. The volley confused the enemy. I then ordered a charge with bayonets, and on moved our gallant boys."[36]

The wounded Col. B.D. Fry became confident in the opportunity of a Southern victory at Gettysburg and shouted for his men to move forward, refusing to have them carry him away, as he was certain the fight would last little more than five more minutes. His command moved forward and soon became shrouded in the dense smoke and hiding Fry's firsthand observation of the ensuing occurrences.[37]

Federal divisions of Gibbon and Hays opened "a destructive fire" upon the Confederates who returned the fire at once. The struggle between the two armies escalated and "at once became fierce and general."[38]

Archer's Tennessee Brigade members began yelling wildly and pushed into the Federal ranks positioned behind a stone wall. June Kimble explained, "It was here that I again sprang in advance, looked up and down that line, and became an eyewitness of the most vivid and stupendous battle scene ... As far as I could see this same line seemed to move as close and steady as upon the start. On it advanced until, having reached close range of the enemy's protected infantry, withering volleys of musketry, grape, double-charged canister, shot and shell shattered and mutilated as fine a body of Southern heroes as ever trod a battlefield. Still, after practical annihilation, the remnant of these glorious Confederates kept going forward, until they silenced the guns and stood in the works of the enemy. Those of the enemy who remained in the works were prostrated at our feet, practically prisoners, with their arms upon the ground, not firing a shot."[39]

From the First Tennessee, Capt. J.B. Turney described the intensity of the battle: "We were engaged in a desperate hand-to-hand conflict for the possession of the fragile walls of masonry that held out as the sole barrier between the combatants. Each man seemed to pick his foe, and it fell my lot to struggle with a stalwart Federal officer, who made a vicious thrust at my breast. I parried it just in time. Thus for a few moments the contest settled as for a death struggle, and one triumphant shout was given as the Federals in our immediate front and to our right yielded and fled in confusion to a point just back of the crest of the hill ... I now mounted the rock wall and found everything successful to my right, while the center and left of Archer's Brigade had failed. From my position to the right the works were ours, but to the left the enemy was still in possession. Thus the First Tennessee ... occupied a most important position. I decided to throw a column beyond the works and enfilade the lines to my left, and succeeded in taking with me my own company and parts of others. The volleys we fired were effective, and created confusion."[40]

J.H. Moore added his comments: "With our line materially weakened by the loss of those that remained in the road, we pressed on and struck the enemy behind a fence or hastily constructed breastwork, over which the First and about one-half of the Seventh Tennessee regiments passed. The rest of our command who crossed the second fence had not reached the works because of their horseshoe shape, and because the point that they were to have reached was to the rear and left of where we entered. As we encountered the enemy in his works all was excitement. Our men fought with desperation, and succeeded in driving the enemy from his line. It was a hand-to-hand encounter."[41]

Despite the intense Union barrage from seemingly every angle, the Confederates pushed forward, moving "up to the very muzzles of their guns." John Fite appeared to be trailing the back of the brigade by a number of steps. He explained that as he was crossing the last fence, a fresh Union command arrived that caused many of the remaining Seventh Tennessee soldiers to fall to the ground as a means of escaping certain death. This occurred, in Fite's estimation, forty to fifty yards from the bulk of the Yankee army.[42]

Less than two hundred yards constituted the area between the angle and an area of rock-strewn ground. The men of Archer's, Pickett's, and other Confederate units began concentrating their efforts on the small area of real estate.[43]

June Kimble stated that within this area "for five, perhaps ten, minutes we held our ground and looked back for and prayed for support. It came not, and we knew that the battle of Gettysburg was ended. Many of this brave remnant chose to surrender rather than run the gauntlet of the enemy's fire."[44]

J.B. Turney observed those frantic moments as well, recalling them almost four decades later. "By this time, at a distance of only about thirty yards, and behind the crest of the hill, I noted the re-forming of the Federal lines. This necessitated a withdrawal to a position behind the stone wall, and there we joined the balance of the First Tennessee. After a desperate, but unsuccessful, effort to dislodge us, the enemy again retired over the crest of the hill. I then made a second effort to cross the works and enfilade, but by this time our lines, from my position to the left, were being beaten back by a most destructive fire; and as our opposition melted in their front, the enemy turned a deadly fire upon the unprotected squad of First Tennesseans, who, together with a few of Garnett's Virginians, had the second time crossed the works. The artillery as well as the musketry belched forth destruction to our little band, and we were forced to drop back behind the wall. By this time

General Armistead had noted the importance of the position held by the First Tennessee, and was obliquing to his left to reach us. A few moments of waiting brought his recruits to our aid. The general was on foot at the head of his column. I shall ever have a distinct remembrance of the dash and fire that was in him. He threw his hat on his saber, called for the command to follow, and scaled the stone wall. I kept by his side, and with us went the colors of the First Tennessee. Armistead's purpose was to enfilade, as I had attempted. Again we became the targets for the concentrated fire of the enemy's guns of all sizes and all positions. At the first volley I noticed General Armistead drop his saber, on which still hung his hat, and grasp with his right hand his left arm and stagger as if he were about to fall … Seeing the impossibility of effective work from behind the wall and the shattered condition of our lines, I hastily called the captains of my regiment for conference. Captains Thompson, Hawkins, Arnold, and Alexander responded. While we were conferring, a courier arrived, and, calling for the officer in charge, told me General Lee's orders were to hold my position, as Ewell had broken the lines on the extreme left. These orders settled the question, and brought us face to face with the critical moments of that decisive battle. To the left of the First Tennessee our lines had entirely given way, thus enabling the enemy to concentrate its fire—not only from our center, but from our left—directly upon my command. The heavy artillery on the ridge and that massed on Little Round Top poured destruction into our ranks. Some of the Virginians to our right had already yielded. For ten minutes still we remained the target, and each minute perceptibly weakened our gallant band and made less possible our chance of retreat. All realized that ours was a hopeless chance, yet General Lee desired that we remain, and that was sufficient."[45]

Dick Reid remembered the height of the battle: "Pickett's Division, with Heth's supporting, gave the old Confederate yell and went over the breastworks … and planted their battle flags … The brave Gen. Armistead … his hat on top of his sword, commanding one of the brigades in Pickett's Division, was the first man … to reach Cemetery Heights, and just as he hallooed at Archer's Tennessee Brigade to stand by Virginia he was shot dead."[46]

The sounds of battle were all the wounded Col. B.D. Fry possessed as a means of gauging the Confederate situation. Lying on the ground in a dense cover of smoke, Fry heard Gen. Pettigrew order his staff to rally the troops on the left. A continuous roll of musketry began, an occasion during which Fry proposed the defenders fired several rounds with only the dead and wounded at their front. John Fite also lay on the ground, expecting to be shot at any moment as the dirt, hurled upward by Federal firing, pelted his body.[47]

Mitchell A. Anderson, Co. K, 7ᵗʰ TN. Filling a lieutenant's vacancy at Gettysburg, this son of Cumberland University's president was killed on July 3, 1863. Courtesy of Paul Gibson.

Fite's response was far from an isolated reaction. Col. Thomas Smyth, First Delaware Infantry, instructed his troops to reserve their fire until the column was within fifty yards, when so effective and incessant was the fire from his line that the advancing Confederates staggered, were thrown into confusion, and finally fled from the field, throwing away their arms in their flight. Others threw themselves to the ground to escape the destructive fire of the Federal infantry.[48]

Along the Confederate line, segments broke with increasing intensity. John McCall remembered how he, like June Kimble, chose to fall back "under terrible fire" rather than face surrender. J.H. Moore called to mind that the ferocity of the hand-to-hand combat was short-lived, "and as victory was about to crown our efforts a large body of troops moved resolutely upon our left flank, and our extreme right at the same time began to give way, as did our left. Still we in the center held the works, but finally, being unsupported, we were forced to fall back. Those of the second line who reached the Emmittsburg road never moved beyond that point to our assistance. We fell back to the lane, which was literally strewn with dead and wounded. The roar of artillery continued, and, mingled with the groans of the wounded and dying, intensified the horrid confusion in the lane."[49]

Moore expressed the utter futility of remaining in the area of the heaviest concentration of Federal defenders. He stated, "From the time we advanced a few yards the artillery continually lessened our ranks, and especially a battery that almost enfiladed us from the right as we neared the lane—a battery that seemed not to have been engaged in the first fire. The artillery that followed up our advance attempted ineffectually to silence this engine of destruction, for at least in my part of our line its effects were equally fatal, if not more so, than all the rest of the artillery directed against us. Those who regained the lane in retreat here for a moment hesitated, but there was no time for deliberation. The combined fire of small arms and artillery was incessantly rained upon us."[50]

Capt. J.B. Turney, 1st TN, saw surrender as his only recourse. When a nearby group of Virginians hoisted a white flag, Turney and those of his regiment who were unable to escape surrendered. With thousands lying dead or seriously wounded all around him, Turney felt fortunate to have only a flesh wound on his neck and "a number of bullet holes in my clothes."[51]

Col. B.D. Fry noted that the end of the lengthy Federal firing was followed with a series of cheers that emphasized the failure of the Confederate attack. Amid the cheering, Col. N.J. George, one of Turney's fellow First Tennessee members, refused to surrender his sword to anyone other than a commissioned officer. He yielded when urged to do so or be "run through" by a bayonet.[52]

John Fite, 7th TN, also became a prisoner, handing over his sword to a major in the Fourteenth Connecticut. In a show of authority, Fite's captor also demanded the scabbard, an item Fite turned over with the explanation that he personally had no future use for it anyway. Both Fite and George would be recorded as surrendering to Maj. T.J. Ellis of the Fourteenth Connecticut Infantry.[53]

Another wounded Tennessee Brigade member to fall into Union hands was Capt. James W. Lockert, Co. K, 14th TN. Nicknamed "Old Ironclad," Lockert had avoided being wounded throughout his company's earlier engagements since bringing with him some 110 men to join the Fourteenth Tennessee and become the Red River Company. Lockert's trademark was his sword, raised high above his head in battle, as his scabbard dragged the ground some four feet behind. The fearless soldier in his late thirties had made it a habit to lead his company into battle. He did so on July 3 and received a wound in his thigh. Originally diagnosed as having a mortal wound, Lockert recovered, only to serve the remainder of the war at Ft. Delaware, Johnson's Island, and Point Lookout as a prisoner of war.[54]

William H. Williamson, Co. H. 7ᵗʰ TN. Recovering from his wounds received at Gaines Mill, Maj. Williamson was wounded and captured at Gettysburg on July 3, 1863. His right arm was amputated and he was sent to Johnson's Island and later to Point Lookout. Practicing law after the war, Williamson allegedly joined a fellow amputee in buying a pair of gloves, with each man using only the one he needed.
Courtesy of Paul Gibson.

The Confederates fleeing the Federal position faced a similar feeling of fear and uncertainty possessed by those recently captured. J.H. Moore, joining men who viewed retreat as the better option, recorded his experience some twenty years later: "Further retreat was as dangerous as the advance. The first fence was again to be crossed, hundreds of yards of open space in full view and within reach of the fire of all arms was to be passed over before we could regain shelter. The plank or slab fence was splintered and riddled, and the very grass was scorched and withered by the heat of shell and bullets. Around me lay forty dead and wounded of the forty-seven of my company that entered the scene of carnage with me. Col. S.G. Shepherd and I and the other survivors hesitated in the lane a moment. It was death or surrender to remain. It seemed almost death to retreat. May be [sic] we could regain our artillery in safety. We chose the latter alternative, and on we sped through the open field, expecting every moment to be shot to the ground. Our condition and experience were not dissimilar to those of hundreds of others."[55]

June Kimble joined others of the Fourteenth Tennessee in deciding to make a break for liberty. Kimble's recollection of setting the lightning speed for the first one hundred yards adds a bit of humor to the otherwise tense situation. Kimble explained, "I realized that I was a good target for those yelling Yankees, and, having a horror of being shot in the back, I faced about and backed out of range, and all without so much as a scratch." Kimble encountered additional men on the retreat and joined some in the rifle pits dug in advance of the original advance on Seminary Ridge. Here, four to a pit, the men formed a skirmish line, awaiting what they felt to be the inevitable Union countercharge.[56]

Kimble's fleeing, perhaps interpreted by some as an act of cowardice, drew praise from M.V. Ingram in a 1908 article. Ingram stated, "It was in the third day's battle of Gettysburg ... that June Kimble, Theo. Hartman, Joe Williams, Emmett McCulloch, John Massie, William M. Daniel, William Green, and a few others of the 14th left to tell the story, stormed the heights of Cemetery Ridge, going over a great stone wall, capturing the enemy's guns, shooting the gunner within fifteen feet of the muzzle as he was ramming his charge to flay them, and took the whole command standing within the enemy's works. The boys, however, did not long enjoy their ... victory. Soon they discovered the enemy's reenforcement [sic] coming in swarms like showers of black locusts, flanking their rear, and with all their daring recklessness they had sense enough to give up the post and retreat in great haste. Some of the boys were captured and made prisoners. Kimble, however, ran for dear life, with bullets flying after him like shower of hail. It was funny as it was serious. McCulloch and Kimble agree in the opinion that but for a mortised post and rail fence that checked the charge of Archer's Tennessee Brigade the Confederates would have won ... Gettysburg ... this mortised post and rail fence checked the charge and confused the whole command when the Federals poured shot and shell into them while they were climbing over it, slaughtering the Confederates by wholesale, breaking their ranks and the force of the charge."[57]

Kimble's return was marked with tragedy in an event that nearly cost his life. Kimble had stopped briefly behind a rock for cover. He noticed a Union soldier with his foot propped upon a rock fifty to sixty feet away and shooting at retreating Confederates. A young member of Armistead's brigade was with Kimble while Kimble fired shots with his Mississippi rifle at the Yankee. Unable to hit his mark, Kimble turned to the Virginian and challenged him to take a shot. The youngster informed Kimble that he'd already tried four times himself and now desired only to return to the Confederate lines. The young man then jumped to his feet, with his back to the Union lines, when Kimble heard the distinct sound of a bullet hitting the youth's head. Kimble debated his own safety momentarily and then, choosing the possibility of death over prison, ran to safety.[58]

The incidents of the return to the Confederate lines are vividly recorded in correspondence sent to J.H. Moore. In a February 8, 1882 letter, Col. Shepherd told Moore, "I remember very distinctly most of the facts ... We came out of the fight together ... when we got back to our artillery we met Gen. Lee, who took me by the hand and said to me: 'Colonel, rally your men and protect our artillery. The fault is mine, but it will all be right in the end.' Whether these were the exact words used by Gen. Lee or not I cannot say, but I can say these are substantially his words."[59]

Moore agreed with Shepherd's recollection of the incident with Gen. Robert E. Lee and recalled the almost immediate and identical conversation Lee held with Gen. Pettigrew. When Lee noticed Pettigrew's arm shattered with grapeshot, he said, "General, I am sorry to see you wounded; go to the rear." Moore recalled the rallying of the shattered ranks of the Confederates around the artillery, awaiting the Union advance Gen. Lee felt would come. Moore said of Lee, "He seemed to be very much agitated, and remained near the center of his original line—close to the artillery in front of Heth's division—for some minutes anxiously watching, with glass in hand, the enemy's line and exposed to their artillery fire. In a few moments Gen. Lee left us and went in the direction of our right. Before he had got very far he was met by Gen. Longstreet ... They staid [sic] there on the highest eminence between our division and the enemy's line nearly an hour—at least it seemed to be—exposed to the ceaseless fire of artillery. While gazing upon them I trembled for their and our safety. Every moment I looked for either or both of them to be torn from their horses, and that too at a time when the exposure was needless."[60]

While the significance of the fences referred to in the recollections of some of the Tennessee Brigade members has been well discussed in other works, the heroic deeds and actions of most men of the brigade have not. In his analysis of the left wing of the Confederate assault column on July 3, 1863, John Purifoy remarked of the entire division and the heroism of the Tennessee Brigade's color-bearers. He stated, "Heth's Division came to a lane enclosed by stout post-and-rail fences. The men rushed over these fences as rapidly as they could and advanced directly upon the enemy's works … Shepard says they were post-and-plank fences … The killed and wounded in the division was very great … Every flag of the brigade except one was captured at or within the works of the enemy. The First Tennessee had three color bearers shot down, the last of whom was at the works and the flag was captured. The 13th Alabama lost three color bearers in the same way, the last of whom was shot down at the works. The 14th Tennessee had four color bearers shot down, the last of whom was at the enemy works. The 7th Tennessee lost three color bearers, the last of whom was at the enemy's works, and its flag was saved only by Capt. A.D. Norris tearing it away from the staff and bringing it our beneath his coat. The 5th Alabama Battalion lost its flag at the enemy's works."[61]

Historian Richard Rollins explained that the battle flag of the Fifth Alabama was captured west of the wall by Capt. William Smith of the First Delaware. Pvt. Bernard McCarren of the First Delaware is credited with the capture of the Thirteenth Alabama flag in the same location. The captor of the First Tennessee's flag is unknown, although it is generally regarded to have been a member of the Fourteenth Connecticut who should receive the distinction for doing so on the Union works. Sgt. Maj. William Hincks of the Fourteenth Connecticut is cited as being the individual who captured the flag of the Fourteenth Tennessee west of the wall.[62]

W.F. Fulton wrote that "the color bearer of the 5th Ala. Batt. was shot down, private Bullock of Co. C. seized the flag and raised it again, when he received a bullet that caused him to drop it. Private Manning of Company B lifted it and shook it out to the breeze when he fell dead in his tracks." Fulton then noted a statement contradictory to most historians in explaining that a private named Gilbert from Co. A of the Fifth Alabama carried the flag from the field.[63]

The failure of the Union defenders to capture the flag of the Seventh Tennessee was due to the bravery and determination of Archibald Norris. Norris's journal made no mention of the extraordinary feat, yet John T. McCall emphasized Norris's heroism in noting that his tearing of the flag from the staff and shielding it within his clothing solely allowed the banner to see further action. Perhaps the greatest accolade for Norris was given in J.H. Moore's 1901 account of the assault. Moore wrote, "I can recall Capt. A. Norris ... when the right was being enveloped and hope gone, tearing the flag from the staff, and retreating with a fragment of his company under a fire so destructive that his escape seemed miraculous. There was no better officer in the Seventh or in any other regiment."[64]

The effective leadership Moore possessed and the relative ease with which he passed praise to his comrades is shown in Moore's review of those in the vicinity of the charge who impressed him. He stated, "Capt. Asa Hill, while cheering on his company, fell mortally wounded; Capt. John Allen, 'the bravest of the brave,' fell where he always was, in 'the thickest of the fight,' with two desperate wounds, thought to be mortal at the time. Lieut. Timberlake fell in the forefront with two severe wounds. Space will not permit me to mention more names, though many more deserve all praise. The rank and file of my own company and, as far as I could see, of others did all that flesh and blood could do to make the assault successful. While my attention was confined principally to my own company, I recall with distinctness the gallant bearing of acting Sergeant Jesse Cage, of Company E ... on my immediate right. He seemed to be oblivious to everything except his full duty as a soldier. His apparent coolness was remarkable. This splendid soldier escaped unscathed in this as well as every other battle in which the Army of Northern Virginia was engaged until the very last, in which he lost a leg. He was a model soldier in war as he is a model Christian gentleman in peace."[65]

Moore's honoring of Asa Hill was reflected in a letter from Hill's former comrade, Capt. F.S. Harris, 7th TN, in a letter Harris wrote to Hill's nephew, J.K. Womack. Speaking of Hill, Moore wrote, "He walked all the way to Gettysburg at the head of his company. When that fatal day and the world's greatest charge was ordered, Capt. Hill stepped to the front smiling, as was his custom on such occasions. He carried his company to the stone wall so well known in that battle. Capt. Alexander, who was perhaps the last man who ever spoke to him, told me afterwards that Capt. Hill stood waving his sword to his men, urging them forward in the face of one hundred pieces of artillery in front, and more than that from Round Top, and three lines of Federal infantry. Capt. Alexander thinks death was instantaneous. He was strictly honest, always courteous, obliging, and was said to be the handsomest man in the regiment."[66]

Capt. Asoph Hill, 7th TN. Killed at Gettysburg on July 3, 1863.
Confederate Veteran.

Remarks for Capt. John Allen, Co. B, 7th TN, were also full of praise. "Capt. Allen was conspicuously brave … He particularly distinguished himself in the desperate charge at Gettysburg … and was there so severely wounded that he was left for dead on the field. His strong vitality pulled him through, however, and after a long time in prison he secured an exchange."[67]

Dr. Henry M. Clarkson, 13th AL, helped establish a field hospital near Herr's Ridge early on July 1. Clarkson eventually used the nearby McPherson barn as his base of operation, treating the wounded of both North and South for approximately three weeks following the battle. For his contributions to the welfare of the troops and recognition from the leadership of both armies, Clarkson's photograph now possesses a spot on the famous Gettysburg Wall of Faces.[68]

Henry Mazyck Clarkson, surgeon, Thirteenth Alabama. Clarkson served the wounded of both North and South following the carnage at Gettysburg. After the war he established a practice in Haymarket, Virginia, where he died in 1915. Courtesy of Gettysburg National Military Park.

June Kimble paid tribute to W.H. McCulloch for his patience, firmness, and Christian principles. McCulloch was a twenty-one-year-old veteran of the war who marched elbow to elbow with Kimble during the July 3 assault on Cemetery Ridge. As the pair joined their comrades in moving to within seventy-five feet of the Union position, they found the roar of cannon and musket fire deafening. Kimble turned to young McCulloch and said, "Billy, stay with us!" to which the young man promptly replied, "I am with you!" As the words left McCulloch's lips, a minié ball pierced his brain, killing him instantly. His body was buried at Gettysburg.[69]

Col. J.H. Moore, 7ᵗʰ TN. Known for his courage and stamina, Moore left his sick bed more than once to join his regiment prior to battle. Moore served the Tennessee Brigade in every battle from Seven Pines to Appomattox. Courtesy of Confederate Veteran.

J.H. Moore, the recipient of honors from a number of individuals, took time to acknowledge the efforts of the Tennessee Brigade and Heth's division, writing, "The Tennessee Brigade was the only in Heth's division that carried their standards into the fortifications on the hill … I am far from being unmindful of the heroism and devotion of other troops in that memorable charge; but in justice to those of Heth's division who fell in the works on Cemetery Hill, in the lane and open field, in the advance or retreat … I cannot be indifferent when Gettysburg is painted without Heth's division prominent in the grand charge. Justice is justice, and fact is fact."[70]

As Moore acknowledged, fact is fact, and the point remains that a number of the men of the Tennessee Brigade returned to the Southern line from which they launched the attack. Here they waited for a Union charge that never took place. That night the Confederates prepared for the uncertain future.

June Kimble briefly mentioned the events of the night of July 3. "About eleven o'clock a staff officer rode up to where we were and asked what command it was. He was told that it was no particular command, and that no officer was present. He then told us to stay there and General Anderson would relieve us. Perhaps an hour later a picket relief came, and each of us went back in search of his command. I soon found the remnant of the 14th Tennessee Regiment reorganized and in the command of Capt. J.M. Dale, of Company C, and Lieut. Charles Mitchell, of Company H. There were about one hundred men out of three hundred and fifty that engaged in that battle. There was but little sleep and poor rest for the weary, battered veterans of Lee's army that night."[71]

Kimble's estimation of casualties is relatively accurate, as the Tennessee Brigade had entered the fight at Gettysburg on July 1, 1863 with 1,048 men. At the end of the July 3 charge, only 371 remained. The casualties included sixteen brigade members killed in some of the most intense fighting of the war. A total of 155 additional members had been wounded. The largest percentage of the missing was comprised of the 517 men who were captured or missing. Seven field officers went into the charge; only two came out. The rest were all wounded and captured. The loss of company officers was nearly in the same proportion. The casualty rate was particularly high in two units of the Tennessee Brigade: the Fifth Alabama and the Fourteenth Tennessee. According to letters and reports of Maj. Van de Graff, the Fifth Alabama had entered the first day's action with 105 men, 7 of whom became casualties on that day. The major stated that in the assault on Cemetery Ridge, his losses were forty-three men. Assuming the accuracy of his figures, the Fifth Alabama sustained a 48 percent casualty rate in the action at Gettysburg.[72]

The Tennessee monument at Gettysburg. Photo by author.

The reverse side of the Tennessee Memorial denotes the state's contributions in terms of casualties. Photo by author.

Dr. C. Wallace Cross explained that 365 of the Fourteenth Tennessee were fit for duty at Gettysburg on July 1, 1863. Only sixty of these men reported for duty on the third; of these, only three remained unharmed at day's end.[73] These numbers disagree slightly with those reported in June Kimble's statements regarding the reorganization of the regiment of the night of the third.

The remnants of the Tennessee Brigade camped the night of July third where they had begun the day, remaining there throughout the fourth. No Federal attack from Gen. Meade's command took place, though the majority of Confederates, as earlier indicated, anticipated, or perhaps even feared, its initiation.

June Kimble recorded one of the best descriptions of the Tennessee Brigade's actions on July 4, 1863, writing, "The morning of the 4th dawned brightly; but it was … seen that on the face of every Confederate … a look of determination and defiance that at once renewed faith in the morale and discipline of those grand old veterans and a blind confidence in our Godlike leader, Robert E. Lee … Whipped? No! There were no cowards there; but the 'Old Guard' was there in part, and Lee, Longstreet, A.P. Hill, Ewell, and Stuart were there to guide and to lead. 'Why, yes, boys, let 'em come on; we'll show 'em that we ain't all dead yet.' Such light banterings escaped from smiling lips all through that long, tense, sweltering fourth day, patiently awaiting the anticipated attack which never came. The most unassuming private wondered what was the matter with the Yanks that they did not come on. They knew their power of resistance, and that their inborn Southern courage, which so often snatched victory out of the very jaws of defeat, would stay with them. On the night of the 4th Lee began his retreat to Hagerstown, Md., without haste or confusion, although the night was dark and stormy."[74]

Kimble's confidence in the Army of Northern Virginia differed from the conception J.H. Moore held of the same group. Moore stated, "We presented a sad contrast in appearance and in spirit when this retreat was undertaken to what we had when we were south of the Rappahannock. Though not subdued, we were not victorious. We had suffered a terrible punishment, yet we reluctantly fell back; and I believe most of our officers opposed this retrograde, even still confident that by acting on the offensive we could render a crushing defeat to the Federals. However, Lee had decided to withdraw, and slowly we worked our way over roads and lanes, in mountain and valley … Many men who had been severely wounded, and even some with arms amputated the day before, to avoid being taken prisoners undertook the journey on foot to Virginia."[75]

Leaving the Gettysburg battlefield behind, the Tennessee Brigade made its way toward the safety of the South. The battle, its phases, and many participants became legendary, leading to one of the most-written-about incidents in world history. One of the most-talked-about incidents of the battle was the Confederate assault of July 3, an event often and commonly referred to as Pickett's Charge. This name became a source of conflict among members of the Army of Northern Virginia and others, North and South.

The misnomer for the Confederate assault reportedly came from a Virginia newspaperman who sought glory for Pickett's command. Statistics prove that North Carolina lost more soldiers in the event than any other Confederate state. Historians have suggested titles such as Longstreet's Assault, Pickett-Pettigrew-Trimble Assault, and others. As to who deserves the claim of first entering the Federal works and/or remaining there for the longest period of time, one need only to examine the facts and eyewitness comments.

Pickett's division had three brigades that were all fresh, none having fought in the battle's previous two days. Pickett was the only general who failed to move forward with his troops, stopping six hundred yards from the stone wall. From this position near the Codori barns, it has been explained, Pickett had a great deal of difficulty and might have been pursuing an impossible task in discerning the movements of his troops. His men, brave as they were, lacked, "a directing mind ... charged with guiding their movements in a great crisis."[76]

Regarding this phase of the argument, LeRoy Farrington, on May 20, 1910, offered the statement, "I have read numerous articles on ... who went farthest, etc., in Pickett's charge, but in every case all credit had been given the Virginia troops. I herewith send you an article on the subject, and one that gives credit to all concerned, especially, though, to Archer's famous Tennessee brigade, whose colors were captured in the Federal works ... The Tennessee brigade had the post of honor; in other words, it was the brigade of direction and the center of the assaulting column."[77]

Jonas Cook, a member of Pettigrew's brigade, noted, "In charging up the slope the Tennessee brigade, Archer's, was the center of the column and the brigade of direction—that is, the other brigades of the column had orders to press on the Tennesseans. Theirs was the post of honor. My brigade, Pettigrew's, was on the immediate left of the Tennessee brigade ... Colonel Fry, who was commanding the Tennessee brigade that day, stepped forward a few paces and, turning so as to face General Pettigrew, saluted with his sword, meanwhile standing in an expectant attitude as if he too had failed to catch the order. At this juncture General Pettigrew shouted at the top of his voice: 'I am dressing on you!' There was great confusion in our ranks and in those to our left, and it was necessary for us to dress on something in order to maintain our alignment. The Tennesseans were moving forward with steady march, and as far as I could see there was not a break in its line except where the shells were plowing through it. My company was next on the left of the first company of the 7th Tennessee. As we moved forward close to the rock fence I observed just to my right and directly in front of the Tennesseans a projected rock wall … Not many of us went over that rock fence." Lt. Col. Morris of the Thirty-seventh North Carolina Regiment explained, "Pettigrew's Brigade and Archer's Tennessee Brigade reached the enemy's works in advance of the other brigades and succeeded in driving the enemy from his works in their front, but were exposed to a flank fire both right and left." A member of Pender's brigade, Capt. S.A. Ashe, added, "Archer's Tennessee Brigade, under Colonel Fry, whose numbers had been greatly reduced in the first day's fight … was the brigade of the direction."[78]

From Lane's brigade, Maj. William Robins wrote, "Lane's North Carolina troops followed Pettigrew's in the charge and crossed the road on the left of the brigade … Scales followed Archer's men … the brigade of direction. As we neared the rock fence Archer's men were confronted by a projected wall, running out from the main fence well down the hill and then turning and joining it again farther up the hill. The projection formed an angle, or salient … We routed the first line of the enemy well in advance of this projected wall … Archer's men in their advance struck this projected wall. It is hard at this distance from the battle to tell just what troops went over the fence, but enough of us got over to break the Federal line."[79]

B.D. Fry, the commander of the Tennessee Brigade explained, "My brigade was the brigade of direction, and, approaching the rock fence, we were leading. Garnett was on our right, and I heard him give the command to dress on my brigade. A moment later he fell. All five of the regimental colors of my brigade reached the enemy's works, any many of my officers and men were killed after passing over it."[80]

Lacking impartiality, J.H. Moore, 7th TN, added, "I can't understand why the Virginians, as a rule, make the statement that Heth's Division retreated or fell back first. The truth is that the center, including the left of Pickett and the right of Heth, were the last to abandon the field. The right and left retreated first because they were flanked. When … I left the field the extreme right of Pickett was passing the brick house in rapid retreat. I suppose the left was also retreating. I never looked that way. My attention was constantly on Round Top from the moment we advanced, for I knew the batteries there could and would rake our lines after we had advanced any considerable distance, and was afraid our right could not stand it … The official reports will successfully refute any disparagement of Heth's Division."[81]

John T. McCall proclaimed, "We want true history, actual facts. All eye witnesses agree that Archer's brigade went as far and stayed as long as any troops either on the right or left."[82]

J.B. Smith, an impartial writer, explained that the First and Seventh Tennessee regiments were the first to breach the Federal position on Cemetery

Hill and that they, along with the Thirty-eighth Virginia that closely followed them, were the only organized regiments to enter "into and beyond the enemy's walls." Smith continued, noting that the Fourteenth Tennessee planted its colors on the stone wall, leaving them there.[83]

A Union officer, Maj. C.A. Richardson, 126th New York Volunteer Infantry, explained to a Tennessee veteran that he helped gather the dead at the battle's conclusion. At and behind the area where Armistead is now honored with a monument, Richardson informed the veteran that he found Tennesseans, Alabamians, and Virginians located in a haphazard manner.[84]

Gen. Louis G. Young, a member of Gen. Pettigrew's staff at Gettysburg, wrote, "The furthermost point reached on the third day is claimed for Archer's command. This claim is made by the Virginians, Tennesseans, and North Carolinians. They were all together and deserve equal praise."[85]

John Purifoy stated, "There is enough glory for all, and credit should not be wholly assumed by any single body of troops in that memorable battle. It is perfectly natural that our gallant comrades who so nobly touched elbows in that noted charge should feel piqued at the frequency of that grand charge as Pickett's. General Pickett's division performed its part nobly, and the writer would … detract from the honors justly due our gallant comrades composing that division."[86]

June Kimble, always proud to proclaim any honor due his beloved Tennessee Brigade, particularly his regiment, the Fourteenth Tennessee, recorded the following: "For several years past most writers have conceded that other troops than Pickett's Division alone constituted the assaulting column in that world-famous charge, and that Heth's Division was the large part of that assaulting column … It has not been a sin of commission so much as omission that makes the survivors of Heth's Division smart under the sting of cruel injustice by the great mass of writers in regard to 'Pickett's charge' … this unfortunate condition was never the result of envy or jealousy, because such miserable sentiments never existed in Confederate ranks; but in their stead love, loyalty, and comradeship glowed throughout the war, and burns to-day as brightly in the hearts of every living and loyal old Confederate … The part that Heth's Division played in what is generally known as 'Pickett's Charge' has never received the praise so well earned and justly due, and it is a lamentable fact. Brave men, however modest, are sensitive and feel the bitterness of neglect or unjust misrepresentation."[87]

Kimble's summary of the justice for the units near and dear to him is full of admiration and pleads for due credit for the group of Tennesseans and Alabamians who fought bravely on the Pennsylvania battlefield. Kimble remarked, "I come now to my own, Archer's Tennessee Brigade, and the 14th Tennessee Regiment. It is at last conceded that Heth's Division constituted an important part of the assaulting column, and that Archer's Tennessee Brigade held the central position in Heth's Division. Future historians therefore must measure out the full share of honors to those troops who led the fight and suffered most. I am sure that today there is not a living Confederate of Heth's Division who would willfully pluck one laurel from the crown of glory won by Pickett's Division. They deserve fully all the tributes laid at their feet. They did their duty nobly, but this verdict must not be marred by injustice to others … For Archer's Tennessee Brigade … the need of praise due it shall be incorporated in the true histories of this wonderful encounter. This brigade, as guide of the assaulting column, held the post of honor, and with all gallantry held it from the beginning to the ending of that mighty death struggle. This glorious band of Tennesseans and Alabamians stood upon the 'high-water' mark on Cemetery Ridge, with the prisoners at its feet, and deliberately turned its guns under the command, 'Boys, shoot to the left!' firing its last volleys into the ranks of reinforcements of the enemy appearing at the crest of the ridge and bearing down upon the exposed left flank of Pettigrew's devoted North Carolinians, who stubbornly fought them back until almost decimated … The devoted remnant of Archer's Brigade was in the works, but all hope for support had passed away. The die was cast and the battle of Gettysburg was ended. Archer's Brigade did its full part. It led the assaulting column as the guiding brigade. It was intended that this column should break the enemy's line at center, and it did so heroically, with a loss of killed and wounded quite unparalleled. In this assault Archer's Brigade … led the advance, was the first to enter the enemy's works and the last to quit those works on that fatal day."[88]

Perhaps the stand of neutrality is the best policy in relation to this issue. Regardless, the issue need not be debated yet should be further memorialized. This direction was perhaps best pursued on the fortieth anniversary of the battle in the words of Southern poet Will Henry Thompson. Thompson penned these words in a work entitled "High Tide at Gettysburg":

A cloud possessed the fallow field,
The gathering battle's smoky shield;
Athwart the gloom the lightning flashed,
And thro' the cloud some horsemen dashed,
And from the heights the thunder pealed.

Then at the brief command of Lee
Moved out that matchless infantry,
With Pickett leading grandly down

To rush against the roaring crown
of those dread heights of destiny

Far heard above the angry guns
A cry across the tumult runs,
The voice that rang thro' Shiloh's woods,
And Chickamauga's solitudes—
The fierce South cheering on her sons.

Ah, how the withering tempest blew
Against the front of Pettigrew!
A khamsin wind that scorched and singed
Like that infernal flame that fringed
The British squares at Waterloo!

A thousand fell where Kemper led;
A thousand died where Garnett bled;
In blinding flame and strangling smoke
The remnant through the batteries broke
And crossed the works with Armistead.

"Once more in glory's van with me!"
Virginia cried to Tennessee;
"We two together, come what may,
Shall stand upon these works today—
The reddest day in history!"

Brave Tennessee! Reckless the way.
Virginia heard her comrade say:
"Close round this rent and riddled rag!"
What time she set her battle flag
Amid the guns of Doubleday.

But who shall break the guards that wait
Before the awful face of Fate?
The tattered standards of the South
Were shriveled at the cannon's mouth,
And all her hopes were desolate.

In vain the Tennessean set
His breast against the bayonet!

In vain Virginia charged and raged,
A tigress in her wrath uncaged,
Till all the hill was red and wet!

Above the bayonets, mixed and crossed,
Men saw a gray, gigantic ghost
Receding through the battle cloud,
And heard across the tempest loud
The death cry of a nation lost!

The brave went down! Without disgrace
They leaped to ruin's red embrace.
They only heard fame's thunders wake,
And saw the dazzling sunburst break
In smiles on Glory's bloody face!

They fell who lifted up a hand
And bade the sun in heaven to stand;
They smote and fell who set the bars
Against the progress of the stars,
And stayed the march of Motherland!

They stood who saw the future come
On through the fight's delirium;
They smote and stood who held the hope
Of nations on that slippery slope,
Amid the cheers of Christendom!

God lives! He forged the iron will
That clutched and held that trembling hill!
God lives and reigns! He built and lent
The heights for Freedom's battlement,
Where floats the flag in triumph still!

Fold up the banners! Smelt the guns!
Love rules. Her gentler purpose runs.
A mighty Mother turns in tears
The pages of her battle years,
Lamenting all her fallen sons![89]

It cannot be overlooked or underemphasized that the Battle of Gettysburg ended Southern hopes of a Northern invasion and caused irreparable damage to the morale of the Confederate nation, nor that it crippled the Army of Northern Virginia for the remainder of the war. A vast majority of the remaining battles of the war were, from the viewpoint of the Confederacy, defensive rather than offensive.

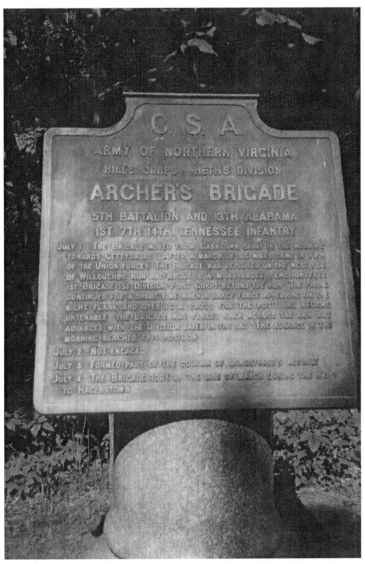

Tennessee Brigade monument at Gettysburg. Photo by author.

CHAPTER FIFTEEN

Imprisonment

The members of the Tennessee Brigade choosing not to retreat from the apparently hopeless situations encountered on July 1 and 3 were, for the most part, unfortunate enough to find themselves prisoners of the Union army. Their adventures were to be documented in letters and family legends.

Brothers Gabriel and Elihu H. Griffin of the Fifth Alabama Infantry Battalion were captured on July 1. Gabriel originally joined the army at the age of twenty and had recently recovered from a wound received a year earlier at Gaines Mill. Following his capture, Gabriel was sent to Ft. Delaware, Delaware, where he died. His body was placed in a mass grave across the river at Finn's Point in Salem, New Jersey.[1]

Elihu Griffin, one of the first Confederate soldiers to be wounded in the early action of July 1, was sent to a Federal hospital to recover. After his wounds healed partially, Griffin was given a parole, due to the hospitals being filled beyond capacity and because Federal doctors concluded that Pvt. Griffin's physical condition presented no further danger to the Union army. Eventually marrying a twenty-three-year-old war widow, Griffin later returned to Confederate service.[2]

Thomas Herndon, captured with Gen. Archer on July 1, arrived at Ft. Delaware at five o'clock in the morning on July 5, 1863. He was marched to the fort from a steamer and was confined to a small upstairs room for the day. The next morning he received his breakfast, bread and coffee, the same ingredients of his supper. Herndon remained at the prison until July 18, at which time he was transferred to Johnson's Island, Ohio.[3] Herndon would spend the duration of the war in the Sandusky, Ohio prison.

B.D. Fry, 13ᵗʰ AL, lay wounded on the field following the Confederate assault of July 3 and was eventually captured. Fry would remain in Union captivity until he was exchanged in April of 1864. Having previously been wounded at Seven Pines, Antietam, and Chancellorsville, Fry declined to allow his fourth wound and term as a prisoner of war to end his military service. Fry's capture was, as he recalled, bittersweet, in that as he was preparing for the infamous charge earlier on the morning of the third, he joked with a color-bearer of the Thirteenth Alabama concerning a saber the latter had attached to the end of his staff. Following his capture, Fry saw a Federal soldier with a deep shoulder wound. Fry felt compelled to inquire of its origin. The Yankee soldier informed Fry that the wound was received from a spear attached to the end of one of the Confederate military colors.⁴

Following his capture, Capt. J.B. Turney, 1ˢᵗ TN, discovered the respect Gen. Lee had among the Federal officers. Turney stated, "We were conducted to the rear, and among the many who came to interview our boys was one of General Jones's aid-de-camps, who, when he came, said he had been inquiring for the officer who stood upon the works so long when the Federals first vacated, and that the soldiers had directed him to me. He then delivered a message of congratulations from his general, which made me feel that I had succeeded in convincing an enemy that I had done my duty. I learned from this officer that the Federals in our front consisted of Hancock's Corps, Burney's Corps, and Doubleday's Division, the latter being in the immediate front of our command. The next morning we were marched twenty-eight miles to Westminster, Md., which distance we were required to cover between the hours of 9 a.m. and 2 p.m. In the afternoon after our arrival we were called upon for details to draw rations. We had no food since the morning before. That same afternoon I was engaged in conversation with some Federal officers, when one asked why we fellows always got the best of an open fight with an equal force. I replied, courteously, that it was the inspiration of a just cause, to which he replied: 'No; it is because you have the greatest military genius of history to lead you. Robert E. Lee combines the organizing capacity of a Marlborough, the intuition of a Turenne, the celerity of a Napoleon, and the tenacity of a Wellington.'"⁵

Col. John Amenas Fite, 7ᵗʰ TN, had escaped death or wounding during the crossing of the stone wall, only to fall into Union hands at the collapse of the attack. Fite was imprisoned at Johnson's Island following a brief incarceration at Ft. Delaware. He remained in captivity until the final days of the war, being released in March 1865.⁶

Fite's recollection of the time following his capture at Gettysburg was filled with a lack of compassion and an abundance of thirst. Fite mentioned in his memoirs that a Union officer and Mason asked for the Masonic strap on Fite's watch as a relic. Fite denied the request, explaining it could be taken only by force. Later Fite and several thousand of his comrades, parched in the July heat, were "allowed" to drink from a creek where Union soldiers were "washing their old sore back horses," and filth abounded. The Confederate officer felt a level of satisfaction after a Union cavalry officer proclaimed to the Confederate prisoners that if they behaved and made no escape attempts they would be treated fairly; otherwise the cavalry would run them down. A fearless captive yelled, "Three cheers for Jeff Davis" at which Fite explained a yell, the likes of which had never been heard on Earth, arose. Following this incident, the Federal officer rode off and the prisoners each received a piece of cornbread and meat before a number of them boarded trains for prison.[7]

Capt. Will Muse, 1ˢᵗ TN, spent the first eighteen days of his confinement in a barn, clinging to life. Muse said he was "on the ground with three holes through me … pronounced dead by our surgeon." Doctor Monroe Jordan, unconvinced of the prognosis, used hot coffee, whiskey, and hot cloths until Muse opened his eyes, revealing a sign of life. After a short stay in New York City, Muse was sent to Johnson's Island, where he spent the next eighteen months.[8]

Point Lookout, Maryland. The prison is in the upper right corner; the lower left spoke buildings are for the sick and wounded. The Potomac River is on the left with the Chesapeake Bay to the right. Courtesy of Point Lookout State Park; Scotland, Maryland.

The details of Gen. Archer's capture on the first day of the Battle of Gettysburg vary to a large extent, yet his prison tenure is well documented. In a July 8, 1863 letter, written one week after his surrender, Gen. Archer noted, "Arrived here at dawn Sunday morning. Am comfortable as could be expected in crowded quarters which receive all the odors of an extensive privy through windows from whence fresh air might have been expected to come …

I shall not suffer the want of exercise or air or any of the unwholesome things of a prison to affect my health or temper and with the blessing of God I will return to the army stronger and better than I left it."[9]

Transferred to Johnson's Island, Archer wrote his mother on July 28 that his comfort had been increased when he was sent from Ft. Delaware, as his new accommodations were much more spacious. Archer continued his plea for a blanket, and he explained that many of his fellow officers lacked even a change of clothes. The general also took time though to acknowledge the receipt of medicine and writing paper from his sister.[10]

Archer's letters during the fall of 1863 grew increasingly distressed and initially focused on the receipt of lemons for his sick comrades and his proclamation of his health being better than it had been since the early stages of the war. By mid-August he complained of his disgust with the books he'd received and stated that he had scoured over their pages to the extent that he had become sick of them. Archer's letter of November 1, written to his mother, began the insight into his disdain for what appeared to be a prolonged prison life with his statement that he saw "no prospect of a speedy exchange."[11]

Archer's contempt for life on Johnson's Island became more evident in a September 21, 1863 communication from Maj. Y.H. Blackwell of the Fifth Missouri Cavalry and a recent parolee. Blackwell forwarded to Secretary of War Seddon an unsigned message from Archer disclosing a count of 1,600 prisoners, 1,200 of whom were officers. With only one battalion guarding the prison, Archer felt its capitulation could be completed with minimal losses among the prisoners. The problem, Archer offered, came in the procurement of steamers to remove the men from the island. To assist with the solution to this problem, Gen. Archer provided the names of three men who would provide armed steamers and crews to carry the Confederates to the safety of Canada. Capt. L W. Allen wrote in his diary that Archer was to command block one, three, and five in a possible storming of the gates in an escape attempt.[12]

Thomas Herndon, 14th TN, likewise grew disenchanted with the conditions he faced on Johnson's Island. Herndon once explained that the water from Lake Erie was pure, the prison sanitary and well governed, and the rations fully capable of maintaining the prisoners' health. An order from US Secretary of War Stanton then cut rations in half, creating unending hunger and suffering. Failing health among the Confederate inmates dramatically increased.[13]

Herndon's journal entry of March 22, 1864 expressed his sadness over the passing of Lt. M.V. Baird of the Seventh Tennessee, a victim of chronic diarrhea. Herndon's poor personal health was the subject of a majority of his November and December 1864 entries. Undoubtedly Herndon's profession of faith on December 31, 1863 had enabled him to survive the humiliating conditions he had to face. His statement of his intention to live as a true Christian showed his sincere intent.[14]

Capt. Will Muse noted in his memoirs that it would be impossible to detail the "eighteen months of hell" he spent in prison. Muse, like Herndon, relied on his faith in God to persevere. He wrote, "The great Creator certainly endowed me with great vitality and ... will power." The cool Northern winds, one quarter rations, and close living quarters bore upon the young soldier as they did upon Jake Anthony, Harry Wright, and Jim Grant, all of his mess in which cooking was shared. Attendance at religious gatherings, theater performances, music and dance schools within the prison compound assisted Muse and others in passing the long hours.[15]

The Johnson's Island compound where misery was so vividly detailed, was sixteen and a half acres in size, containing twelve prisoner blocks and a hospital block. The 130-by-24-foot blocks were two stories high and constituted a proportion of the more than forty buildings, including barns, officer barracks, stables, and a powder magazine that were located outside the stockade.[16]

The photo and diagram show the conditions prisoners faced at Johnson's Island. Gen. Archer paid a guard three hundred dollars and a gold watch in an attempt to gain his freedom from this establishment. In what Archer labeled a "Yankee trick," the guard kept the payment and turned the officer in. After the war, the blockhouse at the main gate served as a hog house and corn fields surrounded the decaying prison barracks. Courtesy of Blue and Gray.

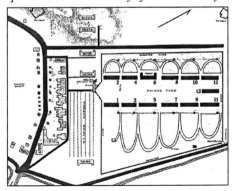

An amazing fact evolving from the conditions and circumstances of the war and prison life is the ability of the participants to extract humor. Robert C. Crouch recorded just such an event: "The prison proper was surrounded with a stockade, on top of which was the sentinel's beat, and on the inside of the stockade, between the buildings occupied by the prisoners and the stockade, was a ditch some four or five feet deep and perhaps six feet wide. Block 1 was perhaps twenty-five feet from the stockade, the ditch between. There were many escapes by prisoners digging tunnels from their quarters to the outside of the stockade. Of the many tunnels dug, I remember particularly one from Block 1. In order to get to the outside of the stockade with this one, it was necessary to go down below the bottom of the ditch spoken of. To dig these tunnels was slow and very laborious. They were made as small as possible, and it seemed that this one was not deep enough for the bottom of the ditch and not large enough. After some of the prisoners had gone through, Captain Cole, of Arkansas, following, got stuck, and the dirt caved in. In order to give those in advance of him time to escape, he made no alarm; but remained stuck in the hole, for how long I have forgotten. The next evening I remember Col. John A. Fite ... and others on the steps of Block 1, relating an account of the escapade to their fellow-prisoners, and concluding the story with a song, two lines of which I can recall:

'And now three cheers for Captain Cole, Who wouldn't holler when he got stuck in the hole.'"[17]

This photo of Robert Crouch was made in the prison by a fellow prisoner and printed on an oyster can. Crouch, a young man from Morristown, Tennessee, joined other prisoners in the great Johnson's Island rat hunt of 1864. Some five hundred rats were killed, skinned, and baked into a form of chicken pie with flour and bacon obtained from bribed guards. Crouch claimed none of the pies were left at the conclusion of the feast. Courtesy of Blue and Gray.

The Johnson's Island hardships encountered among the Tennessee Brigade members were reflected in their counterparts incarcerated at Ft. Delaware. Sgt. J.F. Moore, 14th TN, was captured as Gettysburg on July 1 and moved from Ft. McHenry to Ft. Delaware on July 7, 1863. Moore would remain at the prison, along with others of his regiment, until his release on April 26, 1865.[18]

W.H. Bird, 13th AL, was captured at Gettysburg at the same time that his company's lieutenant, W.H. Pond, and thirteen privates surrendered. Some members of the Thirteenth Alabama Regiment were able to escape to safety, yet a total of some seventy-four fell captive with Gen. Archer. The men of Archer's brigade were marched to Chester, Pennsylvania and moved to Baltimore before arriving at Ft. Delaware on July 4.[19]

The captured Confederates were searched for weapons upon their arrival at Ft. Delaware. This task was completed using two Union soldiers, one of whom searched the prisoners' backpacks while another slapped the men on their hips and breast. W.H. Bird recalled cursing a large Union soldier as he struck Bird across the chest, an act that, even under the situation, caused Bird such embarrassment that he was refrained from using profanity until his dying day. After the search, Bird and his comrades were herded into their barracks, where they found lines of bunks, one over another. Water came from a tank and constantly presented a bad taste and odor. At nine o'clock each morning and three in the afternoon, the men received their two meals, the regular menu being a tin cup of bean soup and two hardtacks with an occasional slice of "some kind of pickled meat."[20]

An excellent description of the conditions encountered at Ft. Delaware is recorded in the 1907 words of Dr. W.H. Moon, 13th AL. Moon's article "Prison Life at Fort Delaware" originally appeared in *Confederate Veteran* and is graciously reprinted here:

> We arrived at Fort Delaware … and were put into newly built barracks consisting of long rows of buildings. The material was all rough and the planks nailed on vertically with strips to cover the openings between. The outer row of buildings formed a square, the doors all opening on the inside except on the south, where the officers were quartered, the backs of their buildings forming our south boundary. From the east side of the square divisions extended westward to within about one hundred feet of the west side, leaving an open way along the front of the outer line of buildings on the west.

Dr. W.H. Moon, Co. I, 13ᵗʰ AL. Captured with Gen. Archer at Gettysburg, Moon spent a great deal of time as a prisoner of war documenting the lifestyle at Ft. Delaware. He later served as an officer of the Alabama U.C.V.; was a Baptist deacon and a Sunday School Superintendent. In 1929 Moon died, leaving his wife of fifty-seven years and eleven children. He was buried, at his request, in his gray uniform and placed in his childhood hometown of Lineville, Alabama. Courtesy of Confederate Veteran.

At the time of our arrival there was much rain, and the island, being formed by the drifting of mud between the two channels at the mouth of Delaware River, soon became a bog where the men had to pass. After the whole place had become a veritable bog, the authorities had plank walks built, which made the passageway better. For three or four months we were supplied with plenty of bread and meat; but as the winter approached our allowance was cut to about half, which was wholly inadequate to supply sufficient nourishment to keep the men from starving and freezing when the cold winter set in. Through the long winter months the men sat in groups upon their bunks or stood leaning against the walls on the sunny side of the buildings, wrapped in their old blankets, conversation generally being about the many good things they had to eat at their homes down in Dixie. The winter was so cold that the ice in the river by the ebb and flow of the tide drifted in to great icebergs, so that when the tide was at low ebb it looked like a vast plain covered with stacks of ice, no water being visible.

A division contained four hundred men and two heaters. Around these crowds would gather in compact mass several deep, so that no one else could get near enough to receive the benefit of the heat. The houses being very open, in cold weather the heat could be felt but a short distance even from a red-hot stove. The prisoners were allowed one suit of clothes, a cheap overcoat, and one inferior blanket to each man. These, with the one heater to two hundred men, were the only protection against the bitter cold winds that swept across the Delaware River and up the bay. One and a quarter miles was said to be the nearest point to land from the isle.

Those who crowded around the stove continually were dubbed stove rats. On very cold days those who spent most of their time on their bunks trying to keep warm would get down in the passway between the bunks, form in column of one or two with as many in the rear as wished to participate, and charge the "stove rats." The hindmost would push those in front until the stove was cleared. The rear ones would then take possession at the stove until another column would form and make a countercharge, when the rear ones of this column would take their turn at the stove. These charges and countercharges would on very cold days sometimes continue for several hours, resulting at times in turning over the red-hot stove on the floor, and this would stop the fun till the stove could be righted and the flames extinguished. When not too cold, others would play cards, make rings from gutta-percha buttons or bones, or work at some other device by which they could earn a pittance to relieve their "starvation rations."

In February we were moved into the old barracks south of where we had been staying These were formerly occupied by commissioned officers, who had been moved to other parts. When we entered these new quarters, the bunks and floor were covered with snow, which we had to clear out before starting up our little heaters. The next morning from our division four corpses were taken, frozen stiff. For four months, during the coldest of the winter, very few of the eight or nine thousand prisoners at Fort Delaware had sufficient food to satisfy their hunger at any time. The Yanks said they were retaliating on us for the way their men were being treated at Andersonville, Ga. On Christmas day I succeeded in getting out on detail to unload a boat of commissaries which consisted of crackers and sugar in barrels, which we were required to roll from the boat landing to the fort. It was impossible for hungry men to roll barrels of sugar so far and keep them whole, consequently there were soon several with the heads out sitting along the passway. As we rolled our barrels to the fort we would in passing these, scoop out a handful of sugar and eat it as we went to and from the fort. In this way we satisfied our hunger and filled our pockets for future use. This, with our half rations, kept off hunger for a few days, when we were again subjected to the torture of cold and hunger for the remainder of the winter.

Quite a number of the older men who required more food to sustain life became very much emaciated, and succumbed to the cold, being found on their bunks in the morning frozen to death. How any survived the ordeal through which we had to pass that winter seems strange to me now. Early every morning we would get down from our bunks and trot around to warm up and get some feeling in our feet, which were benumbed with cold till they felt more like clogs to the legs than feet.

The prevailing diseases were smallpox in winter and measles and diarrhea in summer. From these diseases hundreds died and were buried on the Jersey shore. The manner of burial was to dig a ditch six feet wide and six feet deep, put in three boxes containing corpses one on top of the other, then extend the ditch, using the dirt to cover the boxes.

An amusing incident occurred at one of these burials. There was near the hospital the dead house, where the clothes of the patients who went to the hospital were deposited, as were also the bodies of those who died, for burial the next day. One of the prisoners who was nursing at the hospital concluded to attempt his escape by removing one of the bodies from the box and hiding it under the old clothing, then placing himself in the box and having one of his friends replace the lid, so that it could be easily removed. In this way he, with several corpses, was conveyed in rowboats across the river to the Jersey shore, where all the prisoners who died at Fort Delaware were buried. These burials were attended to by details of prisoners to do the work and a guard to direct and keep the prisoners from making their escape. When they landed on the Jersey shore and were preparing to deposit the boxes in the ditch, the man who had concealed himself forced the lid off the box, jumped to his feet, and ran through the apple orchard which was near by. The detail and Yanks all took to their heels in a different direction, so he had no trouble in making his escape while the stampede was on. As I remember, one or two of the detail made good their escape. Those who knew nothing of the scheme were probably as badly frightened as the Yanks, and made no effort to get away.

Another incident occurred which created considerable excitement among the guard one night. One of the prisoners, an elderly man known as Old Tom, had become demented, and was allowed to roam at will over the island. Occasionally he would lodge in the dead house at night, and on the night of the incident he had taken up his quarters there. As the guard who had just been relieved from duty was passing in front of the dead house, Tom, dressed in long white apparel, moved out through the door, going directly toward the squad. Taking him for the spirit of a dead Rebel, they became frightened and made a break for their quarters, from which they were separated by two canals about twenty feet wide and three or four deep in mud and water. Into these they plunged, making no effort to get to the crossings, which were very narrow. When they reached their quarters, they were all wet and muddy and terribly frightened. An investigation soon revealed the cause of the fright and stampede.[21]

Thirty-eight of the seventy-four men of Moon's regiment, the Thirteenth Alabama, who were captured with Gen. Archer at Gettysburg, died in the hospital or prisoner barracks on Pea Patch Island, the area around Ft. Delaware. These individuals were buried at Finn's Point, New Jersey in the trenches described in Moon's testimony. After having lost some six killed and thirty-nine wounded at Gettysburg, the Thirteenth Alabama's fatality rate at Ft. Delaware proved the statement that capture is no assurance that an individual will sit out the remainder of the war in the safety of a prison camp.[22]

Aerial view of Ft. Delaware. Over thirty-two thousand soldiers were imprisoned here between 1862 and 1865. Courtesy of Fort Delaware Society.

The southwest bastion and moat of Ft. Delaware. Courtesy of the Fort Delaware Society.

Finns Point Cemetery. Many of the Confederates captured at Gettysburg were sent to Ft. Delaware. The thousands who died were buried alongside the Union guards in this cemetery on the nearby New Jersey shore. Courtesy of the Fort Delaware Society.

The Johnson's Island cemetery contains the remains of 206 men who died there. Courtesy of Blue and Gray.

Sutler money was used inside the Johnson's Island stockade to purchase inflated-priced items such as food, clothes, ink, combs, or most other items available in nearby Sandusky stores. Courtesy of Blue and Gray.

CHAPTER SIXTEEN

The Retreat from Gettysburg

The Army of Northern Virginia had been soundly defeated at Gettysburg, ending Lee's initiative of a Northern invasion and beginning a Southward retreat. Having lost their leadership with the capture of Archer and seeing their ranks decimated in the action of July 1 and 3, the remaining members of the Tennessee Brigade fit for service were deeply dismayed. The day after the battle, Lee's army began its retreat, a move that Union general George Meade is rumored to have originally considered a ploy on Lee's part to possibly initiate further action. The retreat was factual, and serving as its rear guard was Heth's division, including the remnants of Archer's Tennessee Brigade.

Meade sent forward cavalry units that harassed the downtrodden Confederates in the early stages of the move from Gettysburg. Historian Edward J. Stackpole explained that Meade's timidity at engaging the Southerners was "suggestive of a clawed lion-tamer gingerly prodding at an escaped beast in an effort to nudge him back into his cage."[1]

Lincoln's open criticism of Meade's hesitance is well known. Meade would later ask to be relieved of his command, yet President Lincoln would contact the general to more fully explain his chastisement of the Federal commander. In a July 14, 1863 letter to Gen. Meade, Lincoln expressed his appreciation to Meade for his defeat of the Confederates but noted the general's failure to pursue the retreating army in a pressing manner and that the enemy was eventually reached and only engaged "by slow degrees."[2]

On July 6, 1863, Gen. Meade informed Maj. Gen. H.W. Halleck, general-in-chief, that Union cavalry had been attacking both flanks of the "crippled" Confederates, inflicting as much injury as possible. Using the Fairfield Pike, the Tennessee Brigade accompanied the Army of Northern Virginia across an almost impassible route until it arrived at Hagerstown, where Gen. Lee "halted and fortified a strong position."³

A.S. Van de Graaff of the Fifth Alabama Battalion wrote his wife from Hagerstown on July 8, 1863, describing the events of the recent past. His words were:

My dear Wife:

I have not been able to send a letter to you since we crossed the river on the 23rd and I know that you must be very uneasy about me. I am well and unwounded.

We marched to Gettysburg, Pa. where we fought on the 1st 2nd & 3rd of July. On the first two days our armies were triumphant; on the last we were badly repulsed in the center and the 3rd Corps badly cut up. I was relieved from duty as Pro. Marshall and went into the battle. On the 1st my Battalion was deployed as Skirmishers and lost only 7 men wounded although we drove the Calvary Pickets & Skirmishers of the Enemy over three miles; during the battle a shell exploded at my feet covering me with dirt and filling my eyes. Our Brigade led the attack, drove the Enemy but being unsupported was forced to fall back. On the 3rd we were in the front line and charged the enemy thru an open field about a mile. Some of the Brigade again reached the top of the Hill and drove the enemy; but again the supporting lines broke and we were drawn back with great loss. The whole corps was routed, and we lost many prisoners. My loss in this battle was 43 of 98 men. Some are prisoners & unhurt. In my old company Tom Barnes was wounded slightly in leg, C.E. Denison taken prisoner, or rather missing. I think he is badly wounded or killed. J.D. Tuerman was shot in the shoulder severely. The Battalion fought well in both battles. I got within 50 yds of the breastworks when our line gave way and being completely exhausted lay down in a lane for 15 or 20 minutes, under a very heavy fire. I then ran out, and succeeded in getting back to our line unhurt, although overheated and broken down. The next evening we fell back and have retreated to this place. We sent our wounded back, but they were all nearly captured by the enemy. Our entire loss must be very heavy. Two wagons from each Reg't was sent back loaded with wounded, and that was attacked and captured by the Calvary of the Enemy. We lost nearly four hundred Wagons. I think we will recross the River as soon as it becomes fordable. We have not heard a word from home, nor indeed any where since we have been over the River. Our army was buoyant and full of life and the repulse wholly unexpected by men & officers. My health has not been good and I am worn out with the exposure and hardships of the last week. I have not been able to change … for ten days, and don't know where we will meet the wagon again. I will write to you every opportunity I meet with, but have little hope of hearing from you soon.

Give my love to all & believe me as ever your affectionate husband

A.S. Van de Graaff[4]

June Kimble recalled the march involved with the retreat and the harassment from Federal cavalry: "Longstreet and Ewell followed the line of retreat upon the right and A. P. Hill on the left. In their disposition it fell to the lot of Heth's Division, under Pettigrew, to cover the rear of Hill's Corps. The retreat was slow, owing to rain and mud, rough mountains, and difficult roads. The enemy's cavalry penetrated this line of march in force and in front of Heth's Division, with the view of capturing the whole division. At this point Fitzhugh Lee's matchless horsemen appeared, and at intervals for two or three days fought them back inch by inch in desperate charge and countercharge. All this time the way was kept open for Heth's Division. About the 8th of July Hagerstown was reached. Here Lee concentrated his retiring columns and calmly awaited the approach of Meade. Here again Lee offered battle, which Meade declined. I am sure that if Meade had attacked a bloody repulse awaited him, because Lee's army was again in its usual fighting trim and ready in spirit to measure lances with the foe."[5]

The photo on the previous page and the one below of Capt. Albert S. Van de Graff, 5ᵗʰ AL, show the effect of war upon a young man. The aging process has made the youngster in civilian clothing almost unrecognizable as the bearded veteran in uniform some three years later. Photos courtesy of Pat Hanson.

Military action was largely insignificant throughout the majority of the retreat, the exception being the aforementioned skirmishes with the harassing Federal cavalry. John T. McCall, 7ᵗʰ TN, reported, "During Lee's retreat from Gettysburg we were detained at Hagerstown, five miles from the Potomac River

… on account of the high waters. The river was swollen, and pontoon boats were brought from Richmond, a distance of over one hundred miles, for a crossing, although most of our wagons had passed over before the rise in the river. Lee's lines extended from the Potomac River to near Hagerstown. Our brigade was on the extreme left of the line. The right moved across first, and left us to cover the retreat. Early on the night of the 13th the army began to cross the river, although it was very dark and a drenching rain poured down."[6]

Maj. Gen. Henry Heth had received orders on the evening of July thirteenth to leave his entrenchments at Hagerstown and advance toward Falling Waters. The artillery of Heth's division moved just before sundown, while Heth deployed skirmishers to his front with the understanding the cavalry would relieve them. The command's progress was minute, as the division halted frequently to allow the passing of wagons and artillery; one cessation lasted two hours. A march of seven miles took twelve hours to accomplish, yet the feat was miraculous in relation to the conditions under which it was carried out. Heth wrote, "The night was entirely dark, and the roads in a dreadful condition … being ankle deep in mud." Approximately two miles from Falling Waters, Heth received orders from A.P. Hill to place his division, including the Tennessee Brigade, on the crest of a hill, along the road extending to Hagerstown. Confederate engineers established artillery placements to the left of the road with an open space to their front through which a half to three-quarter mile unobstructed view existed. Ending the open space was heavy timber. Pender's division was placed to the rear of Heth, who was instructed to place his division in a line of battle.[7]

J.H. Moore remembered, "On that day Heth's division stopped on the road leading to the Potomac … We always kept up a line of battle, and on this occasion halted and formed on the left—the west side of the road. In a part of our front was an old breastwork that had been abandoned long ago." The wagons and artillery began crossing the river while the Tennessee Brigade remained stationery for several hours, having again been chosen to protect the rear of the Army of Northern Virginia.[8]

Capt. William B. Tolley, 1st TN, explained, "This brigade was rear guard to the army, and had marched all night through rain and slush. Upon reaching the Potomac the men had thrown themselves upon the ground for much needed rest, and were lying around loose, when there occurred one of the most thrilling episodes of the war. They had stacked arms and were sleeping in fancied security under the impression that our cavalry was looking after that of the enemy."[9]

John T. McCall added, "We were ordered to stack our guns and rest. Some of our artillery had bogged up, and the men were soon asleep. A few of us were up, when one of the boys called the attention of … J.H. Moore to a troop of cavalry advancing with blue uniforms and Yankee flags; but, supposing Stewart's Cavalry to be behind, Lieut. Moore said not to fire, thinking the flags had been captured."[10]

J.H. Moore described the subsequent events: "On a small eminence on the front of our line Gens. Heth and Pettigrew and several other officers, including myself, were looking back over the route we had traveled, when we noticed a small body of cavalry emerge from a strip of woods, distant about two hundred and fifty yards. After reaching the open space they halted, and the officer in command rode to the front as if to address the men. We observed them closely, and our group concluded they were Confederates. We saw them unfurl a United States flag, but we thought it was a capture that our friends were to carry to us and make some ado over it. Presently they started toward us at a tolerably rapid pace, and when they got within fifty yards of us they advanced at a gallop with drawn sabers, shouting, 'Surrender! Surrender!' Gen. Heth exclaimed, 'It's the enemy's cavalry!' When opposite, they rushed over our little group, using their sabers and firing their pistols, mortally wounding Gen. Pettigrew, and dashed among the infantry, eighteen hundred strong, shouting at the top of their voices, 'Surrender! Surrender!'"[11]

John T. McCall remembered a Federal cavalry major yelling to his men to ride into the Confederates and split their heads. The horsemen struck the Confederates, catching many of them sleeping, and rode over a number of the men, breaking arms and legs. McCall also recalled the Union major "seeing Gen. Pettigrew and staff in a group, dashed up to them and demanded their surrender; and, when they refused to do so, he shot Gen. Pettigrew with his pistol, mortally wounding him. In two or three seconds the major was shot from his horse by one of Gen. Pettigrew's staff officers."[12]

Capt. W.F. Fulton, 5th AL, provided a similar recollection: "I was at the time acting commissary for our battalion … and had a horse to ride, for which I felt sorry because he had been long without food of any kind, and I had ridden him out in the old field back toward Gettysburg and had turned him loose to graze. While watching him enjoy his morning meal my attention was suddenly called to a startling vision on the hill just beyond me. There on that ridge I saw a sight that for a moment paralyzed me. A long line of blue rapidly forming in shape for a charge. It flashed over me in a minute what was going to happen; and I fairly flew toward my comrades, lying stretched out in sleep in an old apple orchard in the edge of the old field, and yelling at the top of my voice: 'Look out! Look out! The Yankees! The Yankees! Look out!' I soon bounded in among the boys, still yelling, and had just time to see them begin to get up and rub their eyes, when the Yankee cavalry came bursting in among us in full tilt, shouting as they waved their carbines: 'Surrender!'"[13]

Heth had incorrectly concluded the cavalry to be Confederate until viewing them with his field glasses from a distance of about 175 yards. Heth and Gen. Pettigrew had restrained the Confederates from firing until that point. Orders for the men to fire rang through the air. At the same time, a Federal cavalry officer issued an order to charge. This initial detachment of Federal cavalry was killed or captured with the exception of a handful of soldiers who escaped.[14]

June Kimble shared Heth's initial conclusion of the presence of a unit of Southern cavalry. He noted, "It had rained during the night, and was still dark and misty. We supposed that Stuart's Cavalry was in our front and that this body was a part of his force. We had no pickets out; there was no fear or concern as to these troops. General Pettigrew was standing in the road observing the front. General Heth, with his head still bound up in the white cloth from his wound of July 1, rode up to Pettigrew, and the two were evidently discussing the situation. Billy Daniels and I were sitting on a little mound constructed for the use of artillery on the left of the road some ten feet from Generals Heth and Pettigrew, and the boys of Archer's Brigade were lounging on the ground twenty or thirty feet from us, many of them asleep. Suddenly a body of horsemen came into the road at the foot of the incline in a sweeping trot. About halfway up they unfurled their pennants, drew sabers, and sprang into a rushing gallop. Daniel and I leaped from the little mound and both exclaiming: 'Look out, boys; the Yanks are on us!' Instantly there was a springing to feet and to guns."[15]

J.H. Moore offered his rendition of the early stages of the confrontation. He wrote, "At first the confusion was great, our officers calling upon their men to form and use the bayonet, at the same time dodging the saber cuts and using their pistols with great effect. Lieut. Baber killed two and Capt. Norris three men. As soon as our men took in the situation, and after they had reached their guns, these daring fellows were quickly dispatched. In the height of the confusion their officer galloped into our midst, and in less time than it takes to relate the circumstance he was riddled with bullets. He was a gallant-looking fellow, riding a magnificent dark-colored horse, but he and his force were to a man either killed or wounded in this quick and rash undertaking. There were not more than one hundred and twenty-five of them, but I will venture to say they came nearer stampeding or capturing a division than they ever did before. Their horses were nearly all killed or so badly crippled as to make them useless. Only two or three were brought off the field, though they were all captured."[16]

William Tolley noted his perception from within the First Tennessee, "Quickly Maj. Buchanan rallied his men and gave the command to fire. Only a very few of the guns would fire, as they were too wet. On rode the Federals, but the Tennesseans, nothing daunted, clubbed their pieces and stood ready to receive them. Some who could not get to their guns actually unhorsed their assailants with fence rails, while the enemy used their sabers. What a grim and unique spectacle! No sound of rattling musketry nor roaring artillery to warn the balance of the army! It was an every-man-for-himself affair. A Federal major, observing Maj. Buchanan, rushed his horse forward, ordering: '… surrender!' but without waiting for response, began shooting at him with his pistol. The major got hold of it and held it to one side until all the shots were exhausted, when the Federal resorted to his saber. All the while Maj. Buchanan had hold of the bridle, walking backwards and leading the horse toward the fence, on which were his own sword and pistol, meanwhile warding off the saber thrusts with the horse's head, receiving, however, several cuts in his hat. Finally—it must have seemed almost an age to him—he reached the fence, and, seizing his own pistol, shot his assailant from his horse."[17]

Capt. W.F. Fulton remembered the events as well: "Of course, it was hard for the poor tired fellows to realize what was to pay, but as the cavalry passed on, after seeing their orders to surrender complied with, they began to wake up and speedily drop in a cartridge, and if the gun wasn't too wet to fire, Mr. Yank was sure to get it in the back; and it was only a short while till they began to scamper back from where they came. Had not the guns and powder been damp that morning, none would have survived that foolhardy charge."[18]

Gen. Pettigrew had received a wounded hand at Gettysburg, possibly affecting the degree of his ability to manage his horse that, during the confusion, reared and fell to the ground with him. At this point the general was struck in his left side by a pistol ball; the wound proved fatal.[19]

June Kimble stated that Gen. Heth whirled his horse to the rear as Gen. Pettigrew backed to the head of Company A of the Fourteenth Tennessee, urging the men to stand their ground. Kimble wrote, "The sharp crack of pistols rang out from the head of the enemy's plunging column, and the brave, noble Pettigrew fell with a mortal wound at the feet of those who had gathered around him, the first victim. Simultaneously a quick volley from the aroused veterans emptied the saddles of the leader and his nearest horsemen."[20]

W.F. Fulton remarked of Gen. Pettigrew, "I was looking at him, riding with his arm in a sling … trying to arouse his weary soldiers, who were asleep after an all-night tramp in rain and mud … from Hagerstown, Md. … and it was in this melee that General Pettigrew, one of North Carolina's great men, was killed." Pettigrew would be carried back to Virginia, where he died of his wounds three days later.[21]

A mortally wounded member of the Seventh Tennessee fell soon after Pettigrew. This constituted the entire loss to Heth's command in the Federal charge. Though thirty-three Federal dead and six wounded were accounted for[22] and the number of Southern casualties was low, the attack was not without Confederate panic.

John T. McCall remarked on the conduct of his comrades of the Seventh Tennessee, "Our men scattered in every direction, most of them leaving their guns in the stack. Seeing an old barn in a field about a hundred yards away, some dozen of us made for it. About six of the Yankees saw us, and here they came with drawn sabers, swearing they would cut our heads off if we didn't surrender. When they struck at us with their sabers we would fall flat on the ground, and before they could check their horse speed we would get some distance from them. A comrade and I got to an old fence, when two of the Yankees saw us and came at us in full speed. We jumped the fence, and before they could get their horses over we were some distance from them. We had it in this way for about five minutes, and were about fifty yards from them, when we found a gun which, fortunately for us, was loaded. They had gotten on each side of the fence, and here they came, yelling. We were hid in the corner of the fence, and when they were within a few steps of us my comrade jumped to his feet and fired at one of them, who threw up his hands and cried out: 'O Jim, I am killed!' His horse ran about a hundred yards, and he fell off dead. His comrade tried to make his escape, but ... was captured."[23]

J.H. Moore recalled the bravery of the Federal cavalrymen, writing, "I talked with one of the survivors of the regiment to which this squadron belonged, and he told me that their officer was promoted only the day before for gallant and meritorious service. My recollection is that it was a part of the Sixth Michigan Cavalry. There was a large body of cavalry a few miles behind this squadron, and we remained at Falling Waters about one hour skirmishing with these. We finally fell back through the woods in line of battle to the river, crossing it with the loss of some stragglers and parts of companies that were detached and lost their way in the woods."[24]

June Kimble remembered a slightly different version of the incident: "The impetus of the charge could not be checked; the rear pressed forward to the front. It became at once a melee, a fierce, bloody, hand-to-hand struggle, and quickly all was over. From one of the wounded I learned that Major Webber was the leader of this squadron of eighty-six men of the 4th Michigan Cavalry. In answer to the inquiry why they rode on us he said they supposed we were only stragglers and they sought to take us in. A fatal mistake, for ... only three escaped. This turmoil lasted about three minutes."[25]

The action to which Moore referred led to a controversy in the years following the battle. Union brigadier general Judson Kilpatrick was said to have captured an infantry brigade at Falling Waters. Gen. Heth explained that Kilpatrick's two cavalry charges had resulted in "the unhorsing of the entire party." Heth was quick to point out that large numbers of stragglers from every brigade who passed over the roads from Gettysburg were captured, yet contrary to Meade's report of Kilpatrick, none captured on July 14 belonged to Heth's command—certainly not the brigade that Kilpatrick claimed. Heth concluded, "We have every reason to be thankful our losses were so small."[26]

The subsequent attacks on other Confederate units left a significant number of Lee's men unable to participate in further action. June Kimble remarked, "The enemy pressed our retreat, and many fell by the wayside from exhaustion. It was shoot, run and load, halt, shoot, and run again, with no let up. About thirty of us agreed to stay together with Lieut. Jim Howard, and we crossed the bridge as it swung loose from the Maryland shore. But before we reached that bridge, when our knees began to tremble and hope was pinning on its wings for a farewell flight, a cannon roared and a shell exploded among the charging columns, another and another, by order of A.P. Hill. Did you ever hear sweet music when you happened to be very tired, somewhat anxious, and just a little bit scared? Talk about your harp of a thousand strings; there was more melody in the roar of that old gun and the pow of that beautiful shell than all the hand organs and Jew's harps in the world put together. It was mesmeric, soothing, exhilarating, inspiring, a nerve restorer ... We had arrived in sight of the Virginia Bluffs, a half or three-quarters of a mile away, when General Hill ordered a couple of pieces of artillery planted on the bluff to open fire upon the enemy ... This faithful handful of Archer's Brigade had fired the last gun as it had fired the first in the Gettysburg campaign. Then we crossed the Potomac back into dear old Virginia." Kimble and his comrades crossed the bridge, topping a bluff that signified their entry into Virginia. Kimble remarked, "What perfect rest we had! I had never slept so well. Gen. A.P. Hill said to his faithful chief courier: 'Let these men sleep until five or six o'clock, then lead them to camp.' Grand old leader and glorious old fighter, he knew what we needed most."[27]

J.H. Moore summed up the Tennessee Brigade's accomplishments of July 1863: "The Tennessee Brigade of Heth's division, composed of the First, Seventh, and Fourteenth Tennessee regiments, the Thirteenth Alabama Regiment, and Fifth Alabama Battalion, began the great battle of Gettysburg, and fought the last battle and skirmish in that memorable retreat from Pennsylvania, and the last the Army of Virginia fought north of the Potomac."[28]

June Kimble added a personal note, stating, "I was among the first of Archer's Brigade to fire a gun in the first day's battle and among the last to fire a gun at Falling Waters. I crossed the enemy's line and stood shoulder to shoulder with my brave comrades of Archer's Brigade inside of the enemy's works at the angle upon Cemetery Ridge. These facts at least should entitle me to some credence, although memory is somewhat treacherous and facts are always remembered differently from different viewpoints. After the lapse of so many years, with, as I feel, all envy or malice or prejudice, if there were any, eliminated by time and the mellowing influence of age and sober reflection, what I have written is due to fairness and justice."[29]

Heth's men once again stood on Virginia soil, where most were safe to seek a good night's rest. Many of Heth's soldiers, ironically, received shoes upon their return to the Old Dominion.[30]

The ramifications of the action at Gettysburg would be felt for months to come. For the Tennessee Brigade, it would, among other aspects, bring about the appointment of a new though temporary leader. Special Order 178, issued on July 19, 1863, gave Brig. Gen. H.H. Walker command of Heth's former brigade. With the severe reduction in numbers among the companies of the Tennessee Brigade, this unit was consolidated with Brockenbrough's Virginians under Walker's leadership.[31] The reception Walker received was less than enthusiastic among the men of Archer's command, who continued to refer to their brigade as Archer's Tennessee Brigade.

After participating in the action at Falling Waters, the Tennessee Brigade again served as the rearguard of the Army of Northern Virginia. This assignment would be conducted as the army moved toward Winchester. Federal cavalry maintained an infrequent contact with the retreating Confederates, though only minor damage was inflicted. South of the Rapidan River, the Tennesseans and other members of Walker's consolidated forces entered camp near Orange Court House, their time there spent primarily in drilling and socialization. An exception to the days of rest came in what had been called "an unfortunate affair, in which the Confederate troops suffered severely"[32]: Bristoe Station.

Lee had ordered Gen. Longstreet's Corps to Tennessee; the Army of the Potomac, in turn, sent the two corps in the same direction. Lee felt the departure of two corps of the enemy could prove to be a proper time to launch an offensive against Meade and possibly capture Washington, D.C. Using J.E.B. Stuart's cavalry as cover, Lee's two remaining corps, under Ewell and A.P. Hill, began moving toward their objective on October 9. By October 11 the Confederates were in Culpepper; Meade began a retreating maneuver to place himself between the Confederates and the US capital. The Tennessee Brigade joined the pursuit of Meade, following him closely until he reached Centerville.[33]

On the fourteenth, Hill's corps was positioned north of Warrenton, where Hill reached a decision to strike and divide the Federal forces that he understood were moving away from the advancing Confederates. Hill clearly heard the rumbling of Federal wagons along the Warrenton and Alexandria Pike, a sound confirming the rumors of a Federal movement. The Tennessee Brigade moved with the remainder of Heth's division and that of Wilcox onto a road toward Greenwich. Gen. Hill detached the Fourteenth Tennessee from the Tennessee Brigade, placing it on his right to serve as skirmishers. The remainder of the Tennessee Brigade formed a line of battle one hundred yards to the rear of Gen. Kirkland along the crest of a hill parallel to Broad Run.[34]

Confederate artillery under Poague opened fire on the Federal wagons, sending them scurrying away. Heth's division, including the Tennessee Brigade, was ordered forward, unaware of the approaching infantry, reacting to the sound of Poague's guns. The oncoming Federals belonged to Maj. Gen. Gouverneur Warren's II Corps, troops who had helped repulse[35] the Confederate assault on Cemetery Hill at Gettysburg on July 3.

Hill, waving his hat and urging the Confederates forward called for protection of Heth's right flank. A large number of stragglers appeared between the two armies, obviously confused by the action. After attempting to pop caps on their empty guns, these tramps and camp followers "broke for the rear in a wild rush," running directly through the Tennessee Brigade.[36]

Two additional divisions of the second corps under Hays and Caldwell arrived as the Union line was strengthened with artillery to the south of the Orange and Alexandria Railroad. Heth's division of four thousand men moved forward at 3:00 p.m., striking the rifles of Brig. Gen. Alexander Webb's men of Warren's Corps. Heth's troops broke the Union line, but the Federal cannon ripped into the charging Confederates of the Tennessee Brigade and two North Carolina brigades. Heth's men began surrendering or retreating in large numbers. Maj. Gen. Anderson's Confederate division arrived as Heth's attack was being carried out. Anderson's artillery chief, Major David McIntosh, had placed seven cannon five hundred yards from the Federal line. These guns fell into Union possession when Heth's troops retreated.

W.F. Fulton recalled the sounds the retreating stragglers made as they were soon joined by large numbers of Heth's division. Confederate officers drew their swords, promising to use them on anyone leaving their ranks. The threats, swords, rifles, and pistols were ineffective as the retreating soldiers and stragglers pushed back those desiring to stand and fight.[37]

Gen. Lee's total losses were heavy; 1,300 men were lost in the "ill-judged attack" and "gross blunder," as participants described the battle. By comparison, Union losses were only 546. Gen. Lee rode over the battlefield with A.P. Hill the following day as the latter poured out his heartfelt apology and explanations for the calamity of the previous day. Lee evidently felt compassion for Hill or perhaps recalled his own misgivings that followed the recent ill-advised assault of July 3 at Gettysburg, as Lee told Hill to bury the poor men and say nothing else about this incident at Bristoe.

No major action took place the following month for the Tennessee Brigade as it went into winter quarters. Meade evidently felt that an attempt to surprise Lee should be made with the possible result of crushing Lee's Army of Northern Virginia. On November 26, Meade began his move, yet Federal troops under Maj. Gen. William French were delayed by heavy rains, the increased size of the Rappahannock, and damaged pontoon bridges that had to be repaired to allow Union artillery to join the infantry. Over the next day and a half, Lee's troops established a strong defensive position at Mine Run, a Rapidan River tributary. W.F. Fulton recalled the Tennessee Brigade's position among Heth's division as "most admirably designed for defense." The natural terrain was strengthened with the digging of earthen defenses and abates. Gen. Meade's subordinates felt the Confederate position was too strong to capture; Meade thus boldly countermanded the earlier order to attack. The Union commander's expectations to be relieved of his duties for his failure to attack would not be immediately carried out. Lee's decision to attack Meade's position following the latter's hesitation resulted in the discovery only of abandoned fire pits.[38]

Thus the Tennessee Brigade, consolidated with Virginians and led by Henry H. Walker, settled into winter quarters for 1863 to 1864. With the exception of a small number of skirmishes and reconnaissance operations, the men saw no action for almost six months.

Following a reconnaissance operation of December 12 through 15, 1863 from Orange Court House to Stauton, Virginia, the Tennessee Brigade found themselves without tents and subjected to the brutal cold and rain and sleet of December 16. As midday of the seventeenth approached, the men found shelter in barns and houses, eventually leaving those to venture to Mount Jackson. The brigade remained there until early 1864. As the winter progressed, the brigade spent time near Cross Keys, returning to Orange Court House in March 1864. During this time, Col. William McComb, recovered from his wounds at Chancellorsville, returned to the Tennessee Brigade and assumed command of the Fourteenth Tennessee. Picket duty and drilling remained the focus of his men during this period.[39]

John D. Adcock, Co. C, 13th AL, wrote his sister on March 14, 1864 from his regiment's camp near Orange Court House. His expression of hope for a near end to the war would prove futile but undoubtedly expressed the feeling of a large number of war-weary soldiers of North and South. Adcock wrote, "I haven't any war news of interest to write. Only the papers say that France has recognized the Southern Confederacy. If that be done, I think we will have peace this year. I would like to have an honorable peace—for I am getting tired of this way of living."[40]

CHAPTER SEVENTEEN

The Wilderness and Spotsylvania

Summer 1864

In early May, 1864, the Tennessee Brigade broke its winter camp when, on May 4, orders were given to cook rations and prepare to move at a moment's notice. Meanwhile, U.S. Grant, the Union army's newly appointed lieutenant general, moved the Army of the Potomac across the Rapidan River. Aware of Grant's intentions, Lee believed a strike against the enemy at the Wilderness would lessen the effectiveness of the Federal army's superior manpower. A.P. Hill's troops, led in the march by Heth's division, reached Mine Run by dark on May 4, 1864. Hill's corps, including the Tennessee Brigade, was to strike Grant's army on the Plank Road while Ewell and Longstreet attacked on two other Chancellorsville-bound routes.[1]

The Fifth Alabama Battalion had been serving as provost guard of Hill's Third Corps since losing half of its two hundred men in the intense fighting at Gettysburg. As the Tennessee Brigade moved out on the morning of May 5, the Fifth Alabama, under the leadership of Capt. Albert Van De Graff, was in line in the rear of Hill's Corps, a frequent provost task intended to reduce the number of stragglers.[2]

The Tennessee Brigade joined the rest of Heth's division and formed a line of battle on the right flank along Orange Plank Road. Prior to this deployment, Federal skirmishers harassed the brigade as it moved forward. Cooke's brigade took the center position, across the road, while Davis's brigade formed to the left. As the afternoon began, a portion of Heth's division took time to establish field works in preparation for battle.[3] The position of the Tennessee Brigade was on Orange Plank Road at the point where it ran in a southwest-northeast direction. Intersecting it at an almost north-south direction was Brock Road.

At approximately three thirty on the afternoon of May 5, 1864, Gen. Lee sent a member of his staff to Gen. Heth, noting the importance of controlling Brock Road. Heth replied that the road could probably be taken, yet he was uncertain as to the possibility of doing so without creating an engagement, an event Gen. Lee sought to avoid.[4]

Breastworks had not been fully established when Heth's troops encountered Federal soldiers approximately ninety yards away. Sgt. Robert Mockbee, 14th TN, remembered the attack occurring in a body of woods containing thick undergrowth. The Union assault was driven back, as was a second, third, fourth, and fifth. The charges upon the Tennessee Brigade's position were not victorious, though they were effective in wearing away the ranks of the decimated brigade. A soldier explained that victory rested on the issue of which army could sustain the most members killed without giving up the fight.[5]

The action in the early stages of the Wilderness campaign brought to mind the following events for William McComb: "The firing was very heavy in our front and just about sunset I found the enemy. So I gave orders to the 14th to change front to rear on left company and deploy to two paces and I never saw the order more perfectly carried out on drill than at this time although we were under heavy fire of the enemy. But it was answered so quickly and the boys moved so promptly into line firing all the time. Our line then laped [sic] the enemy and the enemy in our front fell back with their main line. I mention this movement in detail as it was a little risky to undertake this movement under fire of the enemy ... our boys loved to skirmish and they knew so well how to execute the command that it was a perfect success. The fighting lasted until some time after dark, and we had to hold our position until about one o'clock in the night before we could be relieved by other troops. We then moved to our left but could not get position in the main line. So I went to Genl. Heth and told him the situation and he requested me to go with him to Genl. A.P. Hill and state the situation to him which I did. And Genl. Hill said let the boys lie down and rest as Genl. R.E. Lee had told him a few minutes before Genl. Longstreet would take his place on the front line before day."[6]

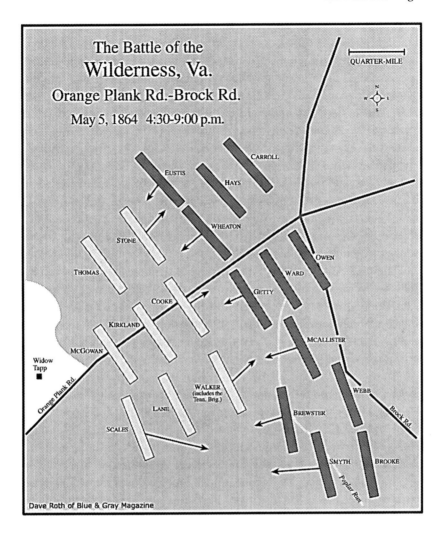

The series of Federal attacks had created a gap between Hill's Second and Third Corps. The Union soldiers, on their final assault, attempted to breach this gap. A.P. Hill had committed all but one of his units to the fight, but he then decided he must also commit that unit to preserve the effectiveness of his line. The Fifth Alabama Battalion had been guarding Federal prisoners but speedily took their number of just 125 members to the front. Moving forward with a rebel yell, the Fifth Alabama surprised the motivated enemy, sealed the gap of the location of the Federal penetration, and prevented a detrimental event for the entire Confederate Army of Northern Virginia.[7]

In numerous places along the battle line, musket wadding sparks ignited brush fires in the dry brush of the Wilderness. Many of the wounded and dying, unable to escape the flames, died from smoke or were burned to death. The noise of screams, cries, and popping undergrowth was horrifically accented by the explosion of cartridges in the boxes of the trapped soldiers.

While the hours passed without relief from Longstreet, the Tennessee Brigade anticipated further Union offensives. Yankees could be heard cutting down trees for use in fortifying their position. Soldiers on the Confederate line pondered the lack of orders to establish their own breastworks. Heth's seasoned veterans of the Tennessee Brigade rolled up their blankets and oil clothes at the break of dawn, using their intuition in preparing for the inevitable assault. A musket volley accompanied yells from the Federal lines as the Confederates jumped to their feet and armed themselves. The ensuing chaos resulted in the disintegration of Confederate regimental order and alignment. The Union assault led to a running retreat of Heth's division.[8]

William McComb explained the action of the morning of May 6, 1864: "There was an open space in our front and I could see the enemy advancing … 150 yards apart and they moved down on our position in splendid order and we were in no position to resist such a charge … and then fell back. And it was a wilderness sure enough and the enemy thinking they had a 'picknick' [sic] and when they got into this wilderness of bushes they got terribly mixed up and in about ¼ of a mile we met Longstreet's line of battle … moving in splendid order and we formed in Longstreet's rear. In a few minutes they struck the enemy and the order was given to charge and there was a Rebel yell sure enough. The enemy were mixed up in the bushes and they were in no condition to resist the charge and they … in a perfect panic … made very little resistance and the result was they were driven far beyond where we were in the morning or the night before and we captured over a 1,000 prisoners. So this was one time it was fortunate Longstreet was a little late coming into the fight. But when they got there they put up a good fight and the loss on our side was nothing like as heavy as it would have been if Longstreet … had … taken our position before day … hand to hand fighting during the day and some fighting the next day but Grant concluded the Wilderness was not a good place to handle 125,000 men and commenced his movement to Spotsylvania."[9]

The retreat of the Confederates had not been filled with total disorder, as many have implied. As Texas soldiers opened their ranks for the passage of the fleeing Tennessee Brigade, supposedly Walker's Virginia Brigade was the answer to the question as to which unit the retreating soldiers belonged. A member of the Fourteenth Tennessee was recognized among members of the advancing ranks of the Texans who asked when the soldier had been transferred from Archer's Tennessee Brigade. Texans would joke with

Tennesseans throughout the remainder of the war that the latter "ran through the Wilderness."[10]

Not all Texans felt the Tennesseans lacked fortitude during the Battle of the Wilderness. A Texas-led debate started in 1895 as to which dark-skinned "Spaniard" brought the Tennesseans "out of the Wilderness in good order." J.K. Miller attempted to settle the debate, writing, "On the morning of May 6th, '64, at the battle of the Wilderness. Col. Shepard, of the Seventh Tennessee, spent the night with me recently, and it was thought he might have been the 'Spaniard,' I asked him if he was in command and if his men were in order. He said they were, and went on to speak of the morning surprise, and that as he came out the Texans were deploying, and he passed through their middle ... he was the man in command of the Tennesseans."[11]

J.K. Cayce, a Texan, offered another explanation: "You ask if the officer in command thereof was not Lieut.-Col. Shepard of the Seventh Tennessee, Archer's Brigade. The officer was not Col. Shepard, but was Col. J.M. Stone ... of Mississippi, commanding that morning the Second and Eleventh Mississippi, Davis' Brigade, Heth's Division. These men saved the army. Shortly afterwards Gen. Lee rode up, and Gen. Longstreet introduced Col. Stone to him as the man who saved the army. This title Col. Stone modestly declined, saying, 'My boys did it.'"[12]

Capt. F.S. Harris offered yet more detail of the settlement of the argument, stating, "Col. J.M. Stone was then, and is now, everything that his legions of admirers claimed, and I have no doubt 'came out in good order.' However, the gentleman from Hood's old brigade who made the inquiry, states that the man who came out in such perfect order was in command of a Tennessee Regiment—that his complexion was so dark he thought he must be a Spaniard. Col. Stone could not have been commanding a Tennessee regiment, as there were only three Tennessee regiments in the Army of Northern Virginia at that time ... Col. S.G. Shepard, whose complexion was very dark, eyes and skin the regular Castillian hue, with beard and hair long, straight and jet black, commanded the Seventh Tennessee. I can't see how the 'Spaniard' can be any other than Col. Shepard, and the most convincing proof of all is the modest admission of the Colonel ... that it was he."[13]

R. E. McCulloch, 14th TN, effectively summed up the contribution of his regiment and brigade when writing, "The Wilderness ... May ... 1864. Here this gallant band stood in line of battle, without rest, for eighteen hours, beating back the forces of the enemy successively hurled against it."[14]

Darkness and the terrain's condition ended an effective Confederate counter-attack, and the battle of the Wilderness came to an end. With thick undergrowth that often limited visibility to ten feet in any direction, losses on both sides were tremendous. The Army of the Potomac suffered 17,500 casualties in the action, compared to Lee's Army of Northern Virginia that lost 7,500 men. The figures are misleading, for the latter constituted approximately 12 percent of the remainder of Lee's army.[15]

The Federal losses included approximately 6,000 prisoners from the first day's fighting. Several Confederate generals were killed or wounded in the fighting at the Wilderness, including Pickett, Pegram, and Longstreet, whose wounds eliminated his ability to effectively serve for months. He had been wounded following the South Carolinians accidental firing on his staff and him[16] in an event eerily reminiscent of the mortal wounding of Stonewall Jackson one year earlier in the same geographical area.

Gen. Grant's skirmishers found Lee's troops behind new defenses on the morning of May 7. Grant decided to abandon the entanglements of the Wilderness following the supplying of his troops with food and ammunition. Grant's men cheered as they marched south, realizing Grant was determined to finish the fight by moving into Confederate territory as his predecessors had failed to do. Grant's decision was to move his army to Spotsylvania Court House, thirteen miles to the southeast. Ironically Gen. Lee had ordered Longstreet's temporary replacement, Maj. Gen. Richard Anderson, to move to the same area for the purpose of resting his troops.[17]

W.M. McComb held a higher view of the maneuvers, writing, "Our great commander Genl. R. E. Lee seemed to have an intuition of Grant's intentions and marched us very rapidly to Spotsylvania and we got there first. The 14th Reg't marched in front of Archer's Brigade and we were put in position by Genl. Smith, Chief Civil engineer of A. of N.V. and directed by him to fortify our position as well as we could."[18]

J.H. Moore, 7th TN, added, "In addition to Lane on the right our line extended more than a mile further. Beginning on the extreme right of Wilcox's Division our line ran for some distance until a ridge, very much like the Bloody Angle, jutted out, forming a spur. It was fortified and so abrupt was the apex that traverses had to be constructed to protect our men from an enfilading fire. This Angle was occupied by Archer's ... Brigade of Heth's Division. ... Still to the right was another brigade of Heth's Division and next on line receding to the rear and immediately in front of the old Court House were planted about forty or more pieces of artillery, which were protected by a small body of cavalry, posted in supporting distance, but far to the right and rear. This completes the disposition of the troops on our right on the morning of the 12th. It would be an unjust disparagement to ignore the services of the troops on the right, as to them belong a great part of the honor of saving the day ... they indirectly caused the cessation of further attacks on the 'Bloody Angle' ... While I would scrupulously abstain from exaggerating the services of any command, yet I cannot but think that Heth's Division, and particularly Archer's Brigade, can justly feel aggrieved at an account of the battle of Spotsylvania that ignores their invaluable service."[19]

William McComb recalled the Confederate artillery as being on the crest of a ridge 150 yards to the right and rear of the Fourteenth Tennessee. The regiment dropped back to allow the artillery's shot and shell to protect the brigade's front. Rails and logs were gathered for use as breastworks, and the Tennessee Brigade "in a short time ... had a fairly good fortification."[20]

The ensuing events were remembered in the words of a brigade member seventeen years later: "Shrouded in a heavy mist that would soon develop into rain as day was approaching, cloudy and heavy, a deep stillness pervaded ... The works occupied by the Tennessee Brigade extended about fifty yards in front of the general direction of our line and terminated in an acute angle. Immediately in our front, for about fifty yards, was an open space and then there was a pine woods ... about halfpast four in the morning we were aroused by heavy firing on our left. This was about gray dawn. All were aroused and we turned our anxious eyes in the direction of our left, as peal after peal of light arms and artillery advised us of the destructive volleys that were belched forth ... On our left ... So incessant was the fire that nothing living could apparently survive its destruction ... a heavy skirmish firing began in our front, and about the same time the Federal artillery opened on us. This skirmish and artillery fire was kept up until about nine in the morning, when the Federal skirmishers were reinforced and our men were driven in. At this juncture, as our skirmishers were being pressed back, Lieutenant Byrd Wilmouth, who was in command of the skirmishers, supposed to have been the tallest man in the Confederate army, leaped upon our works and ran along as if to get a good view of the action in our front. This act ... I regarded as reckless in the extreme, and, being within speaking distance, I called to him to get down. I knew he was a gallant soldier and that he was needlessly periling his life, for the artillery kept up a constant fire upon us and was planted near enough for grape to reach us. As if unmindful of his great danger he presently hallooed: 'Get ready, boys; there are three lines of coffee coming.' Here the enemy appeared marching in splendid order in three lines of battle. As if elated by the sight of our skirmishers, retreating before them to gain the shelter of our works, they marched steadily and boldly out of the cover of the pines into the open space in front of our works. Undaunted they advanced in the height of military discipline and received without wavering volley after volley, but at length our well-directed fire told on their ranks. Their stout hearts were appalled, their efforts seemed fruitless and they retreated to the cover of the pines."[21]

Men of Burnside's Ninth Corps of US soldiers had hit the left side of Heth's position, an area known as Heth's Salient, and heavy fighting erupted.

The strike was made prior to the implementation of Lee's plan to use Heth's and Wilcox's divisions to relieve the stress placed upon the angle. The first Federal assault upon the Confederate position had created a breach in the line to the left of the Tennessee Brigade. Gen. Gordon suggested that men from other brigades should assist Gen. Edward Johnston in closing the opening in his lines[22], but the Tennessee Brigade had problems of their own.

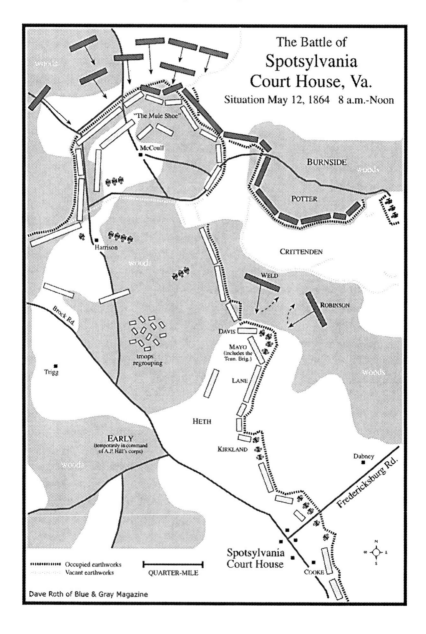

The Battle of
**Spotsylvania
Court House, Va.**
Situation May 12, 1864 8 a.m.-Noon

"The Mule Shoe"

McCoull

BURNSIDE

POTTER

Harrison

CRITTENDEN

WELD

ROBINSON

Brock Rd

DAVIS

MAYO
(includes the
Tenn. Brig.)

troops
regrouping

Trigg

LANE

HETH

EARLY
(temporarily in command
of A.P. Hill's corps)

KIRKLAND

Dabney

Fredericksburg Rd.

Spotsylvania
Court House

COOKE

Occupied earthworks
Vacant earthworks   QUARTER-MILE

Dave Roth of Blue & Gray Magazine

J.H. Moore remarked, "This assault was made while the rain was falling and in the very midst of the contest the rain descended in torrents; indeed, I hardly think I ever witnessed a harder rain. The fire of the enemy's small arms was assisted by his artillery ... the artillery fire was kept up constantly. After the repulse of the enemy, General J.A. Early rode up with his staff to learn, I suppose, how we received this assault. Under this most deadly fire of grape and canister he scanned the scene of conflict sitting on his horse with seeming indifference to the bursting shells tearing their way through the standing trees, shattering and breaking off limb after limb. There the old hero remained studying the situation regardless of the danger, while everyone else sought as secure a position as circumstances would allow. Though the enemy was repulsed with heavy loss he rallied in the pine woods in our front, and again advanced to renew the attack. No time was lost on either side; every man seemed to be nerved to do his whole duty. The constant fire of the artillery seemed to keep up the excitement of a continuous battle, and all was preparation to meet a second assault. In a few minutes the enemy advanced to the open space, but did not entirely emerge from the pine woods. He was checked by the fire of our men in the works, who were assisted by our skirmishers and sharpshooters. The enemy retired and was finally pressed back far into the pine woods by the advance of our division skirmishers and sharpshooters. This ended the attack—two assaults—upon the angle held by the Tennessee Brigade. It is true our loss was comparatively small when we consider the number slain in the Angle on our left. Nevertheless, the attack on the Angle or works held by the Archer Brigade was as determined as that made on the Bloody Angle, while the artillery fire was as great and as incessant ... our loss was less, simply because we had and held our works for protection and we were prepared for the enemy when he made his morning attack upon us. While our loss was comparatively small, that of the enemy was terrible, and had there been no Bloody Angle on our left the Angle held by the Archer Brigade would have been so regarded, as in fact it was by those who assaulted it, as appears form the letter hereinafter quoted."[23]

Moore proceeded to quote a letter from W.J. Jones, who served as a captain in Company I, Eighteenth Vermont Regiment. Moore began, "After the repulse of the second assault our division sharpshooters under Lieutenant F.S. Harris and a heavy skirmish force under Lieutenant Byrd Wilmouth advanced on the enemy and continued the contest in the pine woods in our front. Here, in the very skirts of the woods was the evidence of how terribly destructive was our fire. Though the two assaults had lasted hardly an hour ... Federal dead and wounded lay as thick on the ground as if a battle had raged for a day. Here in the pine woods, on the advance of our skirmishers and sharpshooters, occurred the thrilling and chivalrous scene that the writing of the following letter which was received by Gen. W.W. Estill, of Nashville:

Lebanon, Mo., August 25, 1880

Adjutant General of Tennessee:

Sir: I saw from a St. Louis paper, some weeks since, that a soldier in the Federal army in 1864 found, by writing to you, a friend who saved his life during the war. It was my misfortune to be fearfully wounded at Spotsylvania Court House, Va., on that terrible 12th of May, 1864, in a charge against a Tennessee Brigade in the Confederate army. The Tennessee Brigade occupied what was known afterwards as the Dead Angle, with a strong line of sharpshooters about seventy-five yards in front and about the same distance from our line. I could distinctly see the officer in command of the sharpshooters passing along the line, sending his line. We were ordered to charge about 2 p.m. A terrible battle ensued. The Tennesseans refused to be driven from their position, and after repeated assaults we retired again to our position. But not so with myself. I was left wounded about where the Confederates had their sharpshooters' line. The battalion was thrown to the front under the same officer who had command before and it is of him I now wish to inquire. His line behaved splendidly under the galling fire that our brigade poured into them. When the officer reached me I called to him "in God's name to give me some water." He dropped to his knees and raised my head with his left arm and put a canteen to my mouth. I had hardly finished the draught when a bullet from our troops passed through my throat and blood spurted from my mouth in his canteen and left him untouched. He laid my head down gently saying to himself, "Poor fellow! He has fought his last battle." I remember nothing else after he placed his own blanket under my head until I found myself in one of our hospitals. I do not know the bravest, the coolest and the kindest hearted man I ever saw! The word was passed along our lines often to shoot the tall officer with the broad hat.

I heard one of his men call him Harris or Harrison and he was a very handsome man, perfectly straight, with brown beard, and he wore a very broad hat. I pray God he has survived, for he saved my life. If you don't know him please have this letter published in one of your weekly and daily papers, so that it may reach him or some one who can give me information of him. Pardon the length of this letter.[24]

Moore was pleased to inform the former Union soldier that F.S. Harris, the individual who commanded the sharpshooters on that day, had survived the war and was still alive at the time of Jones's correspondence. Moore also explained that Jones's words depicted that a "bloody angle" existed at the Tennessee Brigade's position. Moore noted the words of British army colonel Freemantle, in whose account of the battle of Spotsylvania in the *Edinburgh Review* called the area a most desperate conflict.[25]

Both McComb and Moore praised the bravery Gen. Lee exhibited in riding along the Confederate lines as the battle raged. Moore explained, "After the second assault had been successfully met by the Tennessee Brigade in the Angle, General Lee rode down our line ... amid heavy artillery firing and stopped within fifty yards of our works. We all shuddered for his safety, and as with one voice we cried 'General Lee to the rear.' Unmindful of our clamors and fears and his imminent danger, he held an animated consultation with Generals Wilcox and McComb, near where the Seventh Tennessee Regiment was stationed, and although I was within fifty yards of him I could not understand what was said. General Lee ... pointed in different directions and then with his right hand and arm made a sweeping motion as if to say, 'Move your men to the right and rear and attack the left flank of the enemy.' Though his gesticulation was quick it did not bespeak nervousness—it rather indicated the promptness ... he expected his command to be executed. At this time, the entire force of sharpshooters of Wilcox's Division, under Lieutenant Harris, together with a strong force of skirmishers, commanded by Lieutenant Byrd Wilmouth, were advanced into the pine woods and gave at least the appearance of a tolerable strong force. This advance of the sharpshooters and skirmishers was but a cover for the real attack—the movement that had been ordered by General Lee ... As General Lee returned toward our left orders were immediately given and two brigades of Wilcox's Division and one brigade of Heth's marched to the rear of our artillery, out of sight of the enemy. The removal of these troops weakened our lines in front of the enemy, but those who were left filled the vacancies as well as could be done. These three brigades moved considerably to the extreme right of our artillery, as a large field was in front of the artillery and extended for some distance to the right, to avoid being seen by the enemy and also to reach a road that led to the woods in front of our artillery ... by a rapid march they soon fell on the left flank of the enemy. The attack was sudden and unexpected and accomplished the result of all successful flank movements ... the enemy was surprised and many prisoners were captured and sent to the rear ... these three brigades met with stubborn resistance and hard fighting they pressed on until they threatened the Federal artillery, when the enemy, to save his artillery and to check this flank movement, withdrew troops from his center and was thereby compelled to desist from further attacks on our center or on the Bloody Angle."[26]

McComb commented, "The command was given ready, aim, fire and I never saw a more effective volley. The enemy's whole line seemed to drop and then the artillery opened on him and those that could left in a hurry and strange to say the enemy made three or four attempts to break our lines at this point during the day but they never came quite as near as they did on the first charge."[27]

Harris added, "The Tennessee Brigade … did not assault the enemy in front of the center Angle, yet they accomplished the same result by forcing the Federals to draw the center, the very troops that were assailing the center or Bloody Angle, and hence we who were on the extreme right claim, after repelling the assaults made on our own part of the line, to have settled by our flank movement the doubtful issue of the repeated attacks on the center … On the morning of the 13th … I saw to our right distant about five hundred yards and about the same distance immediately in front of our artillery, a Federal battery advance at full speed and there in an open field halt. The artillerymen at once took out their horses and sent them to the rear, as much as to say, 'We have come to stay.' This was within full view and within easy reach of our forty pieces. As quick as the horses were started back every man of that battery was seen digging … Presently our artillery opened and as soon as the smoke cleared off, I could see that digging with desperate energy was kept up by the survivors. Death and destruction, I thought, would be the portion of the battery and its brave defenders, for it appeared at times as if their very caissons were literally covered with bursting shells, yet strange to say a few gallant fellows survived the attack of the forty field pieces and amid showers of shot and shell succeeded in throwing up tolerable secure works. They came to stay and they did remain. This was the bravest act of the war."[28]

McComb recalled the Tennessee Brigade's final moments of action at Spotsylvania: "In the preliminary skirmishing we captured a few prisoners and they said they belonged to Genl. Hancock's Div. so this meant we had some fighting to do. But our boys were equal to the emergency and they went in with their usual dash and the 'Rebel yell' and very soon the enemy were in full retreat. The firing and explosion of shells had set the woods on fire and we had to pursue the enemy through fire and smoke and I lost my voice and couldn't give the command halt and for some time had to get Maj. Hick Johnston to command the Reg't. It was not long however for as soon as I got a drink of water and rested a little I was all right. But it was a hot fight for about ¾ … of an hour. This wound up our fighting for the Battle of Spotsylvania."[29]

The fighting at Spotsylvania had cost the Union army approximately seven thousand men. The Confederates had lost four thousand soldiers as prisoners to the Federals and had suffered another irreplaceable five thousand casualties. Union soldiers continued to exhibit Grant's intention to fight to the end on the following day, as Moore's comments related to the determination of the men of the Federal battery displayed.

CHAPTER EIGHTEEN

To Petersburg

The Army of the Potomac had total losses of 31 percent, or thirty-six thousand men, during the early weeks of May 1864. Morale was low, fighting efficiency had diminished, and 50 percent of the army's leadership had fallen into the list of casualties. Lee's Army of Northern Virginia, at the same time, contained less than forty thousand men following its losses at the Wilderness and Spotsylvania. Confederate leadership was also weakened, as eighteen of the forty-three officers at the brigade, division, or corps levels were new to their assignments. A.P. Hill's Third Corps had suffered heavy losses,[1] including the wounded Gen. Walker, replaced on a temporary basis with the assignment of William McComb of the Fourteenth Tennessee as the leader of the Tennessee Brigade.

Hill's corps remained with Anderson's corps at Spotsylvania as Grant and the Federal army continued their southward movement. On May 22, following Lee's orders, Hill's army reached the North Anna River at Butler's Bridge. The march from Spotsylvania was conducted under horrific heat, with the Tennessee Brigade members stopping to fill their canteens with the water from creeks and ponds. The wells they encountered along the way had been already drained by those soldiers marching ahead of them.[2]

William McComb explained the Tennessee Brigade's arrival at North Anna: "When we arrived at Vendor Station, five miles west of Junction we received orders to stop and rest and cook rations. So we marched about ½ mile south of Vendor Station to Little River where there was a small dam and the boys had a fine time bathing. But the next day while the boys were bathing and cooking, it was reported the enemy were crossing the North Anna River about 3 miles west of Vendor … and we had order to drive them back. So the 'long roll' was sounded and formed in line made a detail of men to finish cooking and guard camp and in a few minutes we were 'double quicking' up the RR. The boys were not in a very good humor. You might say they were fighting mad. So as soon as we located the 'blue coats' we formed lines of battle."[3]

Lee placed Hill's Third Corps on the left of a defensive ring with Anderson's First Corps to its right. The line the Confederates formed was an "inverted V" with Hill's Corps anchored on the Little River. Lee felt that the aggressive Grant would divide his army at the river, enabling the Confederates to crush part of the Army of the Potomac before reinforcements could arrive. Unlike the situation faced by the Confederates at Spotsylvania's Bloody Angle, Lee's vulnerable center and ends of the North Anna V were protected by cliffs, swamps, or rivers. The Tennessee Brigade stood to the rear of the three brigades of Kirkland, Walker, and Davis between the Little River and the Virginia Central Railroad.[4]

The Tennessee Brigade experienced only minor attacks in the following days; Grant doubted the wisdom of launching an offensive upon the strong Confederate position. Lee was unable to take advantage of Grant's timidity, as the Confederate commander was confined to his cot, suffering from intestinal inflammation. A.P. Hill had only recently returned from a leave of absence, Ewell was near physical exhaustion, and Anderson had gained his field command only a few weeks before following Longstreet's wounding during the Wilderness fighting. No Confederate leader was capable of taking advantage of the division of the Federal army; therefore, the order to attack was never given.[5]

Although lacking major military significance itself, North Anna had effects upon future events. Lee's inability to attack may have been perceived as unwillingness to fight or as a sign of low Confederate morale. These misconceptions would prove disastrous for Grant at Cold Harbor.[6]

Historian J. Michael Miller explained that Lee had now lost his greatest weapon, maneuverability, with Grant positioning his army within a day's march of Richmond. Lee would be regulated to placing his army between Grant and the Southern capital; the end was now in sight.[7]

Lee's army, now holding a defensive position as strong or stronger than at Fredericksburg, dug trenches at Cold Harbor under the protection of darkness. Fatigued Federal soldiers were to rest for an attack upon the Confederates on the morning of June 3, 1864. Many Union troops, hearing the Southerners digging their trenches, took time to write their names on pieces of paper, which they pinned to their clothes, in order that their dead bodies could be returned to their loved ones.

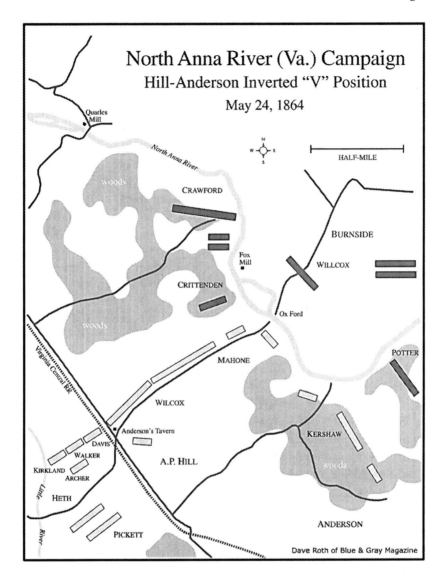

North Anna River (Va.) Campaign
Hill-Anderson Inverted "V" Position
May 24, 1864

Dave Roth of Blue & Gray Magazine

William McComb recorded the events the Tennessee Brigade encountered at Cold Harbor:

> We were put in position on General R.E. Lee's extreme left with instructions to keep the enemy from turning Lee's left flank if possible. There was a rail fence near our front and the boys commenced making a breastwork of the rails and logs but before they had time to put any dirt on the rails the enemy's skirmishers commenced firing on our line ... General Heth and Col Pogue came along the line and

in front of our line there was an open space of probably 300 yards and Col. Pogue was directed to bring in a Battery and put in position in rear of the 14th Tenn. Reg't. The enemy seemed to be putting infantry in place to advance on our line. Col. Pogue brought in a battery as soon as he could but the enemy were advancing in line of battle and a few of the enemy's "Sharpshooters" had gotten to an old house off to our left they commenced firing on the battery as they came into position killing a lot of horses and men and the commanding officers were not able to get a single gun in position to fire. The 22nd Va. Battalion were not in line and I sent an order to the Captain in Command to drive the enemy's sharpshooters from the old house. But they were so slow in starting I directed Capt. Dale who had charge of the Sharpshooters of Archer's Brigade to go at once and drive them away or capture them and then to protect our left and in a very few minutes our boys had the old house and we were not annoyed from that direction again. But by this time the enemy's line of battle was getting uncomfortable near so I gave the order to not fire a shot from the line until the command was given. And when they got within 75 yards the order ready aim fire was given. The enemy's line seemed to drop and in a little while all that could went for the woods and to the rear. In all my fighting experience I never saw our men do better. They kept their nerve and never fired unless they had good aim on the belt of a blue coat. At one time it seemed as if the enemy would march over us and they would if it had not of been for the coolness and courage of our brave boys. Capt. Dale and his men done [sic] noble work in protecting our flank while the above fighting was going.

I will explain a little in regard to the 22nd Va. Battalion. Col. Taylor and Major J.S. Bowles were not with the command and the Capt. in charge was consulting the Com. officers what was best to do and before they got ready to move Capt. Dale and his men had done everything that could be done. The enemy seemed determined to drive us from our position and made several attempts during the day. But they never drove us from the temporary line of breastworks our boys made of rails. In fact they never could force their men over the line of dead blue coats our boys dropped on the first charge. We had some very heavy skirmishing to our left at different time during the day. But we repulsed the enemy at every point and our loss was not so heavy as might have been expected. The artillery company's loss was very heavy ... A few days after this we crossed James River on a pontoon bridge and marched to Petersburg.[8]

The effectiveness of the Confederate fire and casualty rate at Cold Harbor are covered well in other works. The ability of Lincoln, Grant, and Stanton to limit the amount of press the incident received is amazing. The part the Tennessee Brigade played in the Southern victory was not major, yet the wounds it inflicted upon the Northern attackers was indicative of the defensive nature employed during the battle.

F.S. Harris explained, "Fran. Bass, of Company I, Seventh Tennessee, and a sharpshooter for Archer's Brigade, made a remarkable shot. A Federal sharpshooter had wounded several of our men from an ambuscade. Bass, with a pair of field glasses, finally located him in a dense tree, protected by its body. Loading his Enfield carefully, he requested me to go with him to the left to uncover the Yankee. We finally, with the aid of glasses, located him about 500 yards off. At the crack of Bass' gun, he fell from a tree ... Bass ... made wonderful shots ... at the second battle of Cold Harbor."[9]

Harris recalled yet another incident involving sharpshooters from the Tennessee Brigade: "Lain and I were behind an impromptu breastwork at an exposed point. Only one of the enemy seems to have discovered us, but in a very few minutes his bullets were scraping the top of our pile of dirt. Lain held up his hat and Mr. Yank promptly put a bullet through it. His handkerchief on a stick caused a like result. The enemy evidently knew the strength of our breastworks, for he put a ball at least a foot below the top, passing just in front of Lain's nose, and filling his mouth and eyes with Virginia soil. That shot made Lain mad ... Telling me to lie low and amuse Mr. Yank with the handkerchief act, he crawled on his face out of range and disappeared. It was not long before Lain came up smiling. He had killed him over a quarter of a mile distant, and was determined to get his gun and haversack. We found him behind a pile of corded wood with a bullet through his head, while a bright new gun and well-filled haversack were lying beside him. Joining Fran Bass on our return, we had hardly reached our former position, when Lain's keen eye discovered a head just above the same pile of corded wood. Bass took the new Enfield and fired at that head. Soon Joe Hamilton, of Company H, Seventh Tennessee, came to us as 'mad as a wet hen.' Said it was his head we saw. He was looking at us, saw the flash of Bass' gun and dodged just in time, as the bullet cut a chip from the stick where his chin rested."[10]

The June 3, 1864 attack upon the Confederate stronghold had been devastating to Grant's army. The bulk of the attack had lasted less than thirty minutes, with two unsuccessful yet similarly bloody Union assaults upon the position of the Tennessee Brigade being launched later.[11] The two-mile front had caught the Federals in well-prepared killing fields and resulted in their being driven back, despite breaking the Confederate lines at some points. Grant's suicide charges had resulted in 7,000 Union casualties versus only

1,500 for the Confederates. The assault at Cold Harbor haunted Grant for years after the war.

Returning to action from his wounding and capture at Gettysburg in time to participate in the action at Cold Harbor, B.D. Fry observed Gen. Robert E. Lee in a tranquil moment, offering a unique perspective of the great Southern leader from the viewpoint of a man of the Tennessee Brigade. Fry wrote, "On the third day of June, 1864 ... my command, consisting of ten regiments of infantry ... formed during the action the extreme left of our line of battle. On the following day I was ordered to move toward the right; and while riding at the head of my column along a by-road, I observed a group of officers under a spreading oak which stood near the road ... I saw General Lee lying on the grass with his head resting on a saddle over which a cloth had been thrown. He was evidently sleeping soundly, and lay upon his back with one arm across his breast and the other extended by his side ... Turning to my staff, I remarked, 'There is General Lee asleep.' My men were moving at route step, and, as was usual on a march, were laughing, talking, singing, or whistling; but those at the head of the column at once passed the word back, 'Hush, boys, don't make a noise. There is Marse Robert asleep under that tree.' Instantly there was perfect silence, and the long line of bronzed, bearded, and battle-begrimed veterans passed quietly by, each one turning to look at the beloved commander, in whom all felt such unbounded confidence. During the whole war I saw no more striking manifestation of the affection felt by the Confederate soldiers for their great leader. Soon after this I was ordered to another part of the country and never saw him again."[12]

Before Fry's transfer, he was given temporary command of Walker and Archer's brigades on June 9, 1864. Commander of the First Tennessee at that time was Maj. Felix Buchanan; while Col. Sam Sheperd and Col. William McComb led the Seventh and Fourteenth Tennessee regiments respectively.[13]

A series of Federal attacks upon Confederate positions at Petersburg, Virginia had resulted in Southerners under the command of P.G.T. Beauregard creating a number of deep defensive lines, securing Petersburg as a Confederate-held town. Beauregard had fourteen thousand men under his command, too little to resist a serious assault, yet it would be mid-June before Lee recognized the fact that Petersburg was being attacked by the main force of Grant's army.[14]

On June 18, poor communication between Union generals Burnside, Meade, and Warren resulted in Federal troops digging in for a siege of the town. That same day, the Tennessee Brigade reached Petersburg and assumed a position in the near-completed section of earthworks. The goal "to make as strong and complete as any earthworks ever constructed on the American continent" then began. The Tennesseans joined their comrades in weeks of fighting by day and constructing additional breastworks by night. The process would prove to be a lengthy one, as a member of the Tennessee Brigade recalled that as late as March 26, 1865 the earthworks were still being strengthened.[15]

The eruption of powder in a mine and the resulting thirty-foot deep crater are often discussed in historical circles, yet the Tennessee Brigade was not involved in this incident. At the time, the unit was north of the James River but marched some twenty miles the next morning to assist their fellow Confederates.[16]

A group of Tennesseans did gain a unique honor in the defense of Petersburg. James J. Crusman, Co. H, 14th TN, suffered a compound fracture of his thigh at West Point on April 7, 1862 and had resigned due to the resulting disability.[17] The former captain resurfaced at Petersburg in an incident recalled by William McComb:

> Grant came very near getting possession of the city before our arrival, but the old men and boys had organized and repulsed the enemy. And now they felt as if they were safe. Capt. J.J. Crusman of the 14th Tennessee Regiment ... had secured a position in Petersburg and was very active in organizing the old men and boys for the defense of Petersburg and they put up a good fight and repulsed the enemy. But Crussman was quite lame in his broken leg and in some way he was captured the night before we arrived in Petersburg. But the citizens said Capt. Crusman with his bravery and skill saved the day and held the enemy in check until the regular soldiers arrived.[18]

F.S. Harris added, "Soon after Grant's mine exploded near Petersburg in the summer of 1864, an officer in Archer's Tennessee Brigade observed a party of horsemen ascend an eminence far in rear of the Federal lines. He called Capt. Slade, Chief Engineer of A.P. Hill's Corps, who was passing at that moment, and asked him to calculate the distance. Capt. Slade estimated it to be 2,250 yards. Just as one of the men, apparently a general, rode away from the group and stopped on the highest point, the lieutenant took a Whitworth rifle belonging to one of the sharpshooters in that Brigade, trained the gun on him with globe sight, deliberately aimed and fired. The officer fell from his horse, and his staff gathered around him quickly. Two more shots were fired in rapid succession, and three men were carried from that place."[19]

As his former command participated in the daily attacks and counterattacks in the Petersburg area, Gen. James J. Archer remained a prisoner of war. On June 21, 1864, Archer was removed from Johnson's Island and brought to Ft.

Delaware under heavy guard. Archer's guards were instructed not to allow the general to have any communication with any individuals during the move. Archer had heard rumors of the possible transfer for months yet held out little hope of an exchange. Archer continued to assure family members of his recovered health and as late as May 20, 1864 explained that he had a personal physician in one Col. Maxwell of Florida and that field and company officers took special pains to preserve the health of the general and other Confederates.[20]

Arriving at Ft. Delaware on June 24, 1864, Archer wrote his sister that he felt an exchange might be near. His hope for a trip into Southern territory was high, and he urged his family not to fear for his safety. Any situation, he explained, would be "an agreeable change from the monotony of my long confinement." On June 26, Archer would leave Ft. Delaware.[21]

While Gen. Archer made plans to rejoin his brigade, members of his former command began fleeing its ranks around Petersburg. A deserter from Archer's Tennessee Brigade reported to Federal brigadier general R.S. Foster that the corps of Hill and Longstreet were ordered to prepare to move that day at a moment's notice. The units were currently at Deep Bottom, and rumors abounded as to their destination upon leaving there.[22]

Two days earlier, on July 17, the Tennessee Brigade had moved to Chaffin's Bluff. From here Lee felt the brigade and Heth's division could quickly reach the defenses at either Richmond or Petersburg. On the eighteenth, the Tennessee Brigade had passed through Petersburg and moved to the right flank of the Confederate line.[23]

Union colonel George H. Sharpe reported another Archer's Brigade deserter, an Irishman, on August 5, 1864. The individual belonged to the Second Maryland Battalion, a unit that had recently been added to the consolidated brigades of Archer and Walker. The deserter explained that the brigade was now commanded by Col. Mayo of the Forty-Seventh Virginia. The Confederate fears of additional mine explosions such as the one that created the crater were commonplace. Heth's division, stated the Irishman, had gone under arms every night at two o'clock, remaining so until daybreak.[24]

The uniqueness of this deserter is that only one man is recorded to have ever deserted from the ranks of the Second Maryland. Because of the reputation of its members, the regiment would eventually be placed on picket duty, in part to prevent desertion from occurring. The regiment had originally been formed in September 1862 with six companies, comprised largely of men who were left from the remnants of the First Maryland. Officially known as the First Maryland Battalion of Infantry, the unit saw action at Kernstown and Winchester and participated in the heat of battle at Culp's Hill at Gettysburg. After mounting a bayonet charge at Cold Harbor, an event by which Gen. Lee hailed the regiment as saving Richmond, the unit was attached to the Tennessee Brigade. [25]

The Second Maryland would briefly serve under the command of fellow Marylander Brig. Gen. James J. Archer. The general had been assigned to duty with the Army of Northern Virginia via special order 196, dated August 19, 1864. Later that same day, Special Order 197 gave Archer command of the consolidated brigades of his former command and that of Walker, both in Heth's division, Third Corps.[26]

Archer subsequently requested that the Tennessee regiments formerly in Bushrod Johnson's Brigade be transferred to his command. Following a series of correspondence from August 27 through September 23, the request was ultimately denied. Archer, Hill, and Heth favored the move, yet the commanders of the groups involved—the Seventeenth, Twenty-third, Twenty-fifth, Forty-forth, and Sixty-third Tennessee regiments—expressed their and their subordinates opposition to the move.[27] The opposition won out and the request was, at least for the meantime, denied.

Archer's return and the possibility of being joined by men from their home state failed to keep individuals from deserting. Each man who left the ranks of the Tennessee Brigade for the Union army's camps reported consistently decreasing Confederate numbers; one from the Seventh Tennessee informed a Union officer, Lt. Fred L. Manning, that only fifty to sixty men remained in his regiment in the fall of 1864. The deserter claimed that the information had come directly from his own sergeant major.[28]

On the day that Special Order 197 gave Archer command of the consolidated brigades, fighting erupted in the area of Globe Tavern on the southern portion of the Weldon Railroad. Heth's strong defensive line, containing the Tennessee Brigade, crossed the Halifax Road. Heth's brigades worked with the men under Mahone, with Heth striking the Federal center and Mahone driving the Federals from their trenches on the right. During this action, Capt. J.P. Crane, who had assumed command of the Second Maryland at Gettysburg, was killed, giving command to Capt. Duvall of Co. C.[29]

August 20 was filled with both sides attempting to gain the advantage over their opponent. The following day, a Confederate attack failed at every point, resulting in a completely different outcome than two days before. Though the Federal casualties of 4,300 were almost twice the Confederate total of 2,300, Gen. Lee now retained only one supply line for his men. The price of defending Petersburg, though continually growing more expensive, was essential, as the town's fortune was tied to that of Richmond. The latter, as the Confederate capital, must not fall into Union hands.

An August 25 struggle at Reams' Station, a result of what R.T. Mockbee described as "some right hard fighting to get our lines straightened" enabled the Confederates to gain and use a part of the railroad not under Federal control. Heth's and Wilcox's men, aided by Hampton's cavalry[30], soundly defeated Hancock. Confederate losses were only 720, with some 2,700 Federals becoming names and numbers on the casualty lists.

Heth's division, headquartered at the Pickrell House and miles from the troops of the Tennessee Brigade, would spend most of the nine and a half months of the Petersburg siege on the extreme right flank of Hill's Corps. Grant's attempts to encircle the Confederate right caused the division to move from position to position. The Federal gains created a constant trench-warfare method that relied heavily on military intelligence. In mid-September such techniques enabled a detachment of Lee's command to capture 300 prisoners and almost 2,500 cattle, creating taunts directed toward the Union soldiers[31] located in nearby trenches.

Gen. Archer's return to his brigade improved the discipline and attitude among the remaining members of his command. An inspection of the brigade on August 13 found the guns and other military supplies of the Seventh and Fourteenth Tennessee regiments in fair condition. The rusty guns of the Thirteenth Alabama, under Col. Aiken, were reported to be in discreditable order, with the members of companies A and G being greatly neglected in general appearance by their leader, Lt. G.W. Callaway. Gen. A.P. Hill's inspector, Maj. R.J. Wingate, noted the idolization of Archer among the members of his brigade, whom he stated had been unsatisfied since the brigade's consolidation. Archer's ability to harmonize his troops would, as Wingate proposed, be credited with the marked improvement in the brigade's condition by September 23.[32]

Despite Archer's ability to lead his troops and the obvious affection the vast majority of his men held for him, desertions continued within the Tennessee Brigade. Two deserters from the Fourteenth Tennessee reached the Union lines on September 25, detailing the positions of brigades along the Confederate lines. Two days later a deserter from another brigade in Heth's division thoroughly discussed the movement of regiments with the Confederate trenches.[33]

Archer's letters following his release from prison had disclosed the ease with which he had decided between an offer from Gen. Hood to again place him on Hood's staff or the opportunity to return to leadership of the Tennessee Brigade. Once the latter offer was extended, Archer quickly accepted.[34] The impact of his term in prison, added to his poor and almost continuously declining health, present even before his capture, had begun though to take a toll on the brigadier from Maryland. The time he had spent in the deplorable conditions of the Petersburg trenches undoubtedly caused a further decline in Archer's health.

On October 16, 1864, Gen. Archer wrote to Col. W.H. Taylor, requesting a forty-eight-hour leave to Richmond. Archer detailed that for the past two days he had been unable to perform any duty that required even a small amount of physical exertion and that he had business to which he must soon attend. Correspondence from Gen. Heth approved Archer's request, and the general made his way toward Richmond.[35]

Mary Boykin Chesnut, the celebrated Southern diarist and a friend of Gen. Archer's, explained that she was amazed at the level of life taken from Archer during his stay in prison. With half of his life appearing to be gone, Archer's vacant stare and "strange pallid look," wrote Chesnut, had taken away the looks of the man who many referred to as "Sally"[36] because of his near-feminine beauty. Archer's health diminished almost immediately upon his arrival in Richmond, and on October 26, 1864, Gen. James J. Archer died. His body was interred in Richmond's Hollywood Cemetery, where it lies today.

Brig. Gen. James J. Archer's grave in Richmond, Virginia's Hollywood Cemetery. The inscription lists Archer's birthplace and date as well as those of his death. Courtesy of David Gilliam, Hollywood Cemetery.

CHAPTER NINETEEN

The Bitter End

Following Gen. Archer's departure from Petersburg and his subsequent death at Richmond, the Tennessee Brigade participated in action around Petersburg at Burgess Tavern and Dinwiddie Court House. These names would remain in the minds of the men of this brigade for the remainder of their lives. The seemingly profitless confrontations, the cold weather, and the poor conditions of Confederate supplies began making a serious effect upon the morale and health of many of the Petersburg defenders during the winter of 1864–65.

Robert T. Mockbee remembered that the one-sixth rations of "corn meal and rancid pork" created levels of suffering that could be understood only by the participants. Amid the inhumane conditions of the trenches, surrounded by the devastation of the United States' bloodiest war, humanity did exist at Petersburg. William McComb added, "One time we had been fighting in the evening and into the night ... the lines were not over 100 yards apart, one of the Yanks in our front called ... 'Johnnie ... Step and get supper' and the word was passed on both lines and a little while the Yanks and the Johnnies had fires in fair view of each other and if a man on either side had fired a gun he would have been mobbed by his own men. And the next day the lines were fixed permanent, without firing a shot. The soldiers on both sides would fight when the order was given, but during the fall and winter of 1864 and 1865 when there was nothing doing much, the soldiers didn't seem disposed to shoot every time they could see a gray or blue coat as they were in the early part of the war."[1]

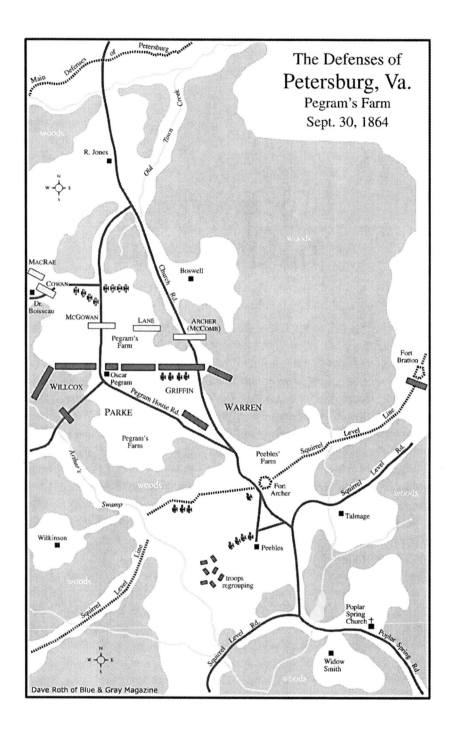

The Defenses of
Petersburg, Va.
Pegram's Farm
Sept. 30, 1864

Dave Roth of Blue & Gray Magazine

Gen. Heth was able to procure supplies such as brandy, hams, canned goods, and cigars for his headquarters. Located along the Boydton Plank Road, Heth's headquarters contained a great deal of goods acquired through a blockade runner named Ficklin.[2] This fact, if known among the soldiers, certainly did little to improve morale or the general fighting spirit.

With the loss of Gen. Archer to death's call, leadership of the Tennessee Brigade was given to William McComb of the Fourteenth Tennessee. McComb, a Pennsylvania native and a millwright by profession, was among the first men to join the Fourteenth Tennessee in 1861. Entering as a first lieutenant in Company L, McComb ascended the ranks in what his comrade June Kimble noted "was rapid and unusual by reason of fatalities among field officers." Years after the war, McComb's January 20, 1865 promotion to brigadier general was viewed as a loss to his regiment rather than high recognition of a true Confederate son. McComb was known for his coolheadedness, bravery, gallantry, and overall leadership skills for being "a leader among his men and a fighter among his enemies."[3]

McComb's size, strength, and fortitude were legendary in the brigade. The newly appointed brigadier, born twenty-eight years before the start of the war, had been wounded at Sharpsburg and Chancellorsville.[4] The latter wound resulted in a furlough that caused his absence at Gettysburg, an event that may well have saved his life, given his proneness to be in the heat of the battle.

In addition to McComb's promotion, the bitter winter of 1864–65 was filled with other changes in assignments within the Tennessee Brigade. Tennessee itself was by then under Federal control, limiting the effectiveness of further recruiting visits of the brigade members. Gen. Robert E. Lee issued another order that gave McComb command of a consolidated group of Tennesseans, the same units Gen. Archer had earlier sought to bring under his command. As well as the First, Seventh, and Fourteenth Tennessee regiments, McComb assumed leadership of the Seventeenth, Twenty-third, Twenty-fifth, Forty-fourth, and Sixty-third Tennessee infantry regiments. The Second Maryland also remained in the Tennessee Brigade, but the Thirteenth Alabama, a long-time affiliate of the organization, was transferred to Gen. W.H. Forney's command on January 9, 1865.[5] McComb now served as the commander of all Tennessee troops in the defense of Petersburg and Richmond. The shuffling of regiments throughout the Confederate army was a vain attempt to maintain the strength of brigades and postpone the inevitable.

Left to right: Capt. John Allen, adjutant general on McComb's staff. He died in 1913. Gen. William McComb, the last brigadier of the Tennessee Brigade, is seated in the middle. Capt. F.S. Harris, leader of the sharpshooters in the Tennessee Brigade, died in 1905. Photo courtesy of Confederate Veteran.

R.T. Mockbee, like many other men of the Tennessee Brigade and the entire Confederate army, endured personal hardships in the winter of 1864–65, spending an entire month in the hospital, suffering from chronic diarrhea. Other brigade members frequently became unable to perform their physical duties that had earlier been simple to complete.[6]

Rufus P. McClain, 7ᵗʰ TN. Brigadier Quartermaster for a brief period, McClain became ill at Petersburg. After the war McClain practiced law and served in the Tennessee State Legislature from 1876 to 1883. Courtesy of Paul Gibson.

As well as prevailing during the time spent in the Petersburg trenches, the Tennessee Brigade suffered heavy losses in the early February action at Hatcher's Run. Gen. Lee had informed Heth to be prepared for an attack. The latter prepared his earthwork defenses and received orders to hit the Union army's Second Corps with the brigades of MacRae, Cooke, and McComb.[7]

Moving from a position northeast of the Rocky Branch, the Tennessee Brigade joined Heth's division in attacking Humphrey's Second Corps. Newlywed Brig. Gen. John Pegram, leading the assault from the west, was killed by a shot to his heart. His funeral was held in the same Richmond church where he had been married just three short weeks earlier. The total losses of Lee's army were near 1,000, with the casualties of the Federal forces reported to be some 1,500 men.[8]

David Dickerson Hamilton, Co. H, 7ᵗʰ TN. Wounded at Seven Pines and Petersburg, Hamilton used crutches for several years after the war ended. His family had mourned his death during the war, yet he returned to serve as a teacher and a father of six children. He died in 1922 at the age of seventy-nine. Courtesy of Confederate Veteran.

The Tennessee Brigade was taken from this position on the trench line to support Gen. Gordon in his assault upon Ft. Stedman. Gordon's attack, though initially successful, was repulsed by a massive Federal counterattack.[9] The Confederate losses here were almost three times the 1,100 of the Union army.

The Tennessee Brigade had undergone a host of personnel changes and had been commanded by a number of individuals. Months in the Petersburg trenches had made the brigade members highly susceptible to disease, while the shelling and skirmishes in the area likewise riddled the ranks and lowered the morale of the suffering Southern troops.

Aaron Alexander, Co. C, Turney's 1st TN. Alexander was wounded twice in the war and received a wound to his left leg near Petersburg on August 18, 1864. The sergeant succumbed to his wound on September 12. Courtesy of Paul Gibson.

The months between June 16, 1864 and April 1, 1865 saw the Tennessee Brigade, in some capacity, participate in a host of events classified as either "actions" or "battles" according to military qualifications. At Globe Tavern, August 18-21, 1864, Heth's division had driven back a Federal division under Ayre. The following day, Union reinforcements had arrived, allowing the Union army to retake most of the lost ground. On the twenty-first, the Confederates were unable to locate a weak point in the Union lines, forcing them to resort to unloading train cars at Stony Creek Station and hauling supplies thirty miles along Boydton Plank Road for use in Petersburg. Though the fight was considered to be a Union victory, Confederate losses of 1,600 were far less than the 4,300 Union casualties. At Ream's Station, Heth's division, on August 25, had successfully attacked and overrun the Federal position, capturing a large number of prisoners, twelve flags, and nine cannon. Maj. Gen. Winfield Scott Hancock's troops had largely lost their fighting effectiveness, as the Union Second Corps was wrecked. The Confederate victory initiated by Heth was one of the few bright spots of the campaign. On April 1, 1865, Gen. McComb and his Tennessee Brigade troops were located in the Confederate line to the right of Percell's battery, with its right flank along the Pole Bridge. Gen. McComb recorded the events of the day: "I had to stretch my command to take the place of Davis in the line and join Wilcox ... on my left. I had about as many men on the skirmish line as I had in the main line." In fact, historian Will Greene noted that the average deployment of A.P. Hill's front troops was 1,300 soldiers per mile, or less than one per yard.[10]

McComb declared, "The firing commenced and continued so long I sent Emmit McCullock to see what was the matter and the firing increased and got so heavy Capt John Allen, my Adj. Gen., said he would go ... I had my horse saddled and Polk Johnson and one courier and myself started to see for ourselves, and just before day is the darkest time in the night and we could hardly see a stump. But I went pretty rapid to the left of my line, or where it had been the evening before, and ... the first thing I knew I was in the midst of blue coats. I ... got my horse headed back to our lines I inquired what command they belonged to and what regiment and some one told me and it was so dark they couldn't tell whether I had on blue or gray. So, I gave the command to follow me and let my horse have the spur and didn't wait for them. I then sent an order to F. S. Harris of 7th Regiment who had command of the skirmish line to come back at once. I then formed as much of the brigade as we could. Polk Johnson was with me and as brave a boy as ever lived. McCulloch and Allen had been taken prisoners. Very soon Harris came in with the boys from the skirmish line and they formed in line with us and in the gray of dawn we charged the enemy. And I never saw our boys make a more gallant charge. We drove the enemy over the branch ... We captured a battery in our line ... and some of the 2nd Maryland had some training in that line and they turned the guns on the enemy ... the enemy were pushing out the road in our rear ... and they would cut us off. We had more prisoners than we had men in our command ... we would have to give them a verbal parole ... as soon as Col. Johnston could get his men together we moved back and the enemy seemed to be glad to get clear of us as they didn't fuss much until we crossed Hatcher's Run. General Cook stayed with us and complimented our boys very highly for the fight we put up to retake the whole line. But it was impossible as Gen. Grant had massed ... men at that point. But after we got in the fight they didn't capture a prisoner ... marched to Amelia Court House where expected to draw rations but through some mistake we didn't find any rations and we had to make a detail and send out in the country along our march to secure something for the boys to eat. They found some corn meal at a mill. The boys were not prepared for making corn bread but we had to do the best we could with the meal. We could manage parched corn better. But we made out on short rations."[11]

R.T. Mockbee recalled that during the final action of April 2, 1865 at Petersburg "some of the bravest and best were sacrificed in the endeavor to accomplish the impossible." As men of the Tennessee Brigade made their way as best they could toward Amelia Court House, many fell captive to the Union army.[12]

A.P. Hill, riding with a courier into a group of Federal infantrymen and demanding their surrender, was shot from his horse. Corporal Mauk, credited with firing the fatal shot at Hill, sent a round in the general's direction, cutting off his thumb, going through his heart, and exiting through his body. Most estimates have the general dying before he hit the ground.[13]

Mauk left the scene, preceded by Sgt. Tucker, Hill's accomplice. Tucker managed to escape to safety, where he met with Gen. Longstreet's staff. He then delivered the message of Hill's death to Gen. Lee, who received the news with tearful eyes.[14] With Hill died another of Lee's last hopes for a successful end to the war for the Confederacy.

Mauk's departure eventually led to an encounter with a group of approximately a half-dozen armed Federal soldiers escorting a like number of unarmed Confederate prisoners. Mauk informed the men, when asked, that a Confederate officer had been killed in the area, and he directed the party in the general direction of the incident. It is an unproven story that the detail may have in fact been a group of Fifth Alabama Battalion soldiers from Hill's headquarters attempting to locate Hill's body. Within the hour of Hill's death, the body was carried to safety. Following a series of burials, Hill's body now rests under his statue at the intersection of Hermitage Road and Laburnum Road in Richmond.[15]

Gen. A.P. Hill was commander of the Third Corps of which the Tennessee Brigade was a member. Hill was killed at Petersburg in the war's latter stages. Photo courtesy of Blue and Gray.

Robert T. Mockbee added further details to the collapse of his brigade and the Confederate lines at Petersburg in an expose written some thirty years after the events. He wrote, "On the fateful morning of April 2, 1865, when the last charge of Lee's army was made in an effort to retake the works, which had been captured and were occupied by the Federals, I was present and participated with probably five or six hundred others left of the old brigade. If there were any who hesitated, I don't remember it. I am willing to accord to Capt. Harris all praise for true bravery, but I know he will say Capt. Norris, of his own regiment, Seventh Tennessee, Capt. H.H. Averitt and Harry Bullock, of the 14th TN, the latter giving up his life in that charge, after going through the whole war unhurt, and scores of other were as brave men as ever lived. Capt. Harris knew those men would fight and go wherever he or Gen. McComb dare lead ... J. Hick Johnson, major commanding the old Fourteenth, who always went into battle smiling, and his noble brother, Polk G. Johnson, acting as aid to Gen. McComb on that day, were there. The latter was one of the most conspicuous figures in that charge ... Soon came the order to close in to left along the breastworks, where we had been deployed ten paces apart all night, that being the strength of Lee's line, at that point, at least. From there we were ordered to move down the line at right angles to the works. Soon the enemy were encountered in force, and the charge was ordered. The Second Maryland Battalion did terrible execution, and the enemy fled back to their main supports, where they had first broken our lines. We followed until reaching Davis' Mississippi Brigade's winter quarters, where we were compelled to halt, on account of the overwhelming numbers that met us. It was there that we lost most of our men, and finally we were forced back toward Hatcher's Run, but contesting every inch of ground against a force double our number in front and overlapping both flanks, until at last the order was given for every man to 'save himself.' The writer and several others made their way to the south side of the railroad, and at a commissary depot found parties in charge of the stores distributing provisions to those who wished them. A large country ham attracted my attention, and soon found a resting-place on my bayonet. We made our way to the Appomattox River, at a point where there was a flouring-mill, and there found Gen. Heth, accompanied by Billy Green, a courier, trying to get across the swollen stream with a message from Gen. Lee to Gen. Gordon, in Petersburg. Green, who was a member of Company A, Fourteenth Tennessee, on detail as courier for Gen. Heth, noticed the old country ham on my bayonet, and, after a hurried consultation with the General, came back to the door, and said, 'Bob, Gen. Heth hasn't had a bite of meat in two days. Won't you give him a piece of that ham?' I gave Gen. Heth half of the ham, and, going by his directions, met the army at Amelia Court House."[16]

J.C. Bingham commented upon the futile attempt of the Tennessee Brigade to regain its lost position on that fateful day. He wrote, "Gen.

McComb ... saw Ferg S. Harris at the head of a detachment of men ... When Harris came up he immediately rushed through our ranks to the front, jerked off his hat, waved it in the air, and struck a brisk trot toward the enemy, hurrahing at the top of this voice. I have often declared, when talking over the events of that ... day ... that the attack and recapture of that redoubt was the last successful advance ever made by any portion of Lee's army, and it was led by Lt. F.S. Harris, of the Seventh Tennessee ... the hottest contested charge ... Tennesseans ever made, not even excepting Gettysburg."[17]

Gen. Heth also praised the bravery of Harris and his men in this last-ditch effort to achieve victory. He explained in a letter to Harris, "Your gallant and well-disciplined sharpshooters, plowing their way in advance of the grand old Tennessee Brigade during the long campaign from the Wilderness to Appomattox, was to me a familiar sight in every battle. I remember well the desperate charge made by McComb's Brigade on that fatal Sunday morning ... when you threw your little battalion of sharpshooters against a division of advancing Federals, and nothing but the most desperate fighting saved you from annihilation."[18]

Remnants of Lee's army reached Amelia Court House on April 4, 1865. Lee's intention in gathering here was to feed his starving army before moving to join other Confederate forces. In a drizzling rain, the Confederates discovered that Lee's message, sent to Richmond before he left Petersburg, had been misunderstood. Rather than food, the commissary department had forwarded ammunition to Lee. The general temporarily halted the retreat to allow his supply wagons to seek food in the area.[19]

Robert T. Mockbee, 14th TN, traveled with twelve to fifteen others through swamps, fields, and byways up and along the Appomattox River. The river was at or near flood stage for most of the journey as Mockbee's group sought some means by which they could place a barrier between themselves and the pursuing Federals. On their side was the fact that the Union troops were being delayed in their action of scouring the country and gathering fugitive Confederates making their way toward Amelia Court House for the ordered assembly.[20]

Mockbee and his comrades spent the night of April 2 on a hill overlooking the river, resuming their march at daybreak. Mockbee added, "As we hurriedly came in sight of the river we perceived the ends of the bridge on each side of it, the flood having carried away all the center. We were greatly disappointed over this, but found about a hundred fellow fugitives gathered just above the bridge, awaiting their turn to be put across in a small bateau, or skiff, with a carrying capacity of about six men at each trip." Mockbee's opportunity came, but not aboard the craft. A young cavalryman offered any taker to lead his horse across the river. Jumping at the chance, Mockbee shed his jacket, empty haversack, blanket, gun, and cartridge box, and rode into the edge of the water upon the horse. Submerging once, the rider and horse "...came up all right and the noble animal made for the other shore, swimming 'like a duck.'" After the Virginia cavalryman crossed the river, he took control of his horse and left for Amelia Court House.[21]

Lee's army crossed the Appomattox River using the bridges at Farmville on the night of April 6. In an attempt to slow the Federal pursuit, the Confederates set fire to the bridges after crossing them. Humphrey's corps of Union troops got to one of the bridges before irreparable damage was caused, saving it and enabling the continuation of the Federal pursuit. Men and animals of the Confederate army were weak from lack of food, the men having started the retreat with one day's rations. The poorly supplied country through which the men moved provided little relief to the troops. Being hungry, sleepy, constantly harassed, and forced to fight while possessing little strength created a march filled with horrors that were pronounced to be among the most terrible on record.[22]

With Lee absent, his general officers held council on the night of April 6. They felt surrender was the best option, with half of their men now too weak to carry their guns and insufficient draught animals for their cannon, which was certain to result in the loss of artillery in an attempt to flee. Gen. Lee, when approached with the idea, disagreed, stating that surrender was not an option as long as a man of the Confederacy remained.[23]

Lee's hopes were lifted on April 7, when his army turned away a Federal cavalry attempt to capture his supply train. Grant sent Lee a note dated that morning, stating his feeling that additional bloodshed could be avoided and that Lee's Army of Northern Virginia was in a hopeless situation and should surrender. Gen. Lee replied with a note asking under what terms the surrender would be granted and stating that he as well desired to cease the useless loss of blood. After dispatching his reply, Gen. Lee continued his retreat under the cover of darkness.[24]

A series of notes on the following day, April 8, revealed Grant's desire and Lee's reluctance to reach an agreement in relation to a possible surrender. Lee's retreat continued toward Appomattox Court House, Virginia. As Lee's spearhead neared the settlement of Appomattox, Union general George Armstrong Custer, with the support of Sheridan, captured twenty-five Confederate cannon and a large number of prisoners and wagons. Lee's last avenue of escape was now closed, and Federal forces closed in from the front and rear.[25]

The Confederates made a last-ditch attempt to break through the Union lines on April 9. If Lee could break the line Sheridan held, escape was a very real possibility and the Southern army's lifespan could be again prolonged.

Initially the Confederate assault caused Sheridan's troops to fall back. The retreating Union cavalry revealed a well-armed line of infantry with bayonets gleaming. Sheridan's horsemen remounted and moved forward as white flags began appearing throughout the Confederate ranks.[26] The fighting, it now appeared, had ended.

William McComb, the last brigadier general of the Tennessee Brigade, recalled the events of those early April days in 1865. He wrote, "The last two nights of the march we didn't pretend to go in regular bivouac we just knaped [sic] a little as we could and on the morning of the 9th we were in sight of the McLean House. We were in full view of the Federal troops at that point. But we didn't know General R.E. Lee at that time was negotiating the surrender of our grand old A. of N.V. and we were making as good a show as we could to the last. But it was all right and under the circumstances our grand old commander Gen. Robert Edward Lee done the right thing."[27]

A one-and-a-half-hour meeting between generals Lee and Grant began at one thirty in the afternoon at the Wilmer McLean House at Appomattox. The Confederate's ability to keep their horses and receive rations was granted; the generals shook hands and Lee departed. The war was now over for the soldiers of Lee's Army of Northern Virginia. Lee's return to his army, defeated yet still proud, was met with tearful soldiers. The relationships established over four years, the comradeship felt for one another, and the admiration a vast majority of the men held for their leaders, their nation, and their now "lost cause," could not be erased with the surrender of their army. The mutual respect the Confederate and Union soldiers held for one another exemplified the forgiveness many across the country failed to exhibit in the years after the war.

The number of men from the Tennessee Brigade surrendering at Appomattox reveals the truly destructive impact the Civil War had upon one of the vast number of units assembled during the struggle. The five most recent additions to the brigade had experienced consolidation with the mainstays of the brigade. The number of those surrendering from each of these was: Seventeenth Tennessee, sixty-eight; Twenty-third Tennessee, fifty-six; Twenty-fifth Tennessee, twenty-five; Forty-fourth Tennessee, fifty-eight; and the Sixty-third Tennessee, seventy-five.[28]

Turney's First Tennessee Provisional Infantry, organized prior to the secession of Tennessee from the United States, surrendered only thirty-eight men, of whom eight officers were present. While the figures fail to accurately match, the list of the paroles at Appomattox for the First Tennessee included: staff, one major, one surgeon, one ordnance sergeant, and one hospital steward. Company A: one captain, one sergeant, and three privates. Company B: one sergeant and one private. Company C: one first lieutenant, one sergeant, two corporals, and one private. Company D: one first lieutenant. Company E:

one corporal and one private. Company F: three privates. Company G: one captain, two sergeants, one corporal, and two privates. Company H: one corporal and one private. Company I: one second lieutenant. And Company K: two sergeants, one corporal, and two privates.[29]

Capt. W.N. Tate, Co. H, 7ᵗʰ TN. Tate fought in approximately thirty-five battles or skirmishes. He served as his company's captain from September 1862 until the war's end without a single day's absence. The latter is quite an accomplishment considering he was left for dead on the field at Gettysburg. Courtesy of Confederate Veteran.

Felix G. Buchanan, 1st TN. Buchanan was noted for his gallantry at Seven Pines, Mechanicsville, and Gaines Mill. He led a detachment of his company at Gettysburg in the moments of Gen. Reynolds's death. Gen. Lee once proclaimed that Buchanan had the distinction of staying with his command more than any regimental officer in the Army of Northern Virginia. After the war, Buchanan returned home and fathered five children. He and his wife were prominent citizens of Lincoln County, TN. Courtesy of Confederate Veteran.

The Seventh Tennessee Infantry Regiment had forty-eight men to surrender at Appomattox, with six of them being officers. Again failing to tally, the breakdown included staff personnel of one lieutenant colonel, one surgeon, one chaplain, one sergeant major, one ordnance sergeant, and two sutlers. Companies A and I reported no one present. Company B: one captain, one first lieutenant, two sergeants, one corporal, and four privates. Company C: three privates. Company D: one sergeant and four privates. Company E: one captain, one sergeant, and four privates. Company F: three sergeants, one corporal, and four privates. Company G: two sergeants. Company H: two sergeants and five privates. Company K: two privates.[30]

Among those surrendering from the Seventh Tennessee was John Close of Company A. Historian Thomas G. Webb wrote that nearly four years earlier John Close had written his friend Wingate Robinson that the men of Company A had lots of fun and some hard times and that he expected to be home in time for a big frolic at Christmas. Now he stood among the ragged, sad-faced, exhausted men with whom he had endured so much and waited his turn to stack his rifle.[31]

The Fourteenth Tennessee Infantry had six officers among a total of forty-one individuals who relinquished their Confederate rights at the village. These included from company A two sergeants and one private. Company B: one sergeant and two privates. Company C: one captain, four sergeants, and two privates. Company D and E: one private each. Company G: one first lieutenant and three privates. Company H: one first lieutenant, two sergeants, two corporals, and one private. Company I: one second lieutenant, one corporal, and one private. Company K: four privates. And Company L: three privates. The staff paroled included one major, one surgeon, one sergeant major, one quartermaster sergeant, and one ordnance sergeant. A total of fifty-nine members of the Second Maryland Battalion were mustered for roll call at Appomattox, with Company A hailing the largest number of troops present with eleven. Company H had only one man present at the surrender.[32]

The unit of the Tennessee Brigade with the largest number of men surrendered at Appomattox was ironically the Fifth Alabama with 128 men. Due to its low numbers following the battle of Gettysburg, the Fifth Alabama had been placed on provost duty. Missing from the ranks of the Fifth Alabama at the brigade's surrender was Jesse H. Hutchins of Company H. Hutchins had enlisted in April of 1861 and served with the Fifth Alabama the entire war. Ironically he was killed during the action of April 8, the last of the war for the battalion.

R.E. McCulloch recalled that at Appomattox his regiment, the Fourteenth Tennessee, "its last battle having been fought, and its duty nobly done ... laid down their arms." Robert T. Mockbee stated the events of Appomattox brought to mind his comrades of the Tennessee Brigade, who "with no stain of dishonor ... furled their battle flags ... turned ... toward their desolated homes to commence life anew."[34]

Roland Swain, Co. H, 7ᵗʰ TN, served as a commissary clerk for the Tennessee Brigade. Swain surrendered at Appomattox. Courtesy of Paul Gibson.

The ability to begin life anew started for many of the Tennessee Brigade members when they walked from Virginia to their homes in Middle Tennessee. Thomas Herndon recorded in his diary that hikes of fifteen miles per day were common, often while the men were exposed to unfavorable weather.[35]

The Appomattox grave of J.H. Hutchins. Courtesy of Patrick Schroeder.

Jack Moore's return home was etched in the memory of a friend, Capt. A. O. P. Nicholson, who shared his friend's dilemma. Nicholson stated, "When the surrender came he was confined in one of the many hospitals of Virginia. It was customary on entering the hospital to take the patient's clothes, and give him instead a long shirt and a pair of woolen socks, until he was convalescent. Shirts were scarce in those days, and the material out of which to make them was scarcer; but the noble women, God bless them! had given up their gowns and chemises to supply this deficiency, and one of the latter had fallen to Jack. When it was learned that Gen. Lee had surrendered, he decided he would make an effort to get home; but when he was ready to give up his hospital toggery, none of his old clothes could be found. Even

309

his hat and shoes were missing, and his entire wardrobe consisted of this low-neck, sleeveless garment and a pair of woolen socks. It was rather an airy costume, even for one of Lee's veterans to start with on a four-hundred mile march, so Jack appealed to one of the lady patrons of the hospital, and when did a Confederate soldier ever appeal to one in vain? She replied that she would go home and see what she could do. She returned with a pair of blue cottonade pants and a wide-brimmed straw hat. The pants belonged to her little fourteen-year-old brother, and the hat was her Sunday one. She had plaited the straw and made it herself. After a hard struggle Jack managed to get inside the pants. They struck him just a little below the knees, leaving exposed a liberal supply of bare legs and feet. They 'fit like wall paper.' He landed some days later at the depot in Nashville; and, while he had added nothing to his traveling costume, he had managed to 'kill' some 'snakes' with the boys, as taking a drink in those days was termed, and was feeling 'rich and reckless' as he walked up town. He walked in the middle of the street, partly from habit and partly because the soft, wet mud felt better to his bare feet than the pavement. Upon reaching the Zollicoffer Barracks, the Maxwell House, a crowd of newsboys and bootblacks were close on his trail and constantly calling to others to 'come and see the wild man.' Jack headed straight for Sandy Carter's, indifferent to the very marked attention being shown him. Carter's was a well-known resort before the war, where … old time gentlemen met to discuss politics, etc., over mint juleps … Judge Joe Guild provided him with every need."[36]

William Frierson Fulton had served in Company A of the Fifth Alabama until paroled on April 12. That evening he and a dozen or his former fellow Tennessee Brigade members began their journey toward Livingston, Alabama. Fulton expressed a feeling of intimidation at being surrounded by "Yankees" and having no gun for protection, as he'd become accustomed to possessing in such situations. Meal and flour were obtained on his journey home and, except for one shoat, served as his diet on his three-week journey home. Fulton's appreciation for the beauty of his surroundings climaxed on May 4, 1865, when his journal entry exclaimed, "Sleeping now on Alabama soil." Soon afterward, Fulton reached his home, attempting to put the war behind him.[37]

While the vast majority of the men who filled the ranks of the Tennessee Brigade served and/or passed into post-war years filled with anonymity, the lives of a number of the veterans of this group of often overlooked Confederates lived well-documented lives. Peter Turney, one of the early leaders of the brigade in times of crisis and the organizer of the First Tennessee Infantry Regiment, survived his life-threatening wound sustained at Fredericksburg to eventually become governor of Tennessee.

*Col. William M. McCall, 7ᵗʰ TN, survived the war to practice law in
Milan and Humboldt, Tennessee. He passed away at the age of eighty.
Courtesy of Confederate Veteran.*

B.D. Fry of the Thirteenth Alabama went to Cuba at the conclusion of the
Civil War and engaged in the tobacco business for several years. He returned
to Alabama, where he served as a school system superintendent. Eventually
he worked and lived in Florida and Richmond, operating a cotton mill and
serving as an officer of Marshall Manufacturing Company. Upon his death
in Richmond on January 21, 1891, Fry was buried in Alabama.[38]

Fergus S. Harris served in Company H of the Seventh Tennessee during
the war, overseeing the sharpshooters of the Tennessee Brigade. After marrying
Lebanon, Tennessee resident Fannie Davis in 1868, Harris fathered two
children. Serving as a state official and as Oklahoma land commissioner,

Harris was an active member of the Christian church and a charter member of the Frank Cheatham Bivouac before passing away at St. Luke's Hospital in Jacksonville, Florida on January 24, 1905 at the age of sixty-four.[39]

Thomas Herndon served in the Fourteenth Tennessee Regiment prior to his capture at Gettysburg. After the war he became a successful Clarksville, Tennessee tobacco dealer and raised two daughters and a son. He married a second time, following his first wife's death. A faithful Methodist and a Mason, he was an active member of the community until his death in his new home of Gulfport, Mississippi in 1918. His obituary, full of accolades, stated, "He had great devotion for family and friends ... a wellstored mind ... He belonged to the age which bred men of positive views, decided character and sensitive responsibility, softened by a politeness and chivalry which marked his contemporaries with unique distinction in this country."[40]

Henry Heth, the division commander of the Tennessee Brigade, lived in Richmond after the war, working in the mining and insurance businesses. In the early 1880s, Heth performed civil engineering duties for the US government and served briefly as a special agent in the Office of Indian Affairs. He died in Washington, D.C. on September 27, 1899 at the age of seventy-three.[41]

John "Jack" J.H. Moore of the Seventh Tennessee passed away in Nashville on September 6, 1906. A practicing lawyer after the war, Moore had been praised for "on more than one occasion left a sick bed to join his regiment when he knew they were going in action, only to return to bed after the battle was fought." Due to his high character, Moore was known even after the war as "Colonel" and served the Confederacy well as a man in his early twenties. Moore had left the United States Naval Academy when the South went to war[42], eventually to write a brief history of his regiment for the preservation of the memory of its contributions.

June Kimble, whose prose compiles a great portion of this work, served in the Fourteenth Tennessee during the war, being promoted several times for his gallantry. Kimble moved with his mother and two brothers to Eastland County, Texas in 1879, serving as editor of the Eastland Chronicle. There he took a great interest in public affairs, primarily in the Democratic Party, for which he served four years as county clerk. Kimble died at the age of sixty-nine in Eastland Texas in April 1911.[43]

Brig. Gen. William McComb was one of the last of his rank to pass away, though during the last years of his life he was forced to walk with a cane because of his many serious wounds.[44] McComb moved to Virginia in 1869, where he engaged in farming until his death on July 21, 1918 at the age of eighty-seven.

Andrew Cherry, Co. G, 14ᵗʰ TN. Cherry is pictured in the uniform he wore when leaving for war in mid-1861. Cherry served until wounded at Hatcher's Run in early 1865. Courtesy of Jerry Ross.

M.T. Ledbetter carried the colors of his beloved Fifth Alabama Battalion into a number of battles and survived two serious wounds. At the time of his death in 1908 at the age of sixty-seven, Ledbetter had spent some twenty years unsuccessfully searching for the flag he had carried into battle. He remained full of faith as a member of the Baptist church and was an active Mason and one of the oldest members in the area around Piedmont, Alabama, where he lived his entire life. His years of collecting and preserving war history[45] are to be praised, as his writings and actions did much to preserve the memory of the Tennessee Brigade.

Dr. William Henry Moon served well as a physician in Company I, Thirteenth Alabama. Moon served as a senior counselor of the Alabama State Medical Association after the war as well as being a member of the College of Counselors for over thirty-five years. He was a deacon in the Goodwater Baptist church and served as the Sunday school superintendent for many years, raising eleven sons and daughters. Following his October 30, 1929 death at the age of eighty-five, his obituary noted, "As a boy … volunteered his all to the Confederacy and faced battle and imprisonment courageously as he met all of life's duties ... He sleeps now near his boyhood home at Lineville, Ala., clothed, by his request, in his beloved gray uniform. Among many floral tributes at his grave, the chaplet of a Southern hero, green tied with Confederate colors, held the place of honor at his head. Christian, patriot, physician, the record of his ... life and noble service is a precious heritage to those he loved."[46]

Archibald Debow Norris left the Seventh Tennessee at war's end and married Sarah Baird on Christmas Day 1866 and raised five children. Norris was a Mason and served as superintendent of public instruction for his home county of Wilson County, Tennessee from 1873 to 1874. He also served two terms as county surveyor and from 1887 to 1899 served in the Tennessee House and Senate. A member of the Methodist Episcopal Church, South, Norris also remained an active farmer, spending time in the banking and insurance businesses as well. Norris died in 1911 at the age of seventy-four.

These men and hundreds more were changed forever in their years spent as members of the Tennessee Brigade. North or South, regardless of feelings invoked by the causes, battles, and personalities of the Civil War, it is because of men such as these that the citizens of our nation, now reunited, cannot and must not forget the men who served their country. The men of the Tennessee Brigade, and the thousands of others who served and died in the American Civil War, must be forever remembered.

The Winchester, Tennessee grave of Peter Turney, organizer and commander of the First Tennessee Infantry Regiment and later a two-term governor of Tennessee. Photo by author.

This marker was placed in memory of the Confederate soldiers from Winchester, Tennessee. The Peter Turney chapter of the United Daughters of the Confederacy erected the marker in 1950. Photo by author.

Franklin County Tennessee's Confederate Memorial Cemetery in Winchester, Tennessee. The marker is inscribed with the words, "In memory of the brave men from the Franklin County area who defended their homeland against Northern Aggression." Photo by author.

This statue graces the town square in Lebanon, Tennessee and is dedicated to the memory of the Confederate veterans of Wilson County, Tennessee and all other true Southern soldiers. A likeness of Gen. Hatton stands on the top. Photo by author.

This monument is located in Cedar Grove Cemetery in Lebanon, Tennessee, the home of many members of the Seventh Tennessee Infantry Regiment. It is dedicated "to the memory of Confederate Soldiers who sleep in this cemetery" and lists the names of dozens of area Confederate veterans. Photo by author.

Confederate Memorial in Clarksville, Tennessee, home of the Fourteenth Tennessee Infantry Regiment. It contains these words: "In honor of the heroes who fell fighting for us in the Army of the Confederate States. Though adverse fortune denied final victory to their undaunted courage, history preserves their fame, made glorious forever." Photo by author.

The 5ᵗʰ Alabama Battalion memorial is located in the "Confederate Rest" section of the Old City Cemetery in Jacksonville, Alabama. The front side praises the men of the unit who gave their lives as members of the Tennessee Brigade. The opposite side, shown on the following page, lists the major battles in which the battalion served while a member of the brigade. Photos by Don Griffin.

ENDNOTES

Abbreviations

C.W.C.C. Civil War Centennial Commission. Nashville, Tennessee. All references are from part one of a two-part set.

O.R.   U.S. War Department. *The War of the Rebellion: A Compilation of the Official Records of the Union and Confederate Armies.* 128 vols. Washington, D.C., 1880-1901.

S.C.V.   Sons of Confederate Veterans.

CHAPTER 1. *War Seeds Are Planted*

1. Corlew, *Tennessee*, p. 287; Patten, *Chronicle*, p. 183.

2. Corlew, *Tennessee*, p. 288; Patten, *Chronicle*, p. 182.

3. Corlew, *Tennessee*, p. 288; Patten, *Chronicle*, p. 183.

4. Corlew, *Tennessee*, p. 289.

5. Ibid, pp. 289-90.

6. Horn, *Tennessee's War*, p. 15; Corlew, *Tennessee*, pp. 290-91.

7. Horn, *Tennessee's War*, p. 15; Corlew, *Tennessee*, p. 290.

8. Thorogood, *"Only County."*

9. Thorogood, *"Only County"*; Fite, *"Peter Turney"* p. 11; Foreman, *"Secession,"* p. 9.

10. Foreman, *"Secession,"* pp. 5-7.

11. Ibid, p. 8.

12. Thorogood, *"Only County."*

13. Ibid.

14. Corlew, *Tennessee*, pp. 291-92.

15. Horn, *Tennessee's War*, p. 16; Corlew, *Tennessee*, p. 292.

16. Thorogood, *"Only County"*; Fite, *"Peter Turney,"* p. 13.

17. Thorogood, *"Only County."*

18. Ibid.

19. Fite, *"Peter Turney"*; Thorogood, *"Only County."*

20. Thorogood, *"Only County."*

21. *"Departure."*

22. Horn, *Tennessee's War*, p. 16.

23. Corlew, *Tennessee*, pp. 292-93.

24. Fisher, *War*, pp. 35-36.

25. Langsdon, *Tennessee*, p. 153; Fisher, *War*, pp. 35-36.

26. Patten, *Chronicle*, p. 188.

27. Horn, *Tennessee's War*, p. 17.

28. Ibid.

29. Horn, *Tennessee's War*, p. 17; Titus, *Picturesque*, p. 99.

30. Corlew, *Tennessee*, p. 153; Fisher, *War*, p. 49; Patten, *Chronicle*, p. 193.

31. Langsdon, *Tennessee*, p. 153; Fisher, *War*, 38; Corlew, *Tennessee*, p. 298.

32. Langsdon, *Tennessee*, p. 153.

33. Patten, *Chronicle*, p. 189; Corlew, *Tennessee*, pp. 288-89; Langsdon, *Tennessee*, p. 154.

34. Ibid.

35. Corlew, *Tennessee*, p. 297.

36. Fisher, *War*, p. 62

37. Joiner, *Tennessee Then and Now*, p. 215.

38. Joiner, *Tennessee Then and Now*, pp. 229-30.

39. Ramsdell, *Southern Confederacy*, p. 58.

40. Corlew, *Tennessee*, p. 324.

41. Ramsdell, *Southern Confederacy*, p. 25.

CHAPTER 2. *Formation of the Tennessee Brigade Regiments*

1. C.W.C.C., *Tennesseeans*, p. 1.

2. C.W.C.C., *Tennesseeans*, pp. 1-2.

3. C.W.C.C., *Tennesseeans*, p. 189; Lindsley, *Military*, p. 227.

4. Porter, *"Tennessee Confederate Regiments."*

5. Porter, *"Tennessee Confederate Regiments"*; C.W.C.C., *Tennesseeans*, pp. 188-89.

6. C.W.C.C., *Tennesseeans*, p. 203; Titus, *Picturesque*, p. 116.

7. Titus, *Picturesque*, p. 117; C.W.C.C. *Tennesseeans*, 203.

8. Titus, *Picturesque*, p. 117; Cross, *Ordeal*, pp. 8-10.

9. Williams, *"Dr. Ben A. Haskins,"* p. 439; Titus, *Picturesque*, p. 100.

10. Tyler, *"Patriotism,"* p. 125.

11. Cross, *Ordeal*, p. 186; Titus, *Picturesque*, p. 100.

12. Butler.

13. Ibid.

14. Ibid.

15. Ibid.

16. Ibid.

17. Ibid.

18. Ibid.

19. Ibid.

20. Ibid.

21. Lacey, *Goodner*, pp. 259-64.

22. Butler.

23. Ibid.

24. Ibid.

25. Cross, *Ordeal*, p. 12; Titus, *Picturesque*, p. 117; Lindsley, *Military*, 227.

26. Butler.

27. McComb, *Tennesseeans*, p. 210.

28. Cross, *Ordeal*, p. 13; C.W.C.C., *Tennesseeans*, p. 172; Lindsley, *Military*, p. 227; Titus, *Picturesque*, p. 117.

29. Butler; Mockbee, *"The 14ʰ Tennessee,"* p. 27.

30. Lindsley, *Military*, p. 228.

31. McComb, *Tennesseeans*, p. 210; Lindsley, *Military*, p. 323.

32. McComb, *Tennesseeans*, p. 210.

33. Butler.

34. Ibid.

35. Ibid.

36. Webb, *Bicentennial History*, p. 371.

37. Mockbee, *"The 14ʰ Tennessee,"* p. 8.

38. Kimble, *"14ʰ Tennessee Glee Club,"* pp. 1-2.

39. Lindsley, *Military*, p. 323.

40. Butler.

41. Ibid.

42. Lindsley, *Military*, p. 228.

43. Lindsley, *Military*, p. 228, Cross, *Ordeal*, p. 20.

44. Lindsley, *Military*, p. 228.

45. Butler.

46. Lindsley, *Military*, pp. 228, 324.

47. Butler.

48. Ibid.

49. McComb, *Tennesseeans*, p. 210.

50. Mockbee, *"The 14ʰ Tennessee,"* p. 9.

51. Fite, *"Short,"* p. 49.

52. Mockbee, *"The 14ʰ Tennessee,"* p. 9.

53. Drane.

54. Ibid.

55. Ibid.

56. Ibid.

57. Ibid.

58. Kimble, *"Gen. Sam Anderson."*

59. Ibid.

60. Butler; C.W.C.C., *Tennesseans*, p. 172.

61. Mockbee, *"The 14ᵗʰ Tennessee,"* p. 6.

CHAPTER 3. *Winter of Indecision, 1861-1862*

1. Butler.

2. Ibid.

3. Ibid.

4. Cross, *Ordeal*, p. 17.

5. Butler.

6. Lindsley, *Military*, p. 229; C.W.C.C., *Tennesseans*, p. 172; Imboden, *North to Antietam,* p. 282.

7. Butler; McComb, *Tennesseans*, pp. 210-11.

8. Butler.

9. Ibid.

10. Ibid.

11. Ibid.

12. Butler; McComb, *Tennesseans*, p. 211.

13. Butler.

14. Ibid.

15. Ibid.

16. Ibid.

17. Butler; McComb, *Tennesseans*, p. 211.

18. Ibid.

19. Butler.

20. McComb, *Tennesseans*, p. 211.

21. Butler.

22. Linsley, *Military*, p. 229; C.W.C.C., *Tennesseeans*, p. 189.

23. McComb, *Tennesseeans*, p. 211.

24. Ibid.

25. Ibid.

26. Butler.

27. McComb, *Tennesseeans*, p. 211; Lindsley, *Military*, pp. 229 and 234; C.W.C.C., *Tennesseeans*, p. 189.

28. Butler.

29. Butler.

30. McComb, *Tennesseeans*, p. 211.

31. Butler.

32. Imboden, *North to Antietam*, p. 283.

33. McComb, *Tennesseeans*, p. 211.

34. Butler.

35. Ibid.

36. Ibid.

37. Ibid.

38. Ibid.

39. Ibid.

40. Mockbee, "*The 14ᵗ Tennessee,*" p. 13; McComb, *Tennesseeans,* p. 211.

41. Butler.

42. Mockbee, "*The 14ᵗ Tennessee,*" p. 14.

43. Butler.

44. Ibid.

45. Ibid.

46. Ibid.

47. McComb, *Tennesseeans*, p. 211.

48. Butler.

49. Ibid.

50. Mockbee, "*The 14ᵗ Tennessee,*" p. 14.

CHAPTER 4. *Realignment*

1. Butler.
2. Ibid.
3. Ibid.
4. Ibid.
5. C.W.C.C., *Tennesseans*, pp. 172-74; Butler.
6. Butler.
7. Ibid.
8. Ibid.
9. McComb, *Tennesseans*, p. 211.
10. Cross, *Ordeal*, p. 23; C.W.C.C., *Tennesseans*, p. 171.
11. C.W.C.C., *Tennesseans*, p. 170.
12. C.W.C.C., *Tennesseans*, p. 171.
13. Thorogood, *"Only County,"* Foreman, *"Secession,"* p. 9.
14. Butler.
15. Ibid.
16. Ibid.
17. Ibid.
18. Ibid.
19. Ibid.
20. C.W.C.C., *Tennesseans*, p. 171.
21. Butler.
22. Ibid.
23. Ibid.
24. Ibid.
25. Ibid.
26. Ibid.
27. Ibid.
28. Ibid.
29. Ibid.
30. Butler; Lindsley, *Military*, p. 229.

31. Kimble, *"At Yorktown."*

32. Ibid.

33. Butler.

34. Lindsley, *Military,* p. 227.

35. Harris, untitled.

36. Tolley, *"Campaigns,"* p. 109.

37. Butler.

38. Cross, *Ordeal,* pp. 104, 117, 147, 156, 160, 197, 267, 276, 282; Herndon, *"Reminiscences,"* p. 5; Mockbee, *"The 14ᵗʰ Tennessee,* p. 14.

CHAPTER 5. *Yorktown*

1. Butler.

2. Ibid.

3. Ibid.

4. Mockbee, *"The 14ᵗʰ Tennessee,"* p. 15; McComb, *Tennesseeans,* p. 211; Herndon, *"Reminiscences,"* p. 6.

5. Lindsley, *Military,* pp. 229-30, 324; Herndon, *"Reminiscences,"* p. 6.

6. Cross, *Ordeal,* p. 116; Mockbee, *"The 14ᵗʰ Tennessee,"* p. 15.

7. Mockbee, *"The 14ᵗʰ Tennessee,"* pp. 15-16.

8. Herndon, *"Reminiscences,"* p. 6.

9. Butler.

10. Butler; McComb, *Tennesseeans,* p. 211; Herndon, *"Reminiscences,"* p. 6.

11. Butler.

12. Kimble, *"Another Story."*

13. Kimble, *"An Ambuscade"*; Cross, *Ordeal,* p. 150.

14. Kimble, *"An Ambuscade."*

15. Ibid.

16. Ibid.

17. Cummings, *"Confederate Heroine,"* p. 91; Donaldson, untitled, p. 164.

18. Butler.

19. Ibid.

20. Clendening, *"Memoirs,"* p. 76.

21. C.W.C.C., *Tennesseeans*, p. 171.

CHAPTER 6. *Hatton's Tenure and Seven Pines*

1. C.W.C.C., *Tennesseeans*, pp. 171 & 189.

2. S.C.V. Camp 723 and fred.net.

3. Kelley, *"Robert Hatton,"* p. 554.

4. Cross, *Ordeal*, p. 25.

5. Lindsley, *Military*, p 230.

6. Kelley, *"Robert Hatton,"* p. 553; Mockbee, *"The 14ᵗʰ Tennessee."*

7. Kelley, *"Robert Hatton,"* p. 553.

8. Barnwell, *"Battle of Seven Pines,"* p. 58.

9. Barnwell, *"Battle of Seven Pines,"* p. 58; Lindsley, *Military*, p. 230; Cross, *Ordeal*, p. 25.

10. Hudson, *"Gustavus W. Smith,"* p. 17.

11. Lindsley, *Military*, p. 230; Hudson, *"Gustavus W. Smith,"* p. 17.

12. Cross, *Ordeal*, p.26; Lindsley, *Military*, p. 230.

13. Cross, *Ordeal*, pp. 26-27.

14. Herndon, *"Reminiscences,"* p. 6.

15. Lindsley, *Military*, p. 230; Herndon, *Reminiscences,* pp. 6; Childs, *"Reminiscences,"* p. 112.

16. Childs, *"Seven Pines,"* p. 19.

17. Herndon, *"Reminiscences,"* p. 7; Childs, *"Reminiscences,"* p. 112; Benton, *"Tennessee Private,"* p. 507.

18. Childs, *"Seven Pines,"* p. 19.

19. Armistead, *"Battle,"* p. 187.

20. Armistead, *"Battle,"* p. 187; Childs, *"Seven Pines."*

21. Lindsley, *Military*, p. 231.

22. Herndon, *"Reminiscences,"* p. 7; Childs, *"Seven Pines,"* p. 20.

23. Childs, *"Seven Pines,"* p. 20; Turney's Muster Roll of Company K.

24. Muse, *"History."*

25. Kelley, *"Robert Hatton,"* p. 553.

26. Lindsley, *Military*, p. 213.

27. Harris, untitled, p. 160.

28. Lindsley, *Military*, p. 231; Fite, *"Memoirs,"* p. 62.

29. Lindsley, *Military*, p. 232; Kelley, *"Robert Hatton,"* p. 554; Childs, *"Seven Pines,"* p. 20.

30. Tennessee S.C.V. Camp 723.

31. Kelley, *"Robert Hatton,"* p. 554.

32. Tate, *"Reminiscences,"* p. 275; Webb, *"Bicentennial,"* p. 271; Watertown, *Phillips Family*, p. 117.

33. Jones, *"Seven Pines,"* p. 506.

34. Jones, *"Seven Pines,"* p. 506; Watertown, *Phillips Family*, p. 117.

35. Jones, *"Seven Pines,"* p. 506.

36. Civil War on line.

CHAPTER 7. *Archer Assumes Control*

1. Wakelyn, *Biographical Dictionary*, p. 76; Harris, *"Archer,"* p. 18; Warner, *Generals*, p. 11.

2. Chesnut, *Diary*, pp. 120-21.

3. Hopkins, *"Archer Letters,"* pp. 74 and 382; Harris, *"Archer,"* p. 18.

4. Hopkins, *"Archer Letters,"* pp. 78-79.

5. Hopkins, *"Archer Letters,"* pp. 78, 80-84.

6. Ibid, pp. 84-85.

7. Ibid, pp. 86-89.

8. Ibid, p. 128.

9. Ibid, pp. 131-32.

10. Ibid, p. 134.

11. Harris, *"Archer,"* p. 18.

12. Lindsley, *"Military,"* p. 232.

13. Fite, *"Short,"* p. 62.

14. Ibid, pp. 62-63.

CHAPTER 8. *Seven Days*

1. Ritter, Historical Memoranda.
2. Porter, *"Calhoun."*
3. Reese, Historical Memoranda.
4. *Nineteenth Georgia Infantry.*
5. Imboden, *North,* pp. 315 & 317.
6. Lindsley, *Military,* p. 232.
7. Katcher, *Battle,* p. 48.
8. Ledbetter, *"Mechanicsville,"* p. 244.
9. Ibid.
10. Fulton, *"Tumbled,"* p. 172.
11. Ledbetter, *"Mechanicsville,"* p. 244; Fulton, *"Tumbled,"* p. 172.
12. Ledbetter, *"Mechanicsville,"* p. 244; Lindsley, *Military,* p. 233; Herndon, *"Reminiscences,"* p. 9.
13. Ledbetter, *"Mechanicsville,"* p. 244; Mockbee, *"The 14ᵗʰ Tennessee,"* p. 16.
14. Fulton, *"Tumbled,"* p. 428.
15. Ibid, pp. 427-28.
16. Fite, *"Short,"* pp. 67-69.
17. McComb, *"Battles,"* p. 161.
18. Lindsley, *Military,* p. 233.
19. Keely, *"Narrative."*
20. Keely, *"Narrative";* Lindsley, *Military,* p. 233.
21. Ledbetter, *"Mechanicsville,"* p. 244.
22. McComb, *"Battles,"* p. 161.
23. Keely, *"Narrative."*
24. Fulton, *"Archer's Brigade,"* p. 301.
25. Tolley, *"Campaigns,"* p. 54; McComb, *"Battles,"* p. 161.
26. *"Tennesseean Killed,"* p. 407.

27. Boze, *"Comrade's Tribute,"* p. 28; Lindsley, *Military,* p. 233; tngennet. org.

28. McComb, *"Battles,"* p. 161.

29. Fulton, *"Archer's Brigade,"* p. 301; Ledbetter, *"Mechanicsville,"* p. 244.

30. Fulton, *"Archer's Brigade,"* p. 301.

31. Tolley, *"Campaigns,"* p. 54.

32. McComb, *"Battles,"* p. 161; Ledbetter, *"Mechanicsville,"* p. 245.

33. Ledbetter, *"Mechanicsville,"* p. 245.

34. Ibid.

35. McComb, *"Battles,"* p. 161; Tolley, *"Campaigns,"* p. 54.

36. McComb, *"Battles,"* p. 161.

37. Benton, *"Tennessee Private,"* p. 507; Cross, *Ordeal,* p. 176.

38. Tolley, *"Campaigns,"* p. 54.

39. McComb, *"Battles,"* p. 161; Benton, *"Tennessee Private,"* p. 507.

40. McComb, *"Battles,"* p. 162; Mockbee, untitled, p. 170.

41. Ledbetter, *Mechanicsville,* p. 245; Lindsley, *Military,* p. 233.

42. Longstreet, *"The Seven Days,"* pp. 399-400.

43. Ibid; McBrien, *Tennessee Brigade,* pp. 333.

44. Ibid.

45. Ibid; Mockbee, *"The 14th Tennessee,"* p. 17.

46. Mockbee, *"The 14th Tennessee,"* p. 17; Lindsley, *Military,* p. 234; McBrien, *Tennessee Brigade,* p. 33; McComb, *"Battles,"* p. 162.

47. McComb, *"Battles,"* p. 162; Busby's Civil War on line.

48. kingwoodcable.com; *"Turney's Muster Roll"*; Blevins, *Sequatchie,* pp. 19-20; Webb, *Bicentennial,* p. 271.

49. *"Fourteenth Tennessee,"* p. 263.

50. Ibid.

CHAPTER 9. *With Stonewall*

1. Lindsley, *Military,* p. 234; Cheeks, *"Rally,"* p. 57.

2. Childs, *"Cedar Run,"* p. 24; Fite, *"Short,"* pp. 69-70.

3. B., *"From the 19".*

4. Lindsley, *Military*, p. 234; Childs, *"Cedar Run,"* p. 24; Cheeks, *"Rally,"* p. 57.

5. Lindsley, *Military*, p. 234; Cheeks, *"Rally,"* pp. 57-60; O.R., Series I, vol. 16,

6. Childs, *"Cedar Run,"* p. 24.

7. Cheeks, *"Rally,"* pp. 61 & 96.

8. Cheeks, *"Rally,"* pp. 96-98; Fite, *"Short,"* p. 70.

9. Ibid.

10. Fite, *"Short,"* p. 70; Childs, *"Cedar Run,"* p. 24.

11. Childs, *"Cedar Run,"* p. 24; Cheeks, *"Rally,"* p. 100.

12. Fite, *"Short,"* p. 70.

13. Childs, *"Cedar Run,"* p. 24.

14. Ibid.

15. Ibid.

16. Fulton, *"Family Record,"* p. 68.

17. Fite, *"Short,"* p. 71.

18. Blevins, *Sequatchie*, p. 19; Cross, *Ordeal*, pp. 37 & 136; fred.net.

19. Cheeks, *"Rally,"* p. 100.

20. Lindsley, *Military*, pp. 234-35.

21. Lindsley, *Military*, p. 235; McBrien, *Tennessee Brigade*, p. 38.

22. McBrien, *Tennessee Brigade*, pp. 38-39; Fulton, *"Incidents,"* p. 451.

23. Fulton, *"Incidents,"* p. 451.

24. McBrien, *Tennessee Brigade*, p. 39; Lindsley, *Military*, p. 235.

25. Fulton, *"Incidents,"* p. 451.

26. Ibid; McBrien, *Tennessee Brigade*, p. 39.

27. Lindsley, *Military*, p. 235; Fulton, *"Family Record,"* p. 64.

28. O.R., Series I, vol. 14, p. 699; Lindsley, *Military*, p. 235.

29. Fulton, *"Incidents"*; Lindsley, *Military*, p. 235.

30. Lindsley, *Military*, p. 235.

31. Fulton, *"Incidents,"* pp. 451-52.

32. Ibid; Lindsley, *Military*, p. 235; O.R. Ser. I, vol. 14, p. 699.

33. *"Fine Shots,"* p. 74.

34. O.R. Ser. I, vol. 14, p. 699; Fulton, *"Family Record,"* p. 70; Lindsley, *Military*, p. 235.

35. Ibid.

36. Lindsley, *Military*, p. 235; Mockbee, *"The 14ᵗ Tennessee,"* p. 19; O.R., Ser. I, vol. 14, p. 700.

37. O.R., Ser. I, vol. 14, p. 700; Lindsley, *Military*, p. 235.

38. Fulton, *"Incidents,"* p. 452.

39. Lindsley, *Military*, p. 235.

40. Lindsley, *Military*, p. 235; O.R., Ser. I, vol. 14, p. 700.

41. O.R. p. 700.

42. O.R. p. 700; Mockbee, *"The 14ᵗ Tennessee,"* p. 19.

43. O.R., p. 700.

44. Hartman, *"With Jackson,"* p. 557.

45. O.R., p. 700.

46. Ibid; Herndon, *"Reminiscences,"* p. 11.

47. O.R., p. 701.

48. Hartman, *"With Jackson,"* p. 557.

49. O.R., p. 701.

50. Hartman, *"With Jackson,"* p.557.

51. O.R., p. 701.

52. Hartman, *"With Jackson,"* p. 557.

53. O.R., p. 701; Herndon, *"Reminiscences,"* p. 11.

54. O.R., p. 701; Cross, *Ordeal*, p. 128.

55. Porter, *"Calhoun."*

56. Herndon, *"Reminiscences,"* p. 11; Cross, *Ordeal*, pp. 151 & 159.

57. O.R., p. 702.

58. O.R., pp. 699 & 702; Webb, *Bicentennial*, p. 272.

59. O.R., p. 702; Cross, *Ordeal*, p. 95.

60. McBrien, *Tennessee Brigade*, p. 45; Fulton, *"Incidents,"* p. 452.

CHAPTER 10. *The Maryland Campaign*

1. Cross, *Ordeal,* pp. 43-44.

2. McBrien, *Tennessee Brigade,* p. 45.

3. McBrien, *Tennessee Brigade,* p. 46; Lindsley, *Military,* p. 236; Mockbee, *"The 14ᵗʰ Tennessee,"* p. 20.

4. Muse, *"History,"* pp. 8-9.

5. O.R., Ser. I, v. 19, p. 1000; Mockbee, *"The 14ᵗʰ Tennessee,"* p. 20; Lindsley, *Military,* p. 236.

6. O.R., Ser. I, v. 19, p. 1000; Mockbee, *"The 14ᵗʰ Tennessee,"* p. 20.

7. O.R., Ser. I, v. 19, p. 1000.

8. Mockbee, *"The 14ᵗʰ Tennessee,"* p. 20; McBrien, *Tennessee Brigade,* p. 46.

9. O.R., Ser. I, v. 19, p. 1000.

10. Ibid; Mockbee, *"The 14ᵗʰ Tennessee,"* p. 20.

11. McBrien, *Tennessee Brigade,* p. 46; O.R., Ser. I, v. 19, p. 1000.

12. Mockbee, *"The 14ᵗʰ Tennessee,"* p. 20; O.R. Ser. I, v. 19, p. 1000.

13. Muse, *"History,"* p. 9.

14. O.R., Ser. I, v. 19, p. 1000; McBrien, *Tennessee Brigade,* p. 46.

15. Ibid.

16. O.R., Ser. I, v. 19, p. 1000.

17. Motlow, *"Campaigns,"* p. 310.

18. McBrien, *Tennessee Brigade,* p. 47; Lindsley, *Military,* p. 237.

19. Mockbee, *"The 14ᵗʰ Tennessee,"* p. 21.

20. McBrien, *Tennessee Brigade,* p. 48.

21. O.R., Ser. I, v. 19, p. 1000.

22. Lindsley, *Military,* p. 236; Mockbee, *"The 14ᵗʰ Tennessee."*

23. Carman, *"Maryland Campaign,"* p. 69.

24. O.R., Ser. I, v. 19, p. 1000.

25. Cross, *Ordeal,* p. 48.

26. Large, *Battle of Antietam,* pp. 179-80.

27. Motlow, *"Campaigns,"* p. 310.

28. Hopkins, *"Archer Letters,"* pp. 140-41.

29. O.R., Ser. I, v. 19, p. 1000; Large, *Battle of Antietam*, pp. 179-80.

30. Motlow, *"Campaigns,"* p. 310.

31. Carman, *"Maryland Campaign,"* p. 69; Lindsley, *Military*, p. 237.

32. Carman, *"Maryland Campaign,"* p. 71.

33. Mockbee, *"Drawn Battle,"* p. 160.

34. Motlow, *"Campaigns,"* p. 310.

35. O.R., Ser. I, v. 19, p. 1000; Lindsley, *Military*, p. 237.

36. Emory, *"Report...Sept. 1862."*

37. Rives obituary, p. 170.

38. Muse, *"History,"* pp. 9-10.

39. O.R. Ser. I, v. 19, p. 1002.

40. Ibid.

41. Motlow, *"Campaigns,"* p. 310.

42. Ibid.

43. O.R. Ser. I, v. 19, p. 1002.

44. Fite, *"Short,"* p. 77; Mockbee, *"The 14ᵗʰ Tennessee,"* p. 22.

45. Fite, *"Short,"* p. 77.

46. Emory, *"Report...Oct. 1862."*

47. Ibid.

48. Ibid.

49. Mockbee, *"The 14ᵗʰ Tennessee,"* p. 22.

50. Ibid, pp. 22-23.

51. Butler.

52. Ibid.

53. Ibid.

CHAPTER 11. *Fredericksburg*

1. O.R., Ser. I, vol. 21, p. 551.

2. Renfroe, *"Model Confederate,"* p. 6.

3. O.R., Ser. I, vol. 21, p. 552.

4. Ibid.

5. Butler.

6. O.R. Ser. I, vol. 21, pp. 552 & 645.

7. Butler.

8. Ibid; Moore, *"Fredericksburg,"* p. 181.

9. Butler.

10. Kimble, *"Company A."*

11. Hopkins, *"Archer Letters,"* p. 141; O.R., Ser. I, vol. 21, p. 650.

12. Hopkins, *"Archer Letters,"* p. 141.

13. O.R., Ser. I, vol. 21, pp. 631 & 656.

14. Ibid; Keely, *"Narrative."*

15. Keely, *"Narrative"*; Moore, *"Fredericksburg,"* p. 182.

16. O.R., Ser. I, vol. 21, pp. 656-57.

17. Johnson, letter to the editor; Mockbee, *"The 14ᵗʰ Tennessee,"* p. 23.

18. Keely, *"Narrative."*

19. Butler.

20. Moore, *"Fredericksburg,"* p. 82.

21. Fite, *"Short,"* p. 86; Thorogood, *"Only County."*

22. Thorogood, *"Only County."*

23. Ibid.

24. Ibid.

25. O.R., Ser. I, vol. 21, p. 657.

26. O.R., Ser. I, vol. 21, pp. 658-661; Cross, *Ordeal*, p. 145.

27. O.R., Ser. I, vol. 21, p. 661.

28. Kimble, *"Company A."*

29. Ibid.

30. O.R., Ser. I, vol. 21, p. 660.

31. McCall, *"Archer,"* p. 19.

32. O.R., Ser. I, vol. 21, p. 659; Butler.

33. Mockbee, *"The 14ᵗʰ Tennessee,"* p. 23; Moore, *"Fredericksburg,"* p. 182.

34. O.R., Ser. I, vol. 21, p. 657.
35. Johnson, letter to the editor.
36. Renfroe, *"Model Confederate,"* pp. 9-10.
37. Ibid.
38. Butler.
39. Hopkins, *"Archer Letters,"* p. 139.
40. O.R., Ser. I, vol. 21, pp. 657 & 672.
41. Ibid, pp. 660-61.
42. Keely, *"Narrative."*
43. Moore, *"Fredericksburg,"* p. 184; Butler.
44. Lindsley, *Military*, p. 238; O.R., Ser. I, vol. 21, pp. 560 & 658.
45. Turney's muster roll.
46. O.R., Ser. I, vol. 21, p. 657.
47. Ibid, pp. 659-61.
48. Ibid.
49. Kimble, *"Company A."*
50. Moore, *"Fredericksburg"*; Fite, *"Short,"* pp. 80-81.
51. Thorogood, *"Only County."*
52. O.R., Ser. I, vol. 21, pp. 657 & 661; Cross, *Ordeal*, p. 151; Herndon, *"Reminiscences,"* p. 12.
53. Keely, *"Narrative."*
54. Moore, *"Fredericksburg,"* p. 183; O.R., Ser. I, vol. 21, p. 658; Hopkins, *"Archer Letters,"* p. 138.
55. Hopkins, *"Archer Letters,"* pp. 138-39.
56. Kimble, *"Company A."*

CHAPTER 12. *Chancellorsville*

1. Lindsley, *Military*, p. 238; Fite, *"Short,"* p. 81; Mockbee, *"The 14[h] Tennessee,"* p. 24.
2. Hopkins, *"Archer Letters,"* p. 140.
3. Mockbee, *"The 14[h] Tennessee,"* pp. 24 & 42.

4. Brock, *"Fry,"* pp. 287-88; Wakelyn, *Biographical,* p. 192; Hopkins, *"Archer Letters,"* pp. 142-43.

5. *"Thirteenth Alabama."*

6. Hopkins, *"Archer Letters,"* p. 142; O. R. Ser. I, vol. 25, p. 1099.

7. Smith, *"Letter...Jan. 22, 1863."*

8. Smith, *"Letter...Feb. 1, 1863."*

9. Ibid.

10. Kimble, *"at Chancellorsville."*

11. Hopkins, *"Archer Letters,"* pp. 141 & 145.

12. Smith, *"Letter...March 8, 1863."*

13. Lindsley, *Military,* p. 238.

14. Butler.

15. Kimble, *"Glee Club."*

16. Bulter; Mockbee, *"The 14* Tennessee,"* p. 24.

17. Kimble, *" at Chancellorsville."*

18. Butler.

19. Childs, *"at Chancellorsville,"* p. 220.

20. Ibid.

21. Butler.

22. O.R., Ser. I, vol. 25, p. 924; Hurst, *"at Chancellorsville,"* p. 261.

23. Butler.

24. Herndon, *"Reminiscences,"* pp. 12-13; Hurst, *"at Chancellorsville,"* pp. 261-62.

25. Lemmon, untitled, pp. 141-42.

26. Childs, *"at Chancellorsville,"* p. 220; Butler.

27. Childs, *"at Chancellorsville,"* pp. 220-21.

28. Butler.

29. Childs, *"at Chancellorsville,"* p. 221.

30. Hurst, *"at Chancellorsville,"* p. 262.

31. Butler.

32. Childs, *"at Chancellorsville,"* p. 221.

33. Hurst, *"at Chancellorsville,"* p. 262.

34. Harris, *"Incidents,"* p. 261.

35. Ibid.

36. Kimble, *"at Chancellorsville."*

37. Mockbee, *"The 14ᵗʰ Tennessee,"* p. 26 & 42; Hopkins, *"Archer Letters,"* pp. 148-49.

38. Fox, letter, p. 410.

39. Childs, *"at Chancellorsville,"* p. 221.

40. Butler.

41. Lindsley, *Military*, pp. 239-40.

42. Kimble, *"at Chancellorsville."*

43. Hurst, *"at Chancellorsville,"* p. 262.

44. *"William Bryan Hutton,"* p. 328.

45. *"Mrs. Eugenia F. Williams,"* p. 477; *"William Bryan Hutton,"* p. 328.

46. Kimble, *"Gus A. Thompkins."*

47. *"Tribute to Maj. John T. Smith."*

48. Ibid.

49. Ibid.

50. Fite, *"Short,"* p. 82.

51. Kimble, *"Battle of Chancellorsville—An Incident."*

CHAPTER 13. *Gettysburg: Day One*

1. Herndon, *"Reminiscences,"* p. 14; Lindsley, *Military*, p. 245; Mockbee, *"The 14ᵗʰ Tennessee,"* p. 26.

2. Herndon, *"Reminiscences,"* p. 14; Mockbee, *"The 14ᵗʰ Tennessee,"* p. 26.

3. Boland, *"Recollections,"* pp. 2-3.

4. Lindsley, *Military*, p. 245; Herndon, *"Reminiscences,"* p. 15; Moon, *"Beginning,"* p. 449.

5. Fite, *"Short,"* p. 85.

6. Meredith, *"First Day,"* p. 183.

7. Fite, *"Short,"* pp. 85-86.

8. Fite, *"Short,"* p. 86; Lindsley, *Military*, p. 245; Bird, *Stories*, p. 6.

9. Purifoy, *"Battle of Gettysburg,"* p. 22; Moore, *"Heth's Division,"* pp. 384-85.

10. Boland, *"Beginning,"* p. 308.

11. O.R., Ser. I, v. 27, p. 637; Moore, *"Heth's Division,"* p. 385.

12. Boland, *"Beginning,"* p. 308.

13. Roth, *"Gettysburg,"* p. 54; Nofi, *Gettysburg Campaign*, p. 58.

14. Fulton, *"The Fifth Alabama,"* p. 379.

15. Bird, *Stories*, p. 6; Moon, *"Beginning,"* p. 449.

16. Moon, *"Beginning,"* p. 449.

17. Boland, *"Beginning,"* p. 308.

18. Hull, *"Gen. John Buford,"* p. 62.

19. Bird, *Stories*, pp. 6-7.

20. Fulton, *"The Fifth Alabama,"* p. 379.

21. Ibid; Purifoy, *"Battle of Gettysburg,"* p. 22.

22. O.R., Ser. I, v. 27, p. 637.

23. Purifoy, *"Battle of Gettysburg,"* p. 22.

24. Moon, *"Beginning,"* p. 449.

25. O.R., Ser. I, v. 27, p. 637.

26. Moon, *"Beginning,"* p. 449.

27. Ibid.

28. Griffin, *"First Confederates to fall,"* pp. 26-27.

29. Harris, *"From Gettysburg,"* pp. 1-2.

30. Swallow, *"The first day,"* pp. 437-39.

31. Purifoy, *"Battle of Gettysburg,"* p. 22.

32. Harris, *"From Gettysburg,"* p. 2.

33. *"Says He Shot."*

34. Moon, *"Beginning,"* pp. 449-50.

35. Swallow, *"The first day";* Wheeler, *Witness to Gettysburg*, p. 126.

36. Coddington, *The Gettysburg Campaign*, p. 269.

37. Wheeler, *Witness to Gettysburg*, p. 126; Moore, *"Heth's Division,"* p. 385.

38. Moore, *"Heth's Division,"* p. 385.

39. Kimble, *"Tennesseeans,"* p. p. 460.

40. Bird, *Stories,* p. 8.

41. Boland, *"Beginning,"* p. 308.

42. Moon, *"Beginning,"* p. 450.

43. Herndon, *"Reminiscences,"* p. 15.

44. Meredith, *"The First Day,"* p. 184.

45. McCall, *"What the Tennesseeans Did,"* p. 2; Titus, *Picturesque,* p. 121.

46. Fulton, *"The Fifth Alabama,"* p. 379; Smith, *"Archer's Brigade."*

47. A.S.R., Letter to the Editor.

48. *"Says He Shot."*

49. Castleberry, *"Thirteenth Alabama,"* p. 338; Mockbee, *"The 14ᵗʰ Tennessee,"* p. 27.

50. Harries, *"The Sword,"* p. 420.

51. Kross, *"General Reynolds,"* p. 20; O.R., Ser. I, v. 27, p. 275.

52. Davis, *The Civil War,* p. 1290; Wheeler, *Witness to Gettysburg,* p. 126.

53. Woodhead, *Voices...Gettysburg,* p. 40.

54. Castleberry, *"Thirteenth Alabama,"* p. 338.

55. Kross, *"General Reynolds,"* p. 20; Bird, *Stories,* pp. 7-8; Herndon, *"Reminiscences,"* p. 15; Mockbee, *"The 14ᵗʰ Tennessee,"* p. 27.

56. Kross, *"General Reynolds,"* p. 20.

57. Meredith, *"The First Day,"* p. 184.

58. Turney, *"The First Tennessee,"* p. 535.

59. Moon, *"Beginning,"* p. 450.

60. Purifoy, *"The Battle of Gettysburg,"* p. 23.

61. Ibid, p. 24.

62. O.R., Ser. I, v. 27, p. 639.

63. Purifoy, *"The Battle of Gettysburg,"* pp. 24-25.

64. Swallow, *"The first day,"* pp. 440-42.

65. Purifoy, *"The Battle of Gettysburg,"* p. 25.

66. Ibid.

67. Nofi, *The Gettysburg Campaign,* p. 68; Meredith, *"The First Day,"* pp. 186-87.

68. Moore, *"Heth's Division,"* p. 387; Kimble, *"Tennesseeans,"* p. 460.

69. Moon, *"Beginning,"* p. 450; Bird, *Stories,* p. 8.

70. Herndon, *"Reminiscences"* pp. 15, 17, 18.

71. Ibid, p. 17.

CHAPTER 14. *Gettysburg: The Third Day*

1. Coffin, *Eyewitness,* p. 99; *Gettysburg: The Confederate High Tide*; p. 126.

2. Ward, *The Civil War,* p. 226.

3. Ibid.

4. Moore, *"Heth's Division,"* p. 387.

5. Tucker, *High Tide,* pp. 222-23; Nofi, *The Gettysburg Campaign,* p. 140.

6. Kimble, *"Tennesseeans,"* p. 460.

7. Ibid.

8. Moore, *"Heth's Division,"* pp. 388-89.

9. Moore, *"Heth's Division,"* p. 389; Fry, *"Pettigrew's Charge,"* p. 92.

10. Fry, *"Pettigrew's Charge,"* p. 92.

11. Reid, *"Incidents,"* p. 508.

12. Ibid.

13. Kimble, *"Tennesseeans,"* p. 460.

14. Turney, *"The First Tennessee,"* p. 536.

15. Fite, *Short,* p. 86.

16. Nofi, *The Gettysburg Campaign,* p. 146.

17. McCall, *"What the Tennesseeans did."*

18. Moore, *"Heth's Division,"* p. 389; Fry, *"Pettigrew's Charge,"* p. 92.

19. Purifoy, *"Confederate Assault,"* p. 227.

20. Kimble, *"Tennesseeans,"* p. 460; O.R., Ser. I, v. 27, p. 373; Moore, *"Heth's Division,"* p. 390; Purifoy, *"Concerning,"* p. 77.

21. Coddington, *Gettysburg Campaign*, pp. 502-03; O.R., Ser. I, v. 27, p. 373.

22. Kimble, *"Tennesseeans,"* p. 460.

23. Fite, *Short*, p. 86; Lindsley, *Military*, p. 249.

24. McCall, *"What the Tennesseeans did."*

25. Reid, *"Incidents,"* p. 508.

26. O.R. Ser. I, v. 27, p. 373.

27. McCall, *"What the Tennesseeans did."*

28. Harris, *"From Gettysburg."*

29. Fry, *"Pettigrew's Charge,"* pp. 92-93; Kimble, *"Tennesseeans,"* p. 460.

30. O.R., Ser. I, v. 27, p. 373.

31. Lindsley, *Military*, p. 250.

32. Fry, *"Pettigrew's Charge,"* p. 93.

33. Turney, *"The First Tennessee,"* p. 536.

34. Lindsley, *Military*, p. 250.

35. McCall, *"What the Tennesseeans did"*; Fite, *Short*, p. 87; Kimble, *"Tennesseeans,"* pp. 460-61.

36. Turney, *"The First Tennessee,"* p. 536.

37. Fry, *"Pettigrew's Charge,"* p. 93.

38. O.R., Ser. I, v. 27, p. 373.

39. Kimble, *"Tennesseeans,"* p. 461.

40. Turney, *"The First Tennessee,"* p. 536.

41. Lindsley, *Military*, p. 250.

42. Fite, *Short*, p. 87; McCall, *"What the Tennesseeans did."*

43. Stewart, *Pickett's Charge*, p. 20.

44. Kimble, *"Tennesseeans,"* p. 461.

45. Turney, *"The First Tennessee,"* pp. 536-37.

46. Reid, *"Incidents,"* p. 508.

47. Fite, *Short,* p. 87; Fry, *"Pettigrew's Charge,"* p. 93.

48. Purifoy, *"Confederate Assault,"* pp. 227-28.

49. Lindsley, *Military,* pp. 250-51; McCall, *"What the Tennesseans did."*

50. Lindsley, *Military,* p. 251.

51. Turney, *"The First Tennessee,"* p. 251.

52. Fite, *Short,* p. 87; Fry, *"Pettigrew's Charge,"* p. 93.

53. Purifoy, *"Confederate Assault,"* p. 228; Fite, *Short,* pp. 87-88.

54. Kimble, *Captain James W. Lockhart.*

55. Lindsley, *Military,* p. 251.

56. Ibid.

57. Ingram, *"Tribute,"* p. 59.

58. Kimble, *Incident at Gettysburg.*

59. Lindsley, *Military,* p. 251.

60. Ibid, pp. 251-52.

61. Purifoy, *"Confederate Assault,"* p. 226.

62. Rollins, *Red Flags,* Appendix A.

63. Fulton, August 10, 1910 letter.

64. Moore, *"Heroism,"* p. 15.

65. Ibid, pp. 15-16.

66. Harris, untitled, p. 160.

67. Allen, *"Five Daughters,"* p. 495.

68. Clarkson information, courtesy of Gettysburg National Military Park.

69. Kimble, *"W.H. McCulloch."*

70. Lindsley, *Military,* p. 252.

71. Kimble, *"Tennesseeans,"* p. 461.

72. Busby's Civil War on line; Purifoy, *"Confederate Assault,"* p. 226; kingwoodcable.com.

73. Cross, *Ordeal,* p. 74.

74. Kimble, *"Tennesseeans,"* p. 461.

75. Lindsley, *Military*, p. 252.

76. Clark, *"Tar Heel Troops."*

77. Polley, *"Testimony,"* p. 524.

78. Ibid, pp. 524-25.

79. Ibid, p. 525.

80. Ibid.

81. Moore, *"Concerning...Gettysburg,"* p. 624.

82. McCall, *"What the Tennesseeans did."*

83. Smith, *"The Charge,"* p. 646.

84. Harris, *"Reply,"* p. 3.

85. Young, *"Comment,"* p. 34.

86. Purifoy, *"Concerning...Gettysburg,"* p. 77.

87. Kimble, *"Tennesseeans,"* p. 462.

88. Ibid, p. 463.

89. Thompson, *"High Tide,"* p. 323.

CHAPTER 15. *Imprisonment*

1. Griffin, *"Among the First Confederates,"* pp. 26-27.

2. Ibid.

3. Herndon, *"Reminiscences,"* p. 12.

4. Wakelyn, *Biographical Dictionary*, pp. 192-93; Brock, *"General Burkett Davenport Fry,"* pp. 286-88; Fry, *"Pettigrew's Charge,"* p. 93.

5. Turney, *"First Tennessee,"* p. 537.

6. White, *"Letters from Prison,"* pp. 140-42.

7. Fite, *Short*, pp. 88-89.

8. Muse, *"History,"* p. 13.

9. *"General's Letter,"* p. 10.

10. Hopkins, *"Archer Letters,"* pp. 356-57.

11. Ibid, pp. 357-58, 363.

12. O.R., Ser. I, v. 6, p. 311; Allen, *"A Plan to Escape,"* pp. 284 & 287.

13. Herndon, *"Reminiscences,"* p. 18.
14. Ibid.
15. Muse, *"History,"* pp. 13-14.
16. Osborne, *"Group plans,"* p. 9.
17. Crouch, *"Humors,"* p. 515.
18. Bennett, Letter of April 26, 2002.
19. Bird, *Stories*, p. 19; *"Prison Fatalities,"* p. 5.
20. Bird, *Stories*, pp. 19-20.
21. Moon, *"Prison Life,"* pp. 212-214.
22. *"Prison Fatalities,"* p. 5.

CHAPTER 16. *The Retreat from Gettysburg*

1. Stackpole, *They Met at Gettysburg*, p. 307.
2. Basler, *Lincoln*, pp. 478-79.
3. O.R., Ser. I, v. 27, pp. 80-81; Mockbee, *"The 14th Tennessee,"* p. 28.
4. Van de Graaff letter.
5. Kimble, *"Tennesseeans,"* p. 461.
6. McCall, *"Battle of Falling Waters,"* p. 406.
7. Heth, *"Report,"* p. 196.
8. Ibid; Lindsley, *Military*, p. 252.
9. Tolley, *"Campaigns,"* p. 109.
10. McCall, *"Battle of Falling Waters,"* p. 406.
11. Lindsley, *Military*, p. 253.
12. McCall, *"Battle of Falling Waters,"* p. 406.
13. Fulton, *"The Fifth Alabama,"* p. 379.
14. Heth, *"Report,"* p. 197.
15. Kimble, *"Tennesseeans,"* p. 462.
16. Lindsley, *Military*, p. 253.
17. Tolley, *"Campaigns,"* p. 109.
18. Fulton, *"The Fifth Alabama,"* pp. 379-80.
19. Heth, *"Report,"* p. 197.

20. Kimble, *"Tennesseeans,"* p. 462.

21. Fulton, *"The Fifth Alabama,"* pp. 379-80.

22. Heth, *"Report,"* p. 197.

23. McCall, *"Battle of Falling Waters,"* p. 406.

24. Lindsley, *Military,* p. 253.

25. Kimble, *"Tennesseeans,"* p. 462.

26. Heth, *"Report,"* pp. 198-99.

27. Kimble, *"Tennesseeans,"* pp. 462-63.

28. Lindsley, *Military,* p. 253.

29. Kimble, *"Tennesseeans,"* p. 463.

30. Mockbee, *"The 14th Tennessee,"* p. 30.

31. O.R., Ser. I, vol. 27, p. 1025.

32. Titus, *Picturesque,* p. 122, Mockbee, *"The 14th Tennessee."*

33. Katcher, *Battle History,* p. 94; Fulton, *War Reminiscences,* p. 107.

34. O.R., Ser. I, v. 29, pp. 426 & 433.

35. Ibid; Katcher, *Battle History,* p. 95.

36. Fulton, *War Reminiscences,* p. 108; O.R., Ser. I, v. 29, p. 426.

37. Fulton, *War Reminiscences,* p. 109.

38. Ibid, pp. 109-110; Katcher, *Battle History,* pp. 96-97.

39. Mockbee, *"The 14th Tennessee,"* pp. 31-32.

40. Adcock, March 14, 1864 letter.

CHAPTER 17. *The Wilderness and Spotsylvania*

1. McBrien, *The Tennessee Brigade,* p. 90; Mockbee, *"The 14th Tennessee,"* p. 32.

2. Radley, *Rebel Watchdog,* p. 43.

3. McBrien, *The Tennessee Brigade,* p. 91.

4. Mockbee, *"The 14th Tennessee,"* p. 42.

5. Ibid.

6. McComb, *"Recollections,"* pp. 3-4.

7. Radley, *Rebel Watchdog,* p. 43.

8. Ibid.

9. McComb, *"Recollections,"* pp. 4-5.

10. Mockbee, *"The 14th Tennessee,"* pp. 35-36.

11. *"What command was it?,"* p. 239.

12. Ibid.

13. Harris, *"Reply,"* p. 334.

14. Lindsley, *Military,* p. 238.

15. Katcher, *Battle History,* pp. 110-111.

16. Ibid; Lossing, *Pictorial Field Book,* p. 303.

17. Lossing, *Pictorial Field Book,* p. 303; Katcher, *Battle History,* p. 112.

18. McComb, *"Recollections,"* p. 5.

19. Moore, *"At Spotsylvania."*

20. McComb, *"Recollections,"* p. 5.

21. Moore, *"At Spotsylvania,"* pp. 5-6.

22. McComb, *"Recollections,"* p. 5; McBrien, *The Tennessee Brigade,* p. 95.

23. Moore, *"At Spotsylvania,"* pp. 6-7.

24. Ibid, pp. 8-9.

25. Ibid, p. 9.

26. Ibid.

27. McComb, *"Recollections,"* p. 6.

28. Moore, *"At Spotsylvania,"* p. 9.

29. McComb, *"Recollections,"* p. 7.

CHAPTER 18. *To Petersburg*

1. Miller, *Blue and Gray,* pp. 13-14.

2. Ibid, pp. 13-19.

3. McComb, *"Recollections,"* p.7.

4. Miller, *Blue and Gray,* pp. 48-49.

5. Ibid, p. 54; McBrien, *The Tennessee Brigade,* p. 98.

6. *"Confrontation on the North Anna,"* p. 76.

7. Miller, *Blue and Gray,* p. 55.

8. McComb, *"Recollections,"* pp. 8-10.

9. *"Fine Shots,"* p. 73.

10. Ibid, pp. 73-74.

11. McBrien, *The Tennessee Brigade*, pp. 99-100.

12. Cook, *"The Last Time I saw General Lee,"* p. 287.

13. McBrien, *The Tennessee Brigade,* p. 100.

14. Katcher, *Battle History,* pp. 128-29.

15. Ibid, p. 129; Mockbee, *"The 14th Tennessee,"* p. 38; Greene, *The Petersburg Campaign,* p. 97.

16. Mockbee, *"The 14th Tennessee,"* p. 38.

17. Cross, *Ordeal,* p. 116.

18. McComb, *"Recollections,"* p. 20.

19. *"Fine Shots,"* p. 73.

20. O.R., Ser. II, v. 7, p. 390; Hopkins, *"Archer Letters,"* pp. 369 & 371.

21. Hopkins, *"Archer Letters,"* pp. 373-74.

22. O.R., Ser. II, v. 7, p. 684.

23. McBrien, *The Tennessee Brigade,* p. 101.

24. O.R., Ser. II, v. 7, p. 54.

25. Clemens, *"History of the 2nd Maryland Infantry,"* pp. 1-2.

26. O.R., Ser. II, v. 7, p. 1189.

27. Ibid, pp. 1284-1287.

28. Ibid, p. 569.

29. Clemens, *"History of the 2nd Maryland Infantry,"* pp. 1-2; McBrien, *The Tennessee Brigade*, pp. 102-103.

30. Mockbee, *"The 14th Tennessee,"* p. 11; McBrien, *The Tennessee Brigade,* p. 103.

31. McBrien, *The Tennessee Brigade,* p. 104; Trudeau, *The Siege of Petersburg,* p. 19.

32. O.R., Ser. I, v. 27, p. 1274.

33. Ibid, pp. 1011-1048.

34. Hopkins, *"Archer Letters,"* p. 379.

35. Ibid, pp. 381-82.

36. Chesnut, *"A Diary from Dixie,"* p. 477.

CHAPTER 19. *The Bitter End*

1. Mockbee, *"The 14ᵗʰ Tennessee,"* pp. 38-39; McComb, *"Recollections,"* p. 11.

2. Greene, *The Petersburg Campaign*, pp. 100-01.

3. Kimble, *"Gen. Wm. McComb."*

4. McBrien, *The Tennessee Brigade*, p. 106; Cross, *Ordeal*, p. 162.

5. McBrien, *The Tennessee Brigade*, pp. 106-07.

6. Mockbee, *"The 14ᵗʰ Tennessee,"* pp. 39 & 43.

7. McBrien, *The Tennessee Brigade*, p. 107; Greene, *The Petersburg Campaign*, p. 145.

8. Ibid.

9. McComb, *"Recollections,"* p. 11.

10. Greene, *The Petersburg Campaign*, p. 257; McBrien, *The Tennessee Brigade*, p. 109; McComb, *"Recollections,"* p. 12.

11. McComb, *"Recollections,"* pp. 12-14.

12. Mockbee, *"The 14ᵗʰ Tennessee,"* p. 39.

13. Greene, *The Petersburg Campaign*, p. 349.

14. Ibid, pp. 350-51.

15. Ibid, pp. 351 & 373.

16. Mockbee, *"Heroes,"* p. 31.

17. *"Last charge,"* p. 565.

18. *"Capt. Fergus S. Harris,"* p. 177.

19. Katcher, *Battle History*, p. 188.

20. Mockbee, *"Crossing River Under Difficulties,"* p. 126.

21. Ibid.

22. Lossing, *Pictorial Field Book*, pp. 554-55.

23. Ibid, p. 555.

24. Ibid, p. 556.

25. Ibid, p. 557.

26. Ibid.

27. McComb, *"Recollections,"* p. 14.

28. Infantry Parole Numbers for the First, Seventh, and Fourteenth Tennessee Regiments.

29. Ibid; McBrien, *The Tennessee Brigade*, p. 111.

30. Ibid.

31. Webb, *A Bicentennial History*, p. 274.

32. Infantry Parole Numbers for the First, Seventh, and Fourteenth Tennessee Regiments; McBrien, *The Tennessee Brigade*, p. 111; Clemens, *"History of the 2ⁿ Maryland Infantry."*

33. McBrien, *The Tennessee Brigade*, p. 111; Calkins, *The Battles of Appomattox Station and Appomattox Court House*, p. 219.

34. Titus, *Picturesque*, p. 122; Mockbee, *"The 14ʰ Tennessee,"* p. 39.

35. Herndon, *"Reminiscences,"* p. 19.

36. Nicholson, *"The Prodigal's Return,"* p. 163.

37. Fulton, *Reminiscences*, pp. 160-178.

38. Brock, *"General Burkett Davenport Fry,"* pp. 286-88.

39. *"Capt. Fergus S. Harris,"* p. 177.

40. *"Captain Herndon Died Yesterday."*

41. Wakelyn, *Biographical Dictionary*, pp. 227-28.

42. *"From Sick Bed to Battle,"* p. 423.

43. *"A Gallant Confederate."*

44. *"General McComb."*

45. *"M.T. Ledbetter,"* p. 89.

46. McLeod, *"Dr. W.H. Moon,"* p. 274.

Bibliography

Adcock, John D., March 14, 1864 Letter to Lucinda Anderson Adcock Jackson. Used with permission of the Alabama Department of Archives and History.

Allen, Capt. John, "Five Daughters of Capt. John C. Allen." *Confederate Veteran,* vol. 9, no. 1, p. 495.

Allen, L.W., "A Plan to Escape," *Southern Historical Society Papers,* vol. 19, 1891, pp. 283-289.

Armistead, Drury L., "The Battle in which General Johnston was Wounded," *Southern Historical Society Papers,* vol. 28, Jan.-Dec. 1890, pp. 185-188.

A.S.R., July 30, 1863 Letter to the Editor of the *Enquirer.* Courtesy of R.L. Krick, Richmond National Military Park.

"B", "From the 19th Georgia," *The Rome Courier,* August 22, 1862. Courtesy of R.L. Krick, Richmond National Military Park.

Barnwell, Robert W., Sr., "The Battle of Seven Pines," *Confederate Veteran,* vol. 36, #2, pp. 58-61.

Basler, Roy P., ed., *Lincoln: Speeches, Letters, Miscellaneous Writings, Presidential Messages and Proclamations, 1859-1865.* Literary Classics of the United States, Inc., New York, NY, 1989.

Bennett, Martha L., April 26, 2002 Letter to Randy Bishop.

Benton, T.H., "A Tennessee Private in Virginia," *Confederate Veteran,* vol. 15, #11, p. 507.

Bird, W.H., *Stories of the Civil War,* Glyocate Print Columbiana, AL, n.d., Courtesy of Gettysburg National Military Park.

Blevins, Jerry, *Sequatchie Valley Soldiers in the Civil War.* October, 1990.

B.M.H., "From Sick Bed to Battle," *Confederate Veteran,* vol. 11, # 9, p. 423.

Boland, E.T., "Beginning of the Battle of Gettysburg," *Confederate Veteran,* vol. 14, pp. 308- 309.

----, "Recollections of Gettysburg," Used with permission of the Alabama Department of Archives and History.

Boze, W.C., "A Comrade's Tribute," *Confederate Veteran,* vol. 5, #1, pp. 28-29.

Brock, R.A., "General Burkett Davenport Fry," *Southern Historical Society Papers,* vol. 28, 1890, pp. 286-288.

Busby, Michael, *Civil War on Line.* All references used with permission of website.

Butler, H. Boyer, ed., *Archibald Debow Norris Civil War Diaries, January 1861-April 1863,* 1999.

Calkins, Chris M., *The Battles of Appomattox Station and Appomattox Court House, April 8-9, 1865.* H.E. Howard, Lynchburg, Virginia, 1987.

"Captain Herndon Died Yesterday." Used with permission of Eleanor S. Brockenbrough Library, The Museum of the Confederacy, Richmond, Virginia.

Carman, Ezra, *The Maryland Campaign of September, 1862.* Used with the permission of Tom Clemens.

Castleberry, W.A., "Thirteenth Alabama—Archer's Brigade," *Confederate Veteran,* vol. 19, #7, p. 338.

Cheeks, Robert C., "Stonewall's 11ᵗʰ Hour Rally," *America's Civil War,* vol. 8, #6, pp. 56-100.

Chesnut, Mary Boykin, *A Diary from Dixie,* Boston: Houghton Mifflin Company, 1905.

Childs, H.T., "Archer's Brigade at Chancellorsville," *Confederate Veteran,* vol. 28, #6, pp. 220-21.

----, "The Battle of Seven Pines," *Confederate Veteran,* vol. 25, #1, pp. 19-20.

----, "Cedar Run Battle as I Saw It," *Confederate Veteran,* vol. 28, #1, p. 24.

----, "Reminiscences of Harris and Hatton," *Confederate Veteran,* vol. 8, #3, pp. 111-112.

Civil War Centennial Commission, *Tennesseeans in the Civil War, A Military History of Confederate and Union units with Available Rosters of Personnel* 2 volumes. Nashville: Civil War Centennial Commission, 1964.

Civil War on line.

Clark, Walter, "Tar Heel Troops Furthest to the Front at Gettysburg," Clippings Portfolio used with permission of Tennessee State Library and Archives.

Clendening, William Alexander, *Memoirs,* courtesy of the Department of the Army, U.S. Army War College and Carlisle Barracks, Carlisle, Pennsylvania. Henry M. Clarkson Biography, Courtesy of Gettysburg National Military Park.

Clemens, Tom, "History of the 2ⁿᵈ Maryland Infantry."

Coddington, Edwin B., *The Gettysburg Campaign: A Study In Command.* Charles Scribner's Sons, New York, 1968.

Coffin, Charles Carleton, *Eyewitness To Gettysburg.* Harper and Brothers-New York, 1889.

"Confrontation on the North Anna," Courtesy of North Anna Visitor's Center.

Cook, Roy Bird, "The Last Time I Saw General Lee," *Confederate Veteran,* vol. 35, #8, p. 287.

Corlew, Robert E., *Tennessee, A Short History.* Knoxville: University of Tennessee Press, 1981.

Randy Bishop

Cross, C. Wallace, Jr., *Ordeal by Fire.* Clarksville: Clarksville Montgomery County Museum, 1990.

Crouch, Robert C., "Humors of Johnson's Island Prison," *Confederate Veteran,* vol. 14, #11, p. 515.

Cummings, C.C., "Confederate Heroine at Williamsburg," *Confederate Veteran,* vol. 4, #3, p. 91.

Davis, Louise, "Unfinished Conversion," Nashville Tennesseean Magazine. February 17, 1946.

Davis, William C. and Wiley I Bell, ed., *The Civil War: The Compact Edition, Fort Sumter to Gettysburg.* Black Dog and Leventhal Publishers, New York, 1981.

"Departure of the Franklin County Regiment," *Franklin County Historical Review,* vol. 8, #1, p. 18.

Donaldson, W.E., untitled, *Confederate Veteran,* vol. 4, #5, p. 164.

Drane Collection, Manuscript Section, Tennessee State Library and Archives, IV-J-3.

Emory, A.G., "Report of the Sick and Wounded—September, 1862." Used with permission of Eleanor S. Brockenbrough Library, Museum of the Confederacy, Richmond, Virginia.

Emory, A.G., "Report of the Sick and Wounded—1st, 7th, 14th Tennessee Regiments—October 1862." Used with permission of Eleanor S. Brockenbrough Library, Museum of the Confederacy, Richmond, Virginia.

"Fine Shots in the Virginia Army," *Confederate Veteran,* vol. 4, #3, pp. 73-74.

"First Tennessee Infantry Paroles," Used with permission of Antietam NMP.

Fisher, Noel C., *War at Every Door: Partisan Politics and Guerilla Violence in East Tennessee, 1860-1869.* Chapel Hill: The University of North Carolina Press, 1997.

Fite, Emily, "Peter Turney: Man of Honor," *Franklin County Historical Review,* vol. 2, #2, June 1971, pp. 1-17.

356

Fite, John, *"Short and uninteresting history of a small and insignificant man."* Reel 5, Manuscript section. Used with permission of the Tennessee State Library and Archives.

Floyd, William C. and Paul Gibson, *The Boys who went to war from Cumberland University: 1861-1865.* Gettysburg, Pennsylvania: Thomas Publications, 2001.

Foreman, Mike, "The Secession of Franklin County," *Franklin County Historical Review*, vol. 8, #1, pp. 3-10.

"Fourteenth Tennessee Infantry Paroles." Used with permission of Antietam NMP.

"Fourteenth Tennessee Regiment," *Confederate Veteran*, vol. 4, #8, p. 263.

Fox, William F., "Letter to F.S. Harris," *Confederate Veteran*, vol. 6, #9, p. 410.

Fred.net

Fry, General B.D., "Pettigrew's Charge at Gettysburg," *Southern Historical Society Papers*, vol. 7, #2, Feb. 1879, pp. 91-93.

Fulton, W.F., August 10, 1910 Letter on file in the Military Records Division of the Department of Archives and History, Montgomery, Alabama.

----, "Archer's Brigade at Cold Harbor," *Confederate Veteran*, vol. 31, #8, pp. 300-01.

----, Family Record and War Reminiscences. Gaithersburg, Maryland: Butternut Press 1913.

----, "The Fifty Alabama Battalion at Gettysburg," *Confederate Veteran*, vol. 31, #10, pp. 379-380.

----, "Incidents of Second Manassas," *Confederate Veteran*, v. 31, #12, pp. 451-52.

----, "Picketing on the Potomac," *Confederate Veteran*, vol. 32, #11, pp. 427-428.

----, "Tumbled too soon," *Confederate Veteran*, vol. 31, #5, pp. 172-173.

"A Gallant Confederate" Used with permission of Eleanor S. Brockenbrough Library, The Museum of the Confederacy, Richmond, Virginia.

"General's Letter" *Fort Delaware Notes*, v. 28, p. 1.

"General McComb," Used with permission of Eleanor S. Brockenbrough Library, The Museum of the Confederacy, Richmond, Virginia.

Gettysburg: The Confederate High Tide, Time Life Books, Inc., Alexandria, Virginia, 1985.

Greene, A. Wilson, *The Final Battle of The Petersburg Campaign: Breaking the Backbone of the Rebellion*. Mason City, IA: Savas Publishing, 2000.

Griffin, Don T., "Among the First Confederates to fall at Gettysburg," *Blue and Gray Magazine*, April 1998, pp. 26-27.

Harries, W.H., "The Sword of Gen. James J. Archer," *Confederate Veteran*, vol. 19, pp. 419-420. "Capt. Fergus S. Harris," *Confederate Veteran*, v. 13, #4, p. 177.

Harris, F.S., *Confederate Veteran*, vol. 9, #4, p. 160.

----, "From Gettysburg," *Lebanon Democrat*, August 10, 1899. Courtesy of Gettysburg National Military Park.

----, "Incidents at Chancellorsville," *Confederate Veteran*, vol. 3, #9, p. 261.

----, "Gen. Jas. J. Archer," *Confederate Veteran*, vol. 3, #1, p. 18.

----, "Reply," *Confederate Veteran*, vol. 3, #11, p. 334.

Haskins, Benjamin, "Gen. James Archer," *Confederate Veteran*, vol. 2, #12, p. 355.

Hartman, Theo. "With Jackson at Second Manassas," *Confederate Veteran*, vol. 24, #12, p. 557.

Herndon, Capt. Thomas, *Diary and Journal, 1863*. Used with permission of the Eleanor S. Brockenbrough Library, The Museum of the Confederacy, Richmond, Virginia.

----, Reminiscences of the Civil War, 1861-1865, pp. 3-19. Used with permission of Eleanor S. Brockenbrough Library, The Museum of the Confederacy, Richmond, Virginia.

Heth, Henry, "Report of Major-General Heth of the Affair at Falling Waters," *Southern Historical Society Papers*, vol. 7, #4, April 1879, pp. 196-199.

Hopkins, C.A. Porter, ed., "The James J. Archer Letters: A Marylander in the Civil War," *Maryland Historical Magazine*, vol. 56; Part 1, pp. 72-93 and 125-149; Part 2, pp. 352-383.

Horn, Stanley F., *Tennessee's War 1861-65.* Tennessee Civil War Centennial Commission, 1965.

Hudson, Leonne M., Ph.D., "Gustavus W. Smith and the Battle of Seven Pines," *Confederate Veteran*, March/April 1993, pp. 15-24.

Hull, Michael D., "The Union Army's most innovative cavalry leader, Brig. Gen. John Buford shines at the Battle of Gettysburg," *America's Civil War*, vol. 10, #1, p. 62

Hurst, John, "Archer's Brigade at Chancellorsville," *Confederate Veteran*, vol. 28, #7, pp. 261-262.

Ingram, M.V., "Tribute to Capt. 'June' Kimble," *Confederate Veteran*, vol. 16, #2, pp. 59-60.

Johnson, W.H., Letter to the editor, *Southern Confederacy*, December 30, 1862.

Joiner, Harry M., *Tennessee Then and Now*, Athens, Alabama, Southern Textbook Publishers, Inc. 1983.

Jones, J.M., "Seven Pines to Prison—Vivid Incidents," *Confederate Veteran*, vol. 11, #11, p. 506.

Katcher, Philip, *Battle History of the Civil War 1861-1865*, New York: Barnes and Noble Books, 2000.

Keely, John, "Narrative of the Campaign of the 19ᵗʰ Georgia Volunteer Infantry," *Atlanta Constitution Magazine*, March 15-April 15, Courtesy of Robert Krick, Richmond, National Battlefield.

Kelley, Rev. D.C., "General Robert Hatton," *Confederate Veteran*, vol. 7, #12, pp. 552-554.

Kimble, June, "An Ambuscade." Used with permission of Eleanor S. Brockenbrough Library, The Museum of the Confederacy, Richmond, Virginia.

----, "Another Story of Gen. Sam Anderson of the Tennessee Brigade." Used with permission of Eleanor S. Brockenbrough Library, The Museum of the Confederacy, Richmond, Virginia.

----, "Archer's Tenn. Brigade at Chancellorsville, May, 3rd, 1863." Used with permission of Eleanor S. Brockenbrough Library, The Museum of the Confederacy, Richmond, Virginia.

----, "At Yorktown." Used with permission of Eleanor S. Brockenbrough Library, The Museum of the Confederacy, Richmond, Virginia.

----, "Battle of Chancellorsville-An Incident." Used with permission of Eleanor S. Brockenbrough Library, The Museum of the Confederacy, Richmond, Virginia.

----, "Capt. James W. Lockhart." Used with permission of Eleanor S. Brockenbrough Library, The Museum of the Confederacy, Richmond, Virginia.

----, "Company 'A' at Fredericksburg Dec. 13th, 1862." Used with permission of Eleanor S. Brockenbrough Library, The Museum of the Confederacy, Richmond, Virginia.

----, "The 14th Tenn. Glee Club." Used with permission of Eleanor S. Brockenbrough Library, The Museum of the Confederacy, Richmond, Virginia.

----, "Gen. Sam Anderson. First Commander of Archer's famous Tennessee Brigade." Used with permission of Eleanor S. Brockenbrough, The Museum of the Confederacy, Richmond, Virginia.

----, "Gen. Wm. McComb." Used with permission of Eleanor S. Brockenbrough Library, The Museum of the Confederacy, Richmond, Virginia.

----, "Gus A. Thompkins." Used with permission of Eleanor S. Brockenbrough Library, The Museum of the Confederacy, Richmond, Virginia.

----, "An Incident at Gettysburg." Used with permission of Eleanor S. Brockenbrough Library, The Museum of the Confederacy, Richmond, Virginia.

----, "Tennesseeans At Gettysburg-The Retreat," *Confederate Veteran*, vol. 18, pp. 460-463.

----, "W.H. McCulloch." Used with permission of Eleanor S. Brockenbrough Library, The Museum of the Confederacy, Richmond, Virginia.

Kingwoodcable.com

"Knew their man—Gen. William McComb," *Confederate Veteran*, vol. 11, #11, pp. 487-488.

Kross, Gary, "General Reynolds to the Rescue," *Blue and Gray Magazine*, vol. 17, #5, pp. 17-22 and 44.

Lacey, Hubert, *The Goodner Family*, Dayton Ohio, 1960.

Langsdon, Phillip, *Tennessee-A Political History*, Franklin, Tennessee: Providence House Publishers, 2000.

Large, Lt. Col. George R. and Joe A Swisher, *Battle of Antietam. The Official History by the Antietam Battlefield Board*. Burd Street Press. Used with permission of Antietam National Battlefield.

"Last Charge of Lee's Army," *Confederate Veteran*, vol. 5, #11, p. 565.

"Ledbetter, M.T.," *Confederate Veteran*, vol. 17, #2, p. 89.

Ledbetter, M.T., "Mechanicsville and Gaines' Mill," *Confederate Veteran*, vol. 1, #6, pp. 244-45.

Lemmon, George, *Southern Historical Society Papers*, vol. 9, #3, pp. 141-142.

Lindsley, John Berrien, ed., *The Military Annals of Tennessee-Confederate*. Nashville: J.N. Lindsley and Company, 1886.

Long, Roger, "Johnson's Island Prison," *Blue and Gray*, pp. 6-62. Feb./ March 1987.

Longstreet, James. "The Seven Days, Including Frayser's Farm." North To Antietam, Battles and Leaders of the Civil War, New York: Castle Books, pp. 396-405.

Lossing, Benson J., *Pictorial Field Book of the Civil War Volume Three Chancellorsville to the Surrender at Appomattox*. The Johns Hopkins University Press, Baltimore and London, 1997.

McBrien, Joe Bennett, *The Tennessee Brigade*, Chattanooga: Hudson Printing and Lithographing Company, 1977.

McCall, John T., "What the Tennesseeans did at Gettysburg," *The Louisville Journal*, 1902. Courtesy of Gettysburg NMP.

----, "Brig. Gen. James J. Archer," *Confederate Veteran*, vol. 3, #1, p. 19.

----, "Seventh Tennessee—Battle of Falling Waters," *Confederate Veteran,* vol. 6, #9, p. 406.

McComb, William, "Tennesseeans in the Mountain Campaign, 1861," *Confederate Veteran,* vol. 22, #5, pp. 210-212.

----, "Recollections." Used with permission of Eleanor S. Brockenbrough Library, The Museum of the Confederacy, Richmond, Virginia.

McLeod, Kelly, "Dr. W.H. Moon," *Confederate Veteran,* vol. 38, #7, p. 274.

Meredith, Jaquelin Marshall, "The First Day at Gettysburg," *Southern Historical Society Papers,* vol. 24, Jan.-Dec. 1896, pp. 182-87.

Miller, J. Michael, *Blue and Gray Magazine,* April 1993, pp. 13-22, 44-55.

Mockbee, R.T., *Confederate Veteran,* vol. 7, #4, p. 170.

----, "Crossing River Under Difficulties," *Confederate Veteran,* vol. 19, #3, p. 126.

----, "The 14ᵗʰ Tennessee Infantry Regiment," *Civil War Regiments: A Journal of the American Civil War,* vol. 5, # 1.

----, "Heroes in last charge of Lee's Army," *Confederate Veteran,* vol. 6, #1, p. 31.

----, "Why Sharpsburg was 'a drawn battle'," *Confederate Veteran,* vol. 26, #4, p. 160.

Moon, Dr. W.H., "Beginning of the battle at Gettysburg," *Confederate Veteran,* vol. 33, #12, pp. 449-450.

----, "Prison Life at Fort Delaware," *Confederate Veteran,* vol. 15, #5, pp. 212-214.

Moore, J.H., "At Spotsylvania," *Philadelphia Weekly Times,* November 26, 1881.

----, "Concerning the Battle of Gettysburg," *Confederate Veteran,* vol. 5, #12, p. 624.

----, "Fredericksburg," *The Southern Bivouac,* vol. 2, #3, August 1886, pp. 179-184.

----, "Heroism in the Battle of Gettysburg," *Confederate Veteran*, vol. 9, #1, pp. 15-16.

----, "Heth's Division at Gettysburg," *The Southern Bivouac*, vol. 3, #9, May 1885, pp. 383-395.

Motlow, Felix, "Campaigns in Northern Virginia," *Confederate Veteran*, vol. 11, #10, p. 310.

Muse, Will J., "History of Captain Will J. Muse," 1907. Microfilm Section, Box 26, Folder 6, Reel 18. Used with permission of the Tennessee State Library and Archives.

Neff, Robert O., *Tennessee's Battered Brigadier*, Hillsboro Press, Franklin, Tennessee, 2000.

Newman, Howard W., "About Reunion of Archer's Brigade," *Confederate Veteran*, vol. 4, p. 338.

Nicholson, Capt. A.O.P., "The Prodigal's Return-Jack Moore," *Confederate Veteran*, vol. 13, #4, p. 163.

Nineteenth Georgia Infantry historical sketch. Used with the permission of the Georgia Department of Archives and History.

Nofi, Albert A., *The Gettysburg Campaign: June and July, 1863*, Gallery Books, New York, 1986.

Norris, Archibald Debow life sketch. Furnished by and used with permission of H. Boyer Butler.

Osborne, Tish, "Group plans to preserve Johnson Island prison site," *The Civil War Courier*, vol. 18, #7, p. 9.

Patten, Cartter, *A Tennessee Chronicle*, Printed in U.S.A., 1953.

Polley, Gen. J.B., "Testimony about battle of Gettysburg," *Confederate Veteran*, vol. 18, #11, p. 524.

Porter, A.N., "Calhoun Sharp Shooters," Historical Memoranda. Used with permission of Alabama Department of Archives and History, Montgomery, Alabama, 1864.

Porter, Col. George C., "Tennessee Confederate Regiments: Seventh Tennessee Infantry-Col. Robert Hatton," Civil War Collection Clippings portfolio I from the Tennessee Library and Archives.

"Prison Fatalities Top Those in Combat," *Fort Delaware Notes*, vol. 26, Jan. 1976, p. 5.

Purifoy, John, "The Battle of Gettysburg, July, 1, 1863," *Confederate Veteran*, vol. 31, pp. 22-25.

----, "Concerning battle of Gettysburg," *Confederate Veteran*, vol. 19, #2, p. 77.

----, "Confederate Assault at Gettysburg, July 3," *Confederate Veteran*, vol. 32, #6, pp. 226-29.

Radley, Kenneth, *Rebel Watchdog The Confederate States Army Provost Guard*, Louisiana State University Press, Baton Rouge, 1989.

Ramsdell, Charles W., *Behind the lines in the Southern Confederacy*, Louisiana State University Press, 1944.

Reese, J.E., Historical Memoranda. Used with permission of Alabama Department of Archives and History, Montgomery, Alabama, 1864.

Reid, Dick, "Incidents of battle at Gettysburg," *Confederate Veteran*, vol. 11, #11, p. 508.

Renfroe, Rev. J.J.D., "A Model Confederate Soldier." Used with permission of the University of North Carolina Library.

Ritter, Wade, Historical Memo of Co. A, 5thAlabama. Used with permission of the Alabama Department of Archives and History, Montgomery, AL, 1864.

Rollins, Richard, *The Damned Red Flags of the Rebellion The Confederate Battle Flag at Gettysburg*, Rank and File Publications, 1997.

Roth, Dave with Gary Kross, "Gettysburg: Attack from the West," *Blue and Gray*, vol. 17, # 5, pp. 51-65.

"Says He Shot Reynolds," *Star and Sentinel*, June 13, 1899. Courtesy of Gettysburg NMP.

Service record for Daniel McCoy, courtesy of Jimmy Jobe, Fort Donelson National Military Park.

"Seventh Tennessee Infantry Paroles," Courtesy of Antietam NMP.

"Sharpshooting in Lee's Army," *Confederate Veteran*, vol. 3, #4, p. 98.

Sifakis, Stewart, *Who was who in the Confederacy*, vol. II of *Who was who in the Civil War*. Facts on File, Inc.,; New York, 1988.

Smith, J.B., "Archer's Brigade," *Milwaukee Sunday Telegraph*, June 20, 1886, Courtesy of Gettysburg NMP.

----, "The Charge at Gettysburg," *Southern Bivouac*, vol. 2, #10, p. 646.

Smith, John T., Letter of January 22, 1863. Courtesy of Eleanor S. Brockenbrough Library, The Museum of the Confederacy, Richmond, VA.

----, Letter of February, 1, 1863. Courtesy of Eleanor S. Brockenbrough Library, The Museum of the Confederacy, Richmond, VA.

----, Letter of March 8, 1863. Courtesy of Eleanor S. Brockenbrough Library, The Museum of the Confederacy, Richmond, VA.

Stackpole, Edward J., *They Met at Gettysburg*, Stackpole Books, Harrisburg, PA, 1956.

"Stephen Turner Rives" *Confederate Veteran*, vol. 26, #4, p. 170.

Stewart, George R., *Pickett's Charge A Microhistory of the final assault at Gettysburg July 3, 1863*. Houghton Mifflin Company, Boston, 1959.

Swallow, W.H., "The First Day at Gettysburg," *Southern Historical Society Papers*, vol. 1, #7, Dec. 1885, pp 436-444.

Tate, W.N., "Reminiscences," *Confederate Veteran*, vol. 6, #6, pp. 275.

Tennessee-scv.org/Camp723 "Tennesseean Killed Near Richmond," *Confederate Veteran*, vol. 21, #8, p. 408.

Thirteenth Alabama Infantry historical sketch. Used with permission of the Alabama Department of Archives and History.

Thompson, Will Henry, "High Tide at Gettysburg," *Confederate Veteran*, vol. 11, p. 323.

Thorogood, J.E., "Only County Ever to Secede From Union is in Tennessee," *Nashville Tennesseean*, September 18, 1932.

Titus, W.P., *Picturesque Clarksville: Past and Present*, 1887.

Tngennet.org

Tolley, Capt. William P., "Campaigns by Army of Northern Virginia," *Confederate Veteran*, vol. 8, #3, pp. 109-110.

----, "That Gaines Mill 'Affair'," *Confederate Veteran*, vol. 7, #2, p. 54.

"Tribute to Maj. John T. Smith." Courtesy of Eleanor S. Brockenbrough Library, The Museum of the Confederacy, Richmond, VA.

Trudeau, Noah Andre, *The Siege of Petersburg*, Eastern National, 1995.

Tucker, Glenn, *High Tide at Gettysburg*, The Bobbs-Merrill Company, Inc. Indianapolis, IN, 1958.

Turney, J.B. "The First Tennessee at Gettysburg," *Confederate Veteran*, vol. 8, pp. 535-537.

"Turney's Muster Roll of Company K, 1"TN." Courtesy of Franklin County Library.

Tyler, Judge C.W., "Patriotism in a Tennessee County," *Confederate Veteran*, vol. 6, #3, p. 125.

United States War Department, *The War of the Rebellion: A Compilation of the Official Records of the Union and Confederate Armies*, 70 volumes in 128 parts (Washington: Government Printing Office, 1880-1901).

Van de Graaff, A. S. letter to his wife, July 8, 1863. Used with permission of Pat Hanson & family members.

Wakelyn, Jon L. *Biographical Dictionary of the Confederacy*, Westport, Connecticut, Greenwood Press, 1977.

Ward, Geoffrey C., Ric Burns and Ken Burns, *The Civil War: An Illustrated History*, Alfred A. Knopf, Inc., NY, 1990.

Warner, Ezra J., *Generals in Gray: Lives of Confederate Commanders*, Louisiana State University Press, 1951.

Watertown, Harry Phillips, *Phillips Family History*, The Lebanon Democrat, Inc. Lebanon, TN, 1935.

Webb, Thomas G., *A Bicentennial History of DeKalb County, Tennessee*, Bradley Printing Company, Smithville, TN, 1995.

"What command was it?," *Confederate Veteran*, vol. 3, #8, p. 239.

Wheeler, Richard, *Witness to Gettysburg*, Harper and Row Publishers, Inc., 1987, p. 364

White, Raymond D., "Colonel John A. Fite's Letters From Prison," *Tennessee Historical Quarterly*, vol. 32, #2, pp. 140-147.

"William Bryan Hutton," *Confederate Veteran*, vol. 8, #7, p. 328.

"Williams, Mrs. Eugenia F.," *Confederate Veteran*, vol. 18, #10, p. 477.

Williams, Nannie H., "Dr. Ben A. Haskins," *Confederate Veteran*, vol. 20, #9, p. 439.

Woodhead, Henry ed., *Voices of the Civil War*, Time Life Books, Alexandria, VA.

Young, Louis G., "Comment on the battle of Gettysburg," *Confederate Veteran*, vol. 19, p. 34.

Mapping Sources

Seven Pines: *To the Gates of Richmond: The Peninsula Campaign* by Stephen W. Sears (Ticknor & Fields, 1992). **Cedar Mountain:** *Stonewall Jackson at Cedar Mountain* by Robert K. Krick (The University Press of North Carolina, 1990). **Second Manassas:** *Return to Bull Run: The Campaign and Battle of Second Manassas* by John J. Hennessy (Simon & Schuster, 1993); "Historical Report on the Troop Movements for the Second Battle of Manassas, August 28 through August 30, 1862" by John Hennessy (United States Department of the Interior, National Park Service, Denver Service Center, Northeast Team, 1985); "The Second Battle of Manassas: Lee Suppresses the 'Miscreant' Pope" by John Hennessy *(Blue & Gray Magazine,* Vol. **IX,** #6). **Sharpsburg (Antietam):** *Blue & Gray Magazine's History and Tour Guide of the Battle of Antietam* (Blue & Gray Enterprises, Inc., 1995); *The Gleam of Bayonets: The Battle of Antietam and the Maryland Campaign of 1862* by James V. Murfin (A. S. Barnes & Co., 1965); *Landscape Turned Red: The Battle of Antietam* by Stephen W. Sears (Ticknor & Fields, 1983). **Fredericksburg:** *The Fredericksburg Campaign: Winter War on the Rappahannock* by Francis Augustin O'Reilly (Louisiana State University Press, 2002); *Drama On the Rappahannock: The Fredericksburg Campaign* by Edward J. Stackpole (The Stackpole Company, 1957). **Chancellorsville:** *Chancellorsville* by Stephen W. Sears (Houghton Mifflin Company, 1996); *Chancellorsville 1863: The Souls of the Brave* by Ernest B. Fergurson (Alfred A. Knopf, 1992); *Chancellorsville: Lee's Greatest Battle* by Edward J. Stackpole (The Stackpole Company, 1958). **Gettysburg:** "Gettysburg Vignettes— Pickett's Charge" by Gary Kross *(Blue & Gray Magazine,* Vol. XVI, #5); "Gettysburg Vignettes—Attack from the West" by Gary Kross *{Blue & Gray Magazine,* Vol. XVII, #5); *Gettysburg—*

July 1 by David G. Martin (Combined Books, 1996). **The Wilderness:** "No Turning Back: The Battle of the Wilderness, Part II: The Fighting on May 6, 1864" by Gregory A. Mertz *(Blue & Gray Magazine,* Vol. XII, #5); *The Battle of the Wilderness, May 5-6, 1864* by Gordon C. Rhea (Louisiana State University Press, 1994); *The Wilderness Campaign* by Edward Steere (Stackpole Books, 1960). **Spotsylvania Court House:** *If It Takes All Summer: The Battle of Spotsylvania Court House* by William D. Matter (The University Press of North Carolina, 1988); *The Battles for Spotsylvania Court House and the Road to Yellow Tavern, May 7-12, 1864* by Gordon C. Rhea (Louisiana State University Press, 1997); "Battle of Spotsylvania Court House," 24 battle maps, historical research by Frank A. O'Reilly, illustrated and produced by Steve Stanley (2000). **North Anna:** "Strike Them A Blow: Lee and Grant at the North Anna River" by J. Michael Miller *(Blue & Gray Magazine,* Vol. X, #4). **Petersburg:** *Richmond Redeemed: The Siege at Petersburg* by Richard J. Sommers (Doubleday, 1981).

Index

357

D

Donaldson, W.E. 356
Drane, (Dr.) Walter 33
Dunbar Cave 19

F

Falling Waters 255, 259, 260, 261,
    347, 348, 358, 362
Fifth (5th) Alabama Inf. 89, 90, 127,
    206, 237
Finn's Point 237, 247
First (1st) TN Inf. x, 7, 27, 34, 52, 54,
    55, 58, 60, 66, 73, 77, 78, 81,
    96, 101, 105, 108, 110, 113,
    115, 117, 120, 122, 127, 128,
    129, 133, 136, 148, 149, 151,
    153, 165, 168, 169, 204, 206,
    211, 212, 213, 214, 215, 217,
    221, 257, 284, 304, 310, 314,
    342, 343, 344, 345, 346, 356,
    366
First Tennessee. *See* Turney's
Fite, John 19, 33, 60, 78, 88, 93, 94,
    105, 110, 136, 153, 172, 176,
    177, 205, 207, 212, 214, 215,
    217, 242, 357
Forbes, William A. 20, 44, 54, 118,
    119
Fort Delaware xi, 197, 243, 246, 247,
    248, 249, 358, 362, 364
Fort Donelson 52, 53, 365
Fort Henry 51
Fourteenth (14th) TN Inf. 18, 19, 20,
    54, 307, 318, 357
Franklin County, TN ix, x, 3, 6, 7, 8,
    9, 54, 55, 159, 315, 356, 357,
    366
Fredericksburg viii, x, 52, 57, 64, 90,
    92, 99, 137, 139, 140, 141, 143,
    144, 148, 151, 153, 154, 155,
    158, 171, 175, 199, 200, 204,
    280, 310, 336, 337, 338, 360,

362, 369
Fry, B.D. 177, 194, 200, 205, 206,
    210, 213, 215, 217, 230, 238,
    284, 311
Fulton, W.F. 92, 93, 96, 97, 110, 111,
    112, 115, 178, 179, 189, 221,
    256, 258, 262, 263

G

Gaines Mill 94, 96, 97, 98, 99, 101,
    218, 237, 306, 366
George, N.J. 116, 122, 148, 217
Gettysburg vii, viii, ix, x, 21, 22, 173,
    175, 176, 177, 178, 179, 180,
    181, 182, 184, 186, 189, 190,
    191, 193, 194, 195, 196, 197,
    199, 201, 204, 211, 213, 214,
    216, 218, 219, 220, 222, 223,
    224, 225, 226, 227, 228, 231,
    232, 234, 235, 238, 239, 243,
    244, 247, 249, 251, 252, 254,
    256, 258, 260, 261, 262, 265,
    284, 286, 287, 293, 302, 305,
    306, 307, 312, 340, 341, 342,
    343, 344, 345, 346, 347, 354,
    355, 356, 357, 358, 359, 360,
    361, 362, 363, 364, 365, 366,
    367, 369
Goodner, John xi, 25, 147, 150, 151
Griffin, Elihu ix, 181, 237
Griffin, Gabriel 237

H

Harper's Ferry 54, 125, 126, 127, 128,
    129, 136
Harris, (Gov.) Isham G. 12, 55
Harris, Fergus (F.S.) 87, 165, 311, 351,
    352, 358
Haskins, Ben 20, 21, 323, 358, 367
Hatton, Robert 25, 54, 67, 70, 79, 80,
    81, 329, 330, 359, 364
Herndon, Thomas 77, 117, 118, 119,
    153, 160, 186, 188, 192, 197,
    237, 240, 308, 312

302, 349, 350, 351, 358, 366, 370

R

Raison, Henry 182
Rapidan River 261, 263, 265
Rappahannock River 137, 139, 140
Renfroe, Nathaniel D. 139, 148, 149
Reynolds, John 178, 180, 182, 184, 185, 190, 195, 306, 342, 361, 364
Romney 41, 46, 47, 50

S

Second (2nd) Maryland Battalion 286, 301, 307
Seventh (7th) TN Inf. 18, 150, 306, 317, 364, 365
Seventh (7th) TN Inf. (7th TN) 25, 80, 166, 169, 209, 216, 295
Seven Days 89, 91, 100, 101, 103, 331, 332, 361
Seven Pines 69, 70, 71, 72, 73, 74, 76, 79, 80, 81, 82, 96, 101, 225, 238, 296, 306, 329, 330, 353, 355, 359, 369
Sharpshooters 90, 206, 282
Shepard, Sam (S.G.) 113, 120, 127, 269
Smith, John T. 156, 158, 169, 171, 340, 366
Spotsylvania 170, 171, 265, 268, 270, 271, 274, 275, 276, 277, 279, 280, 348, 349, 362, 370
Stewart College 20
Sumner County, TN 18, 19

T

Thirteenth (13th) AL 122, 156, 157, 169, 176, 178, 179, 192, 204, 206, 221, 224, 238, 243, 247, 260, 288, 293, 311, 313, 339, 342, 354, 365
Turney, (Col.) Peter 3, 6, 7, 8, 54, 77,

105, 108, 113, 120, 127, 129, 133, 145, 153, 310, 314, 315, 321, 322, 356
Turney, J.B. 193, 205, 211, 212, 213, 214, 217, 238
Turney's First (1st) TN x, 27, 54, 55, 60, 66, 73, 78, 96, 101, 105, 115, 117, 129, 151, 168, 304

V

Van de Graaff, A. S. 252, 253, 347, 366

W

Wilderness 265, 266, 267, 268, 269, 270, 279, 280, 302, 348, 370
Willoughby Run 178, 179, 180, 181, 182, 185, 186, 189, 196
Wilson County, Tennessee 61, 314, 316
Winchester, Tennessee 6, 9, 145, 153, 314, 315

Y

Yorktown 59, 60, 61, 63, 64, 65, 66, 67, 90, 328, 360

About the Author

Randy Bishop teaches American History at Middleton High School and is an adjunct professor for Jackson State Community College. He holds graduate degrees in education and history from the University of Memphis. A long-time Civil War student and collector, Bishop enjoys traveling, reading, and spending time with his family. He is a member of the Sons of Confederate Veterans, the Civil War Preservation Trust, and the Tennessee Civil War Preservation Association. He and his wife Sharon have two sons, Jay and Ben. The author and his family live in Middleton, Tennessee, where he and his wife teach Sunday School. The author has published articles related to the Civil War and family vacation destinations. This is his first book.

Printed in the United States
201232BV00008B/46-87/A

9 781600 080661